INTERMEDIATE

Develomental dyslexia

THOMSON

DEVELOPMENTAL DYSLEXIA

STUDIES IN DISORDERS OF COMMUNICATION

THIRD EDITION

W

WHURR PUBLISHERS
LONDON   JERSEY CITY

© Michael Thomson 1984, 1989, 1990

First published 1984 by
Edward Arnold (Publishers) Ltd
Second edition 1989 published by
Cole and Whurr Limited
Third edition 1990 published by
Whurr Publishers Ltd
19b Compton Terrace, London N1 2UN

Reprinted 1991, 1993, 1994, 1995, 1996, 1997, and 2000

British Library Cataloguing in Publication Data

Thomson, Michael E.
   Developmental dyslexia.-3rd ed.
   1. Children. Dyslexia
   I. Title   II. Series
   618.92'8553

   ISBN 1-870332-70-9

Photoset by Scribe Design, Gillingham, Kent
Printed and bound in Great Britain by Athenæum Press Ltd, Gateshead, Tyne & Wear

To my wife, Rosemary,
with love

Contents

General preface	ix
Preface to the third edition	xi
Acknowledgements	xii

1 Introduction — 1
1.1 Barriers to learning — 2
1.2 The concept of developmental dyslexia — 3
1.3 Emotional correlates of dyslexia — 21
1.4 Sex differences — 26
1.5 Subtypes of dyslexia — 27
1.6 Genetic aspects — 35
1.7 Official attitudes to dyslexia in the UK — 40

2 Case histories — 44
2.1 Case history 1 (I E) — 44
2.2 Case history 2 (M S) — 48
2.3 Case history 3 (D F) — 52
2.4 Case history 4 (identical twins) — 55

3 Etiology — 61
3.1 Introduction — 61
3.2 Neurological perspective — 63
3.3 Cognitive perspective — 86
3.4 Summary — 119

4 Dyslexia as a phenomenon of written language — 121
4.1 Some features of written language — 121
4.2 Models of the written language process — 126
4.3 Reading and spelling behaviour — 134
4.4 Written language and dyslexia: a synthesis — 140

5 Assessment — 144
5.1 Introduction — 144
5.2 'Background' factors — 146
5.3 Assessment of intelligence — 150

5.4 Attainments   164
5.5 Perceptual, motor and memory skills   172
5.6 Screening procedures   173
5.7 Sample reports   178

6   **Remediation: evaluations and assessment**   191
    6.1 The relationship between assessment and remediation   191
    6.2 Evaluating remediation   194

7   **Remediation: principles and techiques**   207
    7.1 General principles of remediation   207
    7.2 Structured written language programmes   214
    7.3 Multi-sensory teaching   219
    7.4 Matching task to learner   226
    7.5 Phonetic teaching   231
    7.6 Essay writing   237
    7.7 The older dyslexic   240
    7.8 Computer-assisted learning and word processing   246
    7.9 Role of the parent in remediation   251

Appendix: Regression equations for IQ, CA and Attainment   255
References   257
Index (Names)   299
Index (Subjects)   305

General preface

This series is the first to approach the problem of language disability as a single field. It attempts to bring together areas of study which have traditionally been treated under separate headings, and to focus on the common problems of analysis, assessment and treatment which characterize them. Its scope therefore includes the specifically linguistic aspects of the work of such areas as speech therapy, remedial teaching, teaching of the deaf and educational psychology, as well as those aspects of mother-tongue and foreign-language teaching which pose similar problems. The research findings and practical techniques from each of these fields can inform the others, and we hope one of the main functions of this series will be to put people from one profession into contact with the analogous situations found in others.

It is therefore not a series about specific syndromes or educationally narrow problems. While the orientation of a volume is naturally towards a single main area, and reflects an author's background, it is editorial policy to ask authors to consider the implications of what they say for the fields with which they have not been primarily concerned. Nor is this a series about disability in general. The medical, social, educational and other factors which enter into a comprehensive evaluation of any problems will not be studied as ends in themselves, but only in so far as they bear directly on the understanding of the nature of the language behaviour involved. The aim is to provide a much needed emphasis on the description and analysis of language as such, and on the provision of specific techniques of therapy or remediation. In this way, we hope to bridge the gap between the theoretical discussion of 'causes' and the practical tasks of treatment—two sides of language disability which it is uncommon to see systematically related.

Despite restricting the area of disability to specifically linguistic matters—and in particular emphasizing problems of the production and comprehension of spoken language—it should be clear that the series' scope goes considerably beyond this. For the first books, we have selected topics which have been particularly neglected in recent years, and which seem most able to benefit from contemporary research in linguistics and its related disciplines, English studies, psychology, sociology and education. Each volume will put its subject matter in perspective, and will provide an introductory slant to its presentation. In this way, we hope to provide specialized studies which can be used as texts for components of teaching courses, as well as material that is directly applicable to the needs of professional workers. It is also hoped that this orientation will place the series within the reach of the interested layman—in particular, the parents or family of the linguistically disabled.

David Crystal
Jean Cooper

Preface to third edition

This third edition of *Developmental Dyslexia* is a response to the rapid development of research and ideas on dyslexia, and the adoption of *Developmental Dyslexia* as a set book for a number of training and diploma courses.

One component of the third edition is therefore an update of research. This includes recent research on demographic studies (Chapter 1), current research on phonological skills (Chapter 3), and some work on the use of the British Ability Scales and subtypes of dyslexia (Chapters 3 and 5). The previous material, including the case histories, general descriptions, overview of research and assessment procedures, remains unchanged.

In response to teacher training needs, and my own experiences at East Court School, the major change in the third edition has been to the 'teaching' component of the book. The previous Chapter 6 has been expanded into two chapters. Previous material has been re-organized, and a good deal of additional information has been added. This is particularly in the area of phonics and word analysis skills, essay planning and writing, the use of computers and word processing and in evaluating teaching programmes.

Michael Thomson April 1989

Acknowledgements

This book could not have been written without the opportunity and training provided by Dr Margaret Newton when I first joined her team at the University of Aston and I am pleased to acknowledge this debt of gratitude and inspiration. I am also grateful to the other colleagues at the Language Development (Dyslexia) Unit at Aston University for their support, shared ideas and the stimulating discussions over the years. In particular, thanks are due to Maggie Cade, June Eaves, Colin Wilsher, Lyn Joffe, Ian Richards and Carolyn Hicks.

Some specific acknowledgements are as follows: Dr C. Wilsher for invaluable discussions on the interpretation of dichotic listening data; Professor and Mrs Miles for providing me with details of the Bangor Teaching Programme; Mrs A. Arkell and Mrs J. Pollock for providing details of the Helen Arkell Centre programme; Dr H. Chasty and Mrs W. Fisher for opportunity to discuss and view the work of the Dyslexia Institute; Dr B. Hornsby for permission to quote from the Alpha to Omega programme.

I would also like to acknowledge the time given to me to complete my book by Bill and Gay Watkins when we were all overstretched in setting up East Court School. My wife, Dr Rosemary Scott, also provided this valuable time, gave support and encouragement throughout and made very valuable suggestions and editorial comments at crucial points.

Thanks are also due to the series editors, Professor D. Crystal and Dr J. Cooper for the mammoth, and very valuable, task of editing and critizing the first draft of the book, and subsequent editorial advice.

I would also like to thank Mrs Maureen Wood for making sense of the first draft and for typing and word processing skills!

Finally, my thanks go to the hundreds of children who I have been in contact with over the years, and about whom this book is written.

The author and publishers would like to thank the following for permission to include copyright material. Full details can be obtained from the captions and references:

Academic Press for Fig. 4.5; The British Psychological Society for Table 1.2; Cornell University and the US Office of Education for Fig. 3.4; *Counsellor* for Table 7.4; The Dyslexia Institute and Wendy Fisher for Fig. 3.6; *Living and Learning* for Table 5.1; NFER/Nelson Publishing Co. for Table 5.1 and University Park Press for Fig. 4.1; Dr Snowling for Fig. 4.6.

1

Introduction

Despite well over 100 years of compulsory education in the United Kingdom, we have failed to achieve the 'universal literacy' so optimistically planned in the 1870 Education Act. Campaigns to alleviate adult illiteracy underline the gap between aspiration and achievement. The following is an extract from the Code of Regulations for Public Elementary Schools, written in 1904, and embodying a philosophy of teaching still prevalent today.

> The purpose of the public elementary school . . . [is to assist] boys and girls, according to their different needs, to fit themselves practically, as well as intellectually, for the work of life. With this purpose in view it will be the aim of the school to train the children carefully in habits of observation and clear reasoning, so that they may gain an intelligent acquaintance with some of the facts and laws of nature; to arouse in them a living interest in the ideals and achievements of mankind, and bring them to some familiarity with the literature and history of their own country; to give them some power over language as an instrument of thought and expression, and, to develop in them such a taste for good reading and thoughtful study as will enable them to increase that knowledge in after years by their own efforts. (Morant 1904 p. 1)

The unspoken assumption in the above is that children attending school would acquire the techniques of written language. However, many surveys report large numbers of children failing to achieve this goal. For example, Kellmer-Pringle, Butler and Davie (1966) in their data on the 1958 Cohort Study involving a longitudinal analysis of various criteria in the school life of children, report that 13.7% of boys and 8.3% of girls scored poorly on group reading tests; and further data, based on basic reading skills, indicated that some 10% of 7 year olds, in the final term of infant schooling, had barely made a start in reading. Clark (1970) in her survey of the County of Dunbarton in Scotland, reported that after 2 years at school, 15% of the children were not yet beyond the earlier stages of reading (a reading quotient less than 85 on the Schonell Graded Reading Tests). Rutter, Tizard and Whitmore (1970) in their study of 'handicap' in the total middle school range of Isle of Wight children, reported that 7.9% of the children were found to be backward in reading, (over 28 months behind chronological age) on the Neale Analysis of Reading Ability. Of these children all who were tested two years later were still backward in reading. Tizard (1974) comments: 'The backward readers were, at best, on the borderline of illiteracy. Furthermore their reading difficulties were remarkably persistent.' He was surprised to find that the progress of intelligent children was not better than that of the educationally backward.

These are just a few examples of the many studies detailing literacy and written language difficulties in the population. Of more immediate importance, however, is the question of why these deficits occur and it would appear that the concept of 'barriers to learning' provides a useful context.

1.1   Barriers to learning

Barriers to learning can be either environmental, or 'intrinsic' to the individual child's development. Eisenberg (1966) describes them as 'socio-psychological' and 'socio-physiological'. Another very general dimension is whether the difficulties are perceived to be located within the child, or within home or school. Ravenette (1968) reports two studies on the attitudes that head teachers take towards reading difficulty in terms of its 'locus of difficulty'. Over half the heads located the difficulty within the child (mainly in terms of a low intelligence) followed by the home and school. In particular, in relation to the home, lack of motivation due to attitudes towards schooling was cited as being a very frequent cause of reading difficulty.

One of the most widely expected and described 'causes' of reading failure is that of the social background of the child. Eisenberg (1966) demonstrated quite clearly the tremendous difference between the incidence of reading disorder in children in a 'metropolis' and children in 'suburbia'. The major difference between these two catchments was in terms of social background as defined by socio-economic class. There was three times the incidence of reading disabilities in the metropolis. The population distributions of the metropolis and the suburban areas were so different that Eisenberg comments that one could almost believe that there were different biological populations represented. Similar findings were observed in the UK. For example, Kellmer-Pringle et al. (1966) found that there were 7% of children in occupational classes 1 and 2 with reading difficulties, 19% in class 3 and 27% in 4 and 5 (see also Douglas et al. (1968), Lovell and Woolsey (1964), Pumfrey and Naylor (1978)).

The above findings are widespread, but explanations for them differ. Fraser (1959) argues that the results are due to the interrelationship between parental encouragement and school achievement. The expectations that parents have about school, and how much they encourage their children to try and succeed at school, may be class linked. Explanations relating to parental encouragement are also given by Valtin (1973) and Davie et al. (1972), linked in this instance to the concept of motivation as a difficulty in reading (Wedell 1977, Gulliford 1969). Deutsch (1963, 1965), however, argues that there is some kind of cultural barrier to learning, in the sense that the lower socio-economic groups have different uses of language which might predispose them to have difficulties in more formal reading, writing and spelling as taught in the typical schools. Others, for example, Labov (1967) and Venezky (1970), argue that these class differences are simply different cultural forms of language use; they are no less rich and sophisticated than those forms of language which are widely accepted and taught by what is predominantly a middle-class teaching profession. Finally, it has also been suggested by Deutsch, as well as by Bereiter and Engleman (1966), that there may be some kind of reduced perceptual experience amongst children from the lower socio-economic groups. This notion, linked to that of 'maternal deprivation', has been described by Rutter (1979) as a form of privation, i.e. reduction in opportunity, or 'rich environment' in so far as cognitive development is involved.

Another important barrier to learning relates to intelligence. Certainly children who have low intelligence do have difficulty in learning to read, write and spell (see e.g. Shakespeare 1975). This is not to say that children who score poorly on IQ tests are completely unable to perform these tasks, and it is sometimes very difficult to define what particular level of IQ is required for an individual to read, write and spell. Children with IQs of less than 50 may be able to 'read' in the sense of being able to decode the words into a sound and say them correctly out loud. This implies a phonological and sound coding strategy. However it is true that they might have difficulty in comprehending the totality of what is read.

A further barrier to learning is that of emotional and psychiatric disturbance which may cause problems in reading, writing and spelling. This often affects a much wider range of learning processes than simply written language, but there are a number of 'emotional' or 'behavioural' disorders which might have important implications for written language—hyperactivity, difficulties in attention, problems of social adjustment, and so on.

It is also accepted, for example Vernon (1971) and Myklebust (1978), that poor reading or written language may be due to a wide variety of factors, including lack of opportunity, inappropriate teaching, being away from school due to illness, frequent change of school, poor curriculum, and 'bad' teaching. There may also be problems due to the senses, i.e. the child might have great difficulty in seeing or in hearing, and therefore have problems in reading, writing and spelling.

A further barrier to learning, largely independent of the above, is that of *developmental dyslexia*.

1.2   The concept of developmental dyslexia

Developmental dyslexia is a severe difficulty with the written form of language independent of intellectual, cultural and emotional causation. It is characterized by the individual's reading, writing and spelling attainments being well below the level expected based on intelligence and chronological age. The difficulty is a cognitive one, affecting those language skills associated with the written form, particularly visual to verbal coding, short-term memory, order perception and sequencing. This definition describes dyslexia as a sub-category of written language problem. Before examining some other definitions it is necessary to review the development of the concept.

1.21   Historical perspective

The term *dyslexia* was originally used to describe various forms of acquired dyslexia, and as such has been investigated for at least 100 years. Kussmaul (1877) used the term *alexia*, or 'word blindness', to distinguish a special type of speech difficulty or aphasia caused by injuries to the left or dominant hemisphere of the brain controlling speech. Berlin (1872) was the first to use the term *dyslexia* as an alternative to 'word blindness'. Dejerine (1871), after post mortem examination of patients with dyslexia, found that: 'There always existed a lesion far back in the posterior temporal region in the left hemisphere where the parietal and occipital lobes come into contiguity.' He also showed that a loss of reading comprehension and writing depended on a left unilateral lesion. Initially, therefore, dyslexia was seen as a specific neurological disorder arising from some acquired brain 'trauma'.

Hinshelwood (1900), however, described a similar disorder not apparently caused by brain injury. He summarized this in a book entitled *Congenital Word-Blindness* (1917). He defined word-blindness as a congenital defect occurring in children with otherwise normal and undamaged brains, characterized by a disability in learning to read so great that it is manifestly due to a pathological condition, and where the attempts to teach the child by ordinary methods failed. Hinshelwood suggested that the disorder resulted from the failure to develop the brain function associated with visual memory of words, letters or figures, particularly connected with the angular gyrus. He also stressed that this was not due to any organic defect. General intelligence and the 'power of observation and reasoning' were found to be normal or above normal, and a further observation was the high incidence of the disability amongst boys.

It is interesting to note some of Hinshelwood's arguments in relation to the way in which he felt that dyslexia was actually caused. He argued that there was a primary register of letters, for example, and an auditory memory system which converted these to visual memory. He postulated that the learner used some kind of analytical or sound coding strategy initially, and finally learnt to read words directly for meaning. This approach echoes very closely indeed some of the current arguments and evidence for the way in which we learn to read, write and spell (see Chapter 3). In particular, Hinshelwood argued that some teaching methods were inappropriate to the dyslexic, and that one needed to help the dyslexic to reach the second stage of this process by letter-by-letter reading, sounding-out using auditory memory to form words, i.e. a *phonetic* approach. This again matches the suggestions made by current writers in relation to teaching the dyslexic, and to notions of auditory memory difficulties in the dyslexic, in terms of etiology (see Chapters 3 and 6).

Further evidence was given by Morgan (1896) and Kerr (1897) who presented case histories of intelligent children who were incapable of learning to read. The following is a typical example, (Morgan 1896 p. 1378):

He (i.e. a 14-year-old boy) has always been a bright and intelligent boy, quick at games and in no way inferior to others of his age. His great difficulty has been—and is now—his inability to learn to read. This inability is so remarkable, and so pronounced, that I have no doubt it is due to some congenital defect.

He has been at school or under tutors since he was 7 years old, and the greatest efforts have been made to teach him to read, but, in spite of this laborious and persistent training, he can only with difficulty spell out words of one syllable. The following is the result of an examination I made a short time since. He knows all his letters, and can write them and read them. . . . In writing his own name he made a mistake, putting 'Precy' for 'Percy', and he did not notice the mistake till his attention was called to it more than once . . . I then asked him to read me a sentence out of an easy child's book. . . . The result was curious. He did not read a single word correctly, with the exception of 'and', 'the', 'of', 'that', etc., the other words seemed to be quite unknown to him, and he could not even make an attempt to pronounce them. . . . He seems to have no power of preserving and storing up the visual impression produced by words—hence the words, though seen, have no significance for him. His visual memory for words is defective or absent; which is equivalent to saying that he is what Kussmaul (1877) has termed 'word blind' (*Caecitas syllabaris et verbalis*).

I may add that the boy is bright and of average intelligence in conversation. His eyes are normal . . . and his eyesight is good. The school-master who had taught him for several years says that he would be the smartest lad in the school if the instruction were entirely oral.

Such case histories have resulted in a generalized picture of the dyslexic children—as have descriptions based on clinical observations.

Another important contribution was that made by Orton (1925 and 1937), although he used a rather convoluted term *strephosymbolia*, literally meaning twisted signs (from the Greek). He put forward a theory in relation to the neurological components of dyslexia, regarding the way in which images could be inverted, reversed, and 'twisted' by competing stores of information in the left and right hemispheres. We shall examine this theory, and current theories that have developed from this early work, in Chapter 3, Section 1. Orton in fact postulated a whole series of developmental disorders, many of which have an echo in today's categories. These include, for example, *developmental word deafness*, in which children have difficulty recognizing the spoken word, and also have delay and distortion of speech, but perfectly normal hearing (a kind of receptive dysphasia or aphasia). He postulated a *developmental motor aphasia* in which there was slow development and disorders of speech but good understanding of spoken words (no word deafness). He also postulated a so-called 'true' child stuttering, in which there were spasms of musculature, developmental apraxias with abnormal clumsiness and a developmental dysgraphia where there where special difficulties in learning to write. The dyslexic category was described initially as *developmental alexia*, an unusual difficulty in learning to read, but with no evidence of accompanying physical, mental or emotional abnormalities. There was normal auditory development, and often a display of good intelligence and imagination in solving their problem of not being able to read. Visual motor and visual skills were normal, and Orton argued that the reading disability took the form of letter and word confusions and reversals, severe spelling difficulties and often difficulties in writing. These descriptions are echoed by current writers, and it was Orton who laid down the foundation for current approaches, which, nonetheless, are not free of problems in definition.

Although these early workers produced a generalized description of 'dyslexia' it was not until more recently that the idea of children having *specific* difficulties was supported by research into types of handicap in the child population. Important evidence, worth examining in detail, is contained in a book based on the Isle of Wight epidemiological study, *Health Education and Behaviour* (Rutter, Tizard and Whitmore 1970), with further published studies by Yule and others widely quoted as support for the notion that there is a category of children having a specific difficulty in reading, as opposed to being just poor readers. The category *specific reading difficulty* is important because as Frith (1981) points out, these studies have shown a specific reading difficulty to be different from a general retardation on statistical, etiological and educational grounds. The importance in this context is that many writers view 'specific reading difficulties' as being synonymous with dyslexia.

The statistical argument for the notion of specific retardation rests on the difference between general backwardness and retardation. Traditionally in remedial education it has been accepted that one describes children whose reading and spelling is at a level with their intellectual abilities, yet behind their chronological age, as being 'backward'. Very simply, a child of 10 with a mental age of 8 and a reading age of 8 would be 'backward'. This is distinguished from the notion of 'retardation' in which a child's reading is behind his so-called potential or mental age. For example a child of 10 with a mental age of 11 and a reading age of 9 would be 2 years 'retarded'. However, there are serious problems in relation to these traditional notions. One relates to standard error of measurement, i.e. the fact that tests have an in-built error in terms of the way they are constructed, so that for a given child the 'true' intelligence or the 'true' reading age may not be that which is given by the test. A more serious problem is the regression effect. This is a statistical effect resulting from *correlations* between two given parameters or variables being less than unity. The correlation is usually around 0.6 between IQ and reading (see for example Yule 1973, Yule and Rutter 1976). This has the effect that if an individual scores poorly on one variable he will tend to score rather higher on another variable. In other words, at the two extreme ends of the population curve, those children who are very intelligent will not necessarily be reading very well, and those children who are very unintelligent will not necessarily be reading very badly. The way around this problem is to use the multiple regression technique where one can provide equations for predicting one variable from another. Typically, one will produce an equation which will predict a child's expected reading age, based on his intelligence and chronological age. This idea of a discrepancy between reading and intelligence is a key notion for the concept of specific reading difficulties, as well as for the diagnosis of dyslexia (see Chapter 6).

The studies by Rutter, Tizard and Whitmore (1970), Yule (1973), Berger, Yule and Rutter (1975), and Yule *et al.* (1974), report the use of multiple regression equations to predict a child's expected reading age from his chronological age and intelligence. These are based on five separate populations—around 1,000 9- and 10-year-olds on the Isle of Wight; the same 9- and 10-year-olds followed up during later years of their schooling; around 1,500 10-year-olds in the ILEA (non-immigrant children); and around 2,000 14-year-olds in the Isle of Wight. The researchers examined the distribution of children with specific reading difficulties, specifically those who were two standard deviations below their predicted reading age, based on regression equations. The theoretical normal curve or distribution should demonstrate 2.28% of children having scores two standard deviations below the norm. This would apply if the children who were poor readers were simply the 'bottom end of a normal continuum or distribution'. In fact what the researchers found was around 3.5% of 10-year-olds and 4.5% of 14-year-olds on the Isle of Wight, and around 6% of 10-year-olds in ILEA. There seemed to be a higher incidence of poor achievers than would be expected from the theoretical distribution—a 'hump' at the bottom end of the normal distribution. Having established that there was an excess of underachievers, the researchers then went on to examine the children with specific reading retardation and those with a general reading backwardness. This was done by looking at intelligence and attainment using the WISC (Wechsler Intelligence Scale for Children) and the Neale Analysis of Reading (either Accuracy or Comprehension). Specific reading retardation was defined as an attainment on the Neale analysis which was 30 months or more below the level predicted on the basis of the child's age and WISC IQ, using a multiple regression equation (Yule 1967). The generally backward readers were those whose attainments were simply 30 months or more below the child's chronological age.

The groups were different on a number of criteria, as shown in Table 1.1.

Table 1.1   Factors in backward and specifically retarded readers

Backward readers	Specific reading retardates
Mean IQ 80	Mean IQ 102
General developmental delays/ abnormalities	Speech and language delays/abnormalities
54% boys	76% boys
Better prognosis	Very poor prognosis
Overt neurological features	Fewer overt neurological features
Frequent organic dysfunctions (e.g. 11% cerebral palsy)	No organic dysfunctions
Motor and praxic difficulties more common	Motor and praxic difficulties less common
Higher incidence of large families	Lower incidence of large families
Higher incidence of low status or disadvantaged homes	Lower incidence of disadvantaged or low status homes

(Developed from Yule and Rutter 1976, Yule *et al*. 1974, Yule 1973, Rutter *et al*. 1970.)

The two groups differed, as might be expected, on intelligence, which was part of the selection procedure. However, there was a great difference in the distribution of sex (boys were more common among the specific retardates). The generally backward readers had a delayed development in many areas such as walking, clumsiness in both fine and gross movements, motor impersistence (difficulty in sustaining a voluntary motor act initiated by verbal commands), poorer on constructional tasks involving copying designs, and so on. There was a general overall delay including speech and language. The children with specific reading retardation, however, seemed to be retarded only in speech and language, and not generally. Yule and Rutter (1976 p. 34) concluded: 'on both contemporaneous and developmental measures, the two types of reading disorder are sufficiently differentiated to argue for the validity of the conceptional distinction'. It is interesting to note that a discrepancy between intelligence and reading behaviour, higher incidence of boys against girls, a delay in language and speech, and the other features are described by many writers as being associated with dyslexia.

In addition, the two types of reading disorder are shown to be different in educational terms, due to the differential prognosis of specific reading retardation and general reading backwardness (Yule 1973). The finding here was that the children with specific reading difficulties in a follow-up study (based on the 10-year-olds in the Isle of Wight) were 6 months behind the children who were generally backward in reading, both in spelling and reading. In other words, the less intelligent children made greater progress in written language, despite both groups being equally retarded (30 months) in the initial stages. It is also interesting to note that the children with specific reading retardation progressed rather better in maths between 10 and 14 years compared to the children who were generally backward. As well as suggesting a difference in educational terms, this finding lends weight to the hypothesis that children who are brighter and yet have an unexpected failure in learning to read have some kind of specific handicap.

Frith (1981) points out that it is precisely the persistence over time and the lack of response to conventional teaching methods that provide the particular test criteria for distinguishing specific from general reading failure. The distinction therefore has very important educational implications.

The above studies provide initial evidence for the notion of a specific learning difficulty, in this case in reading, although Yule (1973) comments on the links between reading and spelling. Yule and Rutter (1976) and Rutter (1978), however, argue that specific reading retardation should be described as such, and not as dyslexia. We shall see that many of the features described above, as well as directional confusion, disorders of temporal orientation, difficulties in naming, sometimes in bizarre spelling errors, and so on, are associated with dyslexia. Indeed Rutter and Yule (1973) in reviewing the evidence of such features in specific reading retardation conclude that most of the characteristics can be found there. They present data consistent with the hypothesis that language difficulties are the unifying factor underlying specific retardation. However, from there on they typically go on to argue that this does not imply that one should use the word *dyslexia* to describe such difficulties. This is mainly on the grounds that there is scanty evidence for biological inheritance (though as we shall see the evidence is not all that scanty), but perhaps more importantly that specific reading retardation is multi-factorially determined, i.e. socio-cultural factors can be important, as well as environmental stimulation, schooling, temperament, personality, and so on. They invoke more or less all the possible reasons for a child having difficulty in learning to read as being associated with specific reading retardation. This, in the present writer's view, negates their initial arguments that the specific reading difficulty is actually different from any other form of difficulty. If one takes such a global interactionist view, one can never be certain whether one is talking about a specific reading disorder. They argue that no studies have demonstrated any clustering of developmental anomalies said to characterize dyslexia, and yet their own studies seem to do just that. Since the above seminal studies were carried out others have examined the notion of children with a specific reading difficulty versus those who are generally backward in reading. A number of studies have focused on the statistical argument based on the so-called 'hump' at the end of the normal distribution. Some writers have criticized Yule and Rutter (1976) by arguing that the higher incidence of under-achievers was due to a statistical artefact (Rodgers 1983, Van der Wessel and Zeger 1985). It is argued that as the ceiling of the Neale Analysis of Reading Ability is around 13, some of the older children were at this ceiling level. This resulted in a negative skew, i.e. an increased portion of children at the bottom end of the normal distribution on the reading test, simply because there were no children who could score over 13. Van der Wessel and Zeger ran computer simulations with artificial ceilings and found that this produced a 'hump' in distribution. They therefore arued that there is no distinction between backward readers and those with specific reading difficulties. Rodgers, in his population study of Glamorgan, found a percentage of 2.29% of under-achievers against the expected 2.28% (two standard deviations) below the norm. Similarly, Jorm et al. (1986) and Share et al. (1987) in their studies in Australian and New Zealand populations respectively did not find an excess of under-achievers. They proposed that a statistical distinction between children with specific reading difficulties and those who are backward in reading could not be replicated. Share et al. go on to argue that some of the other distinctions between specific retardates and those who were generally backward could not be found in their studies. For example, they did not find a higher incidence of boys among specifically retarded children, against those who were generally retarded. Instead they found a higher incidence of boys in both groups of poor readers compared with those who were good readers. Although they found that those with general retardation had a higher incidence of neurological and motor problems than those with specific retardation, they did not find evidence of language delay at 3 years of age. However, they did find that the children with specific retardation had lower WISC Verbal IQs at 9 and poor speech at 7 and 9 years of age.

Set against these recent findings and criticisms are some other studies investigating populations which have found differences. For example Fredman and Stevenson (1988), examining around 1500 7½ year olds and 1500 11 year olds, found a 'hump' (3.05% and 3.72% for reading and spelling). In addition they found an excess of under-achievers (specific retardates) in the reading of non-words at 11 years of age. The reading of non-words, as shown in Chapter 3, relates to the ability of an individual to apply grapheme/phoneme correspondence rules of phonological skills to the task of reading. The authors suggest that this interesting finding argues for focus on process and strategy in reading difficulties rather than on statistical arguments in terms of population frequencies. Miles and Haslum (1986), examining the Child Health Education cohorts, based on the births of 1970, present data looking at 'dyslexia indicators'. These are largely based on the Bangor Dyslexia Test, and they found a much higher incidence of 'dyslexia positive' scores among those specifically retarded readers who were 2–3 standard deviations below the norm. This is based on nearly 1300 children and they suggested that dyslexia therefore forms an 'anomalous population' and is not part of a normal variation.

Tyler and Elliott (1988), utilizing the standardization of the British Ability Scales, identified specific learning difficulties by regression equation. They found similar sex ratios to the Yule and Rutter studies and argued for a specific learning difficulty against general reading difficulty distinction.

Despite the seeming controversy and variation in population data that these studies show, it is important not to get too obsessed or bogged down with the statistical arguments. It is more important to focus on the process involved in the dyslexic individual, in terms of the underlying cognitive weaknesses, or their inappropriate learning strategies, and link these to a theoretical framework. Here the evidence is clearer. For example, in Jorm et al.'s (1986) study, although they did not find a classic 'hump' they did find that the children identified as being specifically retarded, based on regression equations, were weaker at letter naming, phonemic awareness, sentence memory, colour naming and other features. These skills, as we shall see in Chapter 3, are particularly associated with weaknesses that experimental studies have identified. In addition, findings such as Fredman and Stevenson's (1988) that non-word reading can also form an excess of under-achievers does not argue for a continuum of reading difficulties based on phonological skills, as Bryant and Bradley (1985) would argue. Stevenson specifically argues that his data are evidence against the notion of a continuum of difficulties. Ellis and Large (1988), in their longitudinal study, found that children with specific reading difficultes were weaker at items such as phonological coding, short-term memory and naming, compared to better readers. Children with general reading difficulties were weaker on almost all of their 44 variables.

It is also important to recognize that the absence of a 'hump' does not argue against an etiologically distinct group of children with learning difficulties. This point is made by Fredman and Stevenson (1988), as well as Snowling (1987) and Frith (1985); both Snowling and Frith make the point that there is abundant evidence of qualitative differences between children with specific reading difficulties and normal readers of similar levels of reading skill. These statistical or population studies become additionally problematic when one is examining relatively small groups. It is more fruitful to examine the cognitive profiles and specific subskills of the dyslexic, and to place all of this into a developmental perspective. These are themes that will be taken up later.

1.22   Problems of definition

The terminology used has been briefly mentioned above, and an examination of definitions is useful here. The definition on page 3 used the phrase *developmental dyslexia* to distinguish this form of dyslexia from that of *acquired* dyslexia. There is a good deal of literature appertaining to individuals who have learnt to read, write and spell normally but who, in late childhood or usually when adults, have lost this capacity due to some kind of acquired disorder. This is not developmental, but *acquired* dyslexia (see Chapter 3, Section 1). The word *developmental* implies that the child does not acquire reading, writing and spelling very easily, and the problem is in the *initial learning*. It also suggests that dyslexia is a cognitive language disorder of development. The term *dyslexia* is used because this seems to be a simple, short way of describing the child's learning problems. Definitions can become extremely complex, as we shall see later, so let us remember that, etymologically, *dyslexia* simply means 'difficulty with words' (*dys*—'difficulty with' or 'bad' and *lexis*—'words'). This is succinct and to the point. It implies that the problem is not simply reading, but includes spelling, writing and other aspects of language. In fact, the problem, it will be argued, is very much a language difficulty, and needs to be recognized as such. The term can result in misunderstanding, however. Many teachers, presumably owing to the way in which dyslexia is presented in teacher-training colleges, believe that *dyslexia* is a 'medical' term and that therefore the child can never learn to read, write and spell.

Other terminology can further confuse the matter. Terms such as strephosymbolia; acute dyslexia; specific reading retardation; specific dyslexia; specific learning disorder and many others are used to describe the same syndrome. Unless otherwise indicated, I will use the term *dyslexia* to refer to the developmental syndrome defined above and described later. Terms such as reading failure, poor spellers or reading retardation will be used when reporting research findings where the authors themselves have used those terms.

So far we have not described any specific characteristics or features of developmental dyslexia. This is not because dyslexia does not show any such features, but because most of the definitions and early descriptions seem to be rather 'negative'. In other words, by ruling out a whole series of possible reasons for a child having a learning difficulty, one might come to the conclusion that there is a dyslexic problem. Definitions, identification or diagnosis are by exclusion. A typical definition of this type includes the World Federation of Neurology definition of *specific developmental dyslexia*, which states:

> a disorder manifested by difficulty in learning to read, despite conventional instruction, adequate intelligence and socio-cultural opportunity. It is dependent upon fundamental cognitive disabilities which are frequently of constitutional origin (cited in Critchley 1970 p. 11).

A further definition is given in Critchley and Critchley (1978 p. 149):

> Developmental dyslexia is a learning disability which initially shows itself by difficulty in learning to read, and later by erratic spelling and lack of facility in manipulating written as opposed to spoken words. The condition is cognitive in essence, and usually genetically determined. It is not due to intellectual inadequacy, or to lack of socio-cultural opportunity, or to emotional factors, or to any known structural brain defect. It probably represents a specific maturational defect, which tends to lessen as

the child gets older, and is capable of considerable improvement, especially when appropriate remedial help is afforded at the earliest opportunity.

Apart from the references to the fact that dyslexia may be overcome and to a cognitive or constitutional difficulty, this is again a definition by exclusion. Rutter (1978) has criticized this kind of definition, specifically that of the World Federation of Neurology, as a 'logical non-starter'. He argues that one cannot know what 'conventional' instruction is. Does it mean, for example, that a child taught using ITA, or some other form of reading teaching system, cannot be dyslexic? Furthermore, how does one define 'adequate intelligence'—does it mean that dyslexia cannot occur in children who are below average intelligence, and how low an IQ does one have to have before one cannot read at all? He also suggests that the idea of socio-cultural opportunities is not appropriate here either. Does this imply that dyslexia cannot occur in children who come from socio-cultural backgrounds that are not favoured? He particularly argues that negative definitions do not provide conceptual clarity and by ruling out all possible difficulties invoke dyslexia only as a last resort.

A particular problem is the exclusion categories that are used. Typically in relation to intelligence, negative definitions suggest that one should not assume children are dyslexic unless they have an IQ (usually based on the Wechsler Scale, either Performance or Verbal) of more than 90.

One can criticize this notion firstly on the grounds of variability in test performance due to the imperfections of the test instrument itself, i.e. the standard error of measurement in psychometric terms. There are however two other important criticisms. One is that many of the individual intelligence tests have certain items which appear to be specifically difficult for the dyslexic child. We shall examine this in more detail in Chapter 6, but the question is whether these subtests should be used to compute the IQ. This is a very important point, as the Wechsler Scale, for example, has about four subtests which can be shown to be specifically linked to a dyslexic-type learning problem. The second important criticism is that excluding from a dyslexic category all children who have IQs below 90 leads to a logical inconsistency. One is saying that only children who are at least of average intelligence can possibly be dyslexic. But we shall see that dyslexia cuts across all levels of intelligence, whether a genetic or environmental cause is involved. It is of course much easier to *detect* a child with a dyslexic problem if there is a discrepancy between his obvious brightness and his reading, writing and spelling abilities. In many cases if a child is of low intelligence one often assumes that his difficulty is ipso facto due to this cause. However, many children of low intelligence do *not* have difficulties with reading, writing and spelling. It is perfectly possible to define a specific learning problem or dyslexia in children whose IQs are below average.

Other typical definitions of dyslexia exclude sensory functioning as being a cause of the child's reading difficulties. We shall see, however, that some research suggests that there are ocular motor difficulties, or eye movement problems in dyslexia. Similarly, some research suggests severe difficulties in sound discrimination or auditory perception amongst dyslexics. Where should one draw the line over which particular aspects of sensory function should be excluded? This problem will be returned to in Chapters 3 and 6.

Most definitions also exclude brain damage, or neurological dysfunction, as a part of dyslexia, but again (see Chapter 3) some theories suggest there is a minimal neurological dysfunction, or so called 'soft' neurological signs in the dyslexic, and it becomes a moot point as to when a constitutional difference in the central nervous system becomes different from definitive tissue damage or where gross handicaps shade into more circumscribed behavioural effects.

Furthermore, how does one define the *opportunities* for learning? How long must children be exposed to school before one can assume that they will learn to read, write and spell appropriately? How does one evaluate the aspects of teaching methodology in terms of whether they are appropriate for a child to learn? In relation to other environmental determinants, how does one evaluate social adjustment and home background in relation to whether they are 'suitable' for written language learning? The measures we have are very gross indeed, and may not pin-point more subtle difficulties which might have had a very serious effect on written language learning.

There are also difficulties in defining what kinds of teaching experiences characterize adequate opportunity for learning and thus many of the so-called exclusionary items are multi-factorial and interactional. The child with a dyslexic problem may be easier to identify if everything else is 'normal', but this does not necessarily mean that children cannot have other forms of difficulty which can interact with their dyslexia.

In response to the above criticisms, especially those by Rutter (1978), Eisenberg (1978) argues that one can define negatively and this does have utility. He cites his own (1967 pp. 33–4) definitions: operationally, specific reading disability may be defined as failure to learn to read with normal proficiency despite conventional instruction, a culturally adequate home, proper motivation, intact senses, normal intelligence and freedom from gross neurological deficit. He argues that one can define normal performance in terms of the child falling below average on a standardized task, bearing in mind statistical, chronological and mental age considerations. He also suggests that conventional instruction simply means that the child has had some teaching within very broadly accepted criteria. This does not mean that children with idiosyncratic teaching may not have dyslexia, just that there are some basic requirements such as exposure to the written language, opportunity to read books, and so on, which are important. In relation to cultural background, he suggests that there needs to be a reasonable development of vocabulary and agrees that there is a link between school achievement and social class factors. However he argues that there is a difference between defining a so-called 'pure' case of dyslexia in order to undertake research, and a clinical assessment, where one would include the diagnosis of dyslexia in children from lower socio-economic levels. In respect to intact senses, he suggests that it is remarkable how little sensory acuity is required for learning to read provided that the handicap is recognized and dealt with appropriately. So again, one need not necessarily exclude children with sensory defects of various sorts from a diagnosis of dyslexia. According to Benton (1978) in order not to confuse dyslexia with other forms of reading behaviour, one must first establish it as a clinical entity in negative terms, and then finally provide more detailed classifications, and sub-types.

The reader is referred to Wheeler and Watkins (1979) who provide a review of definitions. In addition the reader is referred to the definition at the beginning of Section 1.2, which is the operational definition used throughout this book.

1.23   Incidence

The incidence of specific learning difficulties or dyslexia in the population has important educational implications in terms of the resources that need to be allocated, but also has important educational policy implications with respect to the Government's and other attitudes towards dyslexia.

The figure of 3.5 to 6% reported by Yule *et al.* 1974 represents a very substantial number of children who were identified according to clearly defined criteria. There are many other estimates. Satz *et al.* (1978), for example, suggest that about 15% of children have specific learning difficulties, which represents about 8 million children in the United States alone (Kline 1972). The 15% figure is also reported by Myklebust cf. Celdric 1970; Kellmer-Pringle *et al.* 1966 and Gaddes (1976) in Canada, the UK and France respectively. However, these figures may include children who are not strictly defined as having dyslexia.

The problem really is what criteria—and in particular what 'cut-off'—to use. Traditionally any child who is two years behind his chronological age in reading is deemed to have a severe difficulty. This, of course, ignores the relationship between reading and intelligence as described previously and will include children who have reading difficulties due to backwardness and other forms of learning problem. Another serious point is the inappropriateness of a fixed criterion in development. In particular, Gaddes (1976) makes the point that a two-year retardation at different ages means different things; he quotes studies using the Wide Range Achievement test at various ages. For example at 6 years, 1% of the population are 2 years retarded, and at 7 years 2%, and the percentage increases up to 19 years where 25% of the population are retarded in reading in the sense of being 2 years behind their chronological age. Applying this fixed criterion is obviously an absurdity. In dyslexia there is also an increasing lag between reading, writing and spelling performance against chronological age as the child gets older. We shall examine this in more detail in Chapters 3 and 6. One implication of this is that, due to the way reading is tested, it is impossible for a child of 6 to have a reading age 2 years retarded, as most reading age tests only go down to 6 years. On the other hand a child at the other extreme, with a chronological age of 15, is being given reading tests that are aimed at a maximum of 13 years as a reading age. Similar arguments apply to spelling and other forms of attainment tests. Being 2 years retarded in reading at 15 years old means that one can read very competently for everyday use, and indeed would be able to read most texts required for secondary school learning. On the other hand being 2 years retarded at age 9 represents a much more serious problem in respect of the child's own development. Two years retarded at age 7 means that the child is a non-starter, and has little attainment to speak of at all.

It is important to bear all these points in mind when trying to devise criteria by which to define a population from which one can draw conclusions about incidence. Another important consideration concerns children who may be intelligent but under-functioning, yet whose reading and spelling in absolute terms are not behind their chronological age. The use of regression equations does to some extent circumvent this interpretative difficulty, but it is often the case that bright children whose reading and spelling may be more or less up to their chronological age are not perceived as having a learning difficulty by local authorities and teachers, who comment that there are many children who are reading and spelling much worse. This is a reasonable comment in relation to the kind of resources available, and because a child is brighter, he is not more deserving of remedial education or special help. However this does not detract from the fact that these children are not being recognized as having a learning problem, and are not given appropriate help.

Other estimates of incidence are also given. For example Klasen (1972), in reviewing some of the studies, reports figures between 20 to 25%, Silver and Hagin (1960) suggest between 2 and 25%, and Bender (1957) 5 to 15%, whereas Rabinovitch (1968), and Keeney and Keeney (1968) suggest around 10%. Bannatyne (1971), basing his work on the ITPA Standardization Samples, suggests a figure of 2%, Tarnopol and Tarnopol (1976), in reviewing the incidence of dyslexia around the world, suggest that around 8% is the median figure quoted for retarded readers. Thomson and Newton (1979), in their studies validating the Aston Index, found around 9% who could be described as having a dyslexic-type problem as opposed to other forms of reading difficulty. Farnham-Diggory (1978) quotes the 1970 US Centre for National Statistics as suggesting around 2.6% having specific learning difficulties and Clark (1970), in her study in Dunbartonshire, found around 5% who were 1 to 2 years retarded, and yet had average IQs (and who presumably showed more specific difficulties).

There are some interesting suggestions that these figures will vary very much depending on the particular age at which the children are referred. Owen et al. (1971), for example, suggest that there is a peak of children referred for learning difficulties between 8 and 11 years. They quote data demonstrating that of the 2% referred for remedial education, 4% are 6-year-olds, 10% 7-year-olds, 57% 8- to 11-year-olds and around 18% 11- to 16-year-olds. In other words there may be an underestimate of learning disabilities at the younger, and possibly the older, age ranges due to the referral system. (This, of course, assumes that there is not some sudden onset of dyslexia at 8 years old, and a sudden decline in dyslexia at 15!)

Even at a conservative estimate the practical implications of the above figures are quite dramatic. Assuming the middle of the Isle of Wight and Inner London estimates or the lowest end of the other estimates, i.e. around 5%, we have a substantial problem. In other words the problem is not, as various Governmental

Reports would have us believe, a very small problem besetting a minority of children, but quite a substantial difficulty. What this means is that, in a class of 25 children, there will be around two dyslexic children. In a primary school, around 10 or more, and in a large comprehensive school of 1,500 there will be around 60 children having dyslexic problems. Based on the current child population (OPCS 1981), there are some 394,300 children having dyslexic problems in the UK!

The above is based on conservative estimates of incidence. There are many more children whose retardation is not as severe as 30 months, but who nevertheless are seriously under-functioning and require some remediation, and specialist remedial provision is, in my experience, woefully inadequate.

1.24   Signs and symptoms

Before examing some of the itemized descriptions made by various writers on dyslexia, a thumbnail sketch of a dyslexic individual is presented. This is a description based on my own clinical experience of dyslexic children and, although it is idiosyncratic in that sense, does reflect typical findings described in the literature.

Referral may take place at almost any age, but usually there is a peak of referrals around 9, 10 or 11, after the child has been some years at school, and has consistently failed to acquire reading, writing and spelling. Often it is felt that there is a problem which cannot be readily explained, or is puzzling to the teachers or parents. This is not to say that children are not referred or identified at other stages. Many observant teachers or parents may refer earlier, in order to identify 'at risk' childen so that they can provide appropriate first teaching and thus circumvent difficulties. Similarly there is another small peak of referrals at the time of transfer to secondary school, and another peak around examination times.

Typically, the dyslexic child will come from any socio-economic level, with a range of family attitudes towards school and learning. Developmental milestones will have been within normal limits, although language may well have been delayed. In particular there may have been slight phonological or articulatory difficulties persisting beyond the 'norm'. These might be spoonerisms which may persevere into later childhood and even adulthood. The child may manifest these speech difficulties during the childhood years, particularly the confusion of (θ/f) and (r/w), and in some cases there may be some difficulty in expressing ideas fluently in spoken language. However, the child's use of language in reiation to aspects of vocabulary, verbal reasoning, understanding of events, and other intellectual skills associated with higher linguistic functioning is within normal limits, or may well be exceptionally high. (However, it is a mistake to assume that *all* dyslexic children are highly intelligent.)

This point of discrepancy between the child's perfectly adequate and sometimes above-average oral ability in understanding, and his poor developing written language skills is one of the first signs to parents and teachers that something is amiss. A child may be bright, intelligent, able to answer questions and (as far as parents and teachers are concerned) appear to have no apparent difficulty in coping with early aspects of school work. Over the first year the child may be a bit slow in acquiring the alphabet and aspects of sight vocabulary, but parents may have been told not to worry as the child will develop in due course. By about 7 or so, the child has barely made a start in reading and spelling, and has become demotivated. As the child gets older, if he is not given appropriate help with reading, writing and spelling, these will lag further and further behind chronological age.

It is now that the long and tortuous misery of many dyslexic children's school career begins. The child, while recognizing that he can understand the classwork as well as his peers, begins to recognize also that he is not learning to read, write and spell as well as they are. He is faced with his own failure in written language every day, and one has only to draw a parallel with the adult situation to realize how serious this is for his own self-esteem. Imagine having to go to work every day and being confronted with a job which you found impossible to master. Not only do you find the job difficult, but you are completely unable to understand its first principles. You would soon develop strategies to avoid having to undertake that task—namely getting another job! Unfortunately for the child he is not able to undertake simple avoidance. He is stuck with an educational system which expects that he must read, write and spell. If he does not, he may be labelled 'stupid', 'thick', a 'dunce', and be unable to obtain any kind of qualifications in order to succeed in our literate society. A feature associated with dyslexia, then, is a secondary anxiety problem, which may manifest itself in a number of ways. The child may become anxious and withdrawn, or may become rather aggressive and 'play up'. These difficulties can cause tensions in the family, particularly if there is a younger child who is succeeding well at school. The older child may resent this, therefore placing stress on inter-sibling relationships.

There may well be other reading and spelling problems in the child's family, either other diagnosed dyslexic cases, or parents with a spelling difficulty or who were late readers themselves. The child himself will have a problem in reading. This can be characterized by slow and non-fluent reading, regressive eye movements, losing his place, reading from the middle of words, or non-recognition of letters. Reading errors will include confusions of letter order (e.g. *bread* for *beard*) occasional reversals of letters or whole words, *(b/d, on/no)*—although these errors are not as frequent amongst dyslexics as is commonly believed. Other errors include telescoping of sounds, and inability to read phonologically: the child may be unable to sound out words correctly, to blend them, or to break them down into whole units. Some illustrations of these kinds of errors are given in the case histories in Chapter 2.

As well as difficulties in reading, it is important to recognize the other problems associated with attainments. This applies particularly to spelling and to written language. The child will often have greater difficulty in spelling than in reading, and have difficulty in expressing ideas fluently in written form. Spelling may be either phonetic, the child being able to follow his own speech, but unable to remember or 'internalize' spelling patterns, or sometimes it may be totally bizarre, i.e. unrelated to the written language system. It is difficult to describe what one means by 'bizarre' spelling without recourse to example. Here are a few: *raul/urchins*; *kss/snake*; *gars/gasket*; *mocke/smoke*; *hg/have*; *fuda/thunder*;

wueen/walking; *tars/trumpet*; *iriteap/terrific*; *brioth/brown*; *ping/painting*; *teds/maids*. Some of these are clearly approximations to sounds, and the reader with a little linguistic training may attempt an analysis of these phoneme realizations! Of course not all dyslexic children produce such strange realization; others may be phonetic *wayt/wait*, or omission *gog/gong*, etc.

All of this has a profound affect on the child's general ability to cope with school. He is unable to read appropriate texts, or books of interest, not only for obtaining information, but also for pleasure. He is unable to express himself in relation to undertaking school work—much is based on being able to write, whether this is in projects or formal essay writing and questions. The child's spelling will tend to militate against work being taken seriously or given higher marks. Sometimes the child may be labelled as educationally sub-normal, or unintelligent. If the child is shown to be intelligent, then he can be described as stubborn, not trying, or lazy. In many cases one hears quite disturbing stories reported about children required to read aloud in front of the whole class, when it is known that they cannot read at all, or being required to learn long lists of spellings and then being put into detention because they were unable to get 100% the next day. Inappropriate diagnoses are sometimes used to describe the child's learning problems, often based on the erroneous assumption that he is maladjusted. Particularly common is the suggestion that the parents are over-anxious, worrying, and therefore transmitting this to their child, who is somehow deliberately not learning in order to get at his parents.

As well as reading, writing and spelling difficulties, the dyslexic child may typically have problems with arithmetic, such as tables, basic operations, and place value. In some cases, however, the child may have a good mathematical ability, in the sense that he may understand concepts in maths quite well: it is the manipulation of the number symbols that is his problem. Other dyslexic difficulties include problems in aspects of short-term memory: the child may forget instructions, such as, 'go out of the door, go up the stairs, go to the second drawer down and take out the book on the left'. Typically the child comes down having only reached half way up the stairs, to say 'what did you say I should get?' Further difficulties relating to this include problems in remembering a series of numbers, such as a telephone number, for any length of time. This contrasts markedly with the ability of the child to remember things in long-term memory; events long past can be remembered perfectly well. We shall examine memory in some detail in Chapter 3.

In many cases the child will have difficulties with some of the more complex manipulative skills, such as doing up shoelaces or buttons. These difficulties can persist quite late into life. On the other hand this kind of problem may be in marked contrast with the child's very good ability in visuo-spatial skills—for example, being able to assemble models very quickly and easily, in form-boards and Lego. Usually the child assembles from pictures, rather than follow the directions in model making!

We can now look at more formal descriptions of signs and symptoms. As there are almost as many lists of signs and symptoms as there are authors writing about dyslexia, it would be tedious to mention every one. Presented here are a few of the more common views from British and American authors. It should be noted at this point that none of the following features is necessarily exclusive, nor do all the characteristics have to occur in every dyslexic child. These are simply observations associated with children having dyslexic problems. Some children who are good readers, writers and spellers may have similar kinds of difficulties, and some children who are severely dyslexic may not have all of them. What is suggested by the authors is that these particular features occur much more frequently in dylsexic children, and that they have theoretical and diagnostic significance.

Newton (1970) describes the following behavioural features:

1 Persistent reversal and disordering of letters (e.g. *b* and *d*), syllables, words *(saw/was)* and word order when reading, writing and occasionally speaking
2 Mirror imaging of letters and words
3 Inability to perceive, code and subsequently retain a consistent meaningful symbolic image
4 The consequent inability to retrieve and express a relevant meaningful output of linguistic material
5 Severe spelling disorder
6 Non-resolution of hand, ear and eye dominance
7 Late development of spoken language in early childhood
8 Difficulties with sequencing, order and direction
9 Sometimes motor clumsiness, sometimes hyperactivity and occasionally superior ability in spatial skills in direct contrast with the disability in linguistic skills.

Miles (1974) regards the following as signs of dyslexia (many of these signs form part of the Bangor Dyslexia Test, which will be discussed in Chapter Six):

1 Discrepancy between intellectual level and performance in spelling
2 Bizarre spelling
3 Confusion of *b* and *d* in either reading or writing, or both
4 Difficulty in distinguishing between left and right
5 Difficulty in repeating polysyllable words, such as preliminary, philosophical or statistical
6 Difficulty in repeating digits in reverse order (and other defects of short-term memory)
7 Inability to do subtractions except with 'concrete' aids
8 Difficulty in memorizing tables
9 Losing the place when reciting tables
10 A history of clumsiness, late walking or late talking.

Bannatyne (1971) describes the following as major characteristics (again not all need to be present):

1 Often poor auditory discrimination of vowels

2 Inadequate phoneme/grapheme sequencing memory (for matching)
3 Poor sound blending and auditory closure
4 Mildly deficient development
5 Maturational lag in language function
6 Reasonably efficient visual spatial ability
7 Unlateralized gaze when reading
8 Mirror imaging and writing of letters
9 Directional configuration in constancy, also causing mirror imaging of letters
10 Difficulties in associating verbal labels to directional concepts, but no visual spatial disorientation of any kind
11 Visual spelling difficulties
12 Poor self-concept.

Vellutino (1979) describes the following 'correlated characteristics'. These are identifying characteristics occurring in a dyslexic, and is based on a literature review in which he describes these as being those mentioned most often:

1 Boys are observed to have reading problems more frequently than girls, the ratio generally exceeding 4:1
2 The incidence of reading difficulties in the families of dyslexics has been found to be specifically significant
3 Dyslexics have been observed to have difficulty in other forms of representational learning, such as telling the time, naming the months and seasons of the year, or days of the week, and distinguishing left from right or up from down
4 The appearance of neurological softsigns (abnormal reflexes, minor coordination problems, deviant EEG patterns and so on), has been reported in both clinical and laboratory studies of dyslexia, reinforcing the suggestion that reading problems in some children may be associated with a neurological disorder
5 There is some evidence that dyslexia significantly correlates with a history of developmental problems, particularly in one or more aspects of language.

Finally a systematic review of the area of signs and symptoms is given by Wheeler and Watkins (1979), who found the following to be common across well over 20 different descriptive features of dyslexics:

1 Directional confusion (left/right)
2 Writing and spelling impairment
3 Finger differentiation problems
4 Visual perception deficiencies
5 Handedness and cerebral dominance abnormalities
6 Weakness in memory storage
7 Maternal and natal factors
8 Motor dysfunctions

9 Delayed maturation
10 Delayed speech development
11 Neurological dysfunctions
12 Familial or inherited disability (genetic factors)
13 Sex differences
14 Language delays.

They suggest that the various facets described are not incompatible, or mutually exclusive, rather that they demonstrate ways of sampling dyslexics' difficulties.

In many ways these listings are a little unsatisfactory. While it is clear that they may describe some kind of overall grouping, symptomatology or syndrome, there are a number of problems. Rutter (1978), for example, points out that many of these features are age dependent, in most cases being more common in younger children. Also, some of the features are found in good readers, and one cannot necessarily rule out familial or school influences as being associated with a particular sign. He suggests that one should focus on (1) the failure to acquire skills; (2) the types of skills which are involved, i.e. separating reading and spelling from, say, arithmetic or other school-based tasks; and (3) the importance of separating a specific reading difficulty from a general backwardness in reading.

However, at least in describing the kinds of behaviours associated with dyslexia, we are moving away from a definition by exclusion. Furthermore, the above kinds of checklists can be realistically used by teachers and others involved with dyslexic children in order to try and decide whether a particular child may be worth investigating further.

1.3 Emotional correlates of dyslexia

The acquisition of written language can be a very stressful process for many children; many pressures from both home and school are focused on the child to make him succeed. The dyslexics' difficulties will include the unhappy anxious boy of eight, mis-perceived by teachers; the behavioural disorders of 12 and 13-year-olds referred to the school psychological service for treatment; the so called 'disabled (illiterate) school leaver' described by the Department of Employment; the frustrated science, engineering or medical students unable to present their very able thinking in written form; the referrals to psychiatric hospitals of men in the 30–40 age range whose breakdowns are traced back to inabilities to read and write; and the high incidence of illiteracy amongst young offenders in penal establishments.

In order to illustrate the emotional anxiety reactions associated with the dyslexic problem in particular, two brief cases are described, followed by some general descriptions of stress reactions obtained from my own clinical experience of working with dyslexic children.

Case 1 'John'

John was 10 years old when referred, and had barely any attainments in reading and spelling although he could recognize a few words. He was of above average intelligence, and was diagnosed as dyslexic. When initially assessed on the first session John was anxious and withdrawn, and needed considerable encouragement to attempt anything, continually looking for approval or indications that he was doing the correct thing. He verged on tears when asked to do anything relating to written language, and his parents reported that he often burst into tears after school, and was frequently 'ill' in the morning in order to avoid school. Recently he had started wetting the bed after three years 'dry sleeping'. At school John was often teased about his reading difficulties, and the teacher asked him to read in front of the class along with others. He was isolated from his peer group. He was unable to participate in most classroom activities, and 'remedial work' consisted of learning lists of spellings which he invariably could not remember. Reports from the infant school prior to his 'failure' described him as outgoing, cheerful and intelligent.

Case 2 'David'

David was 15 years old when referred, a physically mature boy who had been suspended from school for threatening the head teacher and generally being disruptive. David was of very superior intelligence, with a reading age of about 12 years, but spelling around the $7\frac{1}{2}$ year level with great difficulty in written expression. He was rather sullen and aggressive at first, but soon revealed a warm and pleasant personality with a tremendous verbal fluency and wide interests. David had given up school as a waste of time, with consequent pressures from his parents, who also reported that he bullied his sister (age 10, a very good reader). School reports from previous years indicated that he contributed considerably in classroom discussions, but written work and homework were very poor. He was reported to be lazy. More recently however, David was making himself very popular with his class-mates by joking and fooling around in class, and at home was associating with a group of youths who had been involved with the juvenile courts.

These descriptions illustrate typical behavioural and emotional reactions to dyslexia. They are reactions to the primary difficulty with written language. The secondary behavioural reactions begin to develop after the child starts to 'fail'. The child is vulnerable in his academic work, but also in social, emotional and personality growth. Often these reactions are seen as the causal factors, but in many cases it is difficult to sort out cause and effect relationships.

Clinical observations of stress reactions tend to fall broadly into two categories; 'under' and 'over' reaction. In 'under' reaction the child withdraws, and manifests extreme anxiety. Many times, the writer has observed children and adults actually trembling and sweating when asked to read, and needing continued encouragement to attempt anything. The individuals' self-opinions are very low, and this generalizes to all aspects of their lives where they consider themselves failures, dunces, and generally useless. Often behaviour regresses to more immature forms, such as bed wetting, thumb sucking, dependence, and so on. The child suffers tremendous stress at school, often trying to avoid it by psychosomatic disorders. Parents frequently report tears and emotional exhaustion at the end of the day. Depression and its associated debilitating effects may also be present. The second reaction type is seen in the child who over-compensates. Deep anxieties are revealed from clinical investigation. Here the individual compensates by being 'successful' in other areas, gaining popularity or attention by classroom disruption. In many cases this is manifested by being the class 'joker', hiding his failure under a 'couldn't care less' attitude and 'silly' behaviour. Sometimes this leads to aggression towards other children. Some children may show more extreme behaviour such as stealing, truancy, continued aggression and the rejection of the whole school (and authority) system. A generally hostile attitude to society may result. Older children can develop more serious patterns of delinquency.

Unrecognized and not helped, both groups typically leave school without qualifications, drift without employment and become what the Department of Employment terms 'disabled school leavers'. The highly intelligent child, or those with very supportive families or sympathetic schools 'get by' but are often under-achievers, failing to attain their potential, and may suffer a lifetime of frustration. Family stresses are also associated with dyslexia. One such is guilt arising from the assumption (often perpetuated by professional workers) that the family is at fault, and parental upbringing is poor. Sibling hostilities are magnified. The child may be pressurized by high achieving families to 'try harder' and not be 'lazy'. Ironically these pressures can be exacerbated by parents who had similar problems themselves, but who, misunderstanding the nature of the difficulty, and not wishing similar miseries to beset their children, demand further effort and provide unrealistic work schedules at home.

There is a good deal of research linking various emotional adjustment and anxiety reactions to reading difficulties (see Thomson 1978b and Thomson and Hartley 1980 for a review). The problem is sorting out cause and effect, which can only be undertaken by longitudinal studies of children from an early age, or by epidemiological investigations of total child populations. The Isle of Wight study undertook the latter by determining whether the children with both conditions (behaviour problems and reading backwardness) had more in common with children who show reading retardation alone, or with children who show antisocial disorder alone. This was done by splitting the antisocial children into two groups: competent and poor readers. The antisocial poor readers tended to share the same developmental characteristics as the well-adjusted poor readers; that is, family history of reading backwardness, delay in speech development, articulation defects, clumsiness, motor incoordination, imperfect right/left differentiation and perceptual difficulties. It therefore seemed unlikely that the reading problem was of a different nature in the two groups. Moreover, it was found that competent readers in the antisocial group were associated with broken homes, whereas poor readers in the antisocial group were not. This seems to add support for the theory of reading disability being the primary factor in behavioural problems.

More recent population studies have also examined this relationship. Jorm *et al.* (1986) found that children with specific reading retardation, as defined by regression equation, did not have the associated behaviour problems that those with a general reading difficulty had. McGee *et al.* (1986), in their longitudinal study of 5–11 year olds, did not find such clear-cut results. Using the Rutter Behavioural Scale they found that both backward and specifically retarded readers had a higher incidence of behaviour difficulties as rated by parents and teachers. However, the children with specific difficulties developed these behavioural problems as they grew older, suggesting that this was a reaction to their learning difficulties.

As well as anxiety and behaviour problems the dyslexic typically also lacks self-esteem or has poor self-concept (e.g. Rosenthal 1973, Thomson and Hartley 1980). In remediation it is important to recognize these components of dyslexia. Many authorities assume that the emotional problem is a primary difficulty and reading and spelling problems result from that. Typically the child may be given a programme of psychotherapy or behaviour modification in order to improve adjustment, behavioural or emotional difficulties. Occasionally he might be referred to a school or unit for the maladjusted. Indeed in many cases this behaviour difficulty may clear up for that temporary time, but as the initial cause of his emotional problem has not been obviated, once the child returns to the situation where written language skills are expected, behaviour difficulties return.

Obviously there is a need for both remediation and appropriate recognition and help to overcome behavioural difficulties if they are not to reappear. This would mean a structured teaching programme in relation to written language, as well as some kind of therapeutic teaching (providing emotional support, opportunities for success). In the writer's experience, if the child has been dyslexic, and his difficulties are recognized and given appropriate remedial help, his behavioural, emotional and anxiety problems often disappear very rapidly indeed.

Indeed, we have recently completed a study at East Court, examining the effects of specialized teaching on self-esteem. Children were assessed using the Battle (1981) Culture-free Self-esteem Inventory. The children were all dyslexic and formed three groups.

1 Interviewees: these were children attending for interview for a place at a specialized school of dyslexics. All those included in the study were offered places at the school, and therefore represent a sample who, although they had not attended the school, were similar to those already at the school. Mean age was 9 years 5 months.
2 Fifteen children chosen at random who had attended the school for 6 months. Mean age was 10 years 5 months.
3 Fifteen children, chosen at random, who had attended the school for 18 months. Mean age was 12 years 0 months.

The total self-esteem scores are shown as function of time at school in Figure 1.1 and the results of the subcategories for the self-esteem scales are shown in Table 1.2.

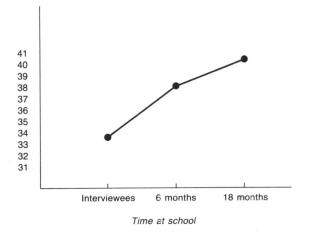

Figure 1.1   Self-esteem scores as a function of time at school

Table 1.2   Percentile points of self-esteem subscales

Subscale	Interviewees	6 months at specialized school	18 months at specialized school
General	50	50	60
Social	32	64	84
Academic	45	77	77
Parental	87	87	87

A significant overall improvement in self-esteem results from receiving help at a specialized school. In general the longer the child is at school the greater his or her self-esteem. The detailed results provide more specific interpretations.

The subscales that show significant improvements across the three groups are the academic and social scales. The general and parental scales do not show significant increases. The main areas of low self-esteem among this sample of dyslexics seem to be in their sense of failure in relation to school work, and their feelings of inferiority in relation to their school peers who are succeeding. Academic self-esteem starts at a little below the 50th centile, but improves to just under the 80th centile from attendance at school. Academic self-esteem seems to reach a high level, and remain there, independent of whether the groups were at school for 6 or 18 months. Social self-esteem, however, starts off at a much lower level and increases through 6 months (64th centile) to 18 months (84th centile). Perhaps this reflects the increasing support the children give each other during their time at school.

General self-esteem is at a moderate level, whereas parental self-esteem is at a high level initially, and remains there. The latter suggests that the problems of children coming to the school are well understood by their parents, who give them support and help.

1.4   Sex differences

There is a good deal of evidence that dyslexia is much more common in boys than in girls. Critchley (1967), for example, in a review of the literature, shows that in populations of children with dyslexia the percentage of boys ranges from 66 to 100. Critchley himself (1970) argues a 4 to 1 ratio of boys to girls, Money (1966) suggests 2 to 1, Rutter *et al*. (1970) 3.3 to 1, Naidoo (1972) 5 to 1, and Goldberg and Schiffman (1972) in a review of literature argue that the frequency varies from 3.3 to 1, to 10 to 1 in favour of a greater male incidence. The differences are therefore well established. What is more debatable is the reason for the sex ratios, and differences in reported incidences of dyslexic difficulties amongst boys.

Goldberg and Schiffman postulate the following as explanations for the sex differences; (1) greater developmental maturity at the age of 6 (the age for starting school in the USA), (2) greater incidence of cerebral trauma in males, (3) greater motivation of females in the learning situation, and (4) secondary emotional conflict in the male associated with factors (1) and (3).

In relation to social and environmental explanations, one fairly obvious point is that, despite the present laws and views on equal opportunity, it is possible that teachers and parents are more concerned about the failure of boys to learn to read, write and spell at school. Perhaps male difficulties in reading are reported more often by teachers? Perhaps parents feel that it is more important for boys to be able to read, write and spell, since they must obtain qualifications for jobs later on, whereas girls 'can always get married'? It is difficult to evaluate this kind of notion in any systematic way. It would depend very much on individual sub-cultural norms, expectations and attitudes towards the behaviour of the sexes.

Other explanations relate to general social interactions, for example, Moseley (1972) found boys more interested in the approval of classmates than in pleasing teachers, and Kellmer-Pringle *et al*. (1966) argue that boys might be less interested in reading than girls, because reading schemes tended to be 'home orientated' whereas their interests focus on the 'world around'.

One therefore cannot rule out social and environmental causes of the male to female ratios. However, a much more likely explanation is in relation to the relative cognitive skills found in the sexes as a result of maturation and development. We have already noted that many dyslexic children have a delay in language, and it is commonly observed that boys show a greater incidence of delayed speech development than girls (Ingram and Reid 1966, Davie *et al*. 1972). Furthermore, girls mature much earlier than boys (Buffery and Gray 1972, and indeed any developmental psychology text book), and there may just simply be a reading readiness or developmental trend here.

More important is the interrelationship between the verbal facility and possibly visuo-spatial skills in the sexes. One established sex difference (Maccoby and Jacklin 1974) is that girls are much better than boys at verbal skills in school ages. Spoken language develops earlier, as well as auditory skills (Kellmer-Pringle et al. 1966). We shall see later on that dyslexia can be linked generally with verbal skills, but more particularly to the notion of verbal encoding and short-term memory. It may be that school-age girls are more likely to be over some kind of threshold in relation to this kind of verbal skill. Another interesting possibility relates to hemisphere function. We shall be examining this in greater detail in Chapter 3, but briefly, there seems to be some kind of link between left-hemisphere language functioning and dyslexia. It is also important to note at this point that the right hemisphere is generally responsible for visuo-spatial functions. Another finding of Maccoby and Jacklin's was that boys tend to be rather better at visuo-spatial functioning. Perhaps an interrelationship between left-hemisphere specialism for language and right-hemisphere specialism for visuo-spatial function is linked in some way to a higher incidence of dyslexic problems in the male.

1.5   Subtypes of dyslexia

The division of dyslexia into subtypes has implications with respect to etiology; and a number of teaching programmes are geared to the assumption that one can divide dyslexics into broad subtypes: for example, the Aston Teaching Portfolio (see Chapter 7) makes the assumption that one can divide children into those having mainly auditory channel deficits or mainly visual channel deficits. It will be seen that there is a great deal of agreement in relation to the kind of problem associated with particular subtypes, and that the main problem lies in the terminology used to describe them.

One of the earliest, and perhaps most influential, attempts to describe subtypes was that by Myklebust and Johnson (1962), also Johnson and Myklebust (1967) Myklebust (1978). They argued for two broad subtypes; *auditory* and *visual* dyslexia. The visual dyslexic has deficiences in visual perception and visual discrimination. They argue that these children can learn through the auditory modalities, given appropriate remediation, and that orientation and sequencing errors are due to visual difficulty. Problems occur in the discrimination of size and form, but also in scanning from left to right, and in recognizing letter clusters. It is suggested that the problem lies in visualization for coding purposes: a child can differentiate between visual shapes, but cannot 'symbolize' these into either sounds or meaningful units. The second subtype is that of the auditory dyslexic. Difficulties are seen to be in discrimination of speech sounds, in sound blending and naming. There are also difficulties in auditory sequencing or serial memory. It is suggested that the children can learn in the visual modality, but that they have a difficulty in analysing sounds or syllables and synthesizing these to form whole words. It is also suggested that they have difficulty in rhyming.

Another attempt at a description of subtypes is that by Ingram (1964) and later Ingram *et al.* (1970). Here it is suggested that there are *audio-phonic*, *visuo-spatial*, and *correlating* difficulties. The audio-phonic dyslexic has difficulties in sound discrimination and sound blending, and is deficient in phonic analysis. Ingram (1964) suggests that there are also speech-to-sound difficulties. The problem lies in synthesizing words from their component sounds, and understanding words and sentences; also, in writing, in terms of finding words and constructing sentences. The visuo-spatial dyslexic has difficulties in visual discrimination and orientation, and difficulties in recognizing simple 'look-and-say' words. There is a failure to recognize letter shapes, and the child tends to guess at words from shapes, confusing reversible letters, transposing letters and syllables, and transposing syllables in words and phrases. Sometimes the child reads backwards. The correlating dyslexic has problems in finding the appropriate speech sounds for individual letters, or groups of letters. The problem here, for example, might be difficulties in recalling the visual form of writing.

One influential and often quoted description is that by Boder (1970, 1971a and b, 1973). This was based on analysing reading and spelling errors in the dyslexic children's performance and produced a classification into *auditory*, *visual* and *mixed* groups. In particular she argues that these categories are not found with reading difficulties due to emotional problems, low intelligence, or environmental handicaps nor among those who do not have reading difficulties at all. The auditory difficulties she describes as *dysphonetic* (63%). The problem here is in letter – sound integration and in learning phonetically. The children approach word learning and spelling in a holistic manner. They have a repertoire of sight words, but spelling bears no resemblance to the words that they attempt to read. There are difficulties in phonic analysis and synthesis. Spelling errors can be illustrated by *alnost* for *almost*, *awlake* for *awake*, *werber* for *remember*. The visual group she terms *dyseidetic* (9%). Here the difficulty is in perceiving words as gestalts. Children can read and spell phonetically but have difficulty in building up sight words and have difficulty in perceiving whole words. Spelling errors include *tok* for *talk*, *uther* for *other*, *muthr* for *mother*. The third group includes children who have mixed difficulties of the auditory and visual kind. This relates to about 22% of her population and the difficulties are both in whole words and in phonic analysis. These children are virtually non-readers. She describes them as being 'alexic', i.e. without any words at all. A further 6% are undetermined.

Mattis, French and Rapin (1975) and Mattis 1978 propose three groups also. The largest group (38%) have auditory difficulties. The problems here are in naming and labelling, and adequate knowledge of syntax. There are some anomic difficulties and also problems in comprehension and speech sound discrimination. The next group of around 37% have various *motor* dysfunctions. These relate particularly to speech articulation difficulties, but they also include visuo-motor (handwriting) problems. Here there are difficulties in graphic motor skills as well as poor sound blending. There is normal receptive language and sound discrimination, however. The smallest group comprises those with *visuo-spatial* difficulty (16%). Here the problem lies in visual discrimination and visual memory, and there may be difficulties on visual retention kinds of test (drawing shapes from memory).

Denckla (1977b) suggests that 54% of dyslexics have a language disturbance with anomia (difficulties in naming), 12% with articulatory and graphomotor disconnection difficulties, and 4% with visual perceptual disorders. In addition, she suggests that there are around 13% with phonemic sequencing difficulties, i.e. poor repetition, characterized by phonemic substitution and mis-sequencing, despite normal naming, comprehension and articulation. A further 10% have verbal memorization disorders, i.e. problems in sentence repetition and verbal paired associate learning. This latter group has no disturbance in any other language skill.

Doehring and Hoshko (1977), in a factor analysis study, suggest three major types of dyslexia. The first has very severe oral reading difficulties, but is quite good at visual and auditory matching. The second type has slow auditory visual letter associations and deficiencies in various matching tasks. The third group has slow auditory visual association of words and syllables, deficient phonic analysis and problems in blending and sequencing. Doehring (1978) has also argued very strongly against the homogeneity of dyslexia. He suggests that these three subtypes should be taken into account in any research.

The majority of the above studies are either observational or (occasionally) based on factor analysis. Vernon (1977a, 1979) undertook a description based on a review of the literature in terms of the kinds of skills required for reading, writing and spelling. She argues that there has been confusion in the literature because dyslexics have been studied as a homogeneous group. Vernon divides dyslexics into five main sub-types. (1) *Difficulties in analysing visual shapes*. Here the children may be unable to read at all, although they could perhaps recognize a few simple words by rote. The problem is mainly in perception in terms of memorizing letter shapes, and analysing and organizing visual information into memory. The problem is not in shape perception *per se*, although there may be some kind of difficulties in memory for complex forms and directional confusion. This applies particularly to younger dyslexics. (2) *Difficulties in analysing whole words into phonemes*. This group has auditory linguistic difficulties. It is associated with late development in learning to speak and understanding speech, and also with poor verbal memory. The children have difficulty in isolating single phonemes from word sounds and are very poor readers. She argues that they are very similar to the auditory dyslexics postulated by others. (3) *Difficulties in the acquisition of grapheme-phoneme associations*. These children have great difficulty in reading and may be unable to read at all if the deficiency is severe. This group has problems in naming, in simple visual-verbal associations, but particularly in abstract symbols (such as graphemes and phonemes). She suggests that this group is similar to that postulated by Ingram, but she also includes Boder's group 1 and Doehring and Hoshko's groups 2 and 3. (4) *Difficulties in grasping irregularities in grapheme and phoneme associations and complex orthography*. The problem here is not in learning the initial association, but in more complex spelling patterns. The children may be inaccurate in perceiving and remembering sequential order of graphemes and phonemes. (5) *Difficulties in grouping single words into phrases and sentences*. The children can recognize individual words, but appear to be deficient in conceptualization, which emerges as difficulties in syntactic and semantic relationship between words in a continuous text.

It may be seen from the above that there is a good deal of similarity and overlap between the various subtypes. Most authors are agreed that there is some kind of auditory linguistic/phonological/language disturbance which affects a majority of dyslexic children. Other types includes some kind of visuo-spatial, visual perception and visual-verbal perception difficulty.

Perhaps the best way of summarizing this is by presenting Ellis's (1981b) attempt at diagramming the categories in functional analysis terms. This is shown in Figure 1.2. Ellis suggests that some of the classifications cannot be standardized easily, and that the kinds of subtypes one can describe depend on the tests used in an investigation. He concludes, as we have done briefly above, that there is always a subgroup of visuo-spatial perceptual problems, and this represents a very small percentage of the population (from 4% to 16%). There is then a subgroup with problems in the phonological coding of visual material, which may be seen in auditory analysis or articulatory analysis, or possibly even in some kind of cross-modality integration problem. Each of these can be subdivided in several ways, and there may be a further group which has both kinds of problems.

There are some interpretation problems, and although these subtypes are fairly well established, it may be that they merely reflect a continuum of dyslexia from severe to mild—i.e. those with grapheme and phoneme association problems may represent a severe form, and those with difficulty in organizing words into sentences a mild form of dyslexia. Also these descriptions suggest that there is a great variability amongst dyslexic children, and variability does not necessarily mean that there are 'subtypes'. The differences between the children may not relate to the causes of reading retardation.

As an example of the problems in interpreting subtypes we shall look at Boder's classification in more detail. This is chosen for two reasons; first, her classification is based on reading and spelling errors, a procedure which I shall be adopting in Chapters 6 and 7; and second, her approach has been very widely quoted and influential. Despite this however, many authors and writers quoting her work do not appear to have looked at her original papers in any great detail. They mainly quote the subtypes without looking at how they were derived.

Her diagnostic assessment procedure involved a word recognition task in which a series of words chosen as being very frequent in standard tests was put into a series of lists. These were then shown (i) quickly as flashcards, and (ii) untimed. She argued that the flashcard approach identified the child's ability to see the word as a 'gestalt'. The ability of the child to read the word in the untimed condition as opposed to the flashcard condition tested the child's ability to analyse phonologically in terms of word analysis and synthesis. Words which were read were then given in spelling tests. These could be divided into *known* words (i.e. those that had been read in sight vocabulary) and unknown words (words that had not been read in sight vocabulary). Boder argues that it is clear that children who

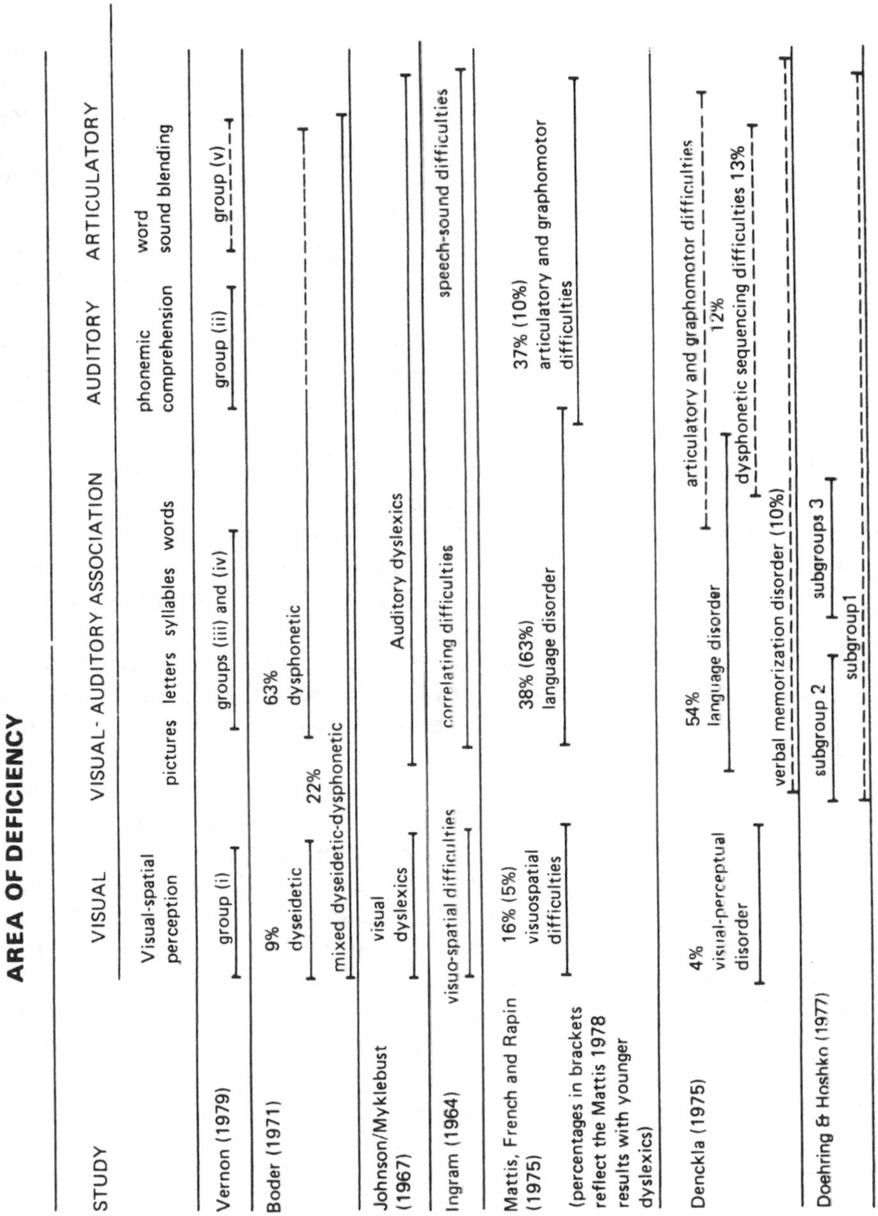

AREA OF DEFICIENCY

STUDY	VISUAL	VISUAL - AUDITORY ASSOCIATION				AUDITORY	ARTICULATORY
	Visual-spatial perception	pictures	letters	syllables	words	phonemic comprehension	word sound blending
Vernon (1979)	group (i)	groups (iii) and (iv)				group (ii)	group (v)
Boder (1971)	9% dyseidetic	63% dysphonetic					
	mixed dyseidetic-dysphonetic 22%						
Johnson/Myklebust (1967)	visual dyslexics	Auditory dyslexics					
Ingram (1964)	visuo-spatial difficulties	correlating difficulties					speech-sound difficulties
Mattis, French and Rapin (1975) (percentages in brackets reflect the Mattis 1978 results with younger dyslexics)	16% (5%) visuospatial difficulties	38% (63%) language disorder				37% (10%) articulatory and graphomotor difficulties	
Denckla (1975)	4% visual-perceptual disorder	54% language disorder			verbal memorization disorder (10%)	articulatory and graphomotor difficulties 12% dysphonetic sequencing difficulties 13%	
Doehring & Hoshko (1977)		subgroup 2 subgroup1		subgroups 3			

Certain classifications in the last three studies are difficult to describe in the terms of this scheme, hence the dotted lines.

Figure 1.2 A functional analysis of the reading process

can spell words that are not in their sight vocabulary are spelling phonetically or phonologically and have good word analysis skills. She also suggests that children who cannot spell words that are in their known vocabulary have 're-visualization problems'. By this she means that they are unable to remember or recreate a visual image of the word and therefore presumably cannot spell it. However the crucial point here is whether individuals actually spell in that kind of way. It may well be that the spelling task involves initially accessing a sound either for letters or for words, and then attaching a visual symbol to that in its motor equivalent or writing plan output. Boder argues that one creates a visual image first and then attaches the sound to that. In fact there are many other kinds of possible explanations for skills involved in spelling (see Frith 1980b), as Boder recognizes.

Further details of the dysphonetic group follow. In their reading they have a limited sight vocabulary, and tend to read the words globally and instantaneously through visual gestalts; there is a problem in deciphering words not in their sight vocabulary; they are unable to sort out or blend letters and syllable units; they make guesses from minimal cues (i.e. the first or last letter) and they substitute words that are similar in meaning but dissimilar phonetically. They spell by sight and not by ear. They are poor spellers and cannot spell words that are unknown in their reading, and they sometimes cannot spell known words as well, due to difficulties in re-visualization. Their spelling is bizarre; often extra letters are added or letters omitted. They have difficulty in analysing auditory cues and translating these into sounds and symbols. Boder gives the following examples of spelling errors for known words: *renber* for *remember*, *dilit* for *delight*, *catteg* for *cottage*, *humen* for *human*. As examples of spelling errors of unknown words we have: *diter* for *dealt*, *slebr* for *scrambled*, *ver* for *varnish*. There are semantic substitution errors such as *funny* for *laugh*, *duck* for *quack*, but she also suggests that in reading the children had difficulty in similar-looking words, e.g. *horse* for *house*, *money* for *monkey*, *stop* for *step*.

Dyseidetic children in their reading are very slow, they have poor identification of visual gestalts, and difficulties in learning what letters look like. They are 'letter blind'. On the other hand they have good auditory memory, they can recite the alphabet, they are analytic and read by ear. They tend to read by auditory analysis and synthesis by sounding out, but have poor sight vocabularies. They can decode phonetically, but may have great difficulty with, words that are irregular, e.g. they may say *loge* for *laugh* or *busynes* for *business*, or *telk* for *talc*. In spelling they spell poorly but not bizarrely. They spell by ear, e.g. *laf* for *laugh*, *burd* for *bird*, *tok* for *talk*. If they spell non-phonetically, this is due to recreating a known word by visualization, according to Boder. The child fails to use his good auditory channels and therefore makes non-phonetic errors, like *glaf* for *laugh*, *glave* for *glue*.

The final group that Boder describes comprises non-readers, or the 'alexic'. This group experiences a great number of d/b, m/n, h/n confusions. The examples she gives from this combined group tend to represent a complete inability to represent sounds with appropriate symbols, e.g. *llk* for *kitten*, *n* for *want*, *ge* for *play*.

We can, initially, criticize Boder's procedure—for example, showing a child a flashcard for about one second does not prevent him from analysing phonetically or phonologically. Jorm (1977) in fact provides evidence that children can identify nonsense words in less than 1.5 seconds. A nonsense word, in order to be read, must be analysed phonetically—it cannot be read in a look-and-say manner directly for meaning. There are also other interpretations of the errors she quotes. First of all, arguing that the dysphonetic group cannot 're-visualize' suggests that it does have some kind of visual problem. Furthermore, while some of Boder's errors are obviously auditory confusions, others are phonetic, e.g. *humen*. She later argues that dyseidetic problems result in phonetic spelling. The omission of syllable units like *rember* for *remember*, if due to a revisualization difficulty, is surely a visual problem. On the other hand, if the child is omitting a single unit because he cannot follow his own speech sounds, this is an auditory/articulatory problem. It seems that we have interpretations that can be argued either way here. Furthermore, similar-looking word errors like *horse* for *house*, and *stop* for *step* could quite well be visual errors. Perhaps the child is making a guess from one or two letters, not because he cannot analyse the sound but because he is making a guess at what it looks like, and is unable to visually analyse the middle part of the word. Both interpretations are perhaps equally likely. Whether the 'dyseidetics' spell phonetically or non-phonetically, one can interpret their spelling errors as fitting the category! Surely if these occurred in a child whom you wanted to classify as having auditory problems, you would suggest that *laf* was an auditory error. Similarly the examples she gives from dyseidetic children include severe confusion of sounds *wur* for *your*, as well as the phonetic attempts she suggests are more common, like *kan* for *cane*, *chans* for *chance*. The question the above examples raise is naturally regarding the reliability of classifications; indeed Felton and Campell (1985), in using naming, word retrieval and the Boder classification system, found that the classifications used tended to be unreliable.

Boder's system is thus based on a very small sample of (presumably carefully selected) errors. These are open to other interpretations. Thus, although her classification seems reasonable one must guard against too simple a division between subtypes.

The majority of the subtypes we have reviewed are based on clinical observation, and there have been very few factor analytical studies in relation to dyslexia on large samples. Naidoo (1972) undertook a cluster analysis and found (i) a speech and language disorder group, (ii) visuo-spatial defects and (iii) a 'genetic' group. Thomson *et al*. (1980) undertook a factor analysis of 523 children, representing a sample of children who had been diagnosed as dyslexic and referred to the Language Development Unit, University of Aston over a number of years. The purpose of the study was to examine underlying features of dyslexia, and then relate these to classification systems, particularly the Vernon classification outlined above. The items that went into this factor analysis were the results of standard tests given to children referred for dyslexic problems at Aston. These included the Wechsler Intelligence Scales, items from the Aston Index, the Neale Analysis of Reading Ability, and the Schonell Reading and Spelling Tests. Other items included common sequences, such as days of the week, months of the year, and identifying left and right. Thomson and Hicks found seven factors—a general written language literacy factor, followed by verbal abilities, coding, visuo-spatial function, labelling, sequencing, and auditory perception factors, paralleling those outlined above by Vernon.

A further way of examining subtypes is to classify children on their reading and spelling errors, and then examine cognitive skills in each group. One such study was undertaken by Thomson (1982b), using the British Ability Scales with dyslexic children. The Scales are described in Chapter 6. The dyslexics were divided into three groups based on their reading and spelling errors, viz *auditory linguistic*, *visuo-spatial* and *mixed*. The children were also divided into three age groups and the percentage of children falling into the three categories is given in Table 1.3. An interesting finding here is the different percentages in the age groups. The younger children have relatively more visuo-spatial problems. This provides some support for Satz *et al.'s* (1978) theory of developmental lag—viz early visuo-spatial difficulties and later auditory-linguistic difficulties (see Chapter Three).

Table 1.3   Percentage of children for subtypes of dyslexia

Age	Auditory linguistic	Visuo-spatial	Mixed/uncertain
8–10;11	45	38	17
11–13;11	52	28	20
14–16;11	61	22	17

From Thomson 1982b.

Some differences were found in relation to the subtests between the groups. For example, the visuo-spatial group scored less well on Block Design and on Speed of Information Processing compared to the auditory-linguistic group. Both groups scored poorly on Short-Term-Memory compared to the norms, however. (See Thomson 1982b for further details.)

Tyler and Elliott (1988), in their cluster analysis of the same data used by Thomson, also found three groups although they gave them slightly different labels. They identified a group of visuo-spatial and linguistic processing difficulties; these included problems in short-term memory and information retrieval. Another group was made up of those with sequential processing difficulties, including problems in Recall of Digits and Speed of Information Processing, and finally a group with holistic retrieval of information problems, i.e. involving some visual–motor memory and word defining difficulties.

Clearly these do not fall into the auditory linguistic and visuo-spatial subtypes mentioned previously, but perhaps this is a matter of labelling. It is always arguable in cluster analysis just what the various subtests used in analysis measure. For example, in the British Ability Scales it is a moot point whether the Immediate Visual Recall subtest measures visual recall or auditory verbal labelling, because in this particular test pictures of items are shown on a card and named. The task is then to recall the items by giving them a name.

It may be seen from the above that one cannot assume a total heterogeneity among individuals classed as dyslexics. There do seem to be a number of fairly valid subtypes in terms of clinical descriptions and in relation to cognitive skills and factor analysis. Whilst not going as far as Seymour (1986) in proposing that this heterogeneity means that one can only investigate individuals, it does mean that we should take into account individual variations. However, as will be seen later there are underlying similarities which justify the description of a syndrome of dyslexia.

1.6   Genetic aspects

The issue of inheritance versus environment as a determinant of human behaviour is controversial and beset by methodological difficulties. This applies particularly to the issue of whether intelligence is inherited or learned. If, as has been suggested in some definitions, dyslexia is constitutionally determined, some evidence for a genetic influence is required. A number of authors do describe a higher incidence of dyslexia amongst siblings, parents and other family members of dyslexic children (e.g. Hinshelwood 1900, Orton 1937). More recently Naidoo (1972) describes a high frequency of similar incidence of reading and of spelling disorders amongst the families of spelling retardates, and Ingram et al. (1970) describes a 40% incidence of reading difficulties amongst families with specifically retarded children against a 25% incidence amongst those who were generally retarded. Yule and Rutter (1976) report that a family history of reading difficulties was three times more likely to occur amongst children who had reading retardation. Silver (1971) reports 30% of families having a history of learning difficulties; and a more systematic study with a control group (Doehring 1968) found 40% of parents with dyslexic children had reading difficulties compared to 10% of a control group. Critchley (1970) also reports a high incidence of specific reading difficulties in families.

These studies, however, are merely suggestive. Many of them suffer from not having control groups. Also, in many cases they merely give anecdotal or reported data from parents rather than actually testing parents and siblings for attainment. Goldberg and Schiffman (1972) argue that there are four major areas which would need to provide evidence in order to suggest a genetic cause for dyslexia. These are (1) Pedigree and family history studies, (2) Twin studies, (3) Persistence of dyslexic disorders throughout life, (4) Biochemical or chromosomal abnormalities. We shall now review some of this evidence, and we shall see that most of the data fall into the first two categories suggested by Goldberg and Schiffman.

First, there are a number of family pedigree studies, the most widely reported of which is that by Hallgren (1950). Using large-scale neurological and educational evaluation, he studied 112 families where the children had dyslexic difficulties. He examined the situations where both parents had a dyslexic problem (3%), where one parent had a dyslexic problem (80%), and where neither parent had a dyslexic problem (17%). He then undertook a Mendelian analysis, and argued for a 'dominant' mode of inheritance, concluding that there was a clear-cut genetic component related to dyslexia. This study has, however, been criticized. For example, Sladen (1971) used Hallgren's data and suggested that there was a variable dominance in the male inheritance and a recessive mode of inheritance in the female. She also argued that the mating of the parents was not 'random'. This is a most important criticism which tends to invalidate the Mendelian analysis: Sladen argues that perhaps an individual who has a reading difficulty might be more likely to marry a similar individual.

A number of quite recent studies have re-examined family and pedigree studies since Hallgren's seminal work. For example, Finucci *et al*. (1976) examined a group of 20 poor readers and looked at their first-degree relatives. 45% of these had reading difficulties, and these difficulties were greater in males. They argued that there was no single clear-cut mode of inheritance, and that reading difficulties were heterogeneous. Owen *et al*. (1971) undertook a large-scale family study. Although they did not specifically look at the dyslexic individual, but a group of children that they described as *educationally handicapped*, this study is worth examining in some detail because the criteria used to define the educationally handicapped overlapped to some extent with those used for a dyslexic group. Low intelligence, emotional problems, and socio-cultural difficulties were ruled out, and the children had specific difficulties. This group was compared to a control group of children who were succeeding academically. The interesting point here was that the control group had an appropriate number and age of siblings in order to match the educationally handicapped poor readers. The first findings by Owen *et al*. were that the siblings of the poor readers had lower reading and spelling performances compared to the control group siblings, and the parents of the poor readers had lower attainments than the parents of the academically successful control group (based on high school English grades). Further, the differences between fathers' performances were highly significant. Based on the Wechsler Intelligence Scales (see Chapter 6) it was also found that the reading-disabled children who had higher Performance (non-verbal) against Verbal IQs, had a high incidence of speech therapy in their history and 35% of their siblings had had a history of speech therapy in the past. Furthermore, the siblings had difficulties in auditory memory as well as sequential difficulties. There seemed to be a 'familial language disability'. It was also found that the reading disabled children *and* their siblings were impaired in the Arithmetic, Information, and Digit Span tests of the Wechsler Scale—a very interesting finding as it relates to the typical profiles associated with dyslexia (see Chapter 6). In addition to these subtests it was also found that the Coding subtest was highly correlated between siblings and reading disabled children.

Decker and De Fries (1980, 1981) also undertook a large-scale family study based on 125 children who had reading disorders. They investigated parents and families and compared them to a matched control group, i.e. one which was matched on siblings who were good readers. This involved over 1,000 individuals. A number of tests were given to the children, as well as to the siblings and members of the family, including the Illinois Test of Psycho-linguistc Abilities, Coding subtests from the Wechsler Scales, and tests of speed and spatial ability. In their 1980 report Decker and De Fries describe a principal component analysis (a type of factor analysis) which revealed three different factors in the test results. These were reading, spatial/reasoning, and coding/speed factors. They found that the parents and siblings that were poor readers were highly correlated on the reading and the coding/speed factor. There was also an interaction between sexes—brothers being more affected than sisters. They found that the males did rather less well on the coding/speed factor and rather better on the spatial reasoning factor, and argued that the results demonstrated the familial nature of the learning difficulties.

In further reporting these data (1981) on the same group of children and controls, they suggested four subtypes within the dyslexic group. The first subtype consisted of poor readers, poor at spatial/reasoning, but good at coding/speed. This group accounted for 23% of the sample and, they suggested, was akin to Boder's dyseidetic group. A second group was poor on reading, poor on coding/speed but good on spatial/reasoning. This accounted for 18% of the sample and possibly represented encoding and short-term memory difficulties. A third group was poor on reading only and good on the other two factors, accounting for 41% of the sample and probably typified a specific reading deficit. The final group was poor on all three of these factors and represented 9% of the sample, this perhaps being a mixed group. Unfortunately these subtypes do not overlap in any clear way with the subtypes described earlier. However, Decker and De Fries argue that the reading disabled group differed from their matched controls, who were good on all three factors; and when they classified the subtypes among siblings and parents they found that there was a much greater concordance of these difficulties in the families of the reading disabled children compared to the controls.

We now turn to Goldberg and Shiffman's second area, that of twin studies. One of the most commonly quoted studies, is by Hermann (1959). He reported studies on 11 monozygotic twins, and 27 dizygotic twins, finding that the monozygotics were 100% concordant with respect to dyslexia; and that the dizygotics were 33% concordant. He concluded that this showed with 'all desirable clarity' that dyslexia was an inherited predisposition. Hermann's results, therefore, powerfully argue for the importance of genetic components in dyslexia. (This would be even more convincing of course if the monozygotic twins had been reared apart, and this is the kind of twin that is looked for particularly in studies of the development of intelligence.) Some recent studies report similar findings. For example, Zerbin-Rudin (1967) reports that 17 monozygotic twins had 100% concordance, whereas 32 dizygotic twins had 12% concordance. Bakwin (1973) found 84% concordance in monozygotic twins and 29% in dizygotic twins. The last study has however been criticized by Finucci (1978) because of the vagueness of the criteria used in relation to reading disabilities (partly from questionnaire and self-report). Stevenson *et al.* (1987), in their study of 285 twins aged 13 years, report little concordance in monozygotes for reading. However, in spelling a heritability rate of 0.53 was recorded, which increased to 0.75 when intelligence was controlled for. They also commented that strong genetic influences on spelling were found when the concordance rates for spelling disabilities were compared for monozygotic and dizygotic pairs.

There have been fewer studies on the last two components cited by Goldberg and Shiffmann. There is evidence that dyslexia persists into adulthood (Rawson 1968,

Yule *et al*. 1974, Silver and Hagin 1964), and some researchers have looked at biochemical correlates of dyslexia. For example, Hughes (1976) suggests high metabolic rates in dyslexics due to high thyroxine levels. Some interesting results in relation to hemisphere function and possible biochemical correlates are described by Wilsher *et al*. (1979) in relation to a drug (Piracetam) facilitating verbal learning in dyslexics.

Finucci (1978) puts forward the following three major conclusions in relation to genetics and dyslexia:

1 That dyslexic difficulties aggregate together in a non-random way within families
2 Reading and spelling performance is lower in the immediate family of those with dyslexic difficulties
3 There is a higher concordance of dyslexia amongst monozygotic twins compared to dizygotic. This is argued to indicate the importance of genetic factors

However, what is unclear at the present time is the particular pattern of transmission. It certainly does not appear to be a straightforward Mendelian kind of inheritance. There do not appear to be any *clear* sex link aspects, although these have been discussed earlier. The evidence suggests a multi-factorial genetic predisposition, and implies some kind of genetic inheritance.

This brings us then to the important consideration of environment versus inherited predispositions. There are many different ways in which the genotype (genetic/chromsomal make-up) can be influenced, and give rise to different phenotypes (the expression in the environment of a particular underlying genetic inheritance). This depends on the interaction between heredity and environment. Owen *et al*. (1978) draws on the concept of canalization (Waddington 1957) in relation to reading difficulties. The notion here is that alternative phenotypes are restricted to one or a few outcomes as a result of canalization. This in turn depends on the degree of genotypic control which is related to the force of deflection and the timing of deflection. In other words there may be some kind of inherited predisposition to develop a dyslexic learning problem. Whether this expresses itself phenotypically, i.e. the child actually has a reading, spelling and writing disorder, will depend to some extent on environmental interactions. However, it is unclear how powerful the genetic influence is. The concept of canalization argues that in some cases there is only restricted number of possible phenotypical outcomes, and this may be the case in dyslexia. On the other hand the genetic predisposition may be fairly wide and there may be a great deal of scope for environmental determinants in the possible development of this predisposition. One crucial point here is that showing dyslexia to be strongly under genotypical control does *not* mean that it cannot be modified by environmental effects. An excellent example of this is Phenylketonurea which has an unequivocal genetic cause, yet the results of that genetic cause can be overcome by appropriate nutritional control of diet. The parallel is that if a dyslexic genotype *always* leads to a learning difficulty, this difficulty could still be overcome by appropriate teaching. I believe this to be a very important point, since much of the early controversy in relation to the acceptance of the concept 'specific learning difficulty' appears to involve some kind of misunderstanding as to the possible implications of accepting that there could be a reading difficulty that is inherited. The early use of the term 'word blind', for example, was rather akin to the notion of 'colour blindness'. The latter is clearly a linked genetic disorder, and is irremediable; the individual will always remain colour blind. This reasoning might also apply to 'word blind,' implying a genetic cause, and could suggest that the child will never learn to read and therefore should simply be written off as unteachable. This, quite rightly, has been unacceptable to remedial teachers and educational authorities in general. As a result they have been very reluctant to accept that there could be any intrinsic learning difficulty. The important point is that whether dyslexia is environmentally or genetically determined, the teaching should be appropriate, and geared to the child's difficulty.

Of course, being 'dyslexic', as defined by difficulties in writing, spelling and reading, cannot be inherited *per se*. Reading is not a biological feature that is inherited. There is some underlying cognitive or neurological deficit which *results* in being unable to read. The studies reviewed above can only indicate in general that dyslexia seems to be an inherited form of difficulty, but cannot pinpoint in detail which particular aspect is inherited.

A final but very important point in this discussion concerns the possibility of social transmission of learning difficulties. The studies which provide evidence to show that there is a high incidence of dyslexic difficulties in parents or siblings, or that parents and siblings score less well than control groups on reading and spelling, could be due to some kind of family expectation, modelling or learning. Perhaps a child is aware that one or both parents has difficulty in reading and spelling and therefore copies this parent's behaviour. Perhaps the family in general terms encourages the child not to perceive school work as being very important. One could imagine a situation in which the attitude of the whole family is not to perceive reading and spelling as important skills. This is a crucial point and must have some kind of answer from those who believe that dyslexia is indeed a genetic predisposition. However, this criticism cannot be levelled at those studies cited above which suggest more subtle cognitive difficulties and differences amongst families and siblings where there is an identified dyslexic child. Some of the psychological and psychometric tests given are not common, and certainly the kinds of tasks are not those that an everyday family would come across. It is difficult to see how a family might in general terms 'reject' the need to do this kind of task. It is also uncertain how social transmission might account for the high concordance in monozygotic twins. On clinical and observational grounds, parents and families whose children are referred for dyslexic-type learning problems are not, in my experience, those who reject the school system, or perceive reading, writing and spelling to be unimportant. Indeed the parents are very anxious to help their children, providing a good deal of encouragement. In order to account for social transmission here, then, one has to postulate the opposite to that described previously, i.e. the child is now having to rebel against his parents by refusing to read, write and spell because they perceive it as being so important! Another very common and important clinical observation in this context is the knowledge that the child has about learning difficulties in the family. In many cases the writer has found that the child was *not* aware that either of his parents could not read, write or spell, or indeed that they had had any difficulties when they were at school. The parents are often ashamed of their learning problems, or more often than not do not want their child to undergo the same stress and difficult schooling that they had. They therefore encourage the child to learn to read from an early age, and hide any learning difficulties that they have had.

1.7   Official attitudes to dyslexia in the UK

The 1944 Education Act put forward 11 categories of handicap entitling children to special education treatment. Learning disabilities, dyslexia or similar categories were not amongst them. Sometimes children were assessed by local authorities and then fitted into the appropriate category or given a 'label'. They might then be sent to a special school, given specialized help by a teacher visiting the school or attend a local centre.

Until recently, in the United Kingdom the only possible categories under which parents could claim help in respect of a dyslexic child were the Educationally Sub-Normal (originally defined as *educationally* retarded, but operationally used as *intellectually* handicapped), and Maladjusted (if parents could show that the 'maladjustment' arose from the child's reading and spelling difficulties). It must be said that obtaining help under these categories for a dyslexic child was rare, and both of these categories are inappropriate anyway. Dyslexic children being given help under the ESN title are usually misdiagnosed or misperceived, and given the label incorrectly. The assumption is often made that because a child cannot read, write or spell he must be intellectually backward, and sometimes intelligent children having a dyslexic problem can remain in a special school with those who are intellectually handicapped or severely sub-normal for the whole of their school career. There is a very important distinction, as we have seen, between those who are 'backward' readers and those who are 'retarded' readers. Similarly the provision for those children who are 'maladjusted' is really aimed at those who have psychiatric disturbance, or whose primary difficulty is maladjustment in behaviour. In the case of the dyslexic, there may well be secondary emotional or adjustment problems, but these arise from a primary difficulty in reading, writing and spelling.

It appears that certain local education authorities did not (and still do not), recognize dyslexia as a specific category of difficulty and, in many cases, the educational needs of children are being overlooked. Ironically the Department of Employment recognizes dyslexia as a category of the 'disabled school leaver'. The Rehabilitation Report on People with Dyslexia (1974) concludes 'we are greatly concerned that the provision for identification of dyslexic children is, at the present time, greatly inadequate'. Indeed the Chronically Sick and Disabled Persons Act (1970) includes a section on children suffering from 'acute' dyslexia, which states that the education authorities should provide the Secretary of State with information on the provision of special educational facilities for children who suffer from acute dyslexia. 'Acute' dyslexia here refers to the severity of the difficulty. However, the 1981 Education Act (which came into force in 1983) has abolished all categories of handicap. The aim is to provide each child with educational facilities suitable to his or her requirements, under the heading 'Special Educational Needs'. We shall examine this act and its implications shortly, but as Wedell (1987) comments, there is still no official definition of 'dyslexia or specific learning difficulties' by the Department of Education and Science.

There have been other government reports addressing the situation arising from the 1944 Education Act. One, the Tizard Report (1972) on children with specific reading difficulties, was the report of the Advisory Committee on Handicapped Children. This report concluded that the word 'dyslexia' did not serve any useful purpose, and that children with dyslexic problems were simply at the lower end of the continuum of those with severe reading difficulties. The Committee preferred the use of the phrase *Specific Reading Difficulty* to describe such problems. The report also criticized the Chronically Sick and Disabled Persons Act for using the words 'acute dyslexia' which the Committee argued was particularly unhelpful. The results of this report, at the time, were fairly negative for the dyslexic child. This was not so much because of the argument over the appropriate label, but rather that the notion of *specific reading difficulties* suggested that the problem was not one that required any specialized help, assessment or identification, but was merely a further kind of reading difficulty. The implication was that there should be extra spelling or extra reading, rather than any specialized remedial programme aimed at the children. In other words rather than focus attention on a specific reading difficulty, which local authorities needed to provide for in addition to the categories of handicap from the 1944 Education Act, it merely allowed local authorities to say there was no such thing as dyslexia, and therefore there was no need to make any provision for this non-entity. From my experience this has been the most common attitude displayed by local authorities.

The next Government Report to look briefly at dyslexia was the Bullock Report (1975). Although this was looking at language in very general terms, it did make some comments about written language learning. The report suggested that there was a small group of children whose difficulties were not accounted for by the previously described so-called barriers to learning. However, this report preferred the term *specific reading retardation* to describe such children.

The Warnock Report (1978), amongst other things, recommended a radical departure from categories of handicap, and also looked briefly at specific learning difficulties. It was argued that this concept described severe and long-term difficulties in reading, writing and spelling, and stressed the importance of early identification and assessment, as well as evaluating different kinds of teaching approaches. One particularly welcome aspect of this description was the recognition of writing and spelling rather than simply reading, as additional problems in dyslexics. The Warnock Report sought to substitute the phrase 'children with learning difficulties' to describe both those categories previously referred to in the 1944 Act as well as those who may have narrow specific educational difficulties (the latter would describe the dyslexic). The identification of particular difficulties experienced by the individual child, and the provision of appropriate help without having to slot each child into a category, is in general terms a worthwhile aim. However there are obviously questions concerning 'special' schools versus 'ordinary' schools, teacher training, resources, identification of needs, types of teacher, etc., which need to be tackled. The Report also stressed the need for research into the assessment of children's learning problems, of 'learning difficulties in reading, writing and spelling'.

The 1981 Education Act has not incorporated all of these recommendations, but it is worth examining some of its features, and what the implications might be for the dyslexic learner. This Act was a direct result of the Warnock report, and may well have a profound effect on Government and LEAs' views of dyslexia. One of the most important parts of the act was the repeal of Sections 33 and 34 of the 1944 Act. This means that the 11 statutory 'types' of handicap do not apply. Instead, each LEA has a duty to provide 'special educational treatment' for pupils who 'suffer from any disability of mind or body'. Dyslexic children may be included, and certainly the attitude of 'not defined in 1944 Act, therefore doesn't exist' will, one hopes, be less prevalent. The crucial point is of course how 'Special Educational Needs' will be applied. According to the Act this will include those children who have a significantly greater difficulty in learning than the majority of children of the same age; or a disability preventing or hindering the child from making use of the educational facilities of a kind usually provided in schools.

The Act lays down that a Local Authority can inform parents that they intend to assess the child for Special Educational Needs under the Act. They must give the parents details of the procedure, a named officer whom the parents can contact and liase with and, in addition, the parents should be informed that they can submit their own evidence. This should be done within 29 days. Alternatively, the parents themselves, under Section 9 of the Act, may request that the Authority undertake assessment for Special Educational Needs. The Act states: 'The Authority must comply with that request unless, where it is in their opinion, unreasonable'. The assessment by a Local Educational Authority (LEA) would normally include a psychological assessment, medical officer's assessment, reports from school and teachers and any other relevant party. If the Local Authority feels that there is a learning difficulty they may produce a Statement, which should outline the educational needs of the child and, in addition, the proposed provision that is going to be made for that child.

It seems clear from the above that appropriate help ought to be made available to the dyslexic child, both in terms of recognition of their difficulties, which clearly fall into the above criteria of educational need, and in terms of appropriate remediation.

Unfortunately, this has not always been the case even following the implementation of this Act. Initially, the Act is not particularly clear about the legal basis for 'dyslexia'. The reader is referred to the BPS Working Party for the Division of Education and Child Psychology (DECP 1983) for further information in debates over legalities. However, experience shows that there is a good deal of scope for interpretation of the Act when it comes to application to individual children. For example, the LEAs, as mentioned above, may decide that a request for an assessment is unreasonable. There then may be disagreement between the evidence the parents present and the assessment by the LEA. There is much more likely to be disagreement between the recommendations for appropriate teaching and the remedial help recommended for the child. In many cases LEAs may recommend a peripatetic teacher, or some sessional help, whereas parents may be hoping for rather more specialized and wider help. Incidentally, most specialists in the field, including the author and others, for example Chasty (1981) and Crowther (1982), feel that dyslexics require a specialist form of skilled teaching, something that is not available in ordinary classrooms at the present time. What is required is a more widespread teacher training for dyslexic learning difficulties. There have been many recent court cases where parents have had to go to court under appeal, in order to try and obtain appropriate education or funding for education for their dyslexic children.

2

Case histories

The features associated with dyslexia which have been described in Chapter 1 can be underlined by recourse to case history. The following examples are from individuals whom I myself have assessed.

2.1 Case history 1 (I E)

The first case not only reflects some of the features outlined in Chapter 1, but also illustrates the practical difficulties in helping the problem by describing a boy's spelling and reading after a two-year period, during which he had had some intensive and specialized remedial help to overcome his dyslexic difficulties.

IE was first referred when he was 8 years old, having failed more or less completely to cope with everyday schooling. The school was sympathetic, but very puzzled over IE's learning problems. They did not feel that he was slow learning, and yet he was manifestly unable to undertake most of the classroom activities which were based on reading and writing. He was not receiving any help from the local authority nor from the school apart from a little bit of extra reading to a classroom auxilliary. Generally, his milestones were within normal limits, apart from a rather late language development. Indeed he had been referred for speech therapy during pre-school and still had residual speech difficulties, e.g. confusions of many consonants, and a slightly 'babyish' speech for his age. Hearing and vision were within normal limits. Although IE himself was rather fidgety in the testing and had some slight attentional difficulties, in general he was able to concentrate well and made good rapport with the tester. I found him a boy of normal personality, although rather quiet and beginning to get very anxious about his own failure in written language learning.

IE had a Full Scale IQ on the British Ability Scales of 105. Generally, the Reasoning subtests were in the average to above average range (both non-verbal and verbal reasoning) and he did particularly well on tests of Spatial Imagery such as Block Design. Generally, conceptualizing and other abilities were average or above average. He did particularly poorly, however, on tests of short-term memory, particularly the Immediate and Delayed Visual Recall subtests and the Recall of Digits subtest. IE also did rather poorly on a test of Matching Letter Like Forms. His Reading and Spelling abilities are summarized below:

(Chronological Age	8 years 0 months)
BAS Word Reading	5 years 5 months
Schonell Graded Word Spelling	non-starter
Neale Analysis of Reading Ability	
Accuracy	6 years 6 months
Rate	below norms
Comprehension	6 years 8 months

Examples of his Free Writing and Spelling are shown in Figures 2.1 and 2.2. Other test results, such as the Jordan and the Aston Index test, showed that IE had difficulties in both visual perception and short-term memory, as well as difficulties in auditory perception.

Following his initial assessment, it was arranged for IE to attend a local centre specializing in helping dyslexic children, as well as suggesting some help for the school that might coordinate with the centre's teaching programme. After this assessment, and a discussion of his difficulties with IE, his parents reported that he became a 'changed boy'. He had a much higher self-esteem and was much more motivated to undertake school work. The local authority also provided some additional help in a peripatetic remedial teacher, and he had a very sympathetic class teacher who, having understood the nature of his problem, went out of her way to provide opportunities for success in the classroom. When seen for a review, 20 months later, IE was still attending the local dyslexic centre and receiving help from the peripatetic teacher. He enjoyed both these visits and his parents reported that

(i)   8 years 0 months

mI tan nah ʋshat wac atamas

(ii)   9 years 8 months

I was wocin don of the Stet andI hud
a sSScreem andI went in to the haws and
I Sur * a man uif a knife

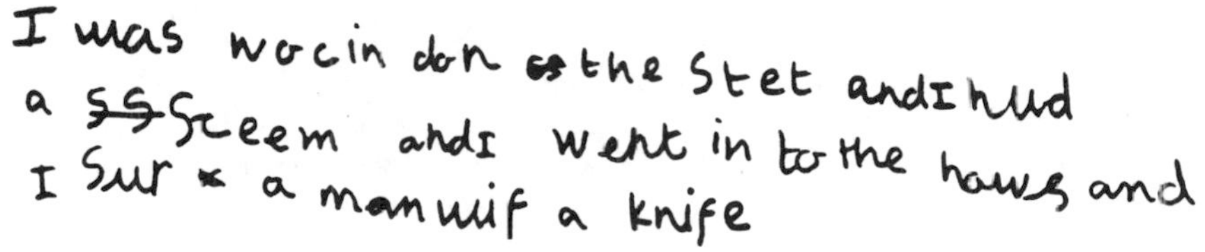

(i)   My favourite hobby is art work and maths

(ii)   I was walking down the street and I heard a scream and I went
into the house and I saw a man with a knife.

Figure 2.1   Free writing of I E

(i)   8 years 0 months

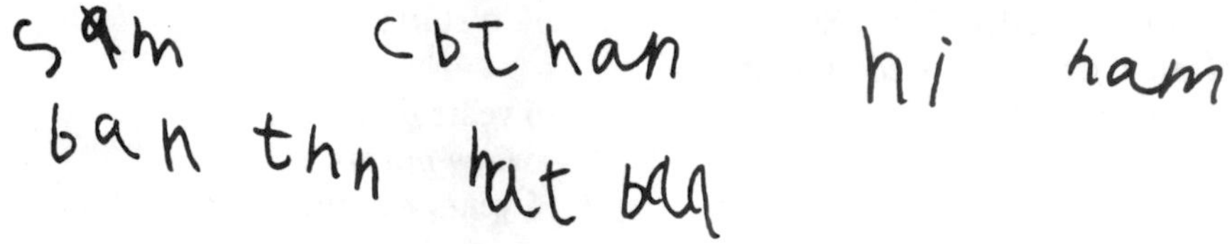

Sam cbthan hi ham
ban thn hat bag

(ii)   9 years 0 months

see cut mat in nan leg dot hat pen

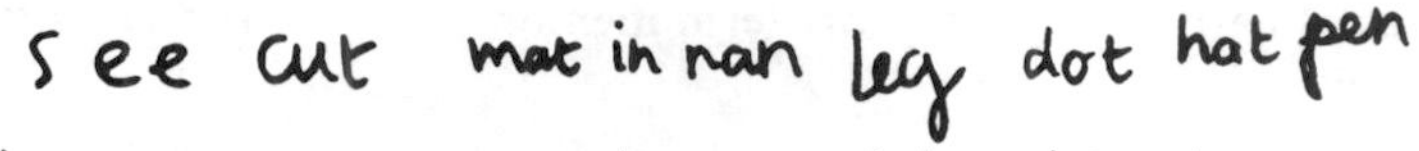

(ii)	see	cut	mat	in	ran	led	lot	hat	pen

Figure 2.2 Spelling of I E

he was well motivated. However, there had been a change of class teacher during the period since he had been seen, and this class teacher was much less sympathetic to IE's difficulties. In some cases, IE was required to read out stories in front of the class, and the result of this was that he was receiving some verbal mockery and occasional physical bullying because he was decribed as being 'thicko' by other children. This resulted in IE's self-esteem and motivation once again taking a plunge and his parents were seriously concerned about his negative attitude building up towards schoolwork.

The following are parts taken from my report written following the review appointment.

In relation to his spelling and writing, for example, [IE]when he was first seen, could not make any sense at all of any sound symbol correspondences, his writing was undecipherable, and bore no relation at all to what he was trying to say. He was only able to spell one word correctly on the spelling test and the other errors included completely random sound symbol correspondence.

Now [IE's] spelling errors have some resemblance to the speech sounds, e.g. *sture* for *story, sic* for *sick* and so on. Other errors include confusions of letter orientation, e.g. *dit* for *bit*, omissions, *duw* for *down*. Similarly, on the Jordan Test, [IE] is now able to identify consonant blends and diagraphs where this was a task completely beyond him before. He had no idea of the relationship between speech and written language. Similarly, his previous assessment suggested very severe visual perceptual difficulties in things such as Visual Matching. He now makes very few mistakes and has most of the basic underlying skills such as sound blending, perception of sounds, visual matching.

His reading strategies are that much more mature—he is able to sound out letters and has a better 'phonic attack', both in identifying individual letters and the occasional diagraph and able to blend them together. This results, however, in a very low Rate of Reading—it takes him a considerable amount of time to sound out the words. For example, for *rabbit*, he sounds out the *r-a* sound laboriously, then the *b* as a *d*, corrected to a *b* and finally the word 'rabbit'. This is typical of his general approach and attack. Occasionally, he makes incorrect uses of context clues by guessing from one or two of the letters, for example, *they heard a scream*, for *they heard a splash*.

IE's performance on the second referral, when he was 9 years 8 months is illustrative of the kind of difficulties besetting dyslexic children. On the one hand his reading and spelling had improved vastly in relation to his reading strategies and approach because of the kind of help he was having, and yet the intractable nature of the problem is illustrated by the fact that he was still over two years retarded in reading, writing and spelling. Dyslexic children can be helped to overcome their learning problems, but it is a slow and laborious process.

IE had at least made a start in reading and spelling, his word recognition skills were around the 7-year level (British Ability Scales Word Reading) and his reading from a story had shown some considerable improvement (in the Neale Analysis). His Reading Accuracy was 7 years 2 months, Reading Comprehension 8 years 2 months, although Reading Rate was still below the norms. The difference between his writing and spelling may be seen by looking at Figures 2.1, and 2.2. Figure 2.3 plots the improvement on various British Ability Scales subtests based on the two assessments. It may be seen that IE's Similarities (verbal reasoning) ability starts off at a higher level than the other abilities (illustrating the specific nature of the dyslexic problem) and then improves steadily over the two-year period. Word Reading was very poor indeed when IE was first seen, but this also improves greatly over the two-year period, illustrating the important effect that the remedial teaching had upon his reading abilities. Although IE's reading has improved tremendously over the two-year period it is still well behind his chronological age. What is of particular interest is that the Recall of Digits and Immediate Visual

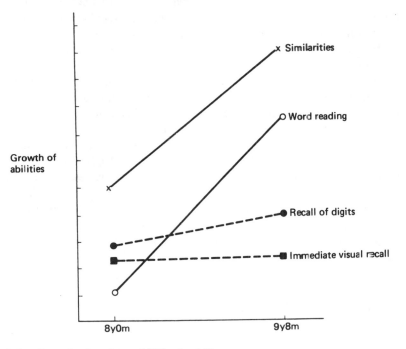

Figure 2.3   Growth of various abilities for I E

Recall subtests (which were particularly poor in IE's case), have not improved at all over the two-year period. There has been a slight increase in abilities in Recall of Digits but in fact IE's performance on Immediate Visual Recall was exactly the same two years later as it had been when he was just under 8 years old. Remediation therefore is overcoming the difficulties, presumably by developing strategies that circumvent memory problems. This also suggests that the dyslexic's problems are some kind of absolute deficit or difficulty rather than a maturational lag, although a conclusion cannot be drawn from one case.

2.2 Case history 2 (M S)

MS was 10½ years old when he was referred for an assessment of his dyslexic difficulties, and is a fairly typical case reflecting many of the problems besetting dyslexic children. He had a younger sister who was succeeding exceptionally well at school, and this caused some difficulties in relation to his own self-image. However, the major problem was that his school did not recognize that he had a learning problem, arguing that his lack of success in reading, writing and spelling was due to him being lazy and not trying.

There had been a long history of learning difficulties in his case, starting from his continued non-attainment at five, six and seven. It was also reported that MS was becoming aggressive at school, being disruptive in class and often fighting in the playground. On the grounds of his bad behaviour he had been referred to the School Psychological Service, where it was felt that he had a behavioural problem. As a result, he was attending, on a day release basis, a local centre for the maladjusted and children with emotional and behavioural difficulties. He was undergoing a series of behaviour modification techniques in order to help alleviate his aggressive and disruptive behaviour.

The interrelationship between emotional difficulties and reading, writing and spelling problems has been mentioned in Chapter 1 and is often difficult to sort out. In MS's case, it was quite clear that his reading difficulties had given rise to his bad behaviour, as he had been a well adjusted boy up to the age of about nine. In fact, prior to that, his teachers had commented on how well behaved he was, and there had been no familial difficulties or trauma that might have resulted in an emotional or behavioural problem. The simple fact was that MS was beginning to perceive himself as a failure, and did not quite understand why he could not attain the apparently simple task that his peer group was attaining. In order to succeed in some kind of fashion, he resorted to aggression and classroom disruption.

The following were some of the basic test results appertaining to MS upon assessment:

CA—10 years 5 months

Weschler Intelligence Scale for Children(R)
  —Full Scale   123
  —Verbal Scale   125
  —Performance Scale   120

Schonell Graded Word Reading	8 years 1 month
Neale Analysis of Reading Ability	
—Accuracy	8 years 6 months
—Rate	7 years 6 months
—Comprehension	9 years 1 month
Vernon Graded Word	
—Spelling	7 years 3 months

On the Wechsler Test, MS scored particularly poorly on the Digit Span and Coding subtests, and rather less well on Arithmetic and Information. In contrast, he scored well on Comprehension, Block Design, Similarities and Picture Completion. This is a profile typically associated with the dyslexic learning difficulty (see Chapter 6). MS also did less well on other tests of short-term memory, and appeared to have difficulty in phonic analysis and auditory processing, as well as in making sense of order and complex orthography. MS also had difficulty in sequencing the months of the year. He wrote with his left hand but did other tasks with his right hand. He was unable to identify left and right directions. Figures 2.4 and 2.5 show his writing and his spelling.

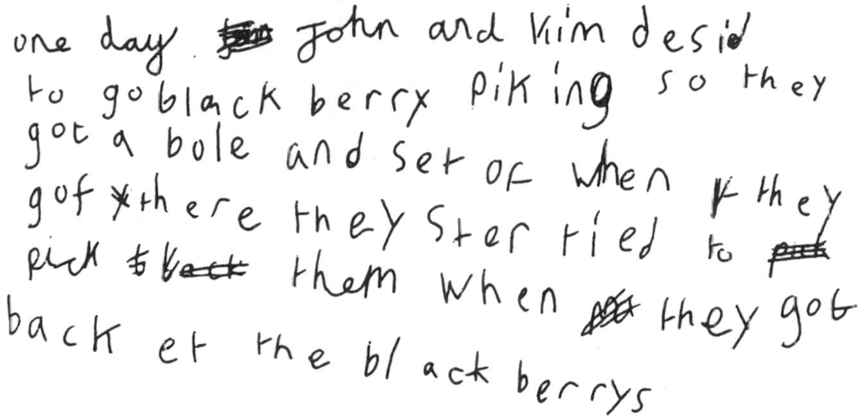

One day John and Kim decided
to go blackberry picking so they
got a bowl and set off, when they
got there they started to
pick them when they got
back (they) ate the blackberries

(Spelling corrected, but not syntax, punctuation, etc.)

Figure 2.4   Free writing of M S

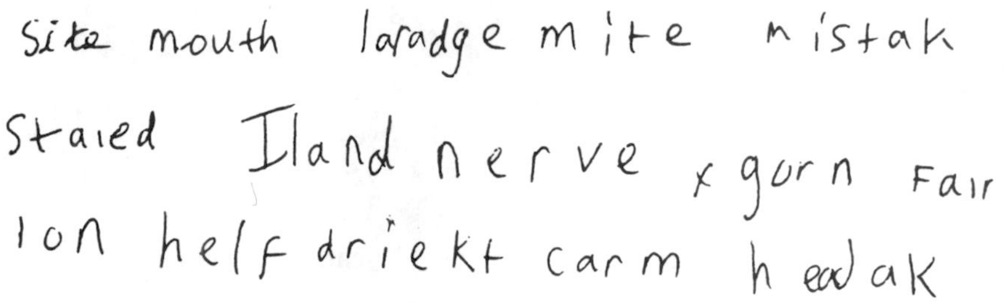

Site mouth laradge mite mistak
Staied Iland nerve x gorn Fair
Ion helf driekt carm hedak

sight	mouth	large	might	mistake
stayed	island	nerve	join	fare
iron	health	direct	calm	headache

Figure 2.5 Spelling of M S

Some further indication of the nature of his difficulties is given by the following excerpts taken from my report on the boy.

On the Word Reading of the British Ability Scales, MS scored at over two years behind his chronological age. Here he was often able to sound out the letters and blend them to form words, but occasionally made errors of omission (e.g. *sad* for *said*). Other errors included confusing letter order (e.g. *sink* for *skin*), mispronunciation, (e.g. *leether* for *leather*), and additions (e.g. *flavour* for *favour*). Towards the ceiling of his ability in reading, MS's attempts at sounding out the words were very slow, laborious and non-fluent.

On the Neale Analysis, MS's reading was somewhat better, as he was able to use context clues, but is still some two years behind his chronological age. This represents a considerable retardation. Although he occasionally had difficulty in understanding aspects of the story, his Reading Comprehension was somewhat better, suggesting that his problem does not lie in the semantic or meaningful aspects of written language, but rather in 'deciphering the symbols'.

On Reading Accuracy, MS made occasional incorrect guesses from context, and errors included substitutions, (e.g. *process* for *progress*) as well as confusions of letter order, or attempted reading from the middle or the end of words, (e.g. *trened* for *returned, sleil* for *skill*). Other errors included word order, (e.g. *stretched out* for *outstretched*), mispronunciations, (e.g. *a wownd* for *wounded*) and, in one story, substituting a word (a name) from a previous story which had apparently been remembered.

Spelling presented an even greater difficulty for MS, being some three years behind his chronological age. Much of MS's spelling was phonetic (e.g. *mite* for *might, carm* for *calm*, or indicated confusions in which particular letters represented the sounds where there was an alternative (e.g. *staid* for *stayed*). Other errors included difficulties in letter order, and confusions of sound (e.g. *driekt* for *direct, helf* for *health*), or incorrect substitutions (e.g. *gorn* for *join*).

MS's major problem seems to be in short-term memory, which may have prevented him internalizing and remembering spelling patterns and rules. This is particularly the case when he has to integrate the sounds with the written symbols and actually produce them in writing.

Not only were MS's reading, spelling and writing behind his chronological age, but also considerably further behind his high-level of thinking ability. The Wechsler Scale placed MS in an above-average/superior range of intelligence, or top 5% of the population. Obviously, his problem does not result from being slow learning, or from general difficulties in understanding spoken language concepts. The important thing here is that normally MS would have been succeeding exceptionally well at school. As well as recognizing his ability, it would have been appropriate to understand how frustrated he had become in being unable to express his good ideas and/or his reasoning abilities in written form.

At any event, after the assessment, the problems were discussed with the boy, and it was explained how these difficulties might be perceived in relation to the nature of the written language, and dyslexia syndrome. Sometimes, it is suggested that to label a child 'dyslexic' is wrong, owing to notions of 'a self-fulfilling hypothesis', i.e. the child would therefore continue to have a difficulty in reading, writing and spelling. The reality seems to be the complete opposite. Explaining to the child what his difficulties are helps him considerably. Indeed, some of the teachers may be helped to understand that it is not poor teaching (which they perhaps suspected in darkest moments) that might have caused the learning disabilities in that child. Parents often report a complete change, almost overnight, in respect of the child's attitude towards school and themselves, following a sympathetic assessment. This is a finding echoed by many of those involved with dyslexic children (e.g. Miles 1974). In the case of MS, his attitude towards school certainly did improve. It was recommended that a structured and appropriate teaching programme be undertaken, and the school began to treat him in a much more appropriate manner. At this point, it would have been nice to say that MS lived happily ever after! However, there is a very sad postscript and ending to this particular case, which is why it was chosen. MS was not given an appropriate teaching programme, although the school tried their best to provide help, and indeed his reading and spelling improved a little over the next year or so. However, the Local Authority still persisted in the notion that his difficulties were emotional in origin. They interpreted the decrease in his disruptive behaviour as resulting from the treatment that he had been receiving at the unit for the maladjusted. (This of course may well have been true, and the very rapid improvement in his self-esteem and behaviour following the assessment and explanation of dyslexic difficulties could have been coincidental.) The Local Authority did not have any resources available for dyslexics, as they did not believe that such a child existed, nor did they have any provision for children with specific learning difficulties. MS's parents then arranged for him to attend an independent centre for dyslexic children. Unfortunately, the Local Authority refused permission for him to attend this and rather than make a legal issue out of the events, his parents decided to withdraw him from the centre. MS's behavioural difficulties returned after a term or so and eventually he ended up before a juvenile court following some rather more serious misdemeanours.

This is not to say that all local authorities hold this kind of view about dyslexia. Many local authorities have good provision and resources available for specific

learning problems. Indeed, some special remedial teams and educational psychologists specifically deal with these problems.

2.3   Case history 3 (DF)

The third case history is that of an adult dyslexic, a Mr DF. DF had left school at 15
with no qualifications or examination passes, and when referred to me was aged 28.
He was working in a factory, and had referred himself, mainly because he felt that
his present employment prospects did not match his hopes. He was working at a
menial task, which he found very boring. He always felt that he had under-
achieved at school, and in many ways felt rather bitter about his school experiences. He had been categorized as 'slow learning' at school, and had been in the
'low band'. He was not encouraged to take examinations and had been given the
impression that the best thing he could do was to leave school at the earliest possible
opportunity.

When I first met DF he was worried and anxious about his own spelling, writing
and reading problems. In many ways he had a 'chip on his shoulder' and was very
defensive. However, on discussing his problems with him in a sympathetic way, it
soon emerged that he thought he might really be 'stupid', and had spent a considerable amount of time trying to hide his written language difficulties from his colleagues and anyone else he came across. As soon as he realized that he was going to
receive a sympathetic ear and that he would not be made fun of, he settled down
and made a very lively rapport during the testing session.

The Wechsler Adult Intelligence Scale (WAIS) placed DF in the superior range
of intelligence (an IQ of around 130). Skills such as reasoning and vocabulary were
exceptionally mature and sophisticated. For example, he was able to define all the
words on the Vocabulary scale from the WAIS, a very rare occurrence. Generally,
his non-verbal scores were slightly lower and this had important implications for
aspects of his learning difficulties (see below). DF's reading abilities based on the
tests given were reasonably good. He could read words quite well, and his comprehension was good, However, on the Neale Analysis, Reading Rate was rather slow,
and reading tended to be a laborious and non-fluent process. This residual difficulty in reading fluency is typical of the adult dyslexic, as are the comments made in
respect of the attitudes that DF adopted towards the world.

It was spelling and writing, however, that presented a very severe difficulty for
DF. His spelling was around the 9-year-old level and gave him a spelling quotient of
less than 70. A sample of his spelling is given in Figure 2.6. Many of his attempts, it
may be noted, are phonetic: he was able to follow the sounds but unable to remember the spelling patterns which represented the particular sounds (e.g. *strate* for
straight, mileon for *million*). Some errors included confusions of sound patterns,
or omissions of consonants (e.g. *crawed* for *crowded, caperrat* for *cooperate*),
and other errors suggested difficulties in 'revisualization' (e.g. *lengthgth* for
length). The latter is obviously perservation of letter combinations, but the key
feature here was the inability of DF to look at the word and realize that there was
something wrong with it, i.e. to have some kind of image of what the word looked

like and to be able to compare that to his actual attempt.

A sample of DF's writing is given in Figure 2.7. An important feature is the discrepancy between his oral and verbal abilities as measured by his intelligence and his ability to express his ideas fluently in written form. One should bear in mind that this is a 28-year-old man with a superior intelligence. While the concepts may be fairly reasonable, it can be seen that there are difficulties in syntax, punctuation and spelling. Errors include omissions, telescoping of sounds, confusions of sound symbol correspondence as well as phonetic attempts.

DF's difficulty appears to be one of 'visual dyslexia' (see discussion of subtypes in Chapter 1). For example, he did very poorly on a Recall of Designs test, and on a test of Immediate Visual Recall, suggesting difficulties in visuo-motor memory. His cognitive difficulties related mainly to errors of short-term memory and coding. On the WAIS he showed a typical 'dyslexic profile' (see Chapter 5), i.e. he had a poor Digit Span or auditory sequential memory ability. He was only able to remember 6 digits forward and 3 in reverse, which is below average for an adult, and very discrepant from his other verbal abilities. On the Performance Scale of the WAIS he did very poorly on the Digit Symbol test, a test involving coding, graphic skills and serial processing (see the description of the Coding test in Chapter 5).

The lack of attainments and complete inappropriateness of DF's job in relation to his intelligence are typical of the adult dyslexic. If he had had the appropriate written language skills, there would have been no difficulty for DF in obtaining 'A' levels and undertaking further education should he have wished to. It was arranged for DF to receive some remedial teaching help with his writing, spelling and aspects of his reading. In respect to his occupation, he was referred to the Department of Employment with a covering letter and report. DF obtained a grant to undertake some appropriate training programmes and, at the same time, he enrolled for some evening classes. It was his intention in due course to enrol for 'O' level or other classes to improve his general education.

As well as the obvious difficulties that DF was having in obtaining suitable employment for his abilities, one of the key elements was his secondary reaction to

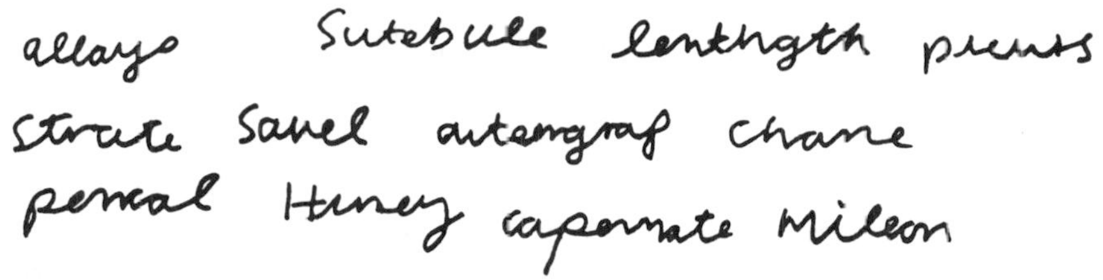

always	suitable	length	paint
straight	shovel	autograph	chair
pencil	honey	co-operate	million

Figure 2.6 Spelling of DF

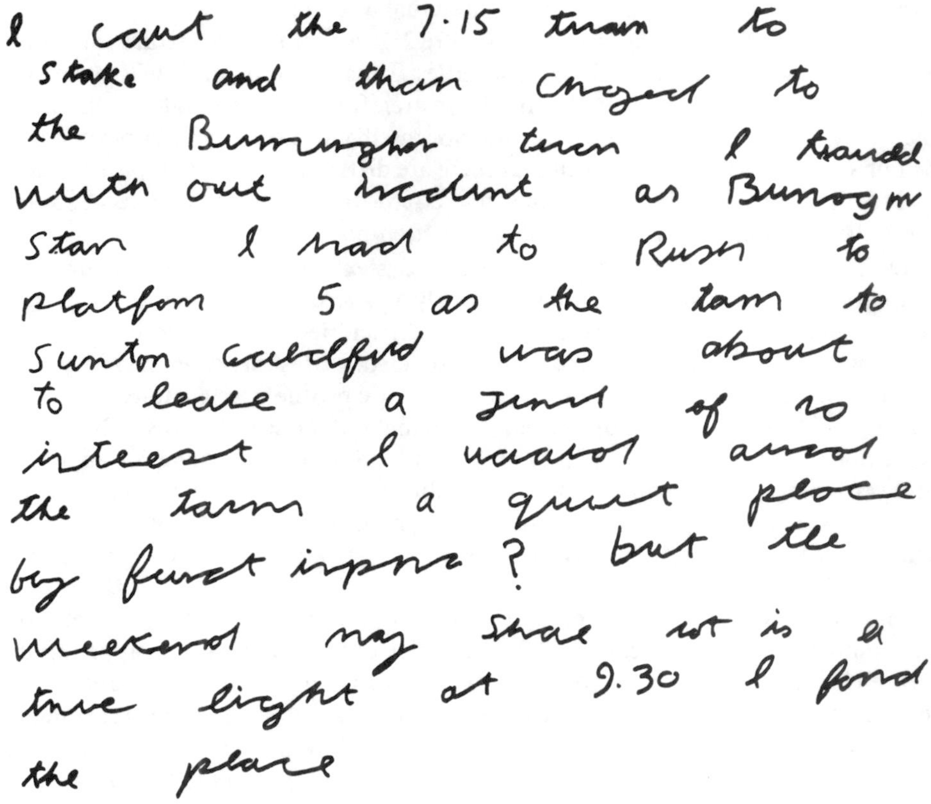

1 caught the 7.15 train to Stoke and then changed to the Birmingham train I travelled without incident as Birmingham station I had to rush to platform 5 as the train to Sutton Coldfield was about to leave a journey of no interest I walked around the town a quiet place by first impression? but the weekend may show it is a true light at 9.30 I found the place.

(Spelling corrected, but not syntax and punctuation.)

Figure 2.7 Free writing of DF

his primary learning problem. Mr DF had become a loner, and had very few friends; he had developed a very 'prickly' personality. This was a defence in case anyone discovered that he could not read, write or spell. At the same time, he was aware that he was intelligent, in the sense of being interested in rather different things to his peer group and colleagues at work. That resulted in a rather over-compensating attitude. He looked down on other people and felt he was superior to them, at the same time secretly knowing that he was 'inferior' because he couldn't write or spell. It has been my experience that many such cases end up in psychiatric hospitals with nervous breakdowns and other personality difficulties. These are just as important components of the learning problem as the dyslexia itself. Both need 'treatment' and understanding help.

2.4   Case history 4 (identical twins)

The final case study illustrates the nature of dyslexic difficulties, but also subtypes of dyslexia and aspects of the genetic component. This is a case of monozygotic twins. What is interesting is to note the apparent subtype differences in a pair of children who have identical chromosomal make-up. This suggests a possible inter-action with an inherited predisposition; the twins are completely concordant in their dyslexia, and yet have different reading and spelling strategies. This is parti-cularly relevant in relation to the concept of canalization which was described in the section on genetics.

Background

The twins, KL and JL, were referred to the writer for assessment of possible dyslexic difficulties. The boys had a history of reading, writing and spelling diffi-culties and, although receiving extra help at school, were making little progress. The local authority was considering sending the children to a special school. Following referral, and interview with the parents, it was established that the boys came from a normal, supportive and loving home background. Developmental milestones were normal apart from a slight delay in language development. Hearing and vision had been tested and were normal. KL was an extended breech and forceps delivery at birth. JL was born first with a relatively normal delivery. The boys' medical history, including blood tests, indicated monozygotic twins, and indeed the children were indistinguishable to me (apart from the fortuitous occur-ence of a pimple on KL's chin!). Both children made easy rapport with me, and cooperated well in the assessment, appearing to enjoy it. KL was rather more expressive in both speech and communication, although rather less confident, often suggesting that his brother 'go first' for the next session. JL had a lower con-centration span.

Assessment Battery

The procedure involved tests routinely given for the assessment of dyslexia, as well as one or two additional items given following an initial inspection of the results. Results of items from the British Ability Scales (BAS), the Neale Analysis of Reading, the Vernon Graded Word Spelling tests, the Aston Index and the Jordan Screening test are presented in Table 2.1.

These results indicate that both children have very similar overall IQs, but that the pattern of sub-abilities making up those IQs are very different. KL has a higher Verbal compared to Visual ability, whereas JL has a much higher Visual as opposed to Verbal ability. This is despite the fact that a number of the subtests are very similar in relation to deficits, e.g. Speed of Information Processing, Word Reading.

KL's profile on the British Ability Scales suggests difficulties in aspects of visual

Table 2.1   Results of assessment tests, case history 4

Results	KL	JL
Age Scores		
CA	8y 6m	8y 6m
Neale Analysis of Reading		
Accuracy	6y 9m	6y 9m
Comprehension	7y 3m	6y 8m
Rate	below norms	6y 9m
Vernon Spelling	5y 7m	5y 7m
BAS Word Reading	6y 3m	6y 5m
British Ability Scales		
General IQ	94	91
Visual IQ	87	96
Verbal IQ	106	86

(IQ calculation from Elliott and Pearson 1980)

Subtests.   T-scores (mean 50 SD 10). IQ equivalents for processes given after brackets if 3 or more subtests given.

	KL	JL
Speed		
Speed of information processing (*vis)	27 (no score)	27 (no score)
Reasoning		
Formal operational thinking (*ver)	52 ⎱	27 (no score) ⎱
Matrices (*vis)	46 ⎰ 102	18 ⎰ 83
Similarities (*ver)	55	50
Spatial imagery		
Block design level (*vis)	47 ⎱	50 ⎱
Block design power (*vis)	45 ⎮	53 ⎮
Rotation of letter like forms (*vis)	47 ⎰ 90	51 ⎰ 102
Visualization of cubes (*vis)	42	50
Perceptual matching		
Verbal tactile (*ver)	n/a but no errors	n/a but no errors
Matching letter like forms (*vis)	38	above norms (min 53)
Short-term memory		
Immediate visual recall (*vis)	29 ⎱	38 ⎱
Delayed visual recall (*vis)	37 ⎮ 82	37 ⎮ 81
Recall of designs (*vis)	46 ⎰	46 ⎰
Recall of digits (*ver)	55	43
Retrieval and application		
Knowledge		
Word definitions (*ver)	50	47
Word reading	32	34

* used to compute IQ
Vis — visual weighting
Ver — verbal weighting
(Elliott and Pearson 1980)

Example reading errors (correct word second)

cook/clock,
me/men,
day/dig,
race/running,
chair/table,
sheep/splash

chalk/clock,
man/men, big/dig,
ran for/fishing,
Paul/Pam

Example of spelling errors

Target:	is	am	do	red	gun	bit	down	milk	bowl	fall
KL	inn	amm	doo	ReR	gnn	bta	ddn	mak	doobl	fol
JL	si	natm	bie	rar	gastin	ballet	beein	nlak	biaue	fal

Target:	potatoes	blue	here
KL	qoqott	doel	HHaeH
JL	petant	balle	hay

Aston Index

Sound blending	Average, (errors refusals)	Poor, errors *pram/peg*, *her/weather*, *pop/pog*, etc.
Sound discrimination	No errors	One error, *bit/pit*
Laterality	Mixed handed, left-eyed	Mixed handed, right-eyed
Months of year	Incorrect	Incorrect
Knowledge of L/R	Poor for age	Poor for age

Jordon test

13. Visual matching	Errors: *tops/spot*, *speech/sheep*, *tarsh/trash*	One error, *sliver/silver*
8. Letter writing from speech	e.g. *Bet/beg*, *mgf/mfpl*	*ben/beg*, *mtpe/mppl*

Alphabet

reading	*d/b, a/q*	*n/i, i/l, e/u, b/d, p/g*
writing	*t/j, s/c, Q/p, b/d*	*s/c, k/q, a/u*

perception. On the Matching of Letter Like Forms, KL did rather poorly. Most of the errors that he made were of a left/right confusion in matching. The fact that he scored reasonably well on the Rotation of Letter Like Forms suggests that the problem is in left/right matching rather than in three-dimensional perception. Block Design, Visualization of Cubes, and Recall of Designs, while within the average range, are rather lower than his performance on the Verbal abilities.

In contrast, JL's abilities on most of these items were rather better than his Verbal abilities. He had some difficulties in the vocabulary tests (Word Definitions). Here his problems were in expressing his ideas fluently in spoken language. In many cases, the writer felt that JL understood the words but could not express exactly what they meant. His responses were rather thin; for example, when asked to define *splash*, he said *water*, and after questioning, *pool* and *blue*, i.e. he was able to provide one or two appropriate associations, but unable to explain exactly what *splash* meant. On Formal Operational Thinking, his difficulties were in understanding the instructions, which are given verbally and are very complex, and trying to describe what a rule might be. For example, he often confused the direction of the logical relationships which are asked for in this test.

There were some similarities in the children. Both were much poorer at Short-Term Memory, which is often associated with dyslexia. Even here, however, there were some differences: JL scored rather poorly on the Recall of Digits, a test of auditory sequential memory, again often a profile cited as being associated with dyslexia (see Chapters 3 and 5), whereas KL did in fact quite well on this test, suggesting no auditory memory difficulties. Both boys did rather poorly on both Immediate and Delayed Visual Recall, which has also been found to be (Thomson 1982b) associated with dyslexia. Although these tests are called 'visual recall', in fact they involve elements of verbal labelling as well (which also has implications for dyslexia, see Chapter 3). This is because the tester gives each object to be remembered a name, encouraging the child to give them verbal labels. In fact, JL actually named each object out loud as he was rehearsing them during the two-minute period—a strategy he would not abandon even though the tester suggested that it was not necessary! This obviously implies a verbal strategy in his case. KL did not do this. When the boys were asked how they recalled the items, JL reported he remembered the names and KL reported that he remembered 'what the objects looked like'. This is interesting, because it suggests that both boys are trying to remember in ways which are opposed to their strength in terms of cognitive skills. They have not developed as yet an appropriate strategy for remembering or undertaking this kind of task.

Both boys also did very poorly on the Speed of Information Processing test, neither being able to get any score at all. This also appears to be a feature of dyslexic difficulties (Thomson 1982b). This test involves crossing out the highest number in a row of numbers under very strictly timed conditions. What this measures is open to debate—possibly serial processing skills, obviously symbol manipulation, possibly graphomotor skills. In the case of these two boys, the difficulties were their inability to decode the symbols appropriately. Neither boy was actually able to identify which was the highest number, because they were unable to identify any numbers, and as a result took over a minute per page.

This profile from the British Ability Scales is confirmed in the other tests. JL, for example, had great difficulty in Sound Blending and made one or two errors in the Sound Discrimination tests, whereas KL's performance here was very good for his age, and error-free. KL, on the other hand, had difficulty in the Visual Matching tasks from the Jordan Test particularly in both letter orientation and letter order. JL's only error here appears to be one of letter order, which one could argue might be an inability to follow his own speech sounds appropriately. The test results are also clearly borne out in the children's reading and spelling errors. As may be seen above, KL's spelling errors very much follow the sounds—they are fairly accurate phonetically and he is obviously representing the speech sounds in some kind of appropriate way. JL, on the other hand, appears to have developed very few appropriate sound symbol correspondences, spelling errors are rather bizarre and he does not appear to be aware that spelling or indeed written language follows or has anything to do with speech sounds. KL also produced more apparent 'visual' errors, i.e. apparent revisualization errors. This is not to say that KL did not produce some odd errors. When both boys were required to do tasks well above their spelling age, as in some of the examples given above, KL also produced spellings which were unrepresentative of the sound system. However, it is the relative incidence of these different kinds of spelling errors in both boys which is striking.

The boys had very similar overall reading ages, except that KL scored rather better on reading comprehension, presumably linked with his better verbal skills. He was however very slow indeed, and worked very hard at decoding letters and words. Errors appear to be guesses from one or two letters, although the *chair/table, race/running* examples suggest some kind of semantic error. JL's reading, in contrast, was less slow, but lower in comprehension score, and errors suggested great sound/symbol confusions. JL therefore appears to have an 'auditory linguistic' deficit in Vernon's (1979) terms, or dysphonetic difficulty in Boder's (1973) terms, whereas KL appears to have a 'visual spatial' (Vernon) or dyseidetic (Boder) difficulty.

The above results provide interesting data in respect to twins in general, and specifically concern the interrelationships between reading disabilities in children who are monozygotic, as well as some suggestive interrelations in visual/auditory classifications of dyslexia. The findings indicate that although the children were very similar—their overall intelligence was within a few IQ points, and their reading and spelling ages were also exactly the same—the whole pattern of their learning profile was remarkably different. Obviously studies looking simply at overall intelligence and reading and spelling ages may assume a much greater concordance amongst twins than actually exists. The children's verbal and visual IQs were almost diametrically opposed; one child has mainly an auditory problem, and the other mainly a visual difficulty. This almost suggests some kind of 'mirror-imaging' of ability, much as one observes in monozygotic twins being left- and right-handed respectively. Whether this relates to genetic development in utero or after birth is impossible to say. It is interesting to note that KL, with the 'visual' problem is left-eyed, which may be related to difficulties due to being 'cross-lateral', although this notion has been criticized (Satz 1976, and also Chapter 3).

Another interesting finding sheds some light on the classification of dyslexics into different kinds of disorder. The implication in the subtypes description is that there are some cognitive differences amongst the children that give rise to differences in reading, writing and spelling disorders. What is suggested by this study is that children having the same genetic complement will develop very different kinds of reading, writing and spelling strategies, and appear to have very different kinds of cognitive skills that underlie these strategies. The evidence here suggests an interaction between the predisposition to have a dyslexic type disorder, early learning, and differential effects of the environment. Perhaps the boys show a disposition to develop cognitively in different ways due to twinning processes but the clear implication is that verbal/visual difficulties are strategies developed by the children in their attempt to cope with the written language system, rather than being some kind of constitutional cognitive difference.

3

Etiology

3.1 Introduction

This chapter will examine the causes or etiology of dyslexia. We can broadly divide these into two areas—*neurological* and *cognitive*. The neurological level of explanation refers to the way in which the brain processes information, and we shall examine ways in which the dyslexic might differ in this process. The neuropsychological organization of the individual will affect his cognitive behaviour. This is much more observable—i.e. what the individual actually does—either in reading and spelling, or in a laboratory task.

The term 'etiology' here is, however, a little misleading as it might imply that by the end of the chapter we will be able to identify the 'cause' of dyslexia. Would that this were the case! What we shall be doing in the forthcoming reviews is picking our way through a vast amount of sometimes contradictory research findings. The best we can do is make some comments in relation to possible correlates of dyslexia, whether this be in terms of a neurological deficit, short-term memory or coding difficulty, or some kind of linguistic problem. The crucial component is how these areas of weakness interact with the written language system.

A recurring theme will be the notion of developmental lag versus deficit. This concept of *delayed* versus *deviant* behaviour is a crucial feature of many other language disorders. Many writers (e.g. Satz and van Nostrand 1973, Satz *et al*. 1978, de Hirsch, Jansky and Langford 1966, Denckla 1977b) suggest that there is a delay in the rate of acquisition of certain developmental skills, e.g. Satz *et al*. relate a delay in the development of the left cerebral hemisphere to reading. Specifically, this kind of model suggests that there is either a delay in cortical hemisphere functioning, preventing the early specialization of language functions, resulting in written language difficulties, or that there is a delay in perceptual and motor skills, resulting in the child not being 'ready' for written language learning in the early stages. Maturational delay implies that there is some kind of 'catch-up' later. Delay in terms of language function suggests that dyslexic individuals are similar to younger children and will eventually catch up either in perceptual and motor skills or in neurological functioning. By contrast, the deficit model (e.g. Doehring 1968, Jorm 1979a, Ellis and Miles 1981) suggests that there is a finite dysfunction, either defined as a cerebral dysfunction (usually suggested as being at some point in the left hemisphere, often the angular gyrus region) or as a deficit in cognitive functioning (e.g. name coding or short-term memory). This implies, in terms of the

61

underlying acquisition of skills, that the child will not necessarily 'catch up'.

Rourke (1976b) presents a discussion of this area, giving examples of maturational lag versus deficit. Two examples are presented here. Figure 3.1 shows a maturational lag paradigm. Here the variable under consideration (for example, reading itself or a perceptual skill) remains at a low level for the first few years and then increases rapidly to catch up with the 'norm'. Figure 3.2 demonstrates a deficit paradigm. Here the skills under consideration do not improve at all, implying a continued weakness in that particular area.

In Rourke's review, he found that one obtained different results depending on the particular tasks examined. For example, tasks such as finger localization (identifying a finger that is touched without looking at it), alphabet learning, and WISC subtests of Object Assembly, Comprehension, Picture Completion and Similarities were associated with a maturational lag. Difficulties associated with a deficit paradigm include poor auditory discrimination, right/left discrimination, auditory-visual and visuo-motor integration, and relatively poor scores on the WISC subtests of Information, Arithmetic, Digit Span and Coding. The latter four WISC subtests are particularly interesting as these are tests associated with dyslexic profiles (see Chapter 5, Section 5.33).

It is useful to consider deficit versus delay notions in respect to etiology, as they have important pedagogic implications: for example, whether to teach a child as if he were just younger, or to teach him differently. However, the situation can be confused when we are considering the reading, writing and spelling processes themselves. In case IE (Chapter 2) reading itself improved over a two-year period, whereas underlying cognitive skills associated with learning problems did not improve. Here we had a deficit *and* a maturational lag paradigm. What happened was that appropriate and good teaching to some extent circumvented the deficit in reading. Positive intervention changed the 'deficit' to a 'delay'.

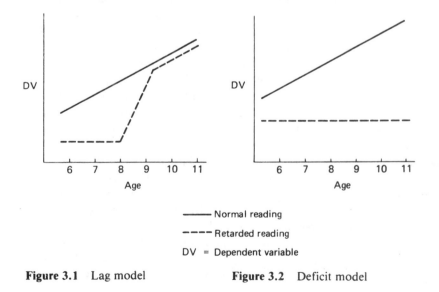

———— Normal reading

– – – – Retarded reading

DV = Dependent variable

Figure 3.1 Lag model   **Figure 3.2** Deficit model

As well as the issue of developmental lag versus deficit, there has been recent discussion regarding the use of appropriate control groups. Until recently most research, particularly in the area of cognitive problems, has matched a group of dyslexic, or backward readers, to 'normal' children of the same age and intellectual level. A point made by Bryant and Bradley (1985), Bryant (1988) and Snowling (1987), among others, is that there is a problem of cause and effect using these kinds of control groups. For example, one might demonstrate that memory for letters in a group of 10-year-old backward readers, reading at the 7-year-old level is weaker than a control group of the same chronological age, where the reading age is 10. Here one cannot parcel out the effects of learning to read on the memory skill. Recent research designs typically involve comparing dyslexics with children who are much younger than themselves but have reached the same level of reading ability. Here, knowing that dyslexics are dealing with reading material at the same level, that they are equally proficient with the printed reading and that their experience of the written language is the same, allows a clearer interpretation of research findings. Any differences that appear between dyslexics in reading age-matched controls are likely to be of greater etiological significance, it is argued. Notwithstanding the above arguments, included in this review of research are studies that include chronological age-matched controls as well as reading or spelling age-matched controls. This is because chronological age controls are, at least, pointing out correlational links between the problems of the dyslexics and the activities in question. It is absurd just to dismiss all previous research on the grounds that it 'could not be taken all that seriously but that, after all is show business' (Bryant 1988, page 109). There are still a number of serious difficulties with reading age-matched controls anyway. For example, one has to take care that the groups are properly matched; and matching for reading or spelling age level would immediately give the dyslexics an advantage in terms of chronological age. Any cause of dyslexia that is some form of developmental lag is therefore masked if dyslexics are compared with controls who are younger. The significance of lag, developmental immaturity or slower development of a particular skill is therefore difficult to tease out. There are some other problems that are discussed later (see Section 3.41 and Chapter 4) and further discussion of this area may be found in Backman, Mamen and Ferguson (1984) and Bryant and Goswami (1986).

3.2 Neurological perspective

3.21 Acquired dyslexia

Although this book is about developmental dyslexia, there is a large literature on psycholinguistic approaches to acquired dyslexia, where neurological dysfunctions are relatively clear cut (see for example Coltheart, Patterson and Marshall 1980, Patterson 1981). A number of studies are currently being undertaken to try to develop parallels between developmental dyslexia and acquired dyslexia, and it is therefore necessary to review some of these findings in the context of a neurological perspective. We can define acquired dyslexia as 'the occurrence of reading deficits in previously literate adults who have suffered neurological damage' (Patterson 1981). An influential attempt at classifying acquired dyslexia is in terms of the types of words in which the patients make errors, particularly in terms of linguistic types such as function versus content words. Marshall and Newcombe (1973), for example, have classified errors into visual errors, grapheme/morpheme transformation errors, and semantic errors, with there being a preponderance of one type of error over another in various types of patients. There is a good deal of variation in the particular terminology and intrepretation in relation to these patients. Most of these classificatory systems are based on the individual's reading single visually presented words which have been varied in a number of ways, for example nonsense words, highly imageable real words, high-frequency vs low-frequency words, content vs function words. Indeed, most of the classificatory systems argue for the existence of two main reading routes (Shallice and Warrington 1980); (i) a phonological encoding route using grapheme to phoneme correspondence rules, or (ii) a direct semantic route.

The three main syndromes are called *deep* (or phonemic), *phonological* and *surface* dyslexia. The deep and phonological dyslexics have great difficulty in using the phonological routes to reading, or are sometimes unable to use this route at all. They appear to use the direct graphemes-to-meaning route, and therefore require a semantic representation of the word before they can obtain a phonological representation of it. They are not able to read non-words (nonsense words). Furthermore, they are unable to read words which they do not understand, as no semantic representation is available for the words (presumably in the same way as no semantic representation is available for a nonsense word).

Deep dyslexics characteristically make semantic errors—typically responses which relate semantically to the stimulus, for example, lecturers read as student. Furthermore, the deep dyslexics are affected by the dimension of imageability/concreteness in the stimuli. Other symptoms include visual errors, where the error response is visually similar to the stimulus; morphological errors, i.e. suffix or prefix adding; and a greater facility with content words as opposed to function words. The phonological dyslexic, while similar to the deep dyslexic, does not make semantic errors, and is not sensitive to the imageability/concreteness dimension of stimuli. Visual errors are made also, but less frequently than in deep dyslexia. There is much less work on phonological dyslexics, and reports are much rarer.

The surface dyslexic seems to rely on the phonological route to reading. A semantic representation may not always be forthcoming; it is possible for a word not to be understood even when it is pronounced correctly (Marcel 1980). They are not sensitive to the semantic dimensions of stimuli, but are affected by characteristics of the graphemic representation—word length and regularity of spelling. Again, few cases so far are reported in the literature.

There have been some attempts to investigate developmental dyslexia in these terms, and certainly an increasing research effort is examining various models of the reading process (e.g. Morton 1979 or Marshall and Newcombe 1973) to try to identify parallels between acquired and developmental dyslexia. Marshall (1982), for example, argues that taxonomies of developmental dyslexia ought to be based on reading errors, not on identifying underlying causes, and that developmental dyslexia may be akin to surface dyslexia. Holmes (1973, 1978) also argues that developmental dyslexia may be similar to surface dyslexia. She suggests that the misreading of developmental dyslexics is comparable to errors made by surface dyslexics. For example, errors such as failure to apply the e rule as in *wage/wag*, *quite/quit* or incorrect realization of *ch* as *k* are similar to Marshall and Newcombe's (1973) assertion that surface dyslexia includes impairment of visual written forms for semantic representation, combined with a letter deficit in relation to knowledge of grapheme and phoneme regularities.

On the other hand, Jorm (1979a) argues that developmental dyslexia may be more akin to deep dyslexia, drawing *functional* parallels between the two conditions. He argues that developmental dyslexics have difficulty in reading nonsense words, greater difficulty in reading low-imagery words against high-imagery words and a tendency to make visual errors in reading. He is therefore arguing for both developmental and deep dyslexics having difficulties in reading via a phonological route. Jorm further states that there are difficulties in interpretation of the errors that Holmes (1978) cites as evidence for partial failure of grapheme-phoneme correspondence; for example *certain* for *cartoons*, *begger* for *badger*, could equally plausible be classified as visual errors.

Coltheart (1982) describes six cases of surface dyslexia, two of which he describes as being developmental dyslexics. This seems to be confusing acquired and developmental dyslexia without even establishing the parallels between the two in an acceptable fashion. Nevertheless, he argues that surface dyslexia exists both in acquired and developmental forms. He argues this because surface dyslexics have impairments of a lexical route, they are better at reading regular words and non-words than irregular words, and he suggests that to some extent everyone is a 'surface dyslexic' because given very rare irregular words they will tend to produce an incorrect pronunciation.

Although the above are some interesting speculations there has been very little systematic work investigating the parallels to date although there is a good deal of work going on. One recent study by Baddeley *et al*. (1982), systematically comparing acquired and developmental dyslexia, used the Patterson and Marcel (1977) techniques to investigate developmental dyslexia. These techniques involved a lexical decision task in which subjects were required to decide whether a series of letters was a word or not. A key feature was whether the words were homophones, e.g. *brane, frute* versus non-words such as *dake, leat*. A second task included reading orthographically regular and irregular non-words. A third task involved reading individual words which were high in imageability, against low-imageability words. It was found that the developmental dyslexics were slower at all the tasks compared to reading age and chronological age controls, but there were no significant interactions. The authors concluded that there was no evidence to support any parallel between deep dyslexia and developmental dyslexia, but that the developmental difficulties were due to some slowness of processing. The use of reading age and chronological age control groups was very important here to control for the effect of reading experience. In relation to the effect of imageability, it was found that dyslexic and reading age group controls were very similar. It was argued that being able to read highly imageable words was a general effect relating to reading, and not necessarily a function of some kind of deficit. However, the authors pointed out that many of the children had been considerably trained in phonics, as they were attending a special school for dyslexics, and the ability to use a grapheme/phoneme route may have therefore been improved by this teaching. Snowling (1983) underlines this point, and suggests that dyslexics who had received phonic training are a totally inappropriate group to use; and that the fact that the dyslexics took longer suggests a phonological weakness.

While the description of acquired dyslexia has been useful in drawing attention to the components of the reading process, I do not think that the kinds of classification systems used will be applicable to developmental dyslexia. This notion of phonological versus direct routes has similarities to the already used classification of auditory versus visual (see Chapter 1). One of the major difficulties in the application of this approach to developmental dyslexia is the great variation in *children's* performance. The types of reading errors given as evidence for sub-categories may be found in the same developmentally dyslexic child at different times, as well as in different children. The impression one gets from reading the acquired dyslexic literature is that these kinds of spelling errors occur, if not 100% of the time in the patients, certainly at a very high frequency. The developmental dyslexic varies from day to day, and attempts to classify reading errors as described above will not be reliable with regard to children.

Another developmental characteristic is the particular strategy used by the child, and this depends greatly on age. The use of control groups has been scarce in the acquired dyslexia literature, despite the fact that it is important to establish whether certain kinds of reading and spelling error are a function of reading development rather than dyslexia. Another important point is that the developmental dyslexic, by definition, is *not* brain damaged, and there is consequently no fixed impairment which might lead to a particular 'route' being deficient. If (as seems somewhat unlikely given the variation in the children), dyslexia could be pinpointed to absolutely *one* specific deficit or cause, there would still be scope for children to develop differential reading, writing and spelling strategies, and therefore presumably different reading, writing and spelling errors.

The notion that developmental dyslexia may be like surface dyslexia (Coltheart 1982, Marshall 1982, Ellis 1979) is based on case reports by Holmes (1973, 1978), Marshall and Newcombe (1973) and Shallice and Warrington (1980), but there are few cases described, and according to Patterson (1981) this is the least understood of the various syndromes. She suggests it would be 'tempting to exclude it from consideration until further cases are identified and described'. A sensitivity to irregularity on the spelling dimension is generally considered to be involved in aspects of surface dyslexia (irregular words causing particular difficulty), and words are often mis-read suggesting inappropriate application of grapheme/phoneme correspondence rules. According to Patterson the particular interest of surface dyslexia is that a set of grapheme/phoneme correspondence rules can be applied without reference to particular lexical items. This can therefore lead to incorrect pronunciation for many English words, including exceptional words like *choir*. (The Schonell Reading test has many examples of these words!) The possibility is that both non-words and words are assembled by segmentation into graphemic counterparts for which their phonological or sound counterparts exist in a lexicon. Reading errors in surface dyslexia are explained by the loss of whole morpheme specifications for some words. For example, Patterson in describing Marcel (1981 p. 168) suggests that:

> in the process of achieving a proununciation for *listen* both normal readers and a patient would at one point obtain a segmentation of *list* plus *en*. For normals, this is overridden by the discovery of the morphemic lexical entry corresponding to the whole word *listen*. The patient lacking this whole graphemic element is left with the *list* plus *en* segmentation, finds phonological realization of these elements and so says *liston* (rather than *lisan*.)

This kind of approach is based on very detailed analysis of individual errors. Bearing in mind the great variation in errors found in the dyslexic, and the need to have appropriate control groups in looking at children, it seems far too early to draw conclusions in relation to acquired versus developmental dyslexia based on this evidence. It is possible that everybody is better at reading words that are regular, and thus the effect in the surface dyslexic is not an abnormal one in relation to dyslexia at all.

Furthermore, many of the errors and experimental analyses reported are based on individual word reading; but one might argue that this is not the same as reading silently for meaning, or even reading aloud from a text. It is important to try and examine reading disorders in relation to the ordinary reading process as well.

I have gone into some detail in describing aspects of acquired dyslexia and their possible relation to developmental dyslexia, mainly because this is becoming a common area of research. These classificatory systems have been very successful, and it is natural that many researchers would like to apply them to developmental dyslexia.

It is important, however, to bear in mind the caveats mentioned above concerning the parallels between acquired and developmental dyslexia. As Morton (1987) comments, the crucial component of the word *development* is change. Children will develop and change over time and any similarities that one can point to between acquired and developmental disorders may be a function of the material itself (e.g. reading matter) rather than the structure of the disorders.

3.22   Minimal neurological dysfunction

Although developmental dyslexia is not due to brain damage, many of the earlier writers on dyslexia, such as Hinshelwood (1917) and Morgan (1896), imply that the children had difficulties that were neurological in origin. More recently, Kinsbourne (1973) describes 'synergism' in dyslexics. This is a motor reflex occurring following a previous movement. For example there might be difficulty in dropping a stick from fingers following grasping and, according to Kinsburne, this suggests a neuro-developmental lag. Rutter *et al.* (1970) comment on a high incidence of neurological signs amongst specific reading retardates. Critchley (1970) gives further examples and details of these 'signs'.

One rather specific syndrome that has been postulated as associated with dyslexia is the Gerstmann syndrome. It has been described in a number of clinical case reports (e.g. Benson and Geschwind 1970, Kinsbourne and Warrington 1963b). The syndrome involves difficulty in right/left orientation, finger agnosia (being unable to move a specific finger on command), agraphia (severe difficulty in copying and writing), and acalculia. A parallel between this syndrome and developmental dyslexia has been suggested by a number of authors (e.g. Satz *et al.* 1976). Croxen and Lytton (1971) found a high incidence of finger localization difficulties and right/left discrimination problems amongst nine- to ten-year-old poor readers (see also Doehring 1968, Finlayson and Reitan 1976). Silver and Hagin (1964) commented that those children showing 'neurological' signs showed less improvement than those without them.

There has been some criticism of such work where there has obviously been some confusion between acquired and developmental dyslexia. Typically neurological 'signs' are reported in studies involving children referred to neurological clinics and the children may therefore be atypical. Rourke (1976b, 1978) points out that although there may be association between these 'signs' and dyslexia, many developmental dyslexics do not show them and therefore the signs cannot be completely causative as they account for minimal variance. Rutter *et al.* (1966), Edwards *et al.* (1971) argue that if the dyslexics are compared to appropriate controls, who are equated for chronological age and intelligence, there is no relationship between academic performance and 'minimal brain dysfunction'. Unfortunately, there has been a great deal of misunderstanding in educational circles in relation to the neurology of reading difficulties and its relation to school children. It can lead to the idea that dyslexia is somehow a 'medical thing'. Sometimes inappropriate screening procedures are used to identify children with learning problems. In pre-school screening, for example, unwarranted assumptions about motor development as manifestation of some kind of neurological difficulty and later reading, writing, and spelling attainment, are often made (see Barnard, Comber and Thomson 1983).

Training procedures based on neurological signs include developing gross motor skills such as throwing and catching, large circular movements on paper, learning to balance by walking on beams and threading beads to overcome tremor. One of the unwarranted assumptions behind many of these teaching programmes is that until one develops these skills it is not worth teaching a child reading, writing and spelling. Such tasks and procedures may be very useful to help a child walk on a beam, to thread beads, to draw properly, or perhaps in general to improve aspects of their motor or perceptual development. However there is little evidence that this will therefore improve reading, writing, and spelling without some specific help and remediation in the area of written language (see Chapter 6).

3.221 Birth history Some authors, e.g. Newton (1970), have commented on the association between at risk birth and dyslexia. Frequently writers refer to only one study—that of Kawi and Pasamanick (1958). A typical comment is that 'Kawi and Pasamanick postulate a continuum of reproductive difficulty from death to learning disorder resulting from post and pre-natal practice'. This study in fact compared the pre, peri and post-natal records of 372 reading disabled children to a control group. They found a much larger percentage of abnormal records amongst the children with reading difficulties—for example 104 birth complications in the reading disabled children compared to 50 in the control group. They also found a birth weight of less than 5.5lbs to be more frequent amongst learning disabled children. However the duration of labour, and the operative procedures that may have been used during labour, did not distinguish the groups. Although this seems a reasonable study there was a 45% drop-out rate in terms of the number of children whose reading and spelling performance was assessed on following up the records. They also refer to heterogeneous groups of children with reading difficulties and did not specifically look at dyslexia.

Balow, Rubin and Rosen (1976) concluded after a review of similar studies that there was no apparent link between pre-natal events and learning disorders. Schulman and Leviton (1978) suggest that many of the results are inconsistent due to differences in the populations which are studied, and the definitions of terms used. Some of the specific features which are suggested by others to be associated with reading disability can be illustrated by referring to a study by Corah et al. (1965) examining anoxia (oxygen deprivation) and its relationship to learning disorders. Anoxia was deemed to have occurred based on signs (in the mother) of anaemia, diabetes, bleeding, prolonged labour, and eclampsia associated with labour. In the infant the signs referred to sleepiness, respiratory delay, delayed labours, weak sucking, poor feeding, and convulsions. Although they found differences in reading at 7 years old when compared to a control group a number of the clinical signs of anoxia could easily be associated with central nervous system damage that was pre-existing (see also Drage et al. 1966). A further complication is illustrated by Douglas et al. (1968) who found that socio-economic backgrounds and family conditions interacted with birth history in terms of its association with reading difficulties. When they controlled for socio-economic background the association disappeared. Similar findings are reported by Robinson and Robinson (1965). A study by Lyle (1970), controlling social class and looking at children where the criteria for selection of children with reading disability seemed to be similar to that for dyslexia, found that developmental variables such as late speech and late locomotion were better predictors of verbal problems than birth difficulties.

The presumed connection between birth history and dyslexia is in the production of minimal neurological dysfunction, rather than gross brain damage *per se*. The above results suggest that there is some association between aspects of birth development and reading difficulties, although its relationship to dyslexia is complicated by socio-economic variables and considerable inconsistency between studies. Schulmann and Leviton (1978) conclude that the mechanisms for production of reading difficulties are unclear. They suggest that reading disabilities might arise from early pre-natal difficulties, or from peri-natal factors, or possibly from both factors combining.

3.222 EEG studies One of the problems about reviewing EEG studies and dyslexia is the definition of dyslexia used in many of the reports. Invariably, there is considerable talk about 'patients' and one can never be sure that the authors are decribing developmental dyslexics, particularly as many studies do not rule out neurological abnormalities. Sometimes the matching of experimental and control samples is poor, for example describing abnormalities 'in samples of dyslexic individuals', without a comparison control group. Further, some 'abnormalities' coexist in the general population and do not have any etiological significance in relation to dyslexia (Hughes 1978). Because of the above this section will be relatively brief and confined to some general comments which are suggestive of further research. Greater emphasis will be placed on hemisphere differences in a later section.

Some authors have referred to EEG abnormalities in dyslexic individuals, e.g. Benton and Bird (1963), Muehl, Knott and Benton (1965), and Hughes (1978), in his survey of the literature, presents the percentages of abnormalities found in EEG records in various groups (see Table 3.1).

Abnormal EEGs include the presence of delta waves, positive spikes, temporal spikes, and occipital slowing. Hughes (1971) suggests that there is a correlation between slowing of the resting record, particularly in the temporal areas of the left hemisphere, and clear organic defects localized in the regions mentioned, and this will therefore result in an associated dyslexia. This clearly refers to acquired rather than developmental dyslexia. Similarly Hughes and Park (1968) refer to occipital slow waves which they suggest relate to visual responsitivity in dyslexia.

Table 3.1 Percentage of abnormalities generalized from summary of studies by Hughes (1977) (based on average weighted means from studies)

Disability	Percentage/Abnormalities
Hyperkinetic	89
Behaviour disturbances	59
Mental retardation	63
Learning disabilities	46
Dyslexia	45

A epilepti-form recording refers to either a sharp wave and spike or a spike and wave complex, and is considered to be evidence of epileptic foci or small epileptic discharges. Here there are considerable differences in reports by various investigators, e.g. Hughes (1971) and Ingram et al. (1970) suggest that these occur vary rarely (6% or 7%) in dyslexic individuals whereas Torres and Ayers (1968) suggest that these are the most common findings amongst dyslexics. Hughes (1978) suggests that 'epilepti-form' findings might occur with specific conditions such as visual perception difficulties, while Green (1961) argues that epileptic discharges are associated with short attention span.

In relation to the alpha rhythm (6 to 10 cycles per second), Hughes (1971) and Newton (1970) described alpha rhythms as being less organized in relation to background, and Sklar et al. (1973) suggested that dyslexics have a different frequency response than normals. Hanley and Sklar (1976) suggest that it is in the left parietal-occipital area that most abnormalities are found in dyslexics.

There are a few studies which used visual and auditory stimuli. Typically a subject views a flash of light from a stroboscope in such a way that the stimulus appears at a strictly regulated time, say one every half-second. A computer of average transience then makes a number of 'sweeps' across the EEG record and averages out the background activity building up an evoked response. This is the cortical response to the stimulus and can be described in terms of various wave forms, frequencies, amplitudes and latencies; it can be a visual evoked response (VER) or an auditory evoked response (AER). Preston et al. (1974), controlling for factors such as intelligence and chronological age, found that the amplitude of the VER was highly correlated with reading disability. Hughes (1971) found low photive responses and depressed amplitudes in the left VER of learning disabled children. Preston et al. (1974) also found low amplitudes, but these were in the early components of the VER. The significance of these findings is rather obscure in relation in dyslexia. Faure et al. (1968) argues that the VER has a vigilance function and others (e.g. Cohen and Walter 1966) relate the VER to the informational content of the stimulus, i.e. to symbolic and meaningful stimuli. All one can suggest here is that there might be some kind of lower cortical response of a vague nature.

Differences in contingent negative variation (CNV) have also been described. The CNV is an expectancy wave obtained from the vertex region of the skull, and seems to be a wave form that is present when an event which is expected is about to occur. According to Dykman et al. (1971) the CNV is reduced in dyslexics and, according to Cohen (1976), absent in younger learning-disabled individuals. Cohen (1980) suggests that dyslexics have less than half the amplitude of CNV compared to control groups and suggests that the CNV difference may be due to attentional processes or deficits in the integration of auditory and visual information. The CNV causes considerable controversy amongst EEG researchers; many find difficulties in establishing the wave and what it measures is uncertain.

Denckla (1978) criticizes the research to date by posing the question, 'these are EEG correlates of what?' For example, in studying children who are both epileptic and dyslexic, one needs normal controls and non-epileptic dyslexics. Too often the studies are measuring dyslexia plus 'something else'. The 'something else' could be gross brain damage, or other neurological dysfunctions. She also argues that we still do not know what a 'normal' EEG is, particularly in relation to the developmental pattern, and that one must develop developmental norms to examine the interrelationship between cause and effect. Connors (1978) makes similar comments and suggests that the data could just as well be interpreted as indicating that there is a high correlation between dyslexia and the *absence* of EEG abnormalities. He sees great significance in the fact that, on examining a number of studies, the more recent they are the less correlation there is between EEG abnormalities and dyslexia.

In conclusion, the concept of some general and unspecific neurological abnormality in developmental dyslexia is not proven. It is more fruitful to focus on some initial theoretical approach and examine the neuropsychological findings in relationship to that. This is the subject of the next section, where the considerable amount of research into the relationship between dyslexia and hemisphere function is reviewed.

3.23   Cerebral dominance and laterality

Orton (1937) was struck by the high incidence of reversals, mirror imaging and disorders of orientation amongst dyslexics. He suggested that these kinds of reading errors related to incomplete dominance, further evidence of which was illateralization and ambidexterity. This incomplete cerebral dominance, he argued, related to a difference in the way the brain was organized in dyslexics. Orton argued that *engrams* or memory traces were stored in left and right hemispheres as mirror images of one another. For example, the word *was* is stored as *was* in the left hemisphere, but would be stored as *saw* in the right hemisphere. For most individuals the left hemisphere was dominant for language functions, and therefore would be engaged and the correct word retrieved when reading or spelling. For dyslexic individuals, who did not have a clear-cut left-hemisphere dominance for language, sometimes the left hemisphere would be accessed, but just as often the right hemisphere. Thus *saw* would be produced as *was* and vice versa. He argued this was due to confusion of competing images. This state of affairs is diagrammed in Figure 3.3.

This simple notion has been since superseded by more sophisticated knowledge of the way in which the brain is organized, although the storing of mirror images has been supported by evidence from animal studies (e.g. Noble 1968, Sperry 1964).

Current views on cortical hemisphere function now generally agree that the left hemisphere is specialized for language and linguistic processing, whereas the right hemisphere is specialized for more spatially oriented types of skills. It is further suggested that the left hemisphere is responsible for analytical, logical and sequential processing of information, or perhaps serial processing. The right hemisphere is also more associated with perception of spatial relationships, depth perception and form perception. It is not proposed to review all of the evidence and the

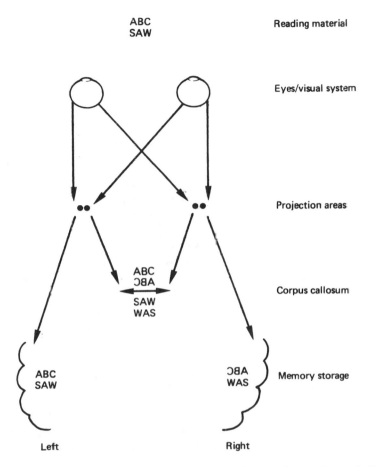

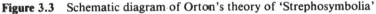

Figure 3.3   Schematic diagram of Orton's theory of 'Strephosymbolia'

interesting findings in this area in any detail (see Dimond and Beaumont 1976 and for an interesting but speculative review, Ornstein 1975). The implications of this model of brain specialization in relation to written language will become clear. Specific details of hemisphere specification are summarized in Table 3.2

Table 3.2   Specialization of hemisphere function in the human brain

Left	Both	Right
Speech and language	Simple motor response	Spatial integration
Complex motor functions	Incidental learning	Calculation
Vigilance	Fatigue phonemes processing	Creative-associative
Paired-associate learning		

Two important sources of evidence for the above specialization of function are dichotic listening and divided visual field experiments. In dichotic listening the subject is presented with auditory material to both ears at the same time. He is then required to report what is heard, or indulge in various other kinds of post-stimulus presentation tasks. Typically a right ear advantage (REA) is found in most normal subjects. For example they may remember numbers that are presented to the right ear better than those that went to the left ear. Kimura (1967), and others, argue that the REA suggests a left hemisphere processing for verbal material as there is a relatively greater functional and anatomical link between the right ear and the left hemisphere and the left ear and the right hemisphere. This contralateral connection between hemisphere control and sensory motor function is of course well known. In divided visual field studies visual stimuli are presented either to the right, or to the left, of a mid line. If the material is located to the right of the mid line, i.e. right visual field, this is transferred directly to the left hemisphere, whereas left visual field information is transferred to the right hemisphere. Typically, verbal material is found to have a right visual field advantage (RVFA), implying left-hemisphere control for language and verbal functions, whereas spatial or less verbally orientated material, e.g. perception of faces, is typically found to have a left visual field advantage (LVFA), implying right-hemisphere control. A number of studies of this kind have been undertaken with dyslexics, and we shall review them shortly.

Following this model of the human brain and these techniques of investigation there are a number of current theories that are put forward to try and account for dyslexia in relation to hemisphere function. These are as follows:

1 A *lack* of cerebral dominance, i.e. lack of left-hemisphere specialization for language. This includes those who would not go as far as saying that there is no dominance at all, but those who argue that there is a less clear-cut dominance of function for language in the dyslexic.
2 A maturational lag or delay in the development of the left-hemisphere specialization for language processing. This is sometimes linked with delay in the perceptual, motor and linguistic skills relating to reading, writing and spelling.
3 A left-hemisphere deficit. This does not imply gross brain damage *per se*, but argues for some dysfunction in the areas of the left hemisphere responsible for written language.
4 Interference in the left-hemisphere functioning by the right hemisphere. This argues for a cerebral organization favouring the right hemisphere at the expense of the left.
5 A disassociation (i.e. lack of integration due to differential processing) of auditory and visual material in different hemispheres.

We shall now review the evidence on hemisphere function and dyslexia, and then evaluate it in the light of the above theories.

3.231 EEG studies First we look at studies on the EEG and its relationship to cerebral asymmetries and cortical hemisphere function, rather than the general components described previously.

Rebert and Wexler (1977) describe asymmetric alpha-rhythms in dyslexic children, and in relation to the VER, Connors (1970) describes asymmetries in the parietal region in dyslexics. Neither of these studies used control groups, and a study by Sobotka and May (1977) describing asymmetries occurring equally in dyslexic *and* control subjects place them in doubt. Newton (1970) compared alpha-rhythm between different hemispheres and found a *greater* asymmetry of function amongst controls. The control groups had much more activity around the angular gyrus region of the left hemisphere whereas dyslexics had equivalence of alpha-rhythm across both hemispheres. She argued, following Orton (1937), that dyslexics did not have a dominant hemisphere for language function. A more recent study by Leisman and Ashkenazi (1980), looking at EEG in the parietal-occipital region, found that controls had a greater concordance between hemi-spheres, whereas the dyslexics were concordant within one hemisphere. Further studies involving CT brain scan found that in controls the left parietal-occipital region was wider compared to the right hemisphere, whereas 6 (out of 8) dyslexics showed no difference between the two hemispheres and 2 of the dyslexics showed a larger right parietal-occipital region compared to the left.

Leisman and Ashkenazi suggest that in the 'normal' condition the right hemi-sphere is subservient or 'slave' to the left hemisphere, whereas in the dyslexics, the two hemispheres act much more independently. This kind of conclusion is similar to one or two suggestions following dichotic listening and divided-field studies.

3.232   Dichotic listening and divided visual field studies Rather than list a cata-logue of results and studies, the major findings are presented in Table 3.3. Here studies which have used verbal stimuli (e.g. digits, words and consonant/vowel syllables), presented auditorally or visually in either paradigm are summarized, in terms of dyslexics versus controls. The column 'greater or no difference' refers to studies where the control group showed a much *greater* REA or RVFA than the dyslexic or where the dyslexic children show *no* ear or visual field advantage com-pared to controls who showed the normal or RVFA.

As far as the dichotic listening is concerned, the studies that report normal REA effects in dyslexics are more or less balanced by those that report LEA, greater REA, or no difference at all. A number of studies, e.g. Keefe and Swinney 1979; Newell and Rugel 1981, report less accurate performance by the dyslexics in overall terms rather than in comparing ear effects. The divided visual field results find fewer RVFA effects in dyslexics compared to LVFA or no difference effects.

Some of the studies report age effects. Bakker *et al.* (1973) suggest that the larger REA in the *older* children (9–11 years) is highly correlated with reading ability. They argue that the results depend on the age of learning to read and relate to dif-ferential strategies. For example, they suggest that the right hemisphere is used in early reading (for feature analysis and visuo-spatial perception), whereas the left hemisphere is used in later reading (e.g. phonological analysis). There have been some sex differences postulated in dichotic listening. In non-dyslexics Kimura (1967) found a greater REA for girls as opposed to boys; however these results are not unchallenged, for example, Knox and Kimura (1970) found similar results in both boys and girls. In relation to *dyslexia*, Bakker *et al.* (1976) suggested a sex x

Table 3.3   Studies showing the results of dichotic listening and divided visual field experiments with dyslexic children

Dichotic listening studies

REA	LEA
Bryden 1970	Zurif and Carson 1970
Yeni-Komshian et al. 1975	Witelson and Rabinovitch 1972
Sparrow 1969	Chasty 1979
Sparrow and Satz 1970	more frequent in
Abigail and Johnson 1976	Satz and Sparrow 1970
McKeever and van Deventer 1975	Sparrow 1969
Witelson 1977	
Capalan 1977	
McRare and Warren 1978	*Greater or no difference*
Sommers and Taylor 1972	
Newell and Rugel 1981	De Haas 1972
Keefe and Swinney 1976	Taylor 1962
Obrzat 1979	Thomson 1976
Leong 1976 younger children	Bakker 1976
Witelson 1976 only	Darby 1974
	Leong 1976
	Witelson 1976
	Satz et al. 1971
	Bakker et al. 1973 older children
	Bakker 1973 only

Divided visual field studies

RVFA	LVFA
Yeni-Komshian et al. 1975	Leavell and Beck 1959
McKeever and Huling 1970	
Satz and van Nostrand 1973	
Keefe and Swinney 1979	*Greater or no difference*
	Marcel et al. 1974
	Marcel and Rajan 1975
	Kershner 1977
	Pirozzolo and Rayner 1977
	Olson 1973 (younger children)

age interaction such that older boys may have greater differential functioning.

In relation to visual field studies, Rourke (1976b) comments that the results are inconsistent and there are problems in attentional scanning, particularly in eye movements when undertaking the task itself. Young and Ellis (1981) suggest that fixation control in divided visual field studies may be very poor, particularly with children. A further argument is that one cannot know in a divided field task if both groups of subjects use the same strategy. The particular stimulus used, i.e. the kind of words, may relate to which hemisphere is engaged. For example, an imageable or concrete word may in fact engage the right hemisphere.

In relation to both kinds of studies, Keefe and Swinney (1979) suggest that most have failed to examine subgroups of dyslexia and indeed have failed to look at individual performances at all. This could account for contradictory results. They argue from their own data that there were two different kinds of lateralization occurring amongst the dyslexics, and researchers should take much greater care in description and selection of subjects. Obrzat (1979) compared the performance of 'dysphonetic', 'dyseidetic' and 'alexic' groups on dichotic and bi-sensory memory tasks. This was based on Boder's classification (see Chapter 1). He found a normal REA in dyslexics except for the dysphonetic group, who had a trend towards a smaller REA compared to controls. The main results suggested that the dysphonetic and alexic groups had a much poorer overall recall compared to the dyseidetic group.

Many of the researchers cited above have developed their own theories based mainly on their own studies, citing (usually selectively!) other studies to support their contentions. The majority of these relate to the theories which we have outlined at the beginning of the section, and we will now examine them in more detail in the light of the evidence.

3.233 Evaluation The first theory, based on Orton's work, claims that dyslexics lack a clear-cut dominant hemisphere for language. The above evidence shows that many dyslexics have normal REA and RVFA, and a simple lack of dominance is difficult to support. Rourke (1976b) suggests that the theory rests on the following premises: (i) retarded readers reverse and mirror image; (ii) reversals and mirror images are correlated with incomplete cerebral dominance; (iii) incomplete cerebral dominance is linked to differences in brain organization, and therefore dyslexics have differences in brain organization. Rourke argues that not all dyslexics make mirror image or reversal errors, and these kinds of confusion do not in fact relate to cerebral dominance at all and may be functions of normal development. Further, notions of developmental plasticity of hemisphere function (e.g. Lenneberg 1967) had not been considered. Satz (1976) in his review asks whether in fact the dichotic and divided visual field studies do in fact measure cerebral dominance (see also Spreen 1978). Satz goes on to say that experimental procedures assume contra-lateral connections and rely on a simple dichotomous brain/hemisphere function. Based on the population characteristics of brain organization given LEA in dichotic listening, the probability of a right brain control for speech is only 0.10. Wilsher (1981) also points out that following the sodium amytal studies directly measuring hemisphere control, e.g. Rasmussen and Milner (1975), there are simply not enough individuals with right-hemisphere control of language to account for the incidence of dyslexia in the population.

The second theory was that of a delay or maturational lag in cerebral dominance. This has been put forward by Satz and his associates, and overlaps with the third theory, i.e. left-hemisphere deficit. Satz *et al.* (1978) argue that the early stages of reading difficulty amongst dyslexics originate in perceptual motor difficulties and that the later problems are more associated with auditory linguistic difficulties. A series of longitudinal studies provides evidence for predictors of changes in perception and motor skills over age that might be related to neuropsychological functioning. The studies have resulted in screening procedures which are described in

Chapter 5. Leong (1976) also argues for a developmental lag in functional cerebral development.

However, there are a number of difficulties in interpreting the data and how they relate to the above theories. Leong (1976) gives the following figures in relation to the correctly reported stimuli in a dichotic listening task.

	R	L
Dyslexics	19	17
Controls	24	19

Similarly, data from Thomson (1976) are shown below. The figures are percentage correct recall for digits:

	R	L
Dyslexics	68	65
Controls	82	68

Leong interprets his data as suggesting a lag in cerebral hemisphere development for language, based on the age groups upon which he obtained some of this data. He comments that both groups show REA but the controls relatively more, and in addition the dyslexics have an overall poorer performance. Thomson (1976) argued that his results showed a less clear-cut dominance of function for language, dyslexics showing no significant REA.

However, these data could easily be interpreted in terms of a deficit model. In Thomson's data, for example, it may be seen that the difference between dyslexics and controls is that the performance of the dyslexics on their right ear is *reduced*. This therefore has the effect of making the right and left ears very similar, i.e. there is no REA. An interpretation of lack or no dominance would be more parsimonious if the dyslexic's percentage were 80 right and 80 left. Similarly, if we look at Leong's results, the performance by the dyslexics and controls on the left ear are much closer than their performance on the right ear. This again suggests that the dyslexics may have an overall difficulty in reporting the digits appearing at the right ear. The implication is for left-hemisphere deficit rather than for functional lag.

Another problem for the maturational lag notion of cerebral dominance is the development of hemisphere specialization. Usually damage to left hemisphere during childhood or before puberty can result in the right hemisphere taking over some of these language functions, rather than both hemispheres being equally likely to develop over time. Segalowitz and Gruber (1972), Rudel (1978), and Moscovitch (1977) argue that experience and maturation affect the development of language in the left hemisphere, not the process of lateralization. Beaumont and Rugg (1978) also argue that there is no direct evidence for the maturation of cerebral lateralization of cerebral processes and they argue that *any* function served by the left hemisphere would be affected if there was a maturational lag. In other words, not just reading, spelling and writing, but many other aspects of verbal skills.

The left-hemisphere deficit model can be based on the same data or evidence that is used to support the maturational lag or the lack of cerebral dominance models, i.e. the studies summarized. Some specific deficits have been suggested. Jorm (1979a) postulates difficulties in the inferior parietal lobule, which may not be fully developed in dyslexics. This is based on comparing the *functional* similarities between developmental dyslexia and acquired dyslexia in terms of the phonological coding difficulties described in the deep and phonemic dyslexics (see Section 3.2). However, there is more direct evidence based on studies which are more carefully controlled than others. Preston *et al.* (1974, 1977), in relation to EEG (VER), showed that all the groups dealt with words in the left hemisphere but the dyslexic's response was faulty over the left angular gyrus. This applied to child and adult dyslexics. Similarly, McKeever and Van Deventer (1975), in their study of divided field presentations and dichotic listening experiments, found that dyslexics had left-hemisphere language dominance effects, but their overall performance was poorer. Wilsher (1979, 1980), using Piracetam (a drug which facilitates left-hemisphere performance), has shown improvement in left-hemisphere abilities of both dyslexics and controls using the drug but *greater* improvement in verbal paired association learning in the dyslexics.

The idea of a left-hemisphere deficit relies on the relative specialisms of the left versus right hemisphere. The left hemisphere is involved in aspects of serial sound production, word fluency and digit span performances, whereas the right hemisphere is involved in block design and model orientation, according to Gordon (1980). He presents evidence that dyslexics and their families do better on the latter (right hemisphere) kinds of tasks. Obrzat (1979) suggests that the right hemisphere is responsible for shape discrimination, and the memorization of visual images which are then transferred to the left hemisphere which 'translates' particular perceptions into speech representations. He argues that *dysphonetic* dyslexics cannot analyse and blend due to a left-hemisphere deficit, but that *dyseidetic* dyslexics have a right-hemisphere deficit and therefore cannot undertake shape discrimination tasks. Heilman *et al.* (1979) argue that the left hemisphere is mainly responsible for converting graphemes into sound, whereas the right hemisphere is more visuo-spatial and is involved in encoding semantic information from pictures, there being no phonological processing. Barry (1981) suggests that the left hemisphere is also involved in lexical access and phonological encoding of visually presented words. (These are key areas suggested as being deficient in a number of studies described later.) The right hemisphere on the other hand is responsible for more concrete words, i.e. those that can be visualized.

We are now beginning to build up a picture of some possible mechanisms that may be involved in relation to cerebral hemisphere function. Our (western) written language orthography involves exactly the kinds of skills that have been mentioned above, such as phonemic encoding, and visual to verbal coding. These are all left-hemisphere skills. In contrast, writing systems such as the pictogram (see Chapter 4), are more likely to involve right-hemisphere processing, i.e. they involve a direct semantic access and visuo-spatial skills. Ornstein (1975) in fact argues that the different western and eastern philosophies are based on the notion of using the left or right hemisphere in one's thinking style. It is the interaction between underlying cerebral functioning or organization and the task required which is relevant.

Although some aspects of the written language system involve right-hemisphere processing (see e.g. Farnham-Diggory 1978) the serial sequencing and naming components are left-hemisphere skills.

The fourth theory mentioned earlier is the concept of interference by the right hemisphere (Witelson 1976, 1977). Witelson's explanation for dyslexic hemisphere difference is rather subtle and intriguing. She developed a test of tactile laterality, (*dichhaptic*) involving dichotomous tactile stimulation using the touch (haptic) sense. Her subjects are given shapes to touch, some of which can be easily coded linguistically, some of which cannot. Based on a number of studies involving this kind of experiment, she develops an argument based on data using dyslexic children. She quotes Levy (1969), suggesting that low spatial ability results from atypical language representation due to the right hemisphere being occupied by the language centre as, for example, in brain damaged patients. Witelson applies this in reverse to dyslexia. She argues that poor language may result from the left hemisphere being taken up with spatial specification. She found, in normal subjects, using nonsense shapes (non-linguistically codable) that the left hand was superior, indicating a right-hemisphere involvement in this task. This did not occur for dyslexics. She argued that this indicated left-hemisphere involvement in spatial skill for dyslexics, i.e. a bilateral representation of spatial abilities. What Witelson is arguing therefore is that the right hemisphere is in some way deficient, i.e. there is no *right* hemisphere specialization for non-linguistic tasks. The left hemisphere therefore takes this on and becomes language impaired. Right-hemisphere type tasks are undertaken in both hemispheres. Witelson also reports sex differences in these tasks, which might account for the higher incidence of male compared to female dyslexics.

The final theory which we listed is based on inter-sensory integration. Geschwind (1962), Sperry (1964), Gazzaniga (1970) and Milner (1971) argue that visual and linguistic components are stored differentially in the hemispheres. Beaumont and Rugg (1978) suggest a functional disassociation between auditory and visual language processing. (Here visual information refers to that which is also linguistically based, i.e. words and verbal material, but visually presented.) They describe mechanisms based on Geschwind's (1974) notion of a disconnection syndrome. Beaumont and Rugg suggest that there is no brain damage as such, but there is a disassociation by bilateralization of visual and verbal processing. By this it is meant that auditory information (i.e. speech sounds) is processed in the left hemisphere as normal, whereas visual information is bi-lateralized rather than being uni-lateralized. There is a delay in linking visual with auditory material. This theory would explain difficulties such as in grapheme/phoneme correspondence, or visual to verbal encoding. Beaumont, Thomson and Rugg (1981) provide some evidence for this in a study specifically designed to test the hypothesis. Generally, dyslexics did have a normal REA or left-hemisphere control for auditory material (although there was a relationship between the severity of the dyslexic problem and a left-ear trend). On the other hand, there was a difference between the controls and dyslexics on the visual field task which matched the hypothesis that Beaumont and Rugg (1978) have put forward.

Thus, a theory of a left-hemisphere deficit *or* a visual-verbal association problem can be supported by the data cited above. However there are a number of methodological criticisms in relation to the tasks used. Kinsbourne and Hiscock (1978) suggest that the literature fails to approach the questions of learning disabilities being linked to anomalous lateralization; as in dichotic listening the REA may be due to expectancy and attentional phenomena. In other words the effects are procedurally specific because of the perceptual 'set' for selective attention. Thus a particular functional area of the brain may process a particular piece of information regardless of the hemisphere initially stimulated by the incoming information. Kinsbourne and Hiscock (1978) argue that dichotic listening techniques are not sufficiently reliable as they are influenced by training a mental set. Further, that this unreliability is particularly prevalent amongst those who have unusual ear advantage scores, i.e. they are more likely to reverse the advantage on retest. Other criticisms have been of perceptual variables, e.g. Studdert-Kennedy and Shankweiler (1970) and Berlin and McNeil (1976) suggest that REA results are a function of temporal synthesis of stimuli and the frequencies used. For example, different results accrue between voiceless stop consonants, which are more intelligible than voiced stop consonants. Also they argue that consonant/vowel combinations and digits do not measure the same neural processes. Some aspects of number are dealt with by the right hemisphere and indeed Joffe (1981) suggests that some dyslexics may employ a strategy using the right hemisphere for number work. This has clear implications for dichotic listening results using digits.

Wilsher (1981) suggests the whole of the encoding process in dichotic listening may be different in dyslexics due to verbal encoding problems and recency effects. He argues that in normal subjects verbal material presented to the left ear is transferred from the right hemisphere to the left hemisphere in order to be processed. Here the right-ear words are encoded first, while the left-ear words are temporarily stored and coded later. In the case of the dyslexic who has a difficulty with verbal encoding it will result in that material being lost. The lack of REA is due to memory weakness and not lateralization.

These methodological difficulties, and indeed the varying interpretations upon the same data, are due to the indirect evidence which we have about hemisphere function. One is only making hypotheses about the way in which the brain works, as the detailed anatomical and biochemical functions which underlie hemisphere differences are not known. However, despite the difficulties outlined above the effects described are real, replicable and relate to an important variation in human behaviour. Indeed some interesting speculations in relation to anatomy are put forward by Geschwind (1982) and Galburda and Kemper (1979). Geschwind argues that there is strong evidence for some kind of physical abnormality in the brain in dyslexics. He suggests that early intra-uterine damage is completely different to brain damage after birth. After birth there is a great plasticity of the nervous system and in early left-hemisphere damage, the right hemisphere may take over the language functions. However he points out that if nerve cells die or fail to reach their target positions in the cortex before birth they will be permanently absent. Cells that survive can now send out dendrites which may fill the positions not taken up by the cells that were damaged during neuronal migration in early development. (Nerve cells after formation migrate to the particular areas of the central nervous-system where they will function later.) So if there is some damage to the nerve cells migrating to the left hemisphere, for example, this will not only have the effect of causing a deficit here but will actually cause an *increase* in the opposite hemisphere due to the right hemisphere dendrites taking up where left-hemisphere cells would normally be. He also states that there is now very good evidence that human brains are anatomically asymmetrical. This applies particularly in the language region, for example Heschl's gyrus in the left hemisphere, which is different in structure to the right hemisphere. In particular there is a much larger upper surface of the temporal lobe (Wernicke's area, the Planum Temporale). The greater size of the latter can be seen with the naked eye in examining brain sections. As well as the gross anatomical differences there are also asymmetries in cell type and structure.

Geschwind and his colleagues argue that dyslexia is in fact an example of a *neuronal migration deficit*. However the evidence is from post-mortem studies of only two dyslexics to date, one of whom had convulsions, and one cannot be sure how typical they are of 'pure' developmental dyslexia.

We are now in a position to make an evaluation of the relative merits of the theories outlined initially in respect of dyslexia and hemisphere functioning. We have seen that a lack of cerebral dominance in the dyslexic is too simplistic an explanation, not only conceptually, but also in that the data do not seem to provide enough evidence. What evidence there is can be reinterpreted in other ways. One would also expect other language functions to be deficient in the dyslexic rather than just reading, and some subtle speech difficulties if there was complete lack of 'dominant' hemisphere function. Direct measures of hemisphere dominance such as sodium amytal cannot account for the relative frequencies of hemisphere dominance in dyslexia.

The maturational lag notions are more difficult to dismiss. The simple idea that the left hemisphere is delayed in its specialization is difficult to maintain. Here one would expect there to be a 'catch-up' and for cortical skills underlying reading to be improved or normal in adulthood. Studies of adult dyslexics do not match this prediction (see, e.g., Wilsher 1980). However an amalgamation of maturational lag and a functional deficit is a more attractive idea. One could argue that during the early stages of development a child develops inappropriate strategies which delays his reading and spelling. The evidence for a functional lag/deficit is fairly strong (e.g. Satz 1976; Bakker 1973). Witelson's work, while having some supportive evidence, seems unnecessarily complex. It seems unnecessary to postulate the left-hemisphere 'deficit' as being due to this hemisphere taking over right-hemisphere functions, rather than being simply 'deficient'. Although complexity is perhaps not a tremendously good reason for rejecting a theory there are arguments for keeping to the most parsimonious and simple explanation. Furthermore, none of Witelson's studies have, to my knowledge, been replicated and one would hope for a good deal more work on this particular approach.

The inter-sensory integration theory is on the other hand perhaps too simple! If there were difficulty in integrating visual with verbal material in a global sense, one would, for example, expect people who have this difficulty to be unable to name everyday objects in their spoken language. This is generally untrue of a dyslexic. One would need to specify detailed functions that might suffer from inter-sensory integration. The evidence is not yet so strong or convincing as to confirm or disconfirm the hypothesis.

While not ruling out some elements of the last two hypotheses, it seems that deficit models coupled with a lag of some kind is the most likely. The deficit model is summarized by Wilsher (1981)

the massive weight of evidence points to a very simple explanation. The reasons dyslexics have difficulty with 'left-hemisphere tasks' (Naming, Coding and Sequencing) is not because they are localized *abnormally*, but because they are localized *normally* and are *dysfunctioning*.

It should be stressed that this does not mean a dysfunctioning left hemisphere in total, as this would obviously include difficulties in speech and all other language forms, but relatively specific connections between sound and written symbol (e.g. naming, lexical access, and acoustic encoding). There may be a slower rate of information processing in these kinds of tasks in the dyslexic.

3.234 Sensory and motor laterality The notion of *laterality* and its association with dyslexia is a contentious one. Here *laterality* refers to handedness, eyedness, footedness and earedness of the individual usually based on some kind of laterality questionnaire. For example, one observes which hand the child uses for writing, for throwing, for dealing cards, for unscrewing a lid and for tapping tasks. In relation to eyedness, the child is observed sighting a telescope, or looking through a hole in a piece of paper. There are various methods of measuring these kinds of features. Orton (1937) was the first to suggest that mixed laterality or mixed handedness was associated in some kind of way with a dyslexic problem. He assumed that mixed laterality related to a less clear-cut 'dominance' of brain function (see above). However the relationship between handedness and hemisphere function is by no means clear (see Dimond and Beaumont 1976, for a review). Generally, it is true that the individual who is completely right-dominant for handedness tasks usually has a left-hemisphere specialization for language. However, the corollary is not true. Although some individuals who are left-dominant for hand have a right-hemisphere control or specialization for language, the majority still have a left-hemisphere function (see also Zangwill 1962). This lack of a clear-cut relationship between handedness, eyedness, footedness, earedness, and cortical hemisphere dominance, is particularly apparent in children, according to Satz (1976).

However, owing to the way in which the sensory and motor mechanisms tend to be controlled by the contra-lateral hemisphere, there might be some interrelationship between the control of these functions and brain dominance. Certainly a number of authors have provided evidence for some kind of interrelationship between dyslexia and mixed laterality. A typical finding is given in Table 3.4.

Table 3.4   Handedness in total population and a dyslexic clinic

	Right	Mixed	Left
Normal population (Annett 1967) (UK)	68	28	4
Dyslexic sample (Thomson *et al*. 1980) n = 530	24	64	11
Normal children (McBurney and Dunn 1976) (USA)	76	11	13

The dyslexic sample compared to both a UK and a USA 'control group' of normal populations has a much higher incidence of mixed handedness. Another suggestion has been that mixed laterality or cross-laterality relates to problems of left/right identification. Cross-laterality refers to the situation where hand and eye are oppositely lateralized, e.g. right-handed, left-eyed. Newton (1974) suggests that this results in difficulty in aspects of seriation, left/right scanning and directionality.

In terms of the simple relationship between laterality and dyslexia the literature is not at all clear. The following report higher incidences of mixed handedness or cross-laterality amongst reading disabled children: Bryden (1970) Critchley (1970), Zangwill (1962), Naidoo (1972), Keefe (1976), Farr and Leigh (1972, based on 12,000 primary school children), Newton (1970), Wheeler (1978), Dunlop *et al.* (1973), Harris (1957), Hecaen and Ajuriaguerra (1964), Ingram (1969). On the other hand, the following authors argue that there is no relationship between the above variables and reading: Hardyck and Petrinovitch (1977), Clark (1970), Rutter *et al.* (1970), Hardyck (1977, 7,000 children), Goldberg and Shiffman (1972), Hart and Fagg (1976), Tinker (1965), Helveston *et al.* (1970), Barlow (1963), Belmont and Birch (1965), Coleman and Deutsch (1964), De Hirsch *et al.* (1966), Satz and Friel (1973), Shankweiler (1963), Sparrow and Satz (1970). One reason for the different findings are the samples used. Samples based on clinical populations—those referred to hospitals, special reading clinics or university research departments—tend to find a higher incidence of mixed laterality associated with a dyslexic problem. Research studies based on large general population samples, with one or two exceptions, tend not to find relationships between handedness and laterality (see also Harris 1979).

Another reason for the inconsistent data may be the lack of detail provided by most of the authors in relation to the kind of laterality measures used. Some of these studies, for example, only refer to left-handedness. Thomson (1975) analysed data on reading retardates and normals based on different criteria for 'abnormal' laterality. He found that when 'left-handed' referred only to writing with the left hand there was no relationship between reading retardation and this criterion. However when the criterion was undertaking two or more tasks with the opposite hand, i.e. mixed-handed, there was a higher incidence of ambidexterity amongst reading retardates. Children who were completely right-dominant and completely left-eyed were not unequally distributed between reading retardates and controls, whereas children who were mixed-eyed or mixed-handed as well as being cross-lateral in some respects were more frequent amongst reading retardates. Different results may be obtained depending on the particular criteria which define the deviant laterality group. Another important point to remember here is that one is talking about relative frequencies. In fact Thomson (1975) provides a probabilistic analysis of the data. While mixed-handedness is more frequent amongst reading retardates it should be borne in mind that some dyslexics will be completely right-dominant, and some good readers will be mixed-handed and cross-lateral. However, we can conclude that some form of mixed laterality does appear to be associated with dyslexia, particularly amongst clinical populations. It is still unclear what mechanisms are in operation, however there appear to be three major notions:

1   Inconsistent laterality reflects a lack of cerebral dominance
2   Inconsistent laterality gives rise to directional confusion and left/right discrimination problems
3   Cross-laterality gives rise to directional confusion, scanning difficulties and may affect hemisphere integration

The first notion we have already argued against, due to the unclear relation between laterality and cerebral dominance.

The second mechanism appears at first sight to be an attractive one, relying on the concept of the left hemisphere being responsible for serial order and directionality. Corbollis and Beale (1976) present some intriguing arguments to suggest that an asymmetric lateralization is an important neuropsychological prerequisite for right/left discrimination, and mirror-image identification. This relates to evidence from Sperry (1964) and others, concerning mirror-image transfer across the corpus callosum between the two hemispheres, and evidence for some kind of mirror image store in the opposite hemisphere (see also Silver and Hagin 1970). However the reader will notice that the acceptance of this assumes mechanism 1 outlined above, i.e. that mixed-handedness and cross-laterality reflect neurological asymmetries (or lack of hemisphere dominance). That logical step is as yet unproven.

The third notion about cross-laterality again is one which has a certain amount of evidence to support it. Zangwill and Blakemore (1972), for example, put forward evidence to suggest that individuals who are left-eye dominant tend to scan from a right to left direction. It is attractive to assume therefore that a very young child scanning from right to left, perceiving a word like 'doll' is in fact reading it as 'llob'. This sort of error is common in young children. For a dyslexic child this kind of error may perseverate due to a left-eye dominance opposite to motor function. We also have the notion of hemisphere integration. Here the idea is that the right hemisphere may control the visual input, whereas the left hemisphere is controlling the motor output, causing delays in integration of visuo-motor function. Wheeler, Watkins and McLaughlin (1977) present evidence to suggest that cross-lateral individuals are slower at information processing in relation to short-term memory (see also Section 3.34). It is difficult to see how left/right confusion per se is linked to inconsistent laterality, but there do appear to be suggestions of difficulties in verbal labelling and information processing, which are key features of the cognitive weakness in dyslexia.

Pedagogically, laterality can be important, particularly in deciding which hand to encourage a child to write with. If the child is left-handed for writing but right-handed for most other tasks I suggest that he be encouraged to write with his right hand, as this is the easiest motor-control system for our left to right language. However, if the child does the majority of tasks or indeed all of the laterality questionnaire tasks with his left hand one would suggest he be allowed to continue to write with his left hand. However, I would not recommend that the child be given an eye-patch or handedness training tasks, and take the view that dominance training has not been proven to have a useful role to perform in the development of cognitive functioning. As we know so little about the way in which the brain develops and matures, it is surely best to change the language to fit the child, rather than change the child to fit the language.

3.3   Cognitive Perspective

3.31   Introduction and information-processing approaches

Cognitive psychology deals with any area of human behaviour that involves some kind of internal representation or 'what goes inside one's head'. It includes thinking, memory, perception and language and each of these can be divided into a number of sub-components. Prior to looking in detail at studies and theories concerning dyslexia, some background in cognitive psychology needs to be outlined. This is necessary to provide a context for the reader. Much of current cognitive theory, including language theory, has developed from the information processing approaches to human behaviour. This takes a functional view of human behaviour (see Underwood 1978; Norman 1976). The assumption is that human beings attend to stimuli in the environment, code these in various ways using cognitive systems such as memory, feature analysis, retrieval, lexical access, and so on. In relation to dyslexia the approach makes the assumption that one can identify various deficiencies in function, for example, in coding or in memory of letter patterns or words. In many cases this information processing approach will involve experimental testing of 'models', i.e. a model of human behaviour from which predictions may be derived. In relation to reading there are many different functional models, as reading is not a single process; it includes, for example, reading single words aloud, reading silently for meaning, and recognizing individual letter patterns. However, an information processing analysis assumes that any task can be analysed into stages, typically processed into a fixed order. This usually begins with sensory input, followed by coding and then output or response. In describing single-word reading one might postulate that a word could be represented in terms of how it looks—its visual features; how it sounds—its phonological features; what it means—its semantic features; and how it is said—its articulatory features. We can then ask what representations are actually used in the process, or what functions are involved in their creation. As an example of this kind of approach we shall look at Mackworth's model (1971, 1972).

Figure 3.4 gives a diagrammatic representation of Mackworth's model. The processes and specific stages assumed to be taking place are indicated by the boxes and the arrows indicate the direction of the process that occur. Mackworth suggests that during a single fixation pause of 250 milliseconds a sensory visual trace of the stimulus element involved is created. Recognition of this input results from matching it to a memory trace of the word leading to an iconic image lasting for a second or longer. Because we learn words in relation to speech, there is the mediation of an articulatory system, i.e. a match to articulatory verbal representation. This gives meaning to written words. From the iconic store words are coded into a short-term memory by a verbal motor program. This short-term memory may last for several seconds, but new input soon erases it. Short-term memory content is stored in long-term memory or it is lost. Meaning at verbal level, such as words and sentences, are stored in the long-term memory, and this will produce expectations of what will come next in reading. This 'feed-back' may influence eye movements in relation to their new fixations and processing of further information. There is similar input in relation to auditory material which will also have to

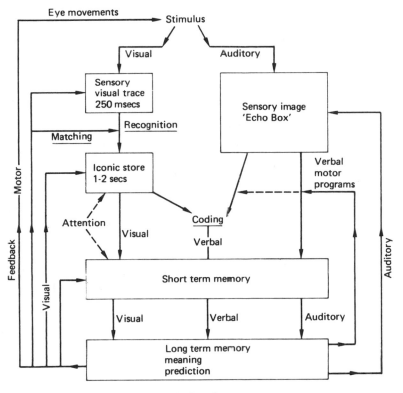

Model of reading process

Figure 3.4 An information processing model of the reading process (Mackworth, 1971)

be encoded. In the following sections we will be looking at evidence for deficits in the sensory visual trace, iconic store, short-term memory, eye movements and verbal coding in dyslexics.

Another simple model is the stage analysis approach. This is illustrated by Figure 3.5. This assumes that one can look at reading in terms of what is sometimes called either a *bottom-up* or *top-down* process. A bottom-up approach assumes that one analyses the physical stage first. In this case it is the visual input in terms of eye movements and consequent coding. This is followed by some kind of sound access or phonological code and finally accessing meaning in terms of the higher-order language elements, for example. A top-down process makes the assumption that one has some kind of knowledge about language first and imposes this knowledge on perception of what we are reading (or indeed writing or spelling).

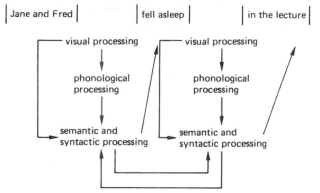

Figure 3.5 Stage analysis model of the reading process

In Figure 3.5, the reading process can involve direct access to meaning, in other words from visual information to semantic and syntactic processing. Alternatively, particularly with beginner readers or difficult texts, a mediational code is used, in this case a sound-based or phonological one. The semantic and syntactic processes guide further visual processing as well as integrating the earlier with the later part of the sentence. In relation to dyslexia the stage analysis model will involve looking at phonological coding in particular, as well as the higher-order language elements.

We have been discussing reading above; this is not because of the lack of importance of spelling and writing in dyslexia, but because most of the research has focused on *reading* difficulties. This is unfortunate, in my opinion. There are however some increasing signs of interest in spelling and writing, both in terms of cognitive models as well as dyslexia, for example Frith (1980b). This research will be mentioned where appropriate.

3.32   Perceptual and motor deficits

This section looks mainly at the sensory input components of the above models, but includes examination of some output elements.

3.321 Visual perception One of the early assumptions about dyslexia was that the difficulties relate to deficiencies in visual perception, particularly directional perception, orientation of shapes, copying of complex designs, difficulties in visual matching and visual discrimination.

In respect to simple visual discrimination Satz *et al.* (1978), as part of their general theory, argue that perceptual and motor deficits are associated with dyslexia in the 5–8 year chronological age range. They suggest that visual recognition and discrimination are the highest predictors of reading achievement. A number of studies in relation to early reading readiness and prediction of reading achievement suggests that matching to standard visual discrimination—i.e. comparing a visual symbol or shape to a possible range of them, is moderately correlated with later reading, e.g. Barrett (1965), Calfee (1977). In respect to elements such as figure – ground discrimination a number of authors, e.g. Elkind *et al.* (1965), Goetzinger *et al.* (1960), Lovell *et al.* (1964), have suggested that poor readers have difficulty in embedded-figures tests—trying to pick out a particular shape against a varied background. The well known series of tests devised by Frostig (1961) examines things such as eye-motor abilities (drawing lines between boundaries); figure – ground (identifying figures against a background); shape constancy (recognizing geometric forms); position in space (reversals and rotations); and spatial relationships (matching simple forms from copying, and drawing in patterns using dots). These are all claimed to be deficient in poor readers. Spatial and directional visual discrimination difficulties are described by Orton (1937) as a key feature of dyslexia, and Silver and Hagin (1970), and Money (1966) argue that these difficulties are related to problems in directional sense or spatial disorientation. Wechsler and Hagin (1964), argue that there is 'axial rotation' conceptional confusion, based on their 'lamb chop' test, where children were asked to match orientations or letter-like forms that were chosen to be nonverbal. However, Spache (1976), in a review of studies, argues that many of the Frostig tests are unreliable and have low predictive scores in relation to reading performance. Further, although there is no doubt that positional and directional confusions occur more frequently in the older dyslexic compared to matched groups (see also Furness 1956, Lyle 1969, Thomson 1982d), this does not specifically tell us that this is due to visual discrimination *per se*.

Vellutino (1979) points out that visual matching tasks involve a memory element in the way that they are given, and that previous knowledge of letters, with memory coding functions, are the most important source of variation in the tasks. He quotes studies such as Curry *et al.* (1973), finding no differences in visual matching if the memory element is removed from the task, or if intelligence is controlled for. Other studies, for example Stanley and Hall (1973), found that there were no difficulties in visual matching and Ellis and Miles (1978) suggest that the difficulties in perception and processing of visual symbols occur only when a verbal label is involved. Vellutino (1979) further argues that left – right confusions are functions of verbal labelling, and that the majority of studies involve some kind of visual to verbal input and do not test visual perception alone. In tasks involving left – right matching, for example, as in the Wechsler and Hagin study, he suggests that the difficulty here may be in the knowledge of how to apply the concept of same and different. The orientation dimension he argues is not crucial for shape identification and that it is the concept of same and different in the matching processes that is important. It is therefore inappropriate learning that is the problem. Vellutino also states that many of the studies refer to 'poor readers' in experimental samples, and do not only deal with dyslexic children. In addition some studies are correlational, i.e. they relate to reading in the general population and are not associated with specific learning difficulties, and many of them fail to control for important variables such as intelligence.

Another commonly quoted reason for dyslexic difficulties is that of visual spatial dysfunction, particularly in copying figures, such as the Bender Gestalt Test, or perhaps in memory for designs, where a complex shape is shown for a few seconds, then removed, and the child is then required to draw it. A number of studies report reading-disabled children having great difficulties in this kind of task, for example Goins (1958), de Hirsch et al. (1966), Koppitz (1958), Crosby (1968). On the other hand a number of studies do not find differences between poor readers on these and similar tasks, for example, Lovell et al. (1964), Symmes and Rapoport (1972), Lyle (1968). Typically the positive findings suggest a 'primitivization' of designs. This means that reading-disabled children would copy dots as a circle; their motor control would be poor; they might have a tendency to 'verticalize' diagonals; or they might invert the whole shape. One of the major problems here is to decide what particular deficit is associated with the child's poor performance at copying shapes. The difficulty might be in the child's actually perceiving the shape and therefore he is copying accurately the shape he actually perceives. On the other hand the child may see the design perfectly well but is unable to represent that design in motor-form. The problem may be a 'graphomotor' one and not a visual perception one. On the other hand the problem may not be in visual or motor areas but in the integration between the visual input and the motor output, i.e. he might see a pattern perfectly well, be able to copy patterns perfectly well but cannot integrate the two. This has important implications for etiology as well as for the kind of remedial teaching that one would recommend for a child, yet we cannot make firm deductions from the tasks given.

Vellutino (1979) also criticizes the studies on the grounds that they often fail to control for intelligence, and therefore one is measuring some kind of intellectual or reasoning-associated factor, i.e. that the visuo-motor reconstruction of spatial arrays measures problem solving or conceptualization. He also points out that cerebral palsied children with severe visuo-motor difficulties can be quite literate and it is difficult to see how these difficulties might affect reading alone. Jansky and de Hirsch (1972), based on the longitudual study on predicting reading, found that letter naming, picture naming (i.e. an oral or language factor) were the most important predictors of reading, but that a visual motor factor associated with things such as drawing of designs was more associated with spelling.

Some authors suggest that these visual perceptual difficulties are linked to age—we have already mentioned Satz in this connection—but Vernon (1979) suggests that the beginner readers require a maturation of perceptual abilities, and this might be associated with certain subtypes of dyslexia (see Chapter 1). Obviously visuo-spatial, visuo-motor, or visual perceptual difficulties would be much more associated with 'visual' kinds of dyslexia. However if the child has difficulty in perceiving directionality of shapes visually one would expect him to have difficulty in recognizing pictures, in finding his way around, in identifying objects, indeed surviving in the everyday visuo-spatial world in which we live. The dyslexic's difficulty seems restricted to the written form, e.g. maps, or to left – right confusion. The evidence for the latter being a labelling difficulty is much stronger, i.e. the child is able to *discriminate* between left and right direction, but is uncertain which side to call left and which side to call right (see discussions on phonological coding later).

Thus in relation to visual *discrimination* and *visuo-motor* difficulties the evidence is unclear at best and in most cases open to a good deal of criticism in relation to dyslexia. Difficulties that *are* observed in the literature are either overall correlations with reading in a population only including dyslexics, or the results could be interpreted in other kinds of ways—for example in terms of memory dysfunctions, verbal labelling difficulties or higher-order conceptual processing. Even when there is strong evidence that there is a visuo-motor or copying difficulty in the dyslexic we are still unsure as to which particular conceptual function is deficient. Benton (1962) concludes in his review of the area 'deficiency of visual form perception is not an important correlate of developmental dyslexia.'

This is not to say that one cannot describe dyslexics as having 'visual problems'—(see for example Chapters 5 and 6), but that the visual problems relate to verbal coding of visual information revisualization skills (i.e. the ability to retain what something looks like in the mind's eye, and correct one's spelling as a result), or in remembering spelling patterns and putting them into the right order.

3.322   Visual sensory store   Some studies have focused on the visual information store and the iconic memory components of reading (see Mackworth's model.) This invariably involves laboratory tasks, as one is examining the initial visual information stored in milliseconds. Stanley (1975), Stanley and Hall (1973), Badcock and Lovegrove (1981) and Lovegrove *et al*. (1980) have found differences in the visual information store in dyslexic children. These studies either relate to visual persistence—i.e. the maintenance of some kind of visual image over time before it fades—or the iconic memory system based on the partial report technique described intitially by Sperling (1960). This latter notion implies that there is a large-capacity memory store that fades very rapidly but from which we can 'read off' information for coding into the next memory system. (See Baddeley, 1976 for descriptions of these system.)

Stanley and his associates argue that a dyslexic's visual persistence is greater than a non-dyslexic's, and if this is the case the visual image will interfere with the next incoming stimulus. Typically, visual information is presented in sequential form such that there is an interval between two successive stimuli (Inter-Stimulus Interval or ISI). The ISI is reported by Stanley and his co-workers to be so much greater in dyslexics that there are difficulties in perceptual integration of the two stimuli. Similar findings are reported by Badcock and Lovegrove (1981) and Lovegrove *et al*. (1978) with stimuli presented in short durations or successive presentations of stimuli. They argue that the basic difficulty in visual functioning is in relation to temporal processing and perception, which gives rise to erratic eye movements in dyslexia (see section 3.325).

On the other hand some studies have found no differences between dyslexics and controls, for example, Vellutino *et al*. (1972 and 1975). Vellutino suggests that where differences are found they may be a response strategy—the dyslexics are more likely to wait until they are sure about the visual display before reporting letters, because the children know that they have difficulties in letter identification. He also argues that verbal factors in letter naming have not been ruled out. A further argument is that reading involves letters and sounds that are stationary, not flashed up onto tachistoscopes in milliseconds. He also points out that despite eye movements being fast enough, visual fusion does not occur in reading, i.e. we do not get grey bands—there is a clearing of vision during eye movements and there must be some kind of adaptive system to compensate for visual images. There are other arguments criticizing the actual experimental procedures involved—these are highly technical and beyond the scope of the present overview.

Studies looking at the iconic memory processes begin to overlap with memory functions. A number of studies have suggested that dyslexics do less well on partial report tasks. For example, Thomson and Wilsher (1979), Alwitt (1963) and Morrison *et al*. (1977) found that dyslexics did less well on 'Sperling' tasks. Briefly this involves flashing up an array of digits or letters, say 4 by 4, and the subjects are then given a cue for one of the rows and are required to report that row. One interpretation of poorer performance of the dyslexics in this kind of task is that they have a smaller memory capacity, but other researchers such as Ellis and Miles (1978) and Done and Miles (1978) using similar tasks, have suggested that this effect only occurs when verbal material is used, and therefore this might be a verbal coding difficulty. Studies on memory will be looked at in more detail in due course.

3.323 Auditory perception Auditory *perception* does not refer to hearing or acuity problems, but to the next stage in terms of auditory discrimination and precursors to auditory coding. In the studies quoted below the assumption is that the children have average or normal auditory acuity. However this is an assumption that cannot always be made with children with learning difficulties. As is described in Chapter 5, there are some children who have subtle difficulties in hearing, such as high-frequency hearing loss, which will make various aspects of auditory perception difficult due to acuity problems. High-frequency hearing loss would result in difficulty in many consonants—for example, /θ/, /s/—whereas low-frequency loss might result in difficulties in vowel sounds and consonants such as /r/, /g/, /b/, /w/.

There has been considerably less work on auditory perceptual difficulties in dyslexic children than on visual perception, based on the assumption that reading is primarily a visual task. Current research on the reading process suggests that this is a dangerous assumption to make, and certainly spelling and writing are not simply visual processes. A common notion is that learning-disabled children have difficulties in auditory discrimination. The words *learning disabled* are used deliberately here, as some studies refer to correlations between discrimination and reading ability in general, or compared normal populations compared with *'poor readers'*, and it is often difficult to generalize from these studies to dyslexia *per se*. Wepman (1960, 1961) suggested that auditory discrimination difficulties were due to developmental lags of speech perception and partly dependent on auditory acuity. Typically a child might have difficulty in discriminating between /pin/ and /pen/. A number of other studies have suggested that there is link between auditory discrimination and reading. For example Goetzinger *et al.* (1960), de Hirsch *et al.*(1966), Silver (1968), Clark (1970), and Valtin (1973) found poor auditory discrimination in bad spellers. Henry (1975), McNinch and Richmond (1972) and Goldberg and Schiffman (1972) found correlations between auditory discrimination and poor reading. On the other hand some studies have not found an association, for example Naidoo (1972) and Dykstra (1966). In a recent literature review Harber (1980) tries to draw a distinction between 'pure' auditory discrimination and tasks involving some kind of memory, auditory analysis (closure) and auditory synthesis (blending). He suggests that there are moderate correlations between auditory discrimination and reading, but more particularly in sound blending where there is good evidence of difficulties in poor readers. However Richardson *et al.* (1977) and Hammill and Larsen (1974) argue that where studies report significant correlations they are 'educationally non-meaningful', i.e. the correlations are low. Indeed Harber found in his own study that only auditory closure and word analysis skills were related, i.e. they reached a correlation which is 'educationally significant' based on Guildford's (1956) notions of statistical significance.

It is useful in looking at auditory discrimination to examine the kinds of tasks used. In the Wepman tasks a series of words is presented and the child is asked to say whether the words are the same or different. Other tasks include saying whether the words rhyme, matching sounds to objects, and so on. Dykstra (1966) found that there were very low correlations between all these kinds of tasks, suggesting that they were not measuring a unitary factor. Morency *et al.* (1970) suggest that difficulties in auditory discrimination are not perceptual but relate to difficulties in articulation. For example, they suggest that as /o/, /s/, /z/, /j/ and /v/ are late in phonological and articulatory development one might expect language or speech delays to give rise to discrimination difficulties. Matthews and Seymour (1981) in fact found that there were no auditory discrimination difficulties amongst poor readers unless there were also articulatory defects. Shankweiler and Liberman (1972) present evidence that discrimination difficulties are a function of presentation, i.e. the child could vocalize them correctly when presented orally, but be unable to read them. Blank (1968) argues that the children are poorer in making same/different judgements, but when they are asked to vocalize rather than to decide whether the words were the same or different they were perfectly able to produce correct responses. In other words the difficulty is not auditory perception or discrimination but in labelling the sounds same or different. It is therefore difficult to interpret exactly what the implications of response might be when dealing with children, particularly with verbal material where there are all kinds of conceptualization and linguistic strategies which might interfere with 'pure' perception. Bradley and Bryant (1978) for example presented children with a series of words, the task being to find the odd one out, e.g. *weed, peel, need, deed,* or *fed, bed, nod.* They found that dyslexic children made many more errors in this task, and that the dyslexics had difficulties in producing rhyming words. They conclude that this '. . . is striking confirmation of their difficulty with *categorizing sounds.* Overall our results strongly suggest that this difficulty could be an important cause of reading failure, (p. 747). The important point here is that the results, while of great interest, could be interpreted in many ways. One is the interpretation given by Bradley and Bryant. Another could be that the children had auditory discrimination difficulties and another interpretation is that they are confused over what rhyming means owing to some general language problem. The latter interpretation might mean for example that the children did not understand the task, and in the case of the first example given above, perhaps assumed that the words were the same because they had an /e/ sound.

Snowling (1987) refers to repetition of words in speech perception. She puts forward the notion of acoustic analysis, with output phonology, in terms of assembling sounds and phonemes together before repeating and also of the use of lexical or semantically orientated skills. She quotes Snowling *et al.* (1986) as finding 'no evidence of difficulties with acoustic analysis, but rather in repeating of non-words amongst dyslexics'; the problem appeared to be associated with phonological skills of the children (see later).

3.324   Inter-sensory integration Another early explanation of reading difficulties is in terms of inter-sensory discrimination, or cross-modal matching. It is typically associated with the work of Birch and Belmont (1964) initiated by Birch in 1962. The basic experimental paradigm involves the cross-modal matching of dot patterns. Typically a set of tap patterns are presented auditorally, varying in terms of the gaps between the taps. The child would then be presented with the task of picking out the matching taps that are presented visually. This might be as follows: test item · · · (auditory) followed by visual stimuli · · · ·, · · · ·, · · · · the child has to pick out the correct sequence to match the auditory stimuli. This paradigm is an auditory – visual integration (AVI) task. Birch and Belmont found that retarded readers did less well at this type of task, and Muehl and Kremenak (1966) found that AVI tasks were highly correlated with reading ability. A number of other studies have supported this finding as well, for example Beery (1967), Bryden (1972), Vande Voort *et al.* (1972).

Vellutino (1979) however argues that children have difficulty in grasping the *concept* of inter-sensory integration (Farnham-Diggory 1972) and that the difficulties are conceptual and not perceptual. Blank and Bridger (1966), and Blank *et al.* (1968) argue that the difficulties are in verbal coding or serial order perception of stimuli rather than inter-sensory integration *per se.* This is based on a series of studies in which they gave temporal and spatial stimuli (matching light flashes to dot patterns) and found no differences between good and poor readers. Then in similar tasks they asked children to describe out loud what they were doing, and found that now there *were* differences between the good and poor readers. They argued therefore that the difficulties were due to verbal mediation, or in translating a speech sequence into a visual sequence (see also Sterritt and Rudnick 1966).

A further criticism is that the early studies failed to control for *intra*-modality integration. In other words the difficulty may simply be in auditory, or visual perception and/or higher-order processing, rather than integrating the two together. Bryant (1975) takes this view, and in fact studies that have controlled for all these possible combinations find rather different results to the early workers. For example Bryden (1972) looked at both temporal and spatial perception matching, both cross-modality and within modality using auditory and visual sequences (nine combinations in all!). He found that the reading retardates scored less well on *all* measures. The difficulties therefore were general and not cross-modal. Similar results have been found by Zigmond (1966), using both verbal and non-verbal tasks. Likely explanations for difficulties in this kind of task are the verbal mediation ones outlined above, but also include difficulties in memory, or in temporal or sequencing perception. Bryant (1975) argues that cross-modal tasks do not parallel reading. Reading involves matching a series of arbitrary symbols, i.e. a visual-to-verbal paired-association kind of task. In studies by Vellutino *et al.* (1973) using non-verbal paired association tasks no differences were found between good and poor readers in visual-to-visual, visual-to-auditory, and auditory-to-auditory matching conditions; but if they included a visual-to-verbal task with nonsense syllables that had to be matched to pictures or letters the retarded readers did less well.

In summary, the notion of inter-sensory integration *per se* appears inadequate as an explanation for dyslexia. Other interpretations can be made to account for the results of experimental work.

3.325   Eye movements Some attention has been given to visual systems that might be involved in reading, particularly the possibility that binocular coordination, faulty scanning, and various ocular motor deficits might be involved in reading difficulties. However most of the evidence suggests that these difficulties are not involved at all in dyslexia. For example, Fox *et al.* (1975) concluded that optometric examinations were not contributory to the diagnosis of severe reading difficulties, Goldberg and Schiffman (1972) quoting the American Academy of Opthalmology suggest that there is no relationship between eye disturbances and dyslexia, Flax (1969) that there are no peripheral eye defects involved, Critchley (1970) that muscle imbalance or binocular fusion do not result in reading difficulties in dyslexics, and Rubino and Minden (1973) that the visual fields are normal in dyslexic children. Some eye defects such as binocular instability (see Drasdo 1972) are clearly related to reading disorders, but the question here is their relation to *dyslexia*.

Some investigations however have found differences between dyslexics and controls. For example Drasdo (1972) found a greater incidence of ametropia in dyslexics, although he is careful not to assign causal links to these refractive errors. More specifically Stein and Fowler (1981) argue for a 'visual' form of dyslexia characterized by unstable ocular motor dominance. This is based on the Dunlop (1972) test in which he describes the eye where ocular motor and retinal signals are linked as the 'dominant' eye. They argue that the neurologically based failure to develop ocular motor dominance gives rise to abnormalities of eye movements. This approach is clearly linked to the neurological theories that we have already reviewed, but provides a mechanism (failure to link eye position and retinal signals) relating dominance to reading.

There is a good deal more work on eye *movements*, as opposed to the general visual systems in dyslexia. Eye movements are an important component of Mackworth's (1971) model in terms of feedback from the higher centres to visual input, as well as relating to the physical analysis stage in reading, in our stage-analysis model. In reading the eye moves in a series of sweeps from left to right across the page (in the English language at any rate), and the movements are characterized by a series of fixations during which time visual information is taken up from the text. Fixations are followed by saccades, which are very quick movements from one fixation point to the next. In the normal case, this results in a characteristic step-like pattern which is illustrated in Figure 3.6.

A number of studies have shown faulty eye movements in dyslexia. These include saccades being too short and quick (Bouma and Legein 1977, Leisman and Schwartz 1976); general evidence for 'faulty eye movement' (Lefton et al. 1978, Nodine and Lang 1971, Getman et al. 1964, Festinger 1972); longer saccadic latencies (Dossetor and Papaioannon 1975, Leservre 1964); an excessive number of fixations, (Gruber 1962, Zangwill and Blakemore 1972, Ciuffreda et al. 1976, Pirozzolo and Rayner 1978, Pavlides 1978); a greater number of regressions (Ciuffreda et al. 1976, Elterman et al. 1980). Regressions here refer to moving the eye backwards along the line in the right-left direction. 'Normal' reading involves a series of movements from left to right involving very few regressions back across the text. The notion here is that dyslexics make a large number of these regressions. Further studies have suggested difficulties in the return sweep—for example, Pirozzolo and Rayner (1978), Pavlides (1978) and Leservre (1964).

A typical finding illustrating the difficulties that dyslexics have in aspects of eye movements is shown in Figure 3.6, based on case studies reported by Pavlides (1978).

There seems little doubt that many dyslexics do show abnormal eye movements when reading; the children often lose their place, regress to earlier parts of the line, apparently pick out letter groups from different parts of the page almost at random, or sometimes skip a line. Young dyslexics may attempt to read from the right-hand margin to the left-hand margin, and some reversals and confusions of word order may well be the result of scanning from right to left (Zangwill and Blakemore 1972).

However the contentious issue is the significance of these eye movements. Goldberg and Arnott (1970) for example argue that the degree of reading comprehension affects eye movement and not the other way round. In other words, poor ocular-motility is a result of poor reading. Similarly Critchley (1970), Vernon (1971), Simon and Ward (1978), and Festinger (1972) all argue that faulty eye movements are a *result* of reading difficulties. Furthermore, many of the difficulties described above need to be put into perspective in relation to what we know about normal reading behaviour. For example, as text difficulty increases there is higher incidence of regressions (Tinker 1958, Griffen *et al*. 1974). Thus normal readers, when reading a text which is very difficult, will tend to move back across

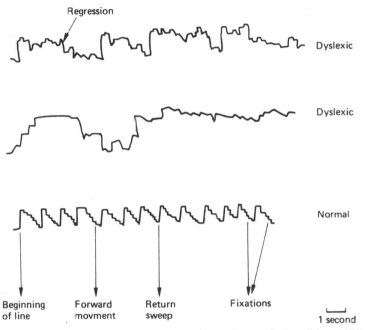

Figure 3.6   Eye movements in dyslexics and normals (Pavlides, 1978)

the page in a right-left direction, checking on a word that they have previously seen. Presumably this is done to provide further information about the meaning of a future word, i.e. trying to work out a complex sentence. Dyslexic children are often reading a story at the limit of their reading skills, and the text is difficult for them. Their eye movements are therefore the result of perfectly normal reading behaviour.

There is also a developmental effect, as average duration of fixations, the number of fixations, and the number of regressions decrease with age. In contrast, the number of words per fixations and their rate of comprehension in words per minute will increase with age (Taylor *et al*. 1960, Gilbert 1953). If there is a maturational lag in dyslexia one might imagine that the children's eye movements would be much less mature and therefore would show a greater number of regressions, and longer fixations, compared to a control group. More importantly however, dyslexic children obviously have lower reading ages and it is likely that many eye movement skills result from experience, exposure and practice in reading. Dyslexic children have had much less practice owing to their less sophisticated reading ability. Furthermore, if eye movement difficulties were causal in dyslexia one would expect these difficulties to show themselves in other tasks. This does not seem to occur; for example, Adler-Grinberg and Stark (1978) found normal rapid saccadic eye movements when dyslexics fixated a meaningless target. Another powerful argument against eye movements as being causal is the many other difficulties that dyslexic children have that are independent of the visual modality, e.g. difficulties in auditory memory, item coding, or in learning to read braille (Rudel *et al.* 1976).

Despite these arguments there are still some researchers who maintain that eye movements are, if not causal, at least highly correlated with dyslexia. Elterman *et al.* (1980) produced evidence to suggest that dyslexic children had difficulties in a symbol-simulation task and suggest some kind of ocular-motor dysfunction. Perhaps the most recent exponent of the notion that eye movements are causal in dyslexia is Pavlides (1981). Pavlides, in a series of carefully controlled studies, presents evidence that there is a difficulty in dyslexics above and beyond textual difficulties and being a 'slow reader'. He argues that most of the previous research was not undertaken in a systematic and controlled manner. He used dyslexics, 'backward' readers (whose problems were due to environmental, intellectual and other causes) and 'advanced' readers, and found differences in terms of increased regressions and longer fixations in dyslexics against all control groups. He argues that this demonstrates that eye movements could be used as a diagnostic guide to dyslexia. More importantly, he then goes on to describe a study where dyslexics were required to track a moving light in left-right and right-left directions. This he argues is a pure sequencing task, and he found similarities in the relative performance of the dyslexics, backward, normal and advanced readers to the reading task itself. He therefore claims that as his data show the dyslexics have increased regressions etc. in a simple light-tracking or sequential task not involving reading, verbal material or texts, the difficulties are primary and not a result of reading difficulties. He concludes that the causal difficulties could be in (a) ocular motor control, or (b) a general sequential deficit or (c) some kind of feedback between the two systems. It appears that he favours a sequential deficit.

The evidence Pavlides provides is impressive, and he does appear to have taken into account difficulties of interpretation due to text difficulties, and levels of reading. It would have been more impressive if he had included children who were matched on reading age but were 'normal', i.e. children who were developmentally much younger in chronological age terms, so that one could investigate the possibility of developmental effects. Pavlides's results have not been replicated at the time of writing, and the studies reported are based on the same 14 dyslexic children. These were selected from 49 children referred to the laboratory as having dyslexic problems. Pavlides argues that only 14 were chosen because they fitted his more stringent criteria of dyslexia. (One assumes that he was not using eye movements as one of the diagnostic criteria!).

In a more recent book (Pavlides and Fisher 1986), Pavlides has moved his position from arguing that eye movements were the key to dyslexia (the underlying cause), to saying that there might be another factor which could account for both eye movement difficulties and the other cognitive problems relating to dyslexia. In addition a number of researchers have failed to replicate his findings—Brown et al. (1983), Olson, Kliegel and Davidson (1983), Stanley, Smith and Howell (1983), and Eskenazi and Diamond (1983) failed to replicate the eye movements.

Therefore, we can conclude that there appear to be some difficulties concerning eye movements in dyslexia; these seem to be a function of some underlying difficulty or of the reading text *per se*, i.e. they are secondary reactions to the learning problem and not the causal factor.

3.33   Sequencing

Although not fitting neatly into either the Mackworth or 'stage analysis' models, most clinical observations and descriptions of dyslexic children state that the children have difficulties in aspects of seriation and sequence. This applies to reciting the days of the week, months of the year or seasons. Thomson and Newton (1979) for example found that 90% of *dyslexic* 10-year-olds could *not* say the months of the year in the correct sequence, whereas 90% of *good* readers at 10 years old *could* do this. Other difficulties reported in the children in respect to sequence include difficulties in letter order, reversals in articulatory speech, in memory for sequentially presented visual and auditory material, tracking tasks, and crossing out numbers, e.g. Johnson and Myklebust (1967) Kirk and McCarthy (1968), Kolers (1970), Bannatyne (1971), Newton and Thomson (1975), Naidoo (1972), Thomson and Wilsher (1979); see also section 3.7 in relation to auditory sequential memory or digit span.

Vernon (1977a) argues that sequential ordering is necessary to the analysis of sequential visual and auditory linguistic structures, in linking visual and auditory material, and in the perception of the regularities in grapheme – phoneme correspondences. Naidoo (1972) suggests that sound blending and other auditory skills are based on sequencing, and Doehring (1968) suggests that sequential processing is important in the serial content of continuous material (viz reading and spelling). Indeed McLeod (1966) in a factor analytic study on the ITPA suggested that an 'integrative' sequencing factor (including auditory vocal associations, auditory vocal sequences, visual motor sequences and digit span) were the largest factor in relation to contribution to reading performance (see also Thomson 1979, Newton and Thomson 1976 and Goldberg and Schiffman 1972).

The problem is what interpretation to make of these observations and findings. Is there a specific sequential deficit associated with dyslexia, as some researchers argue, or is the difficulty only related to memory? Are the difficulties related only to verbal material and verbal coding deficiences which give rise to some kind of apparent sequential deficit? What are the detailed mechanisms in relation to the reading process and these possible sequential difficulties? There have been a number of laboratory studies which have attempted to investigate these areas in more detail and try to tease out the various possibilities outlined above. For example, Corkin (1974) argued that the difficulties arose from a failure to remember the correct serial position of visual or auditory stimuli. He suggests that the difficulty might be in sequence or short-term memory or perhaps some inter-action between the two, and that seriation difficulties are not modality or stimulus specific. Zurif and Carson (1970) found that there was a high correlation between dyslexics' reading performance and temporal-order recall. This affected sound/symbol correspondence but not speech, based on matching tasks in relation to rhythmic patterns (including non-verbal material). They argue that sequential order is one of the most important initial early components of language and under-lies much of language development.

One of the most formalized and detailed theories in relation to sequence is that of Bakker (1967, 1972), Bakker and Schroots (1981). Bakker argues that dyslexic difficulties result from poor temporal-order perception (TOP). He argues that a left-hemisphere deficit gives rise to TOP deficits for verbal stimuli. A typical exper-iment presents three stimuli in serial order and the task of the subject is to indicate the serial position of one of these stimuli subsequently presented, or to repeat the stimuli in various ways. The stimuli include letters, digits, meaningful and non-meaningful pictures, meaningful and non-meaningful shapes. These are presented in various conditions—visual, auditory, or haptic (touch). Early results indicated that there were moderate correlations between TOP and reading. Further that there was a developmental effect and that girls were rather earlier in their develop-ment in this kind of skill. Stimuli not showing a correlation to reading proficiency were the meaningless pictures. TOP scores also correlated well with letter-order errors in reading and writing. Bakker et al. (1981) quote Pierre (1974) as partially replicating their 1970 results—dyslexics of nine and ten years old were poorer than controls on indicating serial position. Bakker and Schroots (1981) also found the TOP test to be a good predictor of reading ability. He then goes on to criticize some of his own work by citing Shankweiler and Liberman (1978), who argue that phonetic coding difficulties give rise to serial order problems. This is based on a study looking at sequential perception of rhyming and non-rhyming material (see below). Bakker also points out that the serial order difficulties may relate to various sub-categories of dyslexia, citing Aaron's (1978) work in relation to digit span. Aaron found that dysphonetic dyslexics did less well on the digit span task than dyseidetic dyslexics. These are based on Boder's (1971a, 1973) classification. However a study by Thomson (1982b) did not find any difference between dyslexics categorized on auditory and visual spelling and reading errors in terms of their digit span.

Vellutino (1979) is critical of Bakker's interpretation and argues that letter naming difficulties are not controlled for, citing Denckla and Rudel's (1976a, b) finding that this is a problem in dyslexic children. This relates of course to item rather than order identification. He also quotes some of his own studies (Vellutino et al. 1973, and Vellutino, Steger, De Setto and Phillips 1975) where there are no differences in sequential memory. He states that there are no differences in visual recall based on graphic reproduction of various verbal and non-verbal stimuli. However he makes the interesting comment that there were difficulties in dyslexics as against controls '. . . when the number of items in a given stimulus began to tax the upper limits of visual short-term memory (five-letter words).' This is interesting because it suggests some kind of interaction between memory and sequential difficulties. Obviously if the memory task is well within the capacity of the individual's span, one should not expect any difficulties. The point here is that where the memory load is too great for the child, sequential difficulties emerge. An interpretation on these lines is suggested by Thomson and Wilsher (1979) and Thomson (1977b) in relation to difficulties in remembering a series of pictures and digits. In one study by Thomson (1977b) dyslexics did not start to make sequential order errors until they had begun to reach their ceiling in terms of memory span.

Vellutino (1979) also criticizes the notion of sequential and serial order deficits on the grounds that serial order and item recall are not separate central nervous system functions, commenting 'it would therefore seem to be an oversimplification to suggest, explicitly or implicitly, that distinct neurological systems are responsible for processing information of each type' (p. 225). He provides no evidence to support this contention. Indeed he cites Estes (1972) who suggests that there *are* two types of coding strategies relating to order and item recall separately, an approach supported by Healy (1974, 1975). Healy (1977) also found support for the possibility that various codes are used, depending on the particular task. For example, phonemic codes are generally employed in temporal order recall tasks, whereas temporal spatial pattern codes are employed in spatial order recall. This is suggestive of phonemic coding involved in reading and hence temporal order recall, whereas temporal spatial pattern codes might be involved in spelling. However the important point here is that there is still some debate amongst cognitive psychologists as to whether there are separate order and item memory strategies. One cannot simply dismiss the notion that there might be a separate order recall strategy which is deficient in dyslexics.

A similar position to Bakker's is taken by Newton and Thomson (1975), Thomson (1977a), and Thomson, Newton and Richards (1979). In trying to illustrate the mechanisms that relate to sequential deficits in written language learning, Thomson (1977a, 1979b) points out that written language is based on a series of arbitrary symbols to be combined in the correct order to produce the large number of possible words that we have in spoken language. Written language is based on a series of phonemic contrasts and a series of graphemic contrasts all involving sequential order. The symbolic and arbitrary nature of this sequential order is rather different to the speech mechanisms which can be analysed in a much more global form (see Chapter 4).

Before leaving this topic, we need to examine briefly the perception of auditory information presented at rapid rates. Tallal (1980) has adapted the work of Tallal and Piercy (1974) in dysphasia and other speech difficulties. Here non-verbal auditory stimuli (tones) are presented. The children are required to give a simple motor response to a temporal sequence. Tallal found that there were no differences between dyslexics and controls at slow rates of stimuli presentation, but differences occurred at fast rates. There was also a correlation between errors made on a non-sense-word reading task which Tallal described as a phonic skill and the errors on the auditory perceptual task. She argues that this suggests a lower level of auditory perception in the dyslexics, which affects phonic skills, and is due to similar deficits to the dysphasic where there are difficulties in phonetic structure, particularly in formant transition perception. She cites Dorman *et al.* (1975) who argue that the first function of a formant transition is to carry phonetic information, but the secondary function is to bind phonemes together in order that phonetic segments at rapid transition rates may be perceived in the correct temporal order as speech. It is the latter difficulty, she argues which affects dysphasics, and in the study quoted here dyslexics also. Tallal however comments on the great divergence of performance amongst the reading-disabled children, stating that 12 of the 20 reading-delayed children performed within normal limits on her auditory perceptual tests. This might of course relate to the notion of different sub-groups of dyslexia once again.

In summary, there is a good deal of evidence for serial order and sequencing difficulties in dyslexic children, although there is some debate over the actual implications and significance of the findings quoted above. Bakker *et al.* (1981) conclude that 'temporal processing of verbal and verbally codifiable information is a predictive and an explanatory factor in reading inability. Whether this factor is either primary or secondary to other functions like linguistic and acoustical analysis has still to be settled' (p. 97).

3.34 Memory

The models outlined earlier (Mackworth and stage analysis) argue for memory components in reading. It is necessary to examine memory in more detail before looking at dyslexia and memory. It is broadly accepted that one can divide memory into various interlinking components or subsystems. These include the initial visual or auditory information store which has a large capacity, but from which information decays very rapidly (within a time-scale of less than one second). We considered some aspects of this memory system under visual perception in Section 3.322. The next memory system is some sort of short-term memory. This is sometimes known as 'short-term memory' 'short-term store', or 'working memory', all of which have slightly different features, but which perform the similar functions of encoding any briefly presented stimuli into a form for later processing and therefore acting as a 'buffer store'. This means that information is rehearsed, changed or transformed into different forms. For example, letters might be transformed into a speech or sound code for the information to be dealt with, or for it to be transferred into a longer-term store for future use. There are many kinds of processes used in relation to short-term memory including retention, perceptual encoding, motor programmes and output, and rehearsal—see Baddeley (1976). A third system is classed as long-term memory or store. This can be divided into information that is stored from an episode in one's own particular life (episodic memory) and memory information required for everyday functions, such as speaking, or understanding what words or concepts are. This is known as semantic memory. It is broadly agreed that long-term memory is a relatively permanent store and that its main features of interest are the encoding or storage of material into the system, and its retrieval and subsequent access.

Short-term memory is usually based on some kind of auditory, phonological or sound code system, whereas long-term memory is based on some kind of meaning or semantic code system. Furthermore, short-term memory is usually assumed to be up to around one minute in duration, whereas long-term memory can be from one minute up to many years. Examples of the way in which short-term memory is used in everyday life includes remembering a telephone number which one has heard long enough to dial and then forgetting it; retaining speech long enough so that one can understand sentences appropriately (being able to remember the beginning part of a speech utterance and relate it to the end part of a speech utterance for example); remembering and carrying tens and units in mental arithmetic tasks; following verbal directions in an unfamiliar town.

In relation to reading and spelling abilities there are many skills that seem to relate to short-term memory. The first is encoding visual information into a verbal store—this might be a speech code in relation to articulation, or in remembering grapheme/phoneme correspondences. Other examples include remembering phoneme/grapheme correspondence rules in order to produce the correct output of letters in spelling; remembering letter-by-letter sounds; reading comprehension in relating visual symbols to speech sound; remembering sounds long enough to blend them in forming words (e.g. c-a-t = cat); being able to correct one's spelling errors by remembering what the whole word or letter combination looks (or sounds) like; being able to copy spellings from the blackboard without having constantly to look up every two seconds or so; maintaining an auditory or visual image of a spelling or reading pattern long enough for it to be internalized and transferred to the long-term memory systems.

Another feature of short-term memory systems is in terms of 'capacity'. It is generally accepted (Miller 1967) that we have a memory capacity of around seven plus-or-minus two 'chunks'. A chunk here is seen to be a coding unit—this might be a digit, a single letter or a whole word. For example, a person might be able to remember around six individually presented letters, and similarly be able to remember about six individually presented words. These words might contain three letters each, and therefore this person is remembering 18 letters—the difference here is that he is coding these letters into whole chunks, rather than remembering them individually (an important notion for remediation, see Chapter 6).

The above brief review sets the context for the research on memory and dyslexia.

3.341 Capacity There is a good deal of evidence that dyslexics do poorly on various kinds of 'span' tasks. These might include Digit Span (Wechsler Scales) or Auditory Sequential Memory (Illinois Test of Psycholinguistic Abilities) or other similar tasks. Similar results have been observed in visual sequential memory task: see Chapter 5 for Wechsler Scale studies and, for example, McLeod (1965),

Huelsman (1970), Rugel (1974), Stanley (1976), Bakker (1972), Nelson and War-rington (1980), Thomson (1982b), Naidoo (1972), Newton and Thomson (1979), Miles and Ellis (1981). In a study reported by Thomson and Wilsher (1979) dyslexics remembered digits from partial report technique (Sperling 1960) as well as simply identifying digits. They argued that there was a much lower information capacity in the dyslexics. This interpretation was based on there being no differences between dyslexics and controls in three-by-three arrays in the partial report task, but differences emerging with increasing size of arrays. This they suggested was due to the dyslexics reaching a capacity that resulted in some kind of overload and therefore doing less well. In addition adult dyslexics were *seven* times slower than controls at 'information absorption', as measured by reading off a series of visually presented digits. Cohen and Netley (1978) also argued that dyslexics had a smaller information processing capacity in short-term memory.

In a later study Cohen and Netley (1981) presented children with a serial running memory task at a very high stimulus presentation rate. They argued that as there was no time for rehearsal, and as poor readers were worse on this task, it was not due to recognition encoding, or rehearsal, but some kind of difficulty in coding serial items in the form of a serial phonological pattern. In other words there is a reduced capacity to encode item *order* into phonological form in a short-term memory system that was already overloaded. This notion of 'encoding' we shall look at in a bit more detail below. A number of other studies have suggested general difficulties in short-term memory in the dyslexics, for example, Masland (1968), Rogers (1969), Senf and Freundl (1971, 1972), Koppitz (1973), Wiig and Roach (1975).

We now have enough evidence to support the notion that dyslexics do less well on various kinds of short-term memory tasks, but we still have not delineated any possible mechanisms. The notion of 'capacity' is not completely explanatory. The idea that dyslexics somehow have a smaller 'bottleneck' through which information can pass implies some kind of differential size of a short-term memory, 'box', a model of short-term memory which has since been superseded (see Baddeley, 1976). The key feature appears to be *verbal* coding. It is perhaps not overall 'capacity' but the particular method of coding, rehearsal strategy or the way in which the dyslexic deals with information that relates to written language learning.

3.342   Coding Lyle and Goyen (1968, 1975) comparing poor and good readers on memory for letters, lines, word shapes, and matching non-verbal shapes found that difficulties related to speed of processing rather than short-term memory unless there was some kind of verbalization required. Vellutino (1979) and his colleagues provide data suggesting that poor readers are as good in copying from visual memory, except where the visual shapes began to look more like the Roman alphabet, and some kind of verbal coding was required. Vellutino goes on to comment later that such difficulties as b/d confusions in dyslexics are not due to them being unable to see them correctly but being unable to remember which particular sound to associate with the letter. This is a theme we shall take up in more detail in a later section, and this idea of naming or coding difficulties is one found by a number of other researchers, for example Denckla and Rudel (1976a and b). It is a moot point whether this difficulty is a problem in verbal encoding, verbal processing, or a problem in short-term memory. Vellutino seems a little confused over this interrelationship, for example, he comments that the performance of dyslexics and normals is comparable in graphic reproduction—except when the configurations tax short-term memory. Spring and Capps (1974) also describe naming difficulties—children were given everyday objects, digits or colours to name, and dyslexics were much slower. They suggest that the problem is entering these names into a working memory programme. Spring and Capps also looked at the scanning techniques of the dyslexic children. They found that the good readers tended to scan from left to right and showed a recency effect (i.e. they tended to remember the later parts of the item better than the earlier parts), whereas only half the dyslexics showed recency effects and these were the same children who did not have a left-right scanning technique.

Other studies have been much more specific in suggesting possible mechanisms in the interrelationship between short-term memory dysfunctions, dyslexia and resultant coding strategies. For example, Farnham-Diggory and Gregg (1975) gave children a memory span and a memory scanning task (letters were given serially in visual and auditory modalities, for example). Poor readers did rather better on the visual tasks but much worse on the auditory tasks. They argue that one possible interpretation of these findings is that the dyslexics are processing the next bit of visual information before the first bit of visual information has been associated with its auditory equivalent. In other words in processing letters, the dyslexics are not immediately accessing the auditory information associated with a visually presented letter in the reading task and by the time they *have* accessed the auditory information they have gone on to the next bit of visual information or letter. This is rather an attractive notion and certainly might describe some of the reading errors observed in dyslexic children.

Another notion in respect to the interrelationship between short-term memory and coding is put forward by Shankweiler *et al.* (1979), and Mann *et al.* (1980). In an earlier study (Liberman and Shankweiler 1978) children were given tasks involving memorizing recurring figures. In other words they were asked what stimulus had been seen before; these included designs, faces and nonsense syllables. The poor readers did worst on nonsense syllables and tended to be somewhat better on the designs. They argued that there were no memory differences in *non-linguistic* information and further that good readers could code phonetically, and hold this coding in short-term memory, whereas the poor readers could not. In their 1979 study good and poor readers were given letters to remember and it was found that although the poor readers as a rule did less well than the good readers, the good readers were more severely penalized when letters actually rhymed, in other words, when there was some kind of phonetic interference. The Mann *et al.* study confirmed these results in sentences and word strings. Here again they found poor readers generally did worst, but the errors amongst the good readers increased to the same level as the poor reader when the stimuli were rhyming. They argued that as the poor readers did *not* use phonetic coding in short-term memory they were not penalized by the rhyming material. Another interesting finding from these studies was that neither semantic nor syntactic components differentiated the groups. In fact what Mann *et al*. had done was to present rhyming and non-rhyming stimuli in meaningful and non-meaningful ways, and also use seven types of sentence reflecting different levels of syntactic complexity. They found no difference between dyslexics and controls on these dimensions, and suggested therefore that the memory problems were manifestations of phonetic coding and not semantic and syntactic coding or long-term memory difficulties.

Jorm (1979a,b) also tries to explain dyslexia in terms of short-term memory deficit, in a way similar to that described above. Jorm points out that access to written words may seem to have two broad routes—a phonological route, based on grapheme – phoneme correspondence rules, and a semantic route going directly from visual input to meaning (see Chapter 4). He argues that phonological recoding difficulties reflect some basic cognitive disability in either auditory/verbal or visual information short-term store, or perhaps both. As the dyslexic children appear to make fewer phonological confusions in tasks outlined in the Shankweiler *et al*. (1979) work the children are not relying on auditory – verbal short-term stores. This suggestion is also supported in recent unpublished work by myself. In this latter study children were given a visual search task with varying backgrounds (auditory or visual similarity). The dyslexics made a significantly greater use of visual code, which implies that they were having difficulty in using an auditory or verbal code. Jorm (1979a,b) argues that the auditory – verbal short-term deficits may also account for serial or sequencing difficulties. Jorm's (1979a,b) analysis has been criticized by Byrne (1981), who suggests that Jorm has ignored evidence on linguistic awareness or lexical access. He suggests that success in acquiring alphabetical orthography relates to identifying speech at the level of phonemes and children need some kind of awareness of phonemic principles to master reading; he cites Gleitman and Rozin (1977), and Kavanagh and Mattingly (1972) in support of this notion. He argues that it is not at all clear that short-term memory difficulties gives rise to this lack of phonemic awareness.

A comprehensive study by Nelson and Warrington (1980) on short-term memory in dyslexia concluded that dyslexics had a 'double deficiency' in aspects of memory. This study was based on taking a whole range of tests following the sorts of evidence upon which theories of short-term and long-term memory systems have been based. Without going into any great detail here, Nelson and Warrington found that dyslexics did less well on digit span, both forward and reverse, on the 'Brown – Peterson Task' involving short-term memory decay, on word knowledge (English Picture Vocabulary Test) and learning new words. However they found dyslexics did just as well as controls on accessing words in semantic memory. Briefly they concluded that the 'double deficiency' related to graphemic – phonemic short-term memory interrelationships, and graphemic – semantic interrelationships. Nelson and Warrington also related their findings to Boder's (1973) classification. They suggested that the graphemic – phonemic deficiency related to the 'dysphonetic' dyslexic, where the graphemic – semantic deficiency related to the 'dyseidetic' dyslexic.

Studies of long-term memory have been rather fewer, possibly because on *a priori* ground one cannot see how dyslexics might have difficulties in long-term memory. Their intellectual abilities are often at least average and there seems to be no difficulty in accessing knowledge. Tasks such as word association, and visual-to-visual matching in long-term memory have not been found to distinguish dyslexics and controls—for example, Budoff and Quinlan (1964), Weinstein and Rabinovitch (1971), Vellutino, Harding *et al.* (1975), Vellutino and Steger *et al.* (1973), Firth (1972), Jorm (1977). However in long-term memory tasks when nonsense syllables and symbols are required, and where verbal coding is involved, some studies have found differences, for example Gascon and Goodglass (1970), Otto (1961), Vellutino (1975). The diferences here seems to be in the initial coding strategies, rather than in long-term memory *per se*. However the Nelson and Warrington study did suggest some difficulties in aspects of long-term memory, particularly word knowledge and new word learning. The idea of word knowledge deficiences was based on the rather lower scores among the dyslexic sample on the English Picture Vocabulary Test.

The above draws attention to one very important and fundamental criticism of much of the research—the methological point of appropriate control groups. Most control groups are matched on chronological age. For example, the dyslexic group might have a chronological age of 10, with a reading age, say, of $7\frac{1}{2}$, whereas the control group's reading and chronological age would both be 10. This means that there might be a $2\frac{1}{2}$ year gap between the reading ages of the two groups. One cannot then be sure that any differences obtained on the dependent variable (i.e. memory test or whatever) are due to dyslexic rather than due to reading experience. Basically the argument goes that learning to read in itself may give rise to certain kinds of skills, not least of which are the ones associated with linguistic elements. Thus the processes of learning to read between, say, seven and ten years old may result in certain phonetic coding skills developing. Furthermore, the kind of information that the children are obtaining from reading a text of reading age $7\frac{1}{2}$, which would include very basic simple words and concepts, is different to that of a reading age of 10 which is almost up to everyday competence (some newspapers have a reading age of around 10 to 11).

The notion of certain perceptual, memory, linguistic or coding skills developing as a result of learning to read is a theme which will be looked at in more detail below. In relation to the memory tasks and the example quoted above, the problem relates to information obtained from reading. Nelson and Warrington used chronologically matched control groups. To compare children's performance on word knowledge, where the reading ages are vastly different, is very inappropriate. The difficulties therefore may not be due to a semantic or long-term memory problem, but simply due to lack of opportunity in obtaining information about words, owing to less experience in reading. One of the most important sources of learning about words is reading (see e.g. Donaldson 1979).

To summarize this section on memory, there is a good deal of agreement as to short-term memory weakness in dyslexics, particularly in serial memory and auditory – verbal coding. We can now place the earlier perceptual difficulties described in the context of a verbal or phonological coding difficulty.

3.35   Verbal processing

It is obviously the case that the difficulties facing the dyslexic are verbal in nature, and in a sense the title of this section is redundant. However we need to be much more specific about the nature of the verbal difficulties facing the individual. The problems manifested by the dyslexic are not in conceptual functions such as spoken language understanding, verbal reasoning, conceptual development and the many other verbal skills which are associated with intelligence and cognitive development.

One can view language as a verbal/symbolic/representational system. The important component here is that of symbolization, i.e. language enables us to transform sensory information into representational units, which are then coded into meaning. This can then relate to 'inner language'. This notion of transforming sensory input into appropriate codes is reminiscent of some of the stage analysis descriptions outlined above, and indeed is something we shall return to when examining models of reading processes in the next chapter. Here we shall consider some aspects of general verbal dysfunctions which might be associated with dyslexia.

There is some evidence that dyslexics do rather less well on the Verbal component of the Wechsler Intelligence Scale for Children (WISC), although this is by no means universally found, as the children may be more heterogeneous. For example, Ingram and Reid (1966) found that their reading-disabled children fell into three main types, based on Verbal/Performance discrepancies on the WISC. Group A (44%) had better Verbal than Performance skills, Group B (25%) had better Performance skills than Verbal, and the rest had similar Verbal and Performance skills. They found that reading impairment was the greatest in Group B, and these also had some minor speech problems. However their reading retardates overlapped considerably with a dysphasic group and many of the children had poor comprehension, very late language development, and speech unintelligble sometimes at four or five years old (see Chapter 5 for further WISC studies). Some researchers, such as Rabinovitch *et al*. (1964) argue for minimal aphasic difficulties in the dyslexic and others (e.g. Montgomery 1981), for articulation difficulties. However, Spreen (1978) points out that if an individual had a general language or verbal impairment he would not have a *specific* developmental dyslexia. This seems a salient point: if all language disorders are associated with dyslexia, what kind of distinction can be drawn between dyslexia and other forms of language disorder? Certainly reading builds on spoken language, and there must be correlations between the ability to use spoken language and reading. Indeed a delay in language may well be a forerunner of dyslexia. But if we are talking about a specific difficulty in reading, writing and spelling, by definition general language must be reasonably complete. This of course applies if the child is scoring reasonably well on an intelligence test, as many dyslexic children do, and there are discrepancies between his intellectual ability and his reading, writing and spelling performance. In particular the notion of a general language or verbal impairment cannot explain very bright adults with excellent language abilities who are dyslexic (see Perlo and Rak 1971), or indeed children who are gifted and yet have a reading, writing and spelling difficulty, see Knabe *et al.* (1970).

However, some argue that dyslexic children have difficulties in verbal learning, see Vellutino (1979), Vellutino, Steger, De Setto and Phillips (1975), Vellutino, Steger, Kaman and De Setto (1975), Vellutino, Harding *et al.* (1975) and Rudel *et al.* (1976). This is based on research where children are given both verbal and non-verbal association tasks whereby they have to learn a nonsense syllable and associate it with a cartoon, or with a novel script. Typically, dyslexic children are found to have problems where visual – verbal learning is required. Furthermore Vellutino suggests that as the dyslexics make more real-word substitutions (e.g. *fog* for *mog*) than controls (who make errors such as *mog/yog*), the dyslexic children have more difficulty in coding phonetically. (This is because in reading these nonsense syllables they are perhaps guessing to produce real words, rather than analysing the sound symbol associations.) Vellutino also cites Blank and Bridger (1964 and 1966) where poor readers have difficulty in verbal classification. He argues that the verbal problem is not conceptual, as the children have good intelligences, but it is in abstracting and generalizing verbal information in tasks such as transfer of learning, and is a subtle language deficit that hampers visual-to-verbal integration.

3.36 Phonological processing

This section focuses mainly on the mediational aspect of the stage analysis model of the reading process outlined on page 88. There is good evidence to suggest that to progress beyond a simple sight vocabulary in reading, i.e. to read complex orthography and develop fluent reading, one needs to decode the visual input (i.e. the letters and the words which are visually presented) into a sound or possibly a speech-based code. This has a number of functions. One is being able to read unfamiliar words and indeed to read nonsense words. However another important function is to enable the visual input to be kept in a holding or short-term memory store in order for the whole of the sentence to be processed syntactically and semantically, i.e. for comprehension to take place. This has obvious implications for some of the short-term memory and sequencing difficulties mentioned, and can be illustrated in Figure 3.7.

This assumption of phonological coding is one over which controversy has arisen amongst the proponents of different theories of the normal reading process. The ability to perform non-lexical phonological encoding is clearly present in the normal reader, otherwise it would be impossible to read non-words or words not previously known to the reader. The question then arises of whether phonological encoding is a necessary stage in the reading of known real words. Some theories of the reading process (e.g. Rubenstein *et al.* 1971) propose that the only mode of access to the internal lexicon is via the phonological representation. Others (e.g. the feature redundancy model proposed by Smith 1971) suggest that, for fluent readers

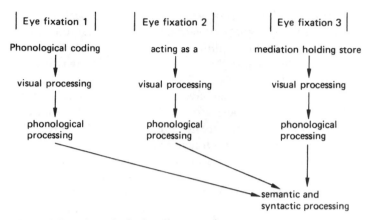

Figure 3.7   Phonological coding as a short-term store

at least, intermediate letter and word recognition need not occur, as meaning is directly accessible from the graphemic representation. Coltheart (1978) and Coltheart *et al*. (1980) argue for the independent functioning of the two routes, citing evidence relating to the performance of normal readers as well as evidence from neuropsychological studies.

In addition to this translation of visual symbols into a phonological code, another important aspect of this mediation stage of reading is phonemic segmentation. In particular Liberman and Shankweiler (1978), Liberman (1971), Mattingly (1972), Savin (1972), and Rozin and Gleitman (1977) argue that decoding printed symbols and establishing phonetic or sound representations of these symbols are key factors relating to the awareness of linguistic structures in speech. This linguistic awareness suggests reading as being secondary to spoken language, and in particular it is the explicit knowledge of phonetic structure that is required if one is to match alphabet symbols to sounds. It is argued that being able to discern that words can be segmented into phonemes, and that graphemes represent these phonemes is an important link between speech and reading and in the development of early reading behaviour. For example it is argued that there is a great difference between distinguishing words such as *pin/pen,* compared to understanding that each word is made up of three independent discrete phoneme units, rather than one acoustic segment. This understanding is a crucial phonemic skill upon which are based phonological strategies in reading. It is an important component of later reading and takes the child beyond simple sight vocabulary and word recognition.

At the simplest level, there is evidence that dyslexic children have difficulty in providing a verbal label or name for visually presented material. Typically (e.g. Denckla and Rudel 1976a, b) the tasks involve rapid naming of stimulus material. For example, the researchers asked the children to name black and white drawings, and it was found that the dyslexics made more errors as well as having longer response latencies. Denckla and Rudel argue that the dyslexics were 'subtly dysphasic'. A later study presented colours, high-frequency lower-case letters, common objects and numerals. Here there were no differences in errors betwen dyslexics and controls, but the dyslexics overall were much slower, particularly in object naming. Denckla and Rudel argue that this slow naming was not due to a generalized 'slowness' in dyslexics, as they scored perfectly well, and indeed rather better, on the timed-test items on the Wechsler Performance Scale. Somewhat similar studies have been undertaken by Spring and Capps (1974) and Spring (1976) in which dyslexics were given rapid naming tasks, and various digit span tasks. The finding here was that dyslexics were slower, as well as being poor on digit span. Spring argues that these difficulties are due to a slow speech-to-motor encoding ability, and that a greater encoding ability would give rise to an improved memory span. The reasoning behind this is that if there is a delay in speech-to-motor encoding, there would be less time for rehearsal, and therefore less time to transfer information to short-term memory. This of course applies to visual – verbal encoding of material such as letters and words. Spring (1976) however found that not only did the slowness of naming tasks account for the variance in his experiments, but also that digit span *per se* accounted for some variance, and therefore speed in naming appeared to be strongly correlated with the recall of digits and possibly short-term memory span overall (see also Eakin and Douglas 1971 and Denckla 1972).

Another experimental paradigm in this context is the use of the 'Posner' task. This investigates the differential coding strategies that are used in identifying, for example, letters. Typically, subjects are given pairs of letters which are physically or nominally matched, for example, AA or Aa. In the former case, all that is required for the subject to recognize that the two letters are the same is a physical match. For the subject to decide that Aa are the same he must name or nominally match (linked to a sound code). Supramaniam and Audley (1976) found that poor readers took much longer to make nominal matches. More systematic studies on this have been undertaken by Ellis and Miles (1978, 1981). They review studies on visual recall, and then present data from their own studies on coding tasks. They argue that there are no difficulties in visual coding, visual code capacity or rate of decay of the visual code in dyslexic children. However they argue for a naming deficiency. It is argued that if the dyslexics have difficulty in naming the word dog as well as naming the *picture* of a dog the difficulty cannot solely be at the level of graphemic pattern recognition for words. They point out that there are no differences found between dyslexics and control groups in non-namable material, as illustrated by Blank and Bridger (1966), Blank *et al*. (1968) and their own studies on the Posner type tasks, where there were no differences in physical or visual matching.

Ellis and Miles argue that the naming difficulties are lexical (i.e. relate to the generation of words or symbols) rather than articulatory (i.e. relating to motor speech patterns). This is based on evidence by Ellis (1980) who suggests that in the tasks used the children were not affected by articulatory suppression. (This is a technique whereby the subject says irrelevant words out aloud so that he cannot use an articulatory based coding strategy.) However, Spring and Capps (1974) claim that the difficulty *is* based on an articulatory naming code problem. The notion here relates to the theoretical model of an articulatory rehearsal loop (Baddeley and Hitch 1974). This is equivalent to a memory span for speech coding and is a temporary storage of phonemic information during reading. Ellis (1981a) reaffirms that he believes the difficulty to be phonological and lexical and suggests a double impairment. The first is in relation to the retrieval of phonology or the application of phoneme and grapheme rules and the second to lexical access and lexical retrieval of pronunciation. These are important studies and interpretations and the reader is referred to the references for more details of the experimental procedures involved.

Frith (1981) intimates that these two interpretations are really part of an overall hypothesis. She suggests that the 'weak' hypothesis argues for a phonological deficit in dyslexics, whereas the 'strong' hypothesis argues for a speech-motor programming deficit, i.e. that dyslexia is some kind of subtype of speech difficulty. This of course relates to an alphabetic system of written language where there is sound/symbol correspondence translation required, as opposed to a logographic system where one can go straight from picture to meaning. The implications for our written language system will be examined in more detail in the next chapter.

Even material thought to be measuring visual memory may sometimes be related to this notion of naming deficits. For example, Hicks (1980) provides evidence that the visual sequential memory subtest of the ITPA does not always measure visual memory but could relate to verbal strategies. First of all she divided a group of normal children into those who used name-coding as opposed to visual-coding strategies and then provided both groups with verbal labels to describe the visual symbols used in this particular test. She found that there was a great improvement in the performance of those who had been visual coders and were now able to use verbal labels. She found that dyslexic children almost invariably used a visual strategy, which she had shown to be inefficient, and on being given an appropriate verbal labelling strategy improved their performance on the test. She argues that the difficulties relate to translating of visual-to-verbal information in short-term memory.

Snowling (1981a) gave dyslexics a reading *and* speaking task. The reading task involved one-syllable non-words and there was no difference between dyslexics and controls, but if there were two-syllable non-words dyslexics were much poorer, particularly if there were a greater number of consonant clusters. These were nonwords such as *molsmit*, and *bigbert*. The importance of using these nonsense words is that this forces the subject to use phoneme – grapheme correspondence rules or a phonological route to read them. They cannot go direct from visual input to meaning. The dyslexics furthermore were more affected by phonological complexity, and when required to say nonsense words had difficulties in articulating them. This, she argued, was a phonemic difficulty based possibly on motor programming in speech. In relation to the speaking tasks she controlled for familiarity by using nonsense words derived from real words, for example, *pedestrian/kebestrian*. Montgomery (1981) also argues that dyslexics have difficulty in articulation and phoneme segmentation. This was based on a task where children had to identify, by indicating which of a number of drawings represented the position of the lips, tongue and other articulators for a given phoneme. She found that it was the awareness of articulation rather than articulation *per se* that differentiated dyslexics and controls.

Shankweiler and Liberman (1972) suggest that dyslexics treat words as unit syllables rather than as containing component parts of the alphabet and Liberman *et al.* (1974) present evidence to suggest one problem amongst poor readers is the difficulty in phonemic segmentation. The problem is isolating phonemes in single-syllable words as well as phonological recoding in short-term memory. This is based on experiments in which they presented rhyming and non-rhyming consonants (e.g. d/g as against d/l). Liberman *et al.* (1977), for example, asked for recall of visually presented consonants which, on the basis of their rhyming, were similar or dissimilar in sound. The argument here is based on Conrad (1964). If the subject is using a phonological, sound or speech-based code he will tend to make more errors when the stimulus material sounds similar, is acoustically confusable or, in this case, rhyming. The results of this and similar studies undertaken by these workers indicated that dyslexics or retarded readers had no difference in recall between the rhyming and non-rhyming words, whereas control groups had greater difficulty in recalling rhyming or acoustically confusable words and letters. This suggested that they were using a speech or auditory based code. Shankweiler and Libermann (1978) found similar results in auditory presentation, and Mark *et al.* (1977) found a similar pattern of results with words. They argue for a phonological memory coding difficulty, i.e. difficulties in employing a phonetic code for effective processing in short-term memory.

Fox and Routh (1980) also argue for a defect in phonemic analysis. They found their disabled readers were unable to segment spoken syllables into individual speech sounds. They suggest problems in word attack skills, particularly in segmenting words into syllables and then syllables into phonemes. Bradley and Bryant (1981) also present data suggesting that dyslexics (or retarded readers at least) have difficulty in detection of rhyme and alliteration, suggesting some kind of phonemic confusion. Legein and Bouma (1981), and Bouma and Legein (1980) suggest difficulties in translating visual information into a speech code. This is based on both foveal and parafoveal recognition involving brief presentation to avoid eye movements. They suggest that visual and articulatory codes are robust, but phonological or sound based codes are deficient in dyslexics. Snowling (1980) gave reading-age matched controls and dyslexics a grapheme-to-phoneme task based on recognition memory for pronounceable non-words which were presented in visual or auditory modalities. These were then required to be recognized in the opposite modality involving decoding across modalities. (She also included a within-modality condition as a control.) She found that the use of grapheme-to-phoneme conversion rules increased with age in the controls but not in the dyslexic group, and that furthermore the dyslexics' reading was based on an increase in their sight vocabulary. The interpretation of this was that dyslexics were mainly reading in a grapheme-to-semantic (direct visual) route, because they have grapheme-to-phoneme or phonological code difficulty. Similar results to Snowling's have been reported by Hicks (1981) in relation to b/d identification. Here the sound/visual coding of b/d in its various forms was presented to dyslexics and controls. It was found that there were deficits in dyslexics in translating the visual input into sound code or name, rather than in visual matching *per se*.

Olson *et al.* (1984) found that this phonetic confusability in rhyming material increased in age for dyslexics but decreased in normal readers. Snowling (1987) argues on the basis of these data that there may be delayed use in the development of the phonological code. Bryant and Bradley (1985) report, in their longitudinal study on 4 year olds, that the ability to pick out rhymes or alliteration (i.e. first letter sounds) was a good predictor of reading ability, independent of IQ and mathematical ability.

These and the other studies mentioned earlier all point to problems in the area of grapheme/phoneme translation phonological coding. This is particularly important in relation to so-called routes to reading and the examination of the written language system and its task demands on the dyslexic child (see Chapter 4).

Now that we have considered some of the evidence in this kind of area, we are in a position to examine some possible mechanisms. Farnham-Diggory and Gregg (1975) suggest that the following processes are involved in aspects of phonetic coding and reading.

1 Visual segmentation and attention
2 Retrieval of auditory associations to the visual component from long-term memory
3 The placement of that association into short-term memory, while attending to the next segment of the word
4 Proceeding sequentially until the end of the word, where the auditory 'particles' are retrieved from long-term memory and then combined

These operations require chunking, i.e. putting together individual or discrete items, whether these be visual or auditory components, into larger units, or in letter combinations which are perceived and matched to an auditory counterpart. Memory span and short-term visual and auditory analysis is also required. The idea that letter-clustering identification representing one 'chunk' of information is intermediate between the alphabet and a whole word is of course related to the notion of redundancy in written language (Gibson 1970, Scheerer-Neuman 1978). By redundancy here we mean that various letter combinations are highly likely to occur in proximity in the English language and therefore we do not need to decode each one individually. Thomson (1979d) found dyslexics to be specifically unable to make use of sequential redundancy in recognition of letter-trigrams. This was related to Smith's models of the reading process where it was argued that the dyslexics were at a stage of using a mediated code, i.e. having to translate each single letter into a sound equivalent rather than being able to use chunking stra-tegies.

Difficulties in the development of grapheme/phoneme correspondence, and impairment in the development of phonological recoding strategies would make it difficult to decode novel words, hence the difficulties dyslexics have with reading. In addition there will be difficulties in retrieving names, and in retaining patterns in relation to phonemic segmentation. The internalization (i.e. relationship to speech sound) of spelling rules or spelling patterns may not have taken place. This failure to internalize spelling patterns, phoneme/grapheme rules, or sequential redundancy, might be due to the failure to transfer this information to long-term memory owing to short-term memory deficits of various sorts, or it might be due to the inefficiency of sound coding in the first place, the information never entering short-term memory let alone being transferred into a long-term memory system. At a simpler level, verbal short-term memory difficulties give rise to problems in phonic blending due to the inability to retain sounds, as well as problems in retaining correct sequence and thus correct pronunciation.

The extent to which the above difficulties can be described as 'phonological process' or 'short-term memory' is a debatable point. Authors such as Snowling (1987) and Bryant and Bradley (1985) make much of the notion of the former as being the main area of weakness. One's own clinical and teaching experience when asking children to remember instructions, remembering where items are around the school and in remembering things that have been taught from lesson to lesson quite clearly point to some weakness in the short-term memory system. Perhaps this is not a real argument, in the sense that phonological processing is quite clearly linked to short-term memory anyway. Ellis (1988), in a longitudinal study taken of children as they are developing their reading process, comments that the acquisition of reading activates phonological processes within short-term memory.

3.37   Syntactic, semantic and lexical factors

We now turn to a brief examination of 'higher order' linguistic functions which we mentioned in our stage analysis model. This is where there is an increasing overlap between spoken and written language, as obviously the semantic and syntactic functions of language are equivalent in both cases. As well as examining syntactic and semantic functions we shall be looking at the notion of lexical access.

Written language is usually seen as secondary to spoken language and one would expect any deficits in syntax to manifest themselves in written language learning also. By definition however dyslexia does not include a gross disability in spoken language and the reader is referred to other books in this series for descriptions of reading and spelling difficulties arising out of a spoken language disorder. However it is possible that there may be subtle difficulties in being sensitive to syntax, and certainly syntactic development is not totally complete when the child learns to read, see e.g. Loban (1963) and Chomsky (1972). In particular Loban's longitudinal study found that there were various linguistic difficulties in poor readers prior to their reading difficulty becoming manifest.

An example to illustrate the relation between possible syntactic difficulties and dyslexic problems is a study by Fry et al. (1970). This examined a group of 7-8-year-old children, and analysed an oral sample based on their description of pictures. They examined communication units, grammatical clauses including modifiers, and the use of transformational rules by the children. They found that the control group had larger speaking vocabularies, and a greater fluency in description of the pictures in terms of output and word categories used. The control group also used a greater syntactic complexity, whereas poor readers tended to use more so-called 'existence' sentences, i.e. simple basic descriptions without detail. The best predictors of reading were the number of different words used, the use of clauses, and predicate positions. In relation to transformational grammar poor readers tended to have poor morphological use, particularly in a greater incidence of subject – verb disagreements as well as using simpler transformational structures. It should be noted that these children were matched on intelligence. Fry *et al.* argued that the less sophisticated use of language gave a smaller number and variety of verbal labels and mediators for coding in relation to the reading process. This links nicely with the previous section in relation to difficulties in verbal labelling or phonological verbal mediation.

There are a few studies specifically in relation to morphological rules, these tending to use the well known measures of the use of rules described by Berko (1958). Brittain (1970) for example found a high correlation between morphological use and reading, and indeed this correlation was higher than between reading and intelligence. Wiig *et al.* (1973) found 9-year-old reading retardates not only were poorer on the use of morphological rules, but tended to produce idiosyncratic and unpredictable kinds of responses, unlike the control group where there was a much clearer pattern of response. Vogel (1974) in a comprehensive study also examined aspects of morphology, various linguistic structures, and use of closure. It was generally concluded that dyslexics were inferior on the use of structural morphology, although it should be noted that this was based on some experimental work rather than a typical linguistic analysis. Clay and Imlach (1971) found poor readers made little use of supra-segmental features such as pitch, stress and so on in word reading. This, they argued, suggested that the children missed out on important linguistic cues.

In relation to aspects of semantic processes, i.e. the extraction of meaning, whether from a single word in a text, we have some evidence which is worth reviewing here. The majority of it however concerns the role of semantic processing in general language functions, for example the interrelationship between deep and surface structures. There is also a good deal of work in relation to semantic processing in the normal reading process, or in groups of unclassified poor readers rather than dylsexics. In particular Goodman (1969), Smith (1971) and Kolers (1975) argue that it is the inability to derive meaning from text which is important in reading difficulties. They argue that phonological or articulatory mediation, i.e. translating the visual input into a sound or speech-based code, is an unnecessary component of reading, and that poor readers have difficulty with reading because they tend to use this kind of strategy. It is suggested that poor readers have problems with comprehension due to poor decoding.

However clinical experience shows that dyslexic children do quite well at comprehension aspects of reading. This is despite very poor decoding skills, and indeed if one supplies the correct words the child has no difficulty in understanding what is meant. Waller (1976) gave reading-disabled children texts based on sentences altered in various ways but with the meaning retained. He found that the retarded readers were unable to remember the exact verbal string (including things such as syntactic markers, tense, and plurality) as well as controls, yet were able to remember the content perfectly well. Golinkoff and Rosinski (1976) found that reading-disabled children were slower on individual word decoding than on understanding based on a semantic interference task.

Perfetti and Lesgold (1978), and Perfetti and Goldman (1976), argued that difficulties in reading and listening comprehension are due to poor coding of information phonetically. In other words there is an equivalence between naming and meaning, as semantic responses are acquired through naming. This then, it is suggested, results from information-processing and short-term memory abilities. For example, remembering word strings verbatim, or remembering specific words and word parts, results in the child being slow to reach a point in comprehension where the exact wording is not needed. So not only is the child poor in exact wording but never reaches a stage of being able to paraphrase and read for meaning directly. This is based on selecting children who were poor on reading comprehension, and suggests a mechanism focusing on the interrelationship between comprehension and some of the mediational, phonological and coding strategies that we have outlined in previous sections. In a series of studies it was argued that there was a specific short-term memory verbal-encoding difficulty, and that poor readers have difficulties in developing effective, immediately accessed linguistic codes. It is difficulties in rapid coding into a short-term memory that result in the children being unable to access higher-order semantic information, rather than actually having difficulty in the latter *per se*.

A further important skill is the use of an internal lexicon or dictionary. This is a series of words stored in long-term memory which need to be accessed to match to the input. There must be some kind of word recognition system therefore which links to a 'semantic' system. The question here is how lexical codes become available. In particular Ellis and Miles (1981) and Ellis (1980) argue that this is a very important component of dyslexic learning problems. They rely heavily on Morton's (1977, 1979, 1980) logogen model of the reading process. Simply, this system suggests that a 'logogen' is essentially a pattern recognizer for words for various inputs. Ellis and Miles suggest the following. (1) Irregular words can be pronounced reliably only if they are in the lexicon (this is because phonological rules enable pronunciation of regular words, but not irregular words). (2) An 'orthographic' strategy of reading requires articulation and some kind of auditory input-pattern recognizer (logogen) before words can be recognized. (3) The visual input-pattern recognizer (logogen), when used in reading, shows a frequency effect (namely high-frequency words are recognized much more quickly than low-frequency words). (4) Non-words can only be processed by the logogen at a lower level and not in direct relation to meaning. They describe the reading process as follows: the child hears and develops a spoken vocabulary whereby there is a direct route from auditory processing to semantic (meaningful) aspects and then to auditory articulatory output. The child then learns to match visual symbols with their spoken equivalent, or he is taught an orthographic strategy which allows him to sound out the correct word to himself. This is therefore mediated by the auditory processing system, his internal speech mechanism making understanding possible. It is argued that the development of visual processing and relating *that* to meaning is dependent on a link between the visual processing logogens and output logogens. This takes the following kind of route: (i) visual input and visual coding, (ii) links to some kind of speech-based output logogen, (iii) links to an articulatory code before speech output actually occurs, (iv) a link to an auditory input logogen, i.e. the auditory processing aspect, and (v) finally to the semantic system (see Chapter 4 for more details of Morton's model).

Deficiences in relation to dyslexia involve tasks which require verbalization, as has been described in the previous section. We would expect deficiences in the so-called visual logogen in dyslexics to affect the information available to the output logogen system and the information to the semantic system. Essentially Ellis and Miles are arguing for difficulties in lexical access, i.e. in word-coding strategies, and some kind of 'disconnection' syndrome. In other words there is a discon- nection between visual-information processing and its auditory equivalent and the subsequent link to the semantic system, requiring lexical access or lexical coding. Although this approach relies heavily on a theoretical and abstract model, and seems unnecessarily complex in many ways, Miles and Ellis (1981) claim that this 'lexical encoding' theory does account for many features of dyslexia. For example the difficulties in dyslexics are not just in reading, but in handling verbalized material, and their theory predicts a slow rate of assimilation of verbal infor- mation. Similarly it would predict greater difficulties in verbal paired-associated learning as has been found by, for example, Done and Miles (1978), and Thomson and Wilsher (1979). Miles and Ellis argue that, in classroom terms, the child requires longer to learn. This might account for some of the difficulties in naming, and the idea of lexical encoding (i.e. visual stimuli being transformed into a lexical entry) might account for difficulties in new complex material becoming mean- ingful. Miles and Ellis then go on to describe other clinical features that they argue might be accounted for by a lexical encoding theory. While some of these are sug- gestive, they seem to the writer to be confused with other simpler notions such as naming problems or short-term memory deficits. For example, they describe the persistence of confusions of b and d in the older dyslexic children as resulting from a lexical encoding problem. However this could quite simply be seen as difficulties in naming responses, i.e. it is not that the child confuses what b and d look like, but they cannot remember what particular sound code to attach to that shape. Although this does seem to be phonological encoding, it does not seem to relate to word or lexical access.

To summarize this section, there is some evidence for certain kinds of semantic and syntactic processing difficulties in dyslexic children, but these do not appear to be very severe. An important consideration is that of cause and effect. Obviously a child who is poor at reading may not develop certain kinds of sophisticated lin- guistic strategies in his reading because of a paucity of reading experience. If one is unable to decode words, how can one make use of redundancy in reading for meaning, or develop appropriate comprehension strategies? All these arguments need to be taken into account if one is trying to postulate some kind of fundamental deficit in respect to higher-order language which may be deficient, rather than demonstrable difficulties in aspects of coding and memory which we have reviewed.

3.4   Summary

This chapter has reviewed some of the more important pieces of research evidence that relate to the etiology of dyslexia. It cannot be claimed that this review is exhaustive, but if nothing else it should have given the reader some idea of the complexities of the issues facing this search for causes.

In relation to the neurological perspective we saw initially that acquired dyslexia does not clearly relate to developmental dyslexia. The electroencephalograph data, both resting records as well as evoked responses, while providing some interesting and suggestive information in terms of the direct physiological mechanisms of brain functions involved, are disappointingly unclear in relation to developmental dyslexia. This is mainly due to confusions over subject definition, as well as considerable debate as to appropriate technology and techniques at the present time. However there were strong suggestions of links between hemisphere function and dyslexia. These were examined in more detail by reviewing studies using dichotic listening and divided visual field techniques. It appears that there is some kind of association between dyslexia and 'abnormal' or certainly 'different' neurological functioning. The word *functioning* is stressed here, as we are not necessarily talking about anatomical differences. It was concluded that dyslexic difficulties might be due to either a left-hemisphere deficit, or possibly some kind of disconnection syndrome between normal processing for auditory material with abnormal processing for visual material. Another possibility which cannot be ruled out is a lag in the maturation of left-hemisphere function for language.

In the cognitive perspective, evidence was reviewed suggesting that the early notions of some kind of visual-perceptual difficulties were open to serious criticism, as were some of the notions of visuo-motor performance difficulties, and inter-sensory integration at least in the form as described in earlier research. However it would appear that *some* dyslexic children might have primary difficulties in these visuo-motor areas.

Eye movement research was also reviewed, and although there are some researchers arguing for primary difficulties in this area, it was concluded that eye movement and eye sequencing difficulties were secondary to the primary problem in decoding the visual symbols into sound, i.e. to the reading process itself. There was a good deal of evidence for difficulties in serial and sequencing skills, particularly where sound encoding is involved. These difficulties were usually associated with some kind of short-term memory problem.

In relation to memory, there is good evidence for weakness here—possibly a memory capacity difficulty in dyslexics, but more likely to be difficulties in short-term strategies used. There is a point where perception, coding and memory overlap with each other; it was suggested that many of the difficulties in aspects of sequencing and memory as cited above relate to verbal encoding and verbal processing. Dyslexic children do not appear to have a general verbal processing difficulty in the sense of being unable to understand or use language, but have difficulties related to various strategies or translating visual input into sound-based or verbal codes. Specifically, aspects of phonological and sound coding were examined in some detail. It appeared that there were difficulties in aspects of segmentation, translation of visual symbols into sound codes, and possibly in translating visual symbols into some kind of articulatory code. Here it was suggested by some authors that there was an overlap between dyslexia and aspects of speech disorders. Certainly there is very strong evidence for some kind of phonological/phonemic/verbal coding difficulty in dyslexic children. This, in many ways, was quite clearly related to problems in using a verbal phonological code in short-term memory, with consequent resulting deficits in the reading, writing and spelling process. Some suggestions on these lines were made. What seems to differ amongst authors in this particular area was the terminology used to describe the deficit. In relation to higher-order language functions these seem to relate to difficulties in coding, although there was some suggestion of problems in lexical or word access and its relation to the semantic system.

4

Dyslexia as a phenomenon of written language

The purpose of this chapter is to place dyslexia in the context of the demands of written language in order that we may pin-point the exact nature of the difficulty facing the child.

4.1 Some features of written language

4.11 Alphabet/symbols

Spoken language is probably commensurate with man as a species, and according to Lenneberg (1967) has biological foundations. The ability to associate sound or visual symbols for communication purposes is not unique to man, of course, but what appears to be unique is the ability to evoke a visual image or cue, with a specific reference, in the absence of the original object. The written alphabet is also very young in historical terms, and one can trace modern writing systems to a few thousand years ago (Gelb 1952). According to Fries (1962), learning to read is a process of transferring the sounds of a message or signal to new signs for the same signals. Written language is therefore a symbolic behaviour, and thus dyslexia is a symbol making disorder. We can view reading (and written language) as part of the general language process, but with particular features.

An important element in western orthography is its alphabetic nature, i.e. vocal signals are made up of recognizable collections of sound contrasts, or phonemes. These segments of sound are strung together sequentially, in what Fries (1962) calls a sequence of phoneme contrasts, to form words. Each language has a finite number of sound contrasts or phonemes; English has about 40 (Lindgren 1965). As we have seen, many dyslexics have difficulty in discriminating between phonemes, particularly vowels, with consequent confusion in their written language. Phonemes in addition may be classified as to whether they are formed by distinctive features which occur in articulatory and/or acoustic functioning. A set of contrasts or features which could characterize the phonemes of all languages can be devised (see Jakobsen et al. 1963).

A segment of sound has phonemic function if it differs from other sounds by at least one distinctive feature.

The order in which sounds are put together to form words, is rule-governed—certain sounds may go together in a sequence, others may not. The legality of sounds depends on their position in words, as well as on morpheme and syllable

121

boundaries. It would appear in general that the spoken language use of phonemes is acquired at a young age, and most children have acquired the use of these structures before they meet the written language system (e.g. Messer 1967, Menyuk 1971). Nevertheless, it is the transfer of these skills to written language which presents a problem for many children.

Another important consideration is the 'arbitrariness' of our written language system. In other words, we use only 26 basic line drawings, or letters, which are combined to represent meanings. Thus when communicating concepts in written form the conventions used are unrelated to the actual event. For example, when communicating the concept of a furry, feline animal used as a pet, we do not draw a picture of a cat; we write instead the symbols *c a t* which have no direct correspondence with the event itself. Other systems are different; there being three main types of writing system—(1) word syllabic (2) syllabic and (3) alphabetic (Gelb 1952). Chinese writing is logographic (word syllabic), and generally a character stands for an object or an event. Some examples of Chinese writing are given in Figure 4.1.

The important point here is that not only do these ideographs have their origins in concrete events or actual picture writing as shown in Figure 4.1, but also that they may be read in any language, i.e. whether German, French, Japanese or English, the appropriate word may be used to describe that particular pictogram. Some languages are mid-way between a pictogram and alphabetic system. For example, Japanese has two broad kinds of syllables—Hiragana and Katakana. The Hiragana is a set of phonetic symbols equivalent to a syllable unit. It has alphabetical connotation in the sense that additions of various sounds or phonemes can change the meaning. For example the symbol for AI means love, whereas that for KAI means shellfish—this is similar to aspects of English where letter patterns have different lexical connotations depending on the letter environment in which they find themselves. It is possible to write Japanese using only syllables, but quite often Chinese-originated characters, called Kanji are used. Kanji provides the base

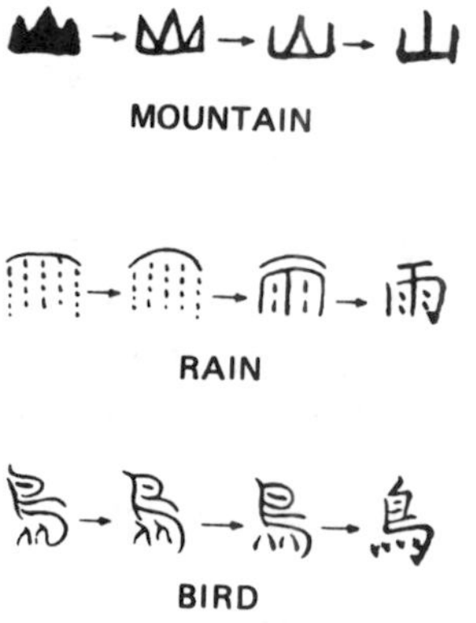

MOUNTAIN

RAIN

BIRD

Figure 4.1 Examples of Chinese phonograms, showing iconic origins (Tzeng and Hung, 1980)

forms of the morphemes, and the syllabaries are used for grammatical markers. The Kanji are very similar to the ideographs shown in Figure 4.1, in the sense that they are iconic.

Some important points arise from a comparison of the various systems. The alphabetic system used in the western world is a combinatorial one; the graphemes and phonemes must be combined to produce words, and thus meanings. It is the phoneme sequence which distinguishes the meanings rather than a unique ideograph or syllabary. A Chinese ideogram may translate into a word or phrase in English. A syllabic sign corresponds to a larger phonological unit than a letter. Combined Kanji and Hiragana is reported to be easier to read than syllabary alone, as the ideographs provide salient graphic units in the test (Sakamoto and Makita 1973). Gibson and Levin (1975 p. 165) comment:

> these findings do not mean that the process of reading is not influenced by the nature of the writing system, but that the outcomes are alike. It seems reasonable that different writing systems which relate to language at different levels will involve attention to and abstraction of different aspects of the orthograhic system. . . . But the skilled readers of one system are able to read as efficiently as skilled readers of another.

A key phrase here is 'different aspects of the orthographic system', because when turning to dyslexic difficulties the situation is somewhat different. Makita (1968) comments on the comparative rarity of reading disorders in Japan, and furthermore (Makita 1974) describes the occurrence of dyslexia amongst children taught only Kanji, or only Katakana script, a much higher incidence of dyslexia is found in the syllabic script (Katakana). He suggests that in Katakana the mode of cognition is similar to decoding and perceiving visual symbols and phonemes. However in Kanji visual perception rests upon a symbol carrying meaning, and is comprehended directly. Rozin *et al.* (1971) showed that dyslexic children (English speakers) could more easily learn Chinese characters.

Sakamoto and Makita (1973) report neurological evidence that in injury to the left hemisphere of the brain the ability to read Katakana is lost before the ability to read Kanji. Geschwind (1962) reported findings by Japanese neurologists that the nature of the writing systems was critical. Thus injury to Broca's area of the left hemisphere resulted in loss of Katakana (syllabic), whereas injury to Wernicke's area results in loss of Kanji (Broca's area involves sound-producing functions, and Wernicke's area comprehension or meaning-related aspects of language.) In addition some recent evidence (Tzeng and Hung 1980) suggests that one finds right visual field advantages for Katakana script, and a trend for left visual advantages for Kanji. The implication here of course is that Katakana has been processed as a left-hemisphere, language or symbolic kind of skill, whereas the pictogram script is being processed as a spatial task. Tzeng and Hung do however make the point that Chinese characters require speech coding of some sort, although not in the same way as a syllabary or alphabetic system might.

Another characteristic of alphabetic systems is remoteness from the perceptual picture of the world which the young child has built up over the first five years of his life. Any basic psychology book will describe the importance of perceptual constancies in the development of a stable perceptual world. Shape constancy for example enables us to retain the central concept of an object in space remaining immutable as an object, despite the fact that its appearance as manifested on the retina will change radically depending on its orientation. This is illustrated in Figure 4.2.

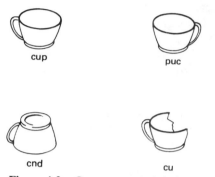

Figure 4.2   Concrete and alphabet representations of 'cup'

The situation when the object is presented in written language form is different, however, as the different orientations of symbols can give us nonsensical represent-ation. This could present considerable confusion to any young learner but *remains* a difficulty for the dyslexic. The matter is further complicated due to many of the 26 symbols used in English being mirror-imaged, or reversed/inverted forms, e.g. b/d/p/q/g; m/w; h/y; s/z; t/f; n/u and many symbols also look or sound alike—a/o, u/o, u/v. Money (1966) suggests that many of the above features such as object constancy, directionality and phoneme-to-grapheme matching are all important components of dyslexic difficulties in relation to left/right processing.

4.12   Orthography

Liberman *et al*. (1980) argue that reading and writing needs (1) phonological matu-rity, and more importantly, (2) the ability to segment orthography and speech. Phonological maturity is the skill of linking an abstract orthography to the phonetic structure which it conveys. Here the reader needs to recognize the written word as equivalent to the lexical store in long-term memory. There must be an orthographic transcription which is equivalent to representation of words in the mental lexicon—they suggest that this might be morphophonological. Here the word is conveyed in a sequence of systematic phonemes divided into constituent morphemes, distinct from pronunciation. They argue that children have immature phonology in the sense that they do not know that representations of words in their personal lexicon match the transcriptions of orthography. Segmentation in ortho-graphy and speech requires a *linguistic awareness* that speech is divisible into pho-nological segments, which represent letters (or syllables). There is a difference between individual alphabet sounds making up the word, and the sound of the word itself. For example, *dog* is made up of one sound, but has three phonological or orthographic segments. The skill here is to know how to divide the sound into three segments. This seems weak in dyslexics (see previous chapter).

This analysis of language into linguistic segments (sentences, phrases, words, syllables and phonemes) is paralleled by the written text, with the difference being that letters and letter clusters are the orthographic units equivalent to the phonemes. The learning of the correspondence between spoken and written forms of language is an important aspect of beginning reading. Thus a child who has not abstracted sets of features and contexts making up the phoneme will find difficulty in learning letter/phoneme correspondences. The ability of children to segment speech into phonemes, syllables and words is thus of some importance. A number of studies (e.g. Savin and Bever 1970, Bruce 1964) find that although children discriminate between distinctive features in usage of language, phonemic analysis is difficult. Instead the syllable unit is used, perhaps as Gibson and Levin (1975) suggest because 'the syllable has characteristics like the presence of stressed vowels and intersyllable pauses which facilitate an abstraction from the speech stress'. The above has implications for the dyslexic learner in that although phonemic analysis is not generally used, the ability to distinguish phonemes is a necessary precursor to syllabification. Chapter 3 reviewed evidence for phonological or phonemic weakness here.

Another aspect of orthography is that auditory/vocal activities occur through time as a sequence of units, unlike static spatial objects (pictures or relationships). This has the important consequence that many of the language conventions are related to the order in which similar sequential units occur, whether they are phonemes, morphemes, words or sentences. However letters and letter sequences do not have consistent phoneme realizations. Bannatyne (1971) states that in English orthography of the vowel phonemes (as distinct from letters), at least 12 can be spelt in eight or more different ways, and all the other phonemes have more than one grapheme equivalent. Furthermore many of the vowel graphemes are interchangeable. Thus the symbol 'a' can represent a minimum of seven separate phonemes, and the letter 'e' stands for seven phonemes, some in common with *a*. The possible permutation and combination of all phoneme/grapheme matchings runs into several hundred. As we have seen, the selection of symbols is arbitrary, and there are few rules to guide the young learner in the sequence of letter for each word. This is particularly difficult, as the letters are discrete or individual sounds which must be blended to form words. The phoneme/visual symbol associations must therefore be learned and remembered, and are difficult to work out from first principles.

There are of course some rules in the development of sound sequences, each language having legal or permissible sequences. In writing, orthographic rules govern sequences and groups. For example, q is followed by u to give /kw/. Other examples include consonant clusters that can appear only at the beginning or at the end of words, e.g. *tr* (beginning) or *ng* (end). There are two considerations in discussing this aspect of written language: (1) the legal letter sequences, and (2) the correspondence between these written sequences and spoken language. For example, Kyostio (1980) comments that Finnish has very close grapheme-to-phoneme correspondences, for example the phoneme /a/ is always spelt *a* whereas in English /a/ might be realized by *ai*, *ay*, *a*, *ea*, and so on. Nevertheless the important fact is that in Finnish one still finds dyslexic difficulties.

Frith (1985) suggests three phases and associated skills in the acquisition of written language—logographic (speech sounds/shapes), alphabetic (chunking letter sounds and morpheme identification) and orthographic (establishing the independence of written language). She argues that a developmental disorder is a failure to advance normally from one phase to another, and dyslexia is a failure to acquire alphabetic skills, with a 'tutored' dyslexic (i.e. one trained in phonics), retaining a partial failure of grapheme – phoneme correspondence rules.

4.2.   Models of the written language process

Having examined some various aspects of the written language system, we now turn to more formal models of the written language learning process. We have already considered one or two examples, particularly a general stage analysis model which we used to illustrate various levels of processing in cognitive terms. We also examined briefly a typical information processing model (Mackworth's). In particular, attention was drawn to the need for phonological coding, for feature analysis in visual perception, for short-term memory (sound coding and holding store), and access to higher-order language units.

4.21   'Psycholinguistic' approaches

The so called *psycholinguistic* approach reflects neo-behaviourist ideas (Osgood and Miron 1963) whereby processes are received and interpreted (decoded) and messages are conceived and articulated. These models were adapted by, for example, Kirk and Kirk (1971) to describe a clinical model of the communication processes which forms the basis of the Illinois Test of Psycholinguistic Abilities. Such models typically describe *levels* (automatic and representation); *processes* such as reception, association and expression and various *channels* or modalities through which information may pass, such as auditory, visual, tactile, motor and vocal. Reception is usually conceived as being sensory, and expression primarily motor. Examining these in any great detail is beyond the scope of this work, but it is worth noticing that of relevance to dyslexic difficulties are the automatic or sequential processes of closure and sequential memory (see also Chapter 5). Those aspects particularly relevant to written language include perceptual decoding in discrimination of sound−symbol systems (distinctive features), sequential memory in relation to sequence of graphemes, or phonemes and order in syntax. Bannatyne (1971) provides a summary of psycholinguistic schemes drawn from various sources. This is given in Table 4.1, with the writer's additions (italicized) to indicate relevance to (i) dyslexia and (ii) written language.

Table 4.1   Summary of psycholinguistic schema

3 Conceptualization representation	4 Thinking/relationship processing	5 Output concept/ imagery planning
Sensori-motor imagery (i) *Sound/symbol association* (ii) *Arbitrary symbols*	Active processing (logical?) of relationships between concepts and images (i) *Good spatial abilities poor verbal and serial abilities* (ii) *Relation of phonology/ graphemes to semantics*	Marshalling thoughts systematically, prior to encoding for communication (i) *Sequential thinking poor* (ii) *Deep structure transformed into ordered surface structure*
2 Identification recognition and recall of data	9 Memory	6 Programming output
Sensori-kinesthetic integration (i) *Difficulties in symbol recognition ie distinctive features* (ii) *Phonological and orthographic rules for distinctive features* Alphabetic system	Visual, auditory motor Kinesthetic/haptic Memory for units Memory for sequences Memory for chunks Short-term memory Long-term memory Recall memory Recognition memory Memory for content (items) Memory for system (relationships) (i) *Poor short term memory particularly for sequence, poor cross-modal integrations* (ii) *Combinatorial system of sequence phoneme/ grapheme*	Motor/kinesthetic sequencing of words Motor/kinesthetic sequencing of actions (i) *Poor sequencing and sometimes motor control/clumsiness* (ii) *Written orthography constrained/directional*
1 Active sensory reception	8 Primary sensori-motor coordination	7 Motor output
Data input; visual auditory, kinesthetic/ haptic (i) *Sensory mechanisms functioning normally* (ii) *Multi-sensory nature of written language*	Motor and sensory feedback between 1 and 7 (i) *Sound/symbol/motor integration often poor* (ii) *Phonemes graphemes meaning involving coordination of modalities*	Voice/vocal Handwriting Doing, action (i) *Motor control difficulties* (ii) *Graphic fluency*

(Modified from Bannatyne 1971)

4.22.   Smith's reading model

Smith (1971) proposes a distinctive-feature model in the identification of letters and words. He uses the term *feature* as an element of a stimulus which, if detected, permits the elimination of some of the alternative categories to which a stimulus might be allocated. He identifies three strategies involved in the reading process—immediate word identification, mediated word identification and comprehension. This is represented in Figure 4.3.

Immediate word identification proceeds directly from discrimination of the features in a visual array to allocation of the array to a category that has a name. This is a similar process to classification of visual stimuli on the basis of concepts. Mediated word identification involves the reader having to learn a category name (a unique cognitive grouping to which particular visual configurations can be allocated together with a name) by some mediating process. This may be phonic, i.e. sounding out, or could be allocation of the array to a category name. Once these relations have been established, the reader can construct a feature list for the named category, so that similar configurations may be allocated to the category in the future. Immediate comprehension involves going directly from the visual features to meaning. Meaning provides a guide to identification of words, as can be seen in a sentence such as 'we should read the minute print on the permit'. Only the meaning of the entire sequence indicates the syntactic role of individual words, which for some words is essential for any decision about intonation. Mediated comprehension requires the prior identification of words.

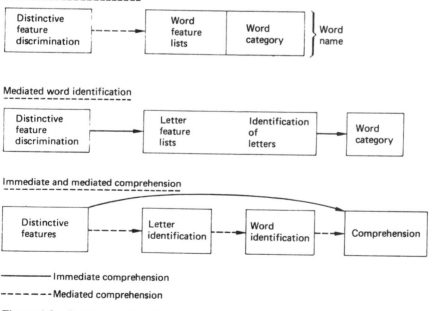

Figure 4.3   Summary of Smith's reading model

These strategies represent a continuum of different levels of skill. The skilled reader relies mainly on immediate comprehension, resorting to mediated processes only when confronted with difficulty or unfamiliar material. The beginning reader, however, has to use the mediated process and consequently his rate of progress is slower and there is a greater burden on his memory. In other words Smith is suggesting that fluent readers move from the surface structure of written language (distinctive features) directly to meaning, whereas beginner readers reach meaning via mediated processes.

4.23   'Phonological' and 'direct' routes to reading

Another way of looking at the written language process (in particular, the reading process), is in terms of possible routes which might be involved in lexical access. A typical model is that based on Marshall's (1982), represented in Figure 4.4.

Marshall argues that there are three routes to reading. Route A is the direct route, which one might describe as a sort of look-and-say approach. This implies that one goes direct from the visual analysis or visual input to meaning. Route B essentially is 'barking at print'. This implies that the individual is reading the words, but not understanding them, i.e. being able to pronounce them, but not representing them in a lexical or semantic system. Route C is the so called 'phonic' route. This involves converting visual representations into some kind of orthographic rule or grapheme – phoneme correspondence which can provide a response. Baron (1977) presents a similar kind of model, suggesting three types of codes: print, sound and meaning. Baron argues that two kinds of path from print

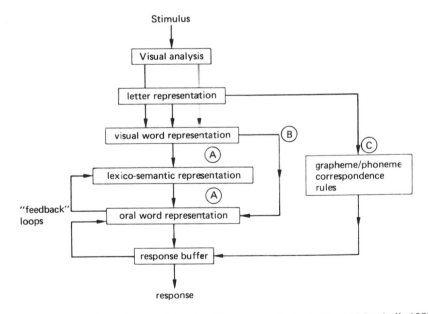

Figure 4.4   Model of word recognition/reading process (adapted from Marshall, 1982)

to sound can be distinguished. One links the whole printed word to the whole spoken word, and the other links part of the printed word (for example letters or groups of letters), to parts of the spoken word (for example, phonemes or groups of phonemes). This path may exist when there are rule-governed correspondences between spelling and sounds as in English.

This dichotomy between reading directly for meaning, and reading via phonological or grapheme rules, is sometimes described as reading like 'Chinese' or reading like 'Phoenicians' respectively. This is based on the idea that Chinese scripts are ideographic, going directly from ideogram to meaning, whereas the Phoenicians are credited with the introduction of alphabetic systems, requiring orthographic or grapheme – phoneme correspondence conversion rules. In relation to dyslexia the evidence we have examined in Chapter 3 suggests problems in grapheme – phoneme conversions, acquisition of orthographic rules, segmentation, verbal encoding, and so on. There do not appear to be any impairments in the visual route analysis stage, or presumably in the visual route to meaning, although this is less clear. In relation to Marshall's model it appears that there may be some difficulties in Route C for a dyslexic. Previously this is what Marshall suggests as equivalent to the surface dyslexic in the acquired dyslexia area (Section 3.1).

4.24   The logogen model

In its simplest form the Logogen Model developed by Morton (1977, 1979, 1980), and described by Morton and Patterson (1980), argues for a grapheme – phoneme conversion route, accessing a response buffer, with extra visual and auditory analyses into a cognitive system. The model is illustrated in Figure 4.5.

Logogens are 'evidence collectors with thresholds' (Morton 1980). When evidence has been collected beyond a certain threshold a code is output to another part of the system. Possible routes to reading can be traced from the visual analysis system to the response buffer which outputs phonological codes. The phonological route links the visual analysis system directly to the response buffer via a series of grapheme – phoneme conversions and is available for reading non-lexical letter strings. The visual input logogen system is a passive categorization system which receives information from the visual analysis system and outputs codes for words (logogens are only available for words and cannot be used for reading non-words). Where an input logogen has collected evidence in excess of a first threshold, it sends a code to the cognitive system, where the appropriate semantics can be found and sent to the output logogen, where a phonological code is obtained. Evidence beyond a second threshold results in a word being sent to the corresponding output logogen.

The separate storage of semantic and phonological information and the existence of the third (input to output logogen) reading route seem to be features which commend the Logogen Model. The Model has been extended to take account of spelling (Morton 1980), and has been examined and described in greater detail in relation to the dyslexic by Ellis and Miles (1981). In the above simplified system the output logogen is responsible for production of articulatory output, i.e. speech.

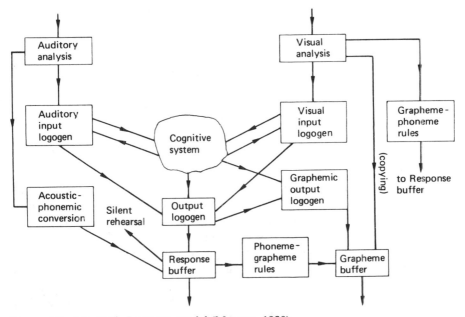

Figure 4.5   Morton's Logogen model (Morton, 1980)

The visual input logogens are pattern recognizers for the linguistic representation of visual material, and auditory input logogens are pattern recognizers for linguistic representations of auditory material. One of the key elements here is the production of a phonological code as described above. The development of phonological coding we know is weak in dyslexics and here there are possible difficulties in relation to the model.

Ellis (1980) and Ellis and Miles (1981) are more specific and argue that there is no deficiency of output logogen in relation to problems in articulatory and coding ability, which they suggest dyslexic children are quite able to do in short-term memory tasks. This is a rather different conclusion to that described by Frith (1981) where, it may be recalled, articulatory or motor programming deficits were postulated. Ellis and Miles refer to aspects of the visual input logogen system, arguing that there are no deficiencies with visual symbols that do not require naming, but if *lexical* encoding is involved there are deficiencies. They relate this to the available strategies for reading a whole word. If a visually presented word activates the visual input logogen, the individual can understand and read that word directly. If the logogen is not available, the only strategy is by synthesis via a phonemic route. This would result in the application of grapheme – phoneme correspondence to different parts of the word and then the resulting representation accessed. It has been suggested that this access requires some kind of implicit speech form, possibly from interactions betwen working memory and the articulatory loop (Baddeley 1979). If, as a result of grapheme – phoneme correspondence application, the word pronunciation is within the reader's heard vocabulary, the word will be understood (via activation of an auditory logogen unit). Ellis and

Miles suggest deficits for the dyslexics in 'visual input lower level logogens', i.e. the mechanism for the production of articulatory representation of word parts, which relates to the motor plan of speech output. (Articulatory coding is the coding of visual input information into a speech-based code, based on some kind of working memory or articulatory system.) They argue that it is the visual-to-input coding rather than articulatory output which is the problem. This they describe as 'disconnection' between the visual pattern recognition system and the internal lexicon.

4.25   Developmental models

The notion of routes to reading, and the complex cognitive models that we have just examined, really need to be placed within a developmental context. This has been attempted by Frith (1985) and by Snowling (1987). In addition Snowling (1987) has presented a model which examines the relationship between spoken and written language processing systems. Basically, she argues that in early development a child's sight vocabulary is stored in a lexicon which links the semantic memory to output phonology, where pronunciations of spoken words are held. Words that are represented in the lexicon are recognized automatically but in order to deal with unfamiliar or new words children will have to develop the letter sound relationships, phonological skills and enter, what Frith terms, the 'alphabetic phase'. This, as one can see, has immediate parallels between the so-called direct route to reading and the grapheme/

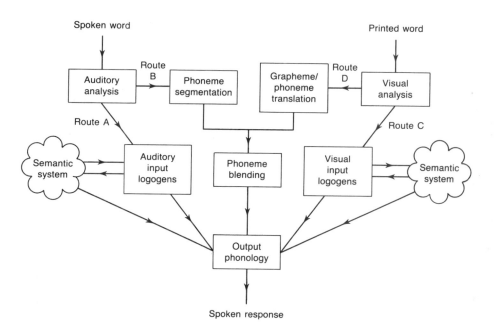

Figure 4.6   Model of the interface between spoken and written language processing system. (From Snowling (1987) with permission)

phoneme conversion that we mentioned previously. Figure 4.6, taken from Snowling (1987), presents a model of these systems. In reading from the printed word one can go through what is labelled 'route C', i.e. visual analysis through visual input logogens (see previous section), to output phonology, i.e. saying the word. This would be the direct or 'look and say' route. Alternatively one can read route D, via grapheme/phoneme translation, i.e. blending the sounds together and then into output phonology and spoken response. Similar routes are proposed for the spoken word, i.e. through sound analysis, straight through to repeating, or through analysing the segments of sounds and producing the word. Obviously unfamiliar words or new words or non-words need to be read through route D, whereas familiar words can be read through route C.

4.26 Spelling

One might think that spelling was a very similar task to reading, apart from it being more of a recall than a recognition task. However a number of writers suggest that this is not the case. A moment's reflection would bear this out. There are many individuals that are exceptionally good readers and yet very poor spellers, and although one might suppose that letter-to-sound coding and sound-to-letter coding might be identical, the evidence argues against this. There are some individuals who have various acquired disorders who can only write or only read, and some are unable to read what they themselves have written (see e.g. Benson and Geschwind 1969, Weigl and Fradis 1977). In particular, spelling may be better than reading where words are spelt in phonologically plausible ways (see Chomsky 1972). Bryant and Bradley (1980) also report that some 7-year-olds could spell what they could not read; they argue that this was due to using a phonological strategy, and suggest that children read on the basis of visual chunks but spell on the basis of phonological segments.

Frith and Frith (1980) present a series of studies examining good readers who were poor spellers, children who were both good readers and good spellers and those that were poor spellers and poor readers. The first group they describe as a disassociation group. Based on the children's performance on nonsense words selected to represent various grapheme-to-phoneme rules it was found that the good readers but poor spellers did less well than the children that were good readers and good spellers (the poor readers and poor spellers also did poorly). They propose that the poor spellers lack grapheme – phoneme correspondence rules although they were able to read perfectly well, and that in the spelling of nonsense words the disassociation group spelt in a more 'phonetically acceptable' way. Their attempts at spelling were ambiguous due to the fact the errors reflected grapheme – phoneme correspondence rules which could be transcribed into various sound patterns. Frith and Frith have also drawn attention to the difference between recall and recognition in spelling and reading. They cite Vingilis et al. (1977) who argued that auditory coding is involved in recall tasks, whereas visual coding is involved in recognition tasks (referring to memory in this case). Also O'Connor and Hermelin (1978) found that sequential items tended to be coded in an auditory manner, whereas spatial arrays tended to be coded in a visual manner (this would be applicable to whole words, for example). The implication here is that there is a sound code used for spelling, in particular, which may well account for the often observed greater difficulties that dyslexic children have in their spelling compared to their reading. Indeed many dyslexic children can overcome their reading difficulties if given appropriate help, and although spelling may be improved to be competent for everyday use it often remains weak.

4.3 Reading and spelling behaviour

We will return briefly to some of the above models at the end of this chapter, but will now examine the direct interrelationship between written language and dyslexic behaviour. Despite the plethora of research into etiology, some of which has been outlined in Chapter 3, there has been amazingly little research on the actual reading and spelling errors of dyslexic children, apart from the observations made and described in Chapters 1 and 2. Most of the research outlined in relation to etiology makes inferences concerning children's written language difficulties based on experiment. Here laboratory tasks or 'quasi written language procedures' are developed in order to isolate specific difficulties. This approach of course has the advantage of controlling all the complex variables that occur when the child is actually reading a story, for example. The drawback however is that the task can be far removed from the real situation.

4.31   Methodological points

Many attempts at error analysis have a number of difficult problems to overcome, (see reviews by Weber 1968 and Spache 1976), and the following are just a few of them. In examining error frequencies the types described are often not uniquely defined, and may not be mutually exclusive. Error types such as 'phonetic' or 'order error', may both occur in a given word. Similarly, it is difficult to agree whether the error should refer to the letter, the syllable unit or word. The interpretation of an error largely depends on who does the analysis. For example, an error such as *on/no* in the dyslexic is often described. This could be a visuo-spatial difficulty in remembering the visual order of the letters, or it could be that the child has difficulty in speech production, which could be phonological or articulatory.

In many cases only a few errors in each category occur in a given child and this makes statistical analysis very difficult as one is left with only a very small percentage of total error types. Furthermore, many statistical analyses are inappropriate owing to the fact that the errors are very rarely normally distributed. In addition to this particular problem, those children who are good readers or spellers tend to produce fewer errors than children who are poor readers and spellers. Therefore the poor readers have a much larger corpus of possible errors from which one can make error classifications.

One of the most difficult areas in relation to error analysis is that of control groups. The question is whether one should match control groups on language (e.g. reading) or chronological age (CA). This is of great importance in relation to reading and spelling errors. The child's exposure to reading and spelling experience or instruction will make a vast difference to the behaviour which one would observe in his reading and spelling performance. The main argument is that we cannot conclude that any differences in dyslexics are due to psychological functioning, as opposed to 'language' practice or experience, unless the dyslexics also differ from matched 'language' age controls. This is undoubtedly an important argument, and yet there are still a number of problems. Matched 'language' age (e.g. spelling age (SA)) controls are not enough on their own either, as (obviously) children differ in many developmental respects quite independent of reading and spelling experience (the matched SA group having a younger CA). Furthermore, a non-significant difference from matched CA controls cannot be simply dismissed as the result of language experience. It remains to be demonstrated, for example, that improving one's reading age from 7 years to 10 years improves one's ability to remember digits, or use a phonological code. More importantly the question as to *why* the child has been delayed in acquiring the experiences of reading development may be overlooked. To take a crude physical analogy: a researcher presented with two children of 10 years, one of whom was able to lift 20lb, and the other only 5lb, and having experimental knowledge that 5lb could be lifted by a child of 6 years, would presumably draw some conclusion based on the muscular strengths of the two children rather than resort to an explanation based on the intervening experiences of gradually learning how to lift 10lb, then 15lb and so on. This is admittedly stretching a point, but one might draw some parallels between physical and cognitive growth. In addition, children who are matched on chronological age to dyslexics will be reading and spelling based on a spoken language vocabulary that is broadly equivalent to their chronological age. Dyslexic children however will be using reading and spelling strategies based on a spoken language this is in advance of their reading and spelling. Fletcher *et al*. (1981) argue that young or beginner readers use graphological and phonological cues much more than later readers, who would tend to use semantic and syntactic features in their written language.

In addition to the above difficulties, there are others that relate to the particular material used. For example, Cromer (1980) argues that presenting oral spelling tests to children and then basing analysis on these will encourage the child to encode the spellings in a 'sound-to-graph manner'. This 'phonological' approach may not be the only way the child spells and therefore one may be missing processes of great interest. On the other hand, spontaneous spelling in free writing will make comparisons difficult when comparing dyslexic children with children without written language difficulties. Further, the particular texts and/or spelling tests used to test these children will not include all the common linguistic structures, whether these be phonological, orthographic or syntactic. Despite some of these difficulties a few studies have been undertaken which relate to some of the features of the written language system which have been outlined earlier on in the chapter.

4.32 Reading

It was suggested in Chapter 3 that dyslexic children have difficulty with grapheme – phoneme correspondence, i.e. visual-to-auditory coding or phonological coding in short-term memory or perception, and in aspects of lexical access. It was also suggested that there is less difficulty in the higher-order elements of written language learning, viz semantic and syntactic functions. Some reading error studies have broadly confirmed these findings.

Thomson (1982d) compared the performance of dyslexic children and two groups of controls (one reading-age matched, the other chronological-age matched) on the Neale Analysis of Reading Ability, looking specifically at Accuracy, Rate and Comprehension. Results are given in Table 4.2.

Table 4.2 Neale Analysis Scores for dyslexics and controls

	Dyslexics	*RA controls*	*CA controls*
CA	12.3	7.8	11.9
Accuracy	8.5	8.2	12.6
Rate	7.6	8.3	13.0+
Comprehension	10.1	8.7	11.10

(from Thomson 1982d)

Dyslexic children scored poorly on Rate of Reading as well as Reading Accuracy, making reading slow and non-fluent for them. However, the interesting finding is that they do relatively well at Comprehension (this in spite of the fact that on the Neale Test one discontinues testing once the child has made a given number of Reading Accuracy errors). This implies that dyslexic children were able to understand almost all that they had read, contrasting with the control groups, whose Comprehension was near CA. The problem appears to be in decoding the symbols rather than accessing meaning.

In respect to error types described as being typical of dyslexics, Shankweiler and Liberman (1978) compared dyslexics with backward readers, i.e. matched on reading age, but who were not chronologically younger. They found that there were no differences in incidence of letter reversals, sequences or in letter orientation. Furthermore, both groups tended to make errors in vowels. However, on further analysis of types of reversal, they found that dyslexic children had a higher incidence (2:1) of horizontal against vertical errors in reversals. In other words, they would tend to reverse *b/d* rather than *b/p*. There was also an asymmetry in their reversals, e.g. they would tend to write *b* for *d* and not *d* for *b*. They argued that there were some differences between dyslexics and controls, but that errors patterns were determined largely by phonetic and orthographic structures of words.

Thomson (1978a) reports a study examining the performance of dyslexics against chronological-age controls, using the Neale Analysis texts. Using Goodman's Taxonomy of Miscues, dyslexics made significantly more errors on graphic and phonemic proximity, while controls made significantly more errors at the bound morpheme, phrase and sentence (deep structure) level. This was interpreted following Smith's (1971) and Goodman's (1969) models of reading, that the dyslexics were still at the mediational stage of reading rather than being able to read directly for comprehension. They had more difficulty with letter and within-word aspects of reading, suggesting more basic grapheme – phoneme difficulties. Syntactic and semantic cues on the other hand seemed to be responded to, and the errors seemed to reflect difficulties in relating orthographic sequences to pronunciation. Kendall and Hood (1979) argue that there are two types of reading-disabled children—those with poor comprehension skills and those with good comprehension and poor word-recognition skills. Dyslexics appear to be the latter group, and Kendall and Hood argue that these use contextual information much better—they made fewer context errors in their study and also tended to read much more slowly. Jorm (1981) undertook a series of studies with children having both reading and spelling difficulties (dyslexic) and those having spelling difficulties only. Although he used only CA controls, he argued that the dyslexics were poor on the use of grapheme – phoneme correspondence rules (based on reading nonsense words and the phonetic accuracy of the spelling), yet did as well as controls on holistic approaches (based on symbol to word association tasks).

One of the key areas here is whether the reading behaviour of dyslexic children is delayed or deviant. If reading behaviour is delayed there are implications for etiology, but would also imply that in relation to remediation one taught the children as if they were younger. On the other hand if the reading errors were deviant, i.e. different from those of younger children who are beginner readers, this suggests that one would have to develop a different kind of teaching method. Unfortunately many of the above studies do not tackle this question as they do not have appropriate control groups. Some initial attempts to address this problem are made by Thomson (1982b) involving the analysis of errors in dyslexics using matched RA controls and matched CA controls. He found evidence for 'delayed' reading (i.e. dyslexics like RA controls) in a tendency to make orthography regular, and there was a gradual decline of this kind of error from RA controls, through dyslexics, to CA controls. Perhaps CA controls make fewer errors of this kind because they have a wider experience and knowledge of reading patterns, and the tendency to assume orthography is regular is due to lack of reading experience. 'Deviant' errors (i.e. different to both controls) were found in dyslexics making significantly more errors on vowels relative to consonants. Difficulties with vowels have been documented by others, e.g. Weber (1970), Shankweiler and Liberman (1972). The latter also argue that there is a greater variation in vowels as they are more fluid and subject to variation across dialect groups, and have different sounds depending on their occurrence with other items. If dyslexics have difficulty in phonological decoding, then additional variations will create a greater difficulty for them.

Temple (1986), in an analysis of error types, found that as far as phonetic type errors were concerned dyslexics were similar to normals of the same spelling age, i.e. they were delayed in their spelling. However, in non-phonetic errors they were outside the normal range, i.e. they had 'deviant' spelling in the sense that they produced more of these non-phonetic errors than those of a similar spelling age.

One particularly interesting feature in Thomson's study was the kind of semantic error made by the groups. There were no significant differences between dyslexics and either group in overall semantic errors. However, the dyslexic group made significantly more errors than both RA controls and CA controls where a visually or graphically completely dissimilar word was introduced: 'large' instead of 'great', or 'roar' instead of 'thunder'. Most of the semantic errors made by the control groups were visually or orthographically similar, e.g. 'accident/incident', 'chase/charged'. The kind of error produced by the dyslexics does suggest difficulties in using a phonological route in much the same kind of way as the 'deep dyslexia' category of acquired disorders, but the errors in the children are of course not invariably produced and can be changed by strategy.

4.33   Spelling

In respect to the number of spelling errors made by dyslexic children, Thomson (1980) compared dyslexics to CA controls and found that the ratio of words to error in dyslexics was 5 to 1, whereas for CA controls it was 35 to 1. Stanley and Watson (1980) also found that there were more spelling errors to words written in free writing and that there was a significant correlation between writing time and the words written in the control group but not in the dyslexic group—this contrasted with drawing time, in which there was no difference at all between controls and dyslexics.

In relation to phonological versus direct routes, Thomson (1980) found that dyslexic children made considerably less use of orthographic rules and perhaps spell like 'Chinese'. The control group had a much more sophisticated linguistic usage which resulted in, for example, more analogy errors, i.e. which appear to relate to knowledge of phonological rules, e.g. *docter* for *doctor* (relating to rules as in *matter* and *litter*), or *onder* for *under* (the rule such as *wonder*, Monday). Dyslexics, perhaps lacking this orthographic knowledge, made significantly fewer errors of this kind.

In relation to some of the serial aspects of written language and some of the short-term memory deficits indicated in Chapter 3, there have been one or two studies which are indicative. Wing and Baddeley (1980) argue that there is no simple short-term memory buffer decay in letter-order errors and that in many cases errors occur in the middle of words and appear to be due to interference effects. They also argue that there are separate processess involved in insertion and reversal errors as opposed to omission and substitution errors, although they do not expand or clarify this point. Nelson (1980), using spelling-age matched controls, found no significant difference between dyslexics and controls on order, phonetically inaccurate and orthographically illegal errors. On the basis of this, she argues that neither sequencing, auditory linguistic or visual problems respectively appear to account for developmental dyslexia. Instead, she argues that the difficulty relates to acquiring spelling knowledge by semantic memory systems.

Thomson (1981) has criticized this study in relation to its assumptions about cognitive function based on error analyses (and vice-versa). For example, many other studies have shown sequencing, acoustic encoding or verbal processing problems (the latter surely auditory linguistic) as being difficult for the dsylexic (see Chapter 3). There is often a gap between error classifications, the child's total reading and spelling performance in context and the cognitive mechanisms proposed by laboratory studies.

Like Thomson's (1978a) study in reading, Frith (1980a) argues that dyslexics make early stage types of errors in spelling, and in addition make errors which are not phonetic, e.g. *couge* for *cough* rather than *coff*. In the study by Thomson (1980) it was also found that dyslexic children had difficulty in the phonological and orthographic aspects of spelling. For example, they made significantly more errors on phonetic substitutions (*rode* for *road*), phoneme realization (e.g. *nise* for *nice*), and letter names. Similar findings were obtained comparing dyslexic spellings to spelling-age controls suggesting that this finding does not relate to language experience (Thomson 1982d). This latter study used cartoons without text, from which children were required to write a story. This provided a context as well as enabling comparisons of similar words. Various forms of phonetic feature were examined. There were no differences between dyslexics and both control groups on voicing. However, dyslexics were different to the chronological age group in nasals and 'other' categories (phonetic features which did not make enough errors to suggest forming a separate category). This suggests, in the case of representing the nasal sound in graphemic form, that dyslexic children are delayed (see also Snowling 1981b). They make more of these types of errors than chronological-age controls, but the same as spelling-age controls. This is of interest because nasals are often some of the latest sounds in phonological development in spoken language, and this suggests that one of the features of dyslexic children's spelling relates to their late language development.

In Thomson's (1982d) study further analysis was based on phonetically accurate (e.g. wayt/wait) and inaccurate (e.g. wta/wait) errors. There were differences between the two groups in using an alternate grapheme. The dyslexic group showed difficulties in using alternative graphemes to represent the sounds, and also in additions or doubling letters. In relation to the latter, following observations and questioning of the children, one possibility is that while the dyslexics may be able to produce a reasonable representation of the sound, they realize that the English language is a complex one, and having failed to automatically access words and orthographic rules will do things like add an 'e', or an extra 'l' just to make certain! One interpretation of the results was that the dyslexics have an array of possible letter representations which may be used to represent a particular phoneme. They then choose any one of these at random and make errors, i.e. this is a phonological coding/lexical access difficulty, as suggested by some of the current cognitive research. What is interesting is that the dyslexic children's errors are not totally random, i.e. they have, for example, the phoneme /k/ represented in a number of ways, *k*, *ck*, *c*, *ch*. These are the kinds of letters that they would substitute for that phoneme. They would not substitute other letters that represent completely different sounds, like /t/ for example. Hence the notion of 'phonetically accurate' spelling. The other interesting feature is of course that the children do not produce their own rule-governed system—their spellings are inconsistent and do not follow the same grapheme representations of the phoneme.

Marcel (1980), examining dyslexic adults and children having a specific learning difficulty, noted problems in initial consonants containing a liquid which was omitted or misplaced. Also voiced stops were sometimes changed, as well as difficulties in terminal, nasal and lateral consonants, which were often omitted. He concludes that many of the adult errors are equivalent to speech deviations of very young children. Haggard (1973) presents evidence that durations of liquids and nasals are reduced in initial and terminal clusters if there is an unvoiced consonant present. This might account for some of the difficulties described by Marcel in relation to speech codes.

Seymour and Porpodas (1980) argue that there are two main channels in spelling—grapheme – phoneme translation and lexical – semantic. Although only using a very small number of children, they undertook a number of tasks, e.g. matching orthographically regular words like *slart* or irregular nonsense words like *lartsa*. They found that dyslexics were poorer at storage or accessing the visual representations of spelling patterns, and although they had a grapheme – phoneme translation route, this was rather slower. The lexical channel however was operational. A previous study by Seymour and Porpodas (1978) suggested a structural coding deficit. Here they argue that spelling involves both spatial and temporal location of letters in horizontal array and in serial order. This structural code is used in generating written or oral spelling. Here they found dyslexics defective in the use of this kind of code, as well as in orientation.

Although the studies on reading and spelling are rather unrelated, we can make a summary of them. It has been shown in many of these studies that dyslexics are rather better at reading comprehension than reading accuracy, and have difficulties in the use of orthographic rules and phonological coding in alphabet, for example. Difficulties also occur in sound or name coding in terms of relating sound to symbols, and there is also evidence of difficulties in acoustic and phonetic analysis, particularly of segmentation and phonological coding. These difficulties suggest problems in perception, phonological processing or short-term memory rather than in syntax or semantics. The implication here is that difficulties do not lie in comprehension and meaning *per se*. The dyslexic's problem seems to relate to the differences between written and spoken language. One might cite in particular Hockett's (1963) 'Duality of Patterning' design feature in language. Here it is the translation of discrete visual symbols into their sound equivalents which appears to be the problem, and this will of course prevent the development of more fluent reading and writing mechanisms relating to higher-order linguistic processes in later aspects of the child's development.

4.4 Written language and dyslexia: a synthesis

Here we shall examine the written language system by *skills analysis*. This will examine some of the features of the written language system, and then look at the consequent *task demands*, in other words the kinds of abilities and skills required of the learner in order to acquire that particular written language feature. While it would be an impossible task to encompass all of the written language system, the writer has tried to examine those features which appear most relevant. A summary is presented in Table 4.3.

The first assumption is that written language is a secondary system based on spoken language. Here difficulties face the dyslexic child. In order to learn to read one has to build up a dictionary of appropriate words—not only meanings, but also their phonological representations which one would need to access in reading and spelling. We have already established that there can be delays in spoken language in the dyslexic, and this may obviously delay the development of the appropriate spoken language skills underlying written language. However in most cases by the time that the dyslexic child begins to learn to read, write and spell, his spoken

Table 4.3 'Skills analysis' and 'task demands' of the English written language system

Skills analysis	Task demands
Written language as second symbol system based on spoken language	Appropriate linguistic skills such as internal lexicon; phonetic representation; short-term memory for segments
Alphabetic system, involving arbitrary symbols with distinctive features	(Linguistic awareness of) grapheme/phoneme correspondences; visual — verbal (phonological) coding/labelling; Visual/Acoustic feature analysis
Directional nature of symbols — both left/right and inverted	Left/right awareness; verbal labelling
Combinatorial script — symbols combined sequentially, varying letter/sound representation	Phonemic coding/segmentation; Short-term memory for sequence; phoneme identification and blending
Orthography rule governed, ordered, represented at lexico-semantic level	Serial and temporal awareness/skills Two apparent routes — (i) application orthographic (symbol/sound) correspondence rules (ii) visual (holistic) analysis to meaning
Reading (word) patterns — sequences of visual to phoneme contrasts	Sequential scanning including sequential memory, visual-to-sound-to-'cognitive' system coding and lexical access
Spelling patterns — sequences sound-to-grapheme contrasts	Lexical access, sound-to-visual coding including sequential memory, output (articulatory) planning
Summary	
Symbolic, auditory, linguistic, temporal, sequential, serial rule governed, analytic	Left hemisphere specialization requiring verbal/phonological encoding; discrete analysis including seriation and sequences, working memory, phonetic segmentation

(Adapted and developed from Thomson, 1978, 1979)

language is competent enough not to provide any serious difficulties in relation to this particular element.

In relation to an alphabetic system, the comments *à propos* different writing systems are most relevant here. In western orthographies the child must be aware that each discrete visual unit represents a sound component in spoken language. In addition there must be some kind of grapheme – phoneme correspondence conversion, i.e. the ability to code visual information into phonological, sound or acoustic codes. This also might be called naming, or verbal labelling. In Chapter 3 we noted that many of these particular skills are shown experimentally to be 'deficient' in the dyslexic child. Here distinctive feature analysis is also required. This might be in the way outlined by Smith (1971), or in terms of information processing at either the early visual analysis or acoustic analysis stages. The child must learn what the appropriate features are for a particular letter identification.

As far as the directional nature of the symbols are concerned, the dyslexic child may have difficulties in directionality itself, or left – right awareness. Another interpretation of these difficulties is in terms of verbal labelling, i.e. the child can identify the direction, but cannot remember which particular name or label applies to the direction.

This alphabetic script is then combined into sequential units. One of the problems here is that these units are not totally consistent. The same combination can give rise to different sounds if they are in different letter environments, or letters in the combinations may function separately. There are differences due to stress, syllable units, and so on. Orthographic or grapheme – phoneme correspondence rules are required. In relation to this component, an element of phonemic or sound coding is required, particularly in relation to segmentation. The child needs to be aware that a number of units are combined, and can be split up in a number of ways. We have seen that the dyslexic child has difficulty in aspects of sound coding, particularly in early stages of short-term memory, in segmentation and in verbal labelling.

Short-term memory and sequencing become increasingly important when we look at the orthography of the written language system. This is rule-governed and refers to grapheme – phoneme correspondence rules, the accepted sequence of letters in a particular language and representations at a higher level. The latter might be termed the lexico-semantic level, i.e. where words are stored and related to their meaning. We continue to have short-term memory processess involved here, particularly serial and temporal awareness. At this stage we can introduce the concept of two routes to meaning which we have described variously under models of the reading process and referred to in the previous chapter. In some dyslexics there may be difficulties in the application of orthographic symbol – sound correspondence rules as we have seen, and this might force them to use a visual approach, with apparent visual analysis errors or, as some research has shown, to use visual coding strategies rather than phonological or sound coding strategies. This leads to difficulties quite early on in the reading process, and sometimes inappropriate ways of attempting to learn to read and spell by application of these rules. The element of phoneme or grapheme contrast also requires sequential scanning and sequential memory.

In relation to spelling the route comes from 'top down', rather than 'bottom up'. The word needs to be accessed initially, then sound-to-visual coding rules applied, again including sequential memory, and finally output. This could be in speech output or in memory systems, such as the articulatory rehearsal loop in short-term memory. This draws attention to some of the research suggesting possible difficulties in articulatory awareness and in pronunciation of complex phonemic segments.

This summary of the written language system draws attention to components of the system that permeate its development. It may be seen that these particular skills are essentially those involved in the left hemisphere. It is here that we need to bring in the review of the work on neurological functioning. One assumes that the written language skills are underpinned by the way in which the brain processes information. Verbal and phonological coding, analysis of discrete items, seriation/sequence, segmentation and working memory in relation to language appear to be associated with the left hemisphere. Deficits or delays in left-hemisphere processing could underlie the weakness in memory and coding.

The so-called deficits result essentially from the task demands of the written language system. We might describe the dyslexic child as having a *learning style* which encompasses skills other than those which appear to be particularly important for written language learning. There would be no difficulty if we as a society did not expect that children read, write and spell. Virtually all the other systems required for everyday life are robust in the dyslexic, apart from some very subtle differences in aspects of language and possibly in other skills involving elements of short-term memory and orientation. Unless we confronted the child with reading, writing and spelling to learn we would be much less aware that there was any learning difficulty or anything indeed amiss with the dyslexic person.

5

Assessment

5.1 Introduction

In this chapter the detailed assessment of the dyslexic individual will be described. This assessment has three major functions:

1 To come to some kind of 'diagnosis', i.e. to determine whether the child has a dyslexic problem and if so, what kind it is. Identifying a child as a dyslexic implies that he is *not* slow learning, primarily maladjusted, or with sensory deficits; thus, teaching methods appropriate for these groups would not be appropriate for dyslexics. Dyslexia requires the use of particular kinds of teaching methodologies (see Chapter 6).
2 To delineate specific difficulties. These might include difficulties in auditory memory, in blending or in visual perception. The implication here is that within the category of being dyslexic there will be greater or lesser degrees of specific difficulty relating to particular aspects of the learning situation. A child might have a complete inability to learn grapheme/phoneme correspondances, or may have more subtle difficulties in learning more complex spelling patterns.
3 To plan remediation. Having identified the particular learning difficulty, the aim is to describe the consequent teaching programmes, where to start in terms of the level of the child's difficulty, what particular techniques and strategies to use, and how to group children.

Tansley and Panckhurst (1981) suggest that assessment should be (i) functional, i.e. to identify what is getting in the way of learning and (ii) descriptive, i.e. to identify what can be done to further learning. Tyson (1970) argues that there are two major approaches to assessment: classification testing, and diagnostic testing. He also refers to the concepts of primary and secondary testing, the former examines actual behaviour, whereas the latter refers to presumed deficits such as perceptual, motor or memory. Another way of looking at the assessment procedure is in terms of the particular approach taken. One approach is psychometric, where the assessment involves test items which have been developed to place children in the context of their chronological and developmental age, for example in intelligence, reading or memory skills. This contrasts with a more informal appraisal based on 'task analysis'. This observes the child's current reading, writing and spelling behaviour (e.g. in terms of errors), and tries to relate this directly to a prescriptive teaching programme. One might refer to this as 'criterion' oriented testing, as opposed to the 'normative' testing of the psychometric approach.

There is some discussion of the most appropriate approach to take in educational psychology practice at the present time. Elliott (1983) provides a good discussion of these approaches, referring to them as *'cognitive'* (psychometric) and *'behavioural'* (criterion orientated). He argues that the focus of cognitive approaches is on the assessment of generalized skills and abilities, whereas the behavioural is on specific skills and abilities. These lead to different questions and implications, summarized in Table 5.1.

He makes the point, with which I agree, that these approaches are not mutually exclusive; both are required to provide a complete picture of the child's problem. We shall therefore examine both methods of assessment, but as dyslexia has been described as a problem mainly within the child's own cognitive development, the

Table 5.1   A framework for assessment

	Cognitive approaches	*Behavioural approaches*
Focus	Generalized skills and abilities.	Specific skills and abilities.
Question	What are the child's cognitive weaknesses and/or strengths?	What has the child failed to learn?
Implication	The problem may be within-child.	The problem may be contextual/environmental.
Methods	Psychometric tests of various cognitive abilities — IQ group factors, specific cognitive functions (e.g. memory) or scholastic abilities. Experimental or observational assessments of specific cognitive abilities.	Criterion-referred or observations, linked to curriculum hierarchies. These are generally developed as an outcome of applied behaviour analysis, task analysis or precision teaching methods.
Outcomes	(a) Reports contain an analysis of the child's problem in terms of the question above. (b) Reports contain recommendations for teaching *method* based upon a consideration of the child's cognitive strengths and/or weaknesses.	(a) Reports are written giving an analysis of the problem in terms of the question above. (b) Reports contain recommendations for teaching *content* based upon task and curriculum analyses.
Limitations	(a) Usually they do not cover specific curriculum content. (b) Implications of cognitive weaknesses and/or strengths for teaching methods are not always clear.	(a) Usually they do not cover generalized problems which the child may have in various cognitive skills. (b) The approaches deal best with basic skills hierarchies and are difficult to apply to complex skills.

(from Elliott 1983)

emphasis will be rather more on the cognitive dimension.

A further approach is related to the laboratory and research studies that have been outlined in Chapter 3. Here one would give the individuals various laboratory tasks that have been shown to identify specific difficulties in dyslexics, and come to some kind of diagnostic interpretation based on this. For example, if one took the view, as does Pavlides (1981), that eye movement is diagnostic, one would use this procedure to classify children as dyslexic. If one were to examine whether the difficulty was in phonological coding, grapheme/phoneme correspondence, or in naming, one might give the laboratory tests that were used by Snowling (1980) or Denckla and Rudel (1976 a and b) for example. However, as the etiological debate is still not totally resolved we shall restrict the discussion to the first two approaches, cognition and behavioural, outlined above.

The diagnostic and assessment procedures that are used in a *'clinical'* situation will be outlined in parallel with those used in a *'classroom'* situation. The implication is that the former would involve clinical and educational psychologists or other professionals who would be able to use the psychologically more complex assessment procedures. In a classroom situation, techniques for teachers, paralleling the psychologist's test batteries, will be described, as well as classroom observation techniques and other procedures to help in planning remedial teaching. In addition, other professional groups, such as speech therapists or medical doctors, would be able to use various parts of the assessment procedures.

5.2 'Background' factors

We saw in Chapter 1 that some definitions of dyslexia are negative in the sense of ruling out other barriers to learning. The examination of these factors is of some importance in assessment. However, a diagnosis by exclusion is not satisfactory, and we need to look at positive features, i.e those associated with dyslexia. We can represent 'negative' and 'positive' features in tabular form (see Table 5.2).

These features therefore represent essential information required for a diagnosis, but also information that provides a basis for identifying the functional nature of the learning difficulty, upon which to base remediation and prescriptive comments. One might describe the 'negative' features as background factors, those that one would want to rule out as being causal in the child's learning problem. However an examination of these background factors does not imply that dyslexia cannot occur amongst children who are slow learning, socially deprived or have sensory (hearing and vision) difficulties. It is much easier to come to a clear-cut diagnosis if none of these factors is operating in the child. If any were operative in the individual, additional teaching procedures would be needed in conjunction with the procedures aimed at the dyslexic problems. A good example of this is in the case of speech or language difficulties, as this difficulty may continue after the child has reached school age and still require speech therapy. It is obviously difficult for the child to relate sound to symbol if his own speech is defective. In addition to remedial teaching, the child would therefore require some kind of help in this area. Another example would be the slow learning

Table 5.2 'Negative' and 'positive' features of dyslexia

Negative or background features
    No sight defects
    No hearing defects
    Not well below average IQ
    No primary emotional disturbance
    No serious lack of schooling
    No serious general health problems
    No gross brain damage
    No socio-cultural deprivation
    No inadequate first teaching.

Positive or specific features
    Discrepancy between intelligence and written language attainments.
    Characteristic WISC (or BAS/ITPA) profile.
    Reading accuracy and fluency, spelling and written expression below that expected based on CA and IQ.
    Delayed and deviant reading/spelling errors — persistent reversals, order errors, bizarre spelling, syllabification difficulties, phonic representation problems etc.
    Confusions of left and right labelling.
    A history of late language development.
    Poor short term memory — e.g. tables, letter pattern retrieval, digit span, instructions and cognitive tasks.
    Difficulties in symbol-sound coding — e.g. alphabet naming tasks.
    Difficulties in sequencing — e.g. auditory/visual sequencing tasks, eye movements, seriation, remembering months of year/days of week.

Also associated:
    Phonological or pronunciation difficulties in speech.
    Similar written language difficulties in the family.
    Mixed handedness or confused laterality.
    Occasionally good spatial skills — using formboards, or lego, model making.

---

child. Here, teaching procedures need to be geared appropriately to the child's intellectual ability—he may have difficulty in comprehending the more complex rules of the English language system and may need some general comprehension and language development work.

In order to examine these background factors the first procedure in assessment is to obtain as much information as possible concerning the child's background, developmental and learning history. The following subsections describe particularly important pieces of information.

5.21 Developmental history

A review of development milestones is necessary to look for general delay which might relate to a child's current intellectual performance, as well as language development. Sometimes it is very difficult to get an appropriate description of language development from parents, as ages at which important language milestones occur may be forgotten. Further, parents are unlikely to be attuned to particularly important events, such as the particular phonology used by the child, the development of two-word grammars, telegraphic speech and so on.

It is worth obtaining information concerning the birth history. Forceps delivery, anoxia, long labours or toxaemia are commonly associated with learning disabilities (but see section 3.1). This is not to say that every child having this kind of birth will have a dyslexic problem, nor that every dyslexic will have some kind of 'at risk' birth condition. All one is doing here is looking for possible neurological damage at this stage. If there is an 'at risk' birth and this is associated with events such as difficulties in early sucking, continued crying and also paediatric involvement during the first year or two of life, one should look carefully at the child's test profile for signs of 'minimal neurological dysfunction'. This category is not tremendously useful in planning teaching programmes, or indeed etiologically (see Chapter 3), but it does form an additional source of information for the clinician.

5.22   Sensory mechanisms

The aim here is simply to check whether the child's ears and eyes have been tested and are within normal limits. As far as vision is concerned the situation is fairly straightforward. If the child has had his eyes tested, this is usually a thorough and appropriate investigation by an optician. In fact, it is very rare that anything other than a gross visual defect will give rise to a learning problem in reading. It is however possible, and is something that needs to be checked.

The situation in respect to hearing is much more complicated. School 'hearing' tests are often rather unreliable. This is due to the nature of the test itself, where the doctor, health visitor, school nurse, or appropriate person will whisper sounds or words to the child across the room. The conditions vary tremendously in terms of the background noise, and the child's attentiveness, to mention only two factors. It is much more appropriate to obtain a thorough audiometric examination in respect to the child, if one is to firmly rule out sensory difficulties. (One should take care not to confuse this with auditory *perceptual* or *coding* difficulties—these are cognitive and not due to the hearing mechanism.)

One gets the impression from working with dyslexic children that many do appear to have some difficulties in the actual auditory input. Indeed an unpublished student project at the University of Aston (Jordon 1979) found evidence for slight high-frequency hearing loss amongst some dyslexic children. Further, children who had hearing loss defined as greater than or equal to 25 decibels in the 8000 Hertz range (either left or right ears) were significantly poorer at spelling than the group of dyslexic children who did not have this level of hearing impairment. This 'hearing impaired' group had many more bizarre errors in spelling. This underlines the importance of obtaining an appropriate and thorough examination of the child's hearing.

5.23   Behavioural/emotional difficulties

It is often difficult to sort out the interrelationship between behavioural difficulties and reading, writing and spelling attainments. As far as the dyslexic is concerned, one is assuming that the behavioural or emotional difficulties are *secondary*, and result from the child's continual failure in written language learning. The important point is to establish, following careful questioning of parents, teachers and others, that the behavioural difficulties developed once the child started to go to school and was confronted with written language learning. Another important point here is to examine all the other attainments. It is difficult to see how an emotional or behavioural difficulty might account for reading, writing and spelling difficulties only, and not give rise to difficulties in other areas of school attainments, such as mathematics, oral class work, and so on. While not wishing to deny that there are emotional and behavioural difficulties that can give rise to learning problems, my experience it is too often used as a superficial and 'instant' reason for the child's difficulties. Some assessment procedures could also be used including the Bristol Social Adjustment Guide, Self-Esteem Inventories (e.g. Coopersmith 1966) or Rutter's Behaviour Rating Scales.

5.24   Educational, medical and social history

A lack of continuous learning experience for the child may well result in delays in written language learning, and frequent changes of school could create this situation. Another feature relates to adequate teaching (assuming the child has been attending the school regularly and not been frequently absent due to chronic illness, for example). The question to ask is 'are the other children succeeding in the child's class?' If the child in question is not succeeding, but others are, and they are treated in the same kind of way by the teacher, one can in general assume that the problem is not due to poor teaching. As well as obtaining information with respect to the child's exposure to learning, it is also important to establish the kind of teaching procedures that have been used. Children who are given mainly 'look-and-say' versus phonic approaches, have been taught 'i t a' or have been exposed to various different kinds of remedial teaching, will obviously have developed different learning strategies.

In relation to medical history an examination of possible medical conditions such as epilepsy, hormonal deficiencies, or hypothyroidism is useful. A 'social' history is particularly important where children come from homes where the first language may not be English. Here there will obviously be difficulties in adapting to early reading, writing and spelling. However, it is important not to dismiss learning problems in children from various ethnic subgroups as being due to difficulties in first-language learning. In respect of social problems of various sorts, if these are severe enough to affect the child's learning, one would expect this to affect ordinary school attainments and not simply reading, writing and spelling. Another aspect of social history is the incidence of learning difficulties amongst the family. This might range from the situation where father has a spelling difficulty, to another member of the family who has been diagnosed as dyslexic. As well as these familial difficulties another feature observed on talking to parents of dyslexic children is the particular kind of 'learning style'. This relates to the high incidence of 'visuo-spatial' occupations amongst the parents. This might include designers, artists, surgeons, engineers at all levels (mechanics, lathe operators, professors). These all seem to suggest abilities in spatial function as opposed to serial, temporal and sequential functioning. Some comments in relation to these skills have been made in earlier chapters.

5.3   Assessment of intelligence

The writer believes that the appropriate assessment of intelligence is one of the most crucial factors in the diagnosis of dyslexia, and is also important in terms of providing descriptive remediation. There seem to be four major functions of an intelligence test given to the dyslexic individual (Thomson 1982a).

1   To obtain a measure of the intellectual level (or IQ) of the child, in order to rule out slow learning or low intelligence as being a cause of written language failure
2   To examine the interrelationship between the child's intellectual level, chronological age and written language attainments, in order to describe any descrepancies between these
3   To obtain a diagnostic profile on the intelligence test used
4   To describe the cognitive functioning of the child, in order to identify areas of deficit and to help plan remediation

Although functions 1 and 2 are linked and functions 3 and 4 are linked, each of these functions can be looked at in turn. The assumption here is that the test used will be one available to a psychologist, or occasionally a speech therapist qualified in using appropriate tests (e.g. ITPA). Later, a description will be given of how similar functions can be achieved with procedures used by, for example, remedial or classroom teachers, medical officers and doctors or other professions associated with learning difficulties in children.

5.31   General intelligence

At first glance this particular function seems fairly straightforward. If the child's overall IQ falls within the average range (above an IQ of 90), one can assume that the child's learning problems do not result from a general slow learning potential or from a general intellectual deficit. If the child's intelligence was very high one would also need to examine whether he was under-functioning in relation to its own 'potential' (see below) as opposed to his chronological age. Intelligence is normally distributed, and Table 5.3 illustrates the distribution of intelligence scores based on the Wechsler Intelligence Scale for Children (WISC), a test very commonly used by educational and clinical psychologists. If a child fell into the 'Dull Normal' or even 'Borderline' category on Full Scale IQ one might still come to a diagnosis of dyslexia, but if a child is well below average it is very difficult to sort out a dyslexic problem from a general cognitive deficiency.

Table 5.3   IQ and intelligence classification from the WISC

IQ	Classification	Percent included	SD*
130 +	Very Superior	2.2	+ 3
120–129	Superior	6.7	+ 2
110–119	Bright Normal	16.1	+ 1
90–109	Average	50.0	0
80– 90	Dull Normal	16.1	–1
70– 79	Borderline	6.7	–2
69	Mental Defective	2.2	–3

* SD = Standard Deviation (from norm)

However, the situation is not quite as simple as this, because dyslexic children do significantly less well on certain subtests in commonly used intelligence tests. This is important for profile analysis, but can affect the evaluation of IQ.

The Wechsler test is divided into two types of scales, Verbal and Performance (or non-verbal). Each of these has a number of subtests. A typical set of results obtained from a dyslexic individual might be those given in Table 5.4. The scaled scores referred to range between 1 and 19. If a child had a scaled score of 10 for all the subtests he would obtain an IQ of around 100.

From the above scaled scores there are some problems in the given Full Scale IQ. Combining all the subtests (i.e. averaging them out to produce a general IQ) can be seriously questioned. The child's abilities range from well below average to well above average. Items such as Digit Span and Coding in particular have been shown by research (see below) to be specifically associated with dyslexia problems. This is rather like measuring a child's intelligence by asking him to read questions and write answers. They are 'dyslexia loaded' items, and one is underestimating the child's abilities. If, in this example, we prorate the IQs above without Information, Arthmetic and Coding (Digit Span is not normally used to compute IQ) we obtain a Full Scale of 109, a Verbal IQ of 106 and a Performance IQ of 112.

On the other hand, to take the child's best abilities and use them to form an IQ creates difficulties also. One might argue that one could do this for all children, and that having low performance on Digit Span and Coding is part of the intellectual performance of the child as defined by the test. Without going into long arguments about the nature of intelligence, it is important to be very cautious about interpreting overall IQ and one should always bear in mind that an intelligence test score is a minimum estimate of the child's overall capacity. Often it may be said that the child has a particular IQ, but if this was prorated without the scores that are particularly poor, one would get a much higher intelligence. This question can be a crucial one if the overall IQ is at the 'Borderline' level as described by the WISC. Many children in my experience have been placed in schools for the educationally sub-normal whereas examination of the subtest scores could result in a better estimate of the childs 'true' intellect. Further, IQ is only one component of a child's behaviour, and is not necessarily stable over time. It is important not to 'label' children based on IQ; tremendous changes can occur in cognitive development.

Table 5.4   Examples of WISC IQs and subtest profiles from a dyslexic child

Verbal IQ — 97		Full scale IQ — 100	Performance IQ — 104
Verbal items	Scaled scores	Performance items	Scaled scores
Information	8	Picture completion	13
Comprehension	12	Picture arrangement	11
Arithmetic	7	Block design	12
Similarities	11	Object assembly	11
Vocabulary	10	Coding	6
Digit span	6		

These issues are important, but beyond the scope of this book—see for example Mittler 1976, Cronbach 1979, and Elliott 1983.

The same kind of situation applies to the British Ability Scales, although there is much less research on the subtest profile. The additional facility in the British Ability Scales is however the ability to compute an IQ equivalent through various different kinds of processes—whether they be Reasoning, Spatial Imagery, or Short-Term Memory. Typically, a dyslexic child scores poorly on Short-Term Memory and one can then say that in general its abilities are low in this area. IQ equivalents for Reasoning and for Spatial Imagery may also be computed. Examples of this approach are given both below and also in the sample report at the end of this chapter. As stated before, the decision about 'correct' IQ can create difficulties if the child is on the borderline area in the above normal distribution. In practice however it is usually easy to rule out slow learning potential as being a possible cause of the child's difficulty.

There is an additional problem with respect to the British Ability Scales (BAS) in computing an overall or general IQ level for the purposes of ruling out slow learning ability. In the manual, it is suggested that a short form IQ be produced from four abilities, namely, Speed of Information Processing, Similarities, Matrices and Recall of Digits. Two of these (Similarities and Matrices) are reasoning tests, the others relate to rather specific functions (see below) in relation to manipulation of symbols and in short-term memory for auditory sequence. The important point here is that one would expect these abilities to be specifically associated with dyslexia, and indeed a study by Thomson (1982b) shows this to be the case. To produce an IQ from four subtests, two of which are specifically 'dyslexia loaded', results in a much lower IQ. The 1983 edition (see also Elliott and Pearson 1980) does however describe an alternative IQ enabling one to compute a Full-Scale, a Visual and a Verbal IQ similar to the Wechsler test. This can involve 10 or 11 subtests, and therefore is less invidious in producing an inappropriate IQ for the dyslexic child. Here only one or two of the subtests will be specifically 'dyslexia loaded' and it is much 'fairer' to use this IQ. Table 5.5 shows various intelligence quotients from Thomson (1982b).

In fairness to the authors, they do point out that if there is any discrepancy

Table 5.5 Intelligence quotients in the British Ability Scales for a sample of dyslexic children

Age Groups	8.0–10.11	11.00–13.11	14.0–16.11
Number	29	29	24
BAS Manual 4 (Short Form IQ)	95	96	99
BAS Elliott and Pearson (1980)			
Full Scale IQ	104	106	105
Visual IQ	104	105	107
Verbal IQ	103	107	103

Note: There are 10 IQ points difference (one SD) between using the two types of IQ computations. It is recommended that the BAS Manual 4, where Matrices, Similarities, Speed of Information Processing and Recall of Digits are given for IQ computation should *not* be used for a dyslexic child.

between abilities (see later), these should not be used to compute an IQ, and one would hope that the tester would take this into account.

As well as the WISC and the BAS, another very common test used in individual assessment procedure is the Illinois Test of Psycholinguistic Abilities (ITPA). Although the ITPA is not strictly an intelligence test, Paraskevopoulos and Kirk (1969) present data showing high correlations between the overall ITPA score and the Stanford-Binet intelligence test. Carroll, J. (1972) argues against the use of the ITPA as a measure of psycholinguistic ability; instead he cites factor analysis studies that indicate high verbal comprehension or verbal intelligence factors. Smith and Marx (1971) also consider that general linguistic or verbal ability accounted for 80% of the variance in ITPA test scores and this was tantamount to general intelligence. They found correlations between the WISC IQs and the ITPA psycholinguistic age of around 0.63, and argue that the ITPA . . . 'is largely a measure of verbal intelligence, with new names for old subtests of intelligence.' The ITPA then could be used as a measure of overall intelligence, certainly for the purpose of ruling out slow learning ability as being the prime reason for a child's difficulties in reading.

5.32   Intelligence and attainments

There are a number of ways of approaching the concept of a discrepancy between written language ability and intelligence. Many of these involve achievement ratios, or complex formulae involving age, chronological age and reading age. Some of these are reviewed by Spache (1976) and by Gaddes (1976), and are heavily criticized. In remedial education a rule of thumb has been to compare the child's chronological age, mental age and reading age. Thus a child of 10 with a mental age of 10 and reading age of 10, will be 'average'. A child of 10 with a mental age of 8, and reading at 8, will be a 'backward' child. Here his reading performance would be at the level one would expect from his intelligence, and although slow learning, he would not have a specific problem. On the other hand, a child of 10, with a mental age of 11 and reading of 9, would be in fact *2 years retarded*. He will have a specific difficulty such that his reading is behind his mental age, the assumption being that his reading age should be at his mental age level. This notion has been seriously criticized, particularly at the extreme ranges of intelligence (very low or very high in IQ terms). These criticisms are based on the interrelationship between reading and spelling in the general population, and the statistical notion of 'regression'. The arguments are outlined by Yule and a number of other authors in a series of papers: Yule *et al*. (1974), Yule and Rutter (1976), Berger *et al*. (1975), Yule (1967). In brief, Yule argues that achievement quotients are unacceptable on both conceptual and statistical grounds. The latter relates to the intercorrelations between reading and spelling in the general population. Usually these are around 0.6 The important thing here is that they are less than unity. It is only if the correlation is in fact 1.0 that the interrelationship between mental, chronological and reading age, as outlined above, applies. If correlations between the two variables are less than unity, obtaining an average score in one measure will result in being underestimated on another; or being well below average on one variable will result in being less inferior on the second variable. This applies particularly one standard deviation outside the mean. In practical terms what this implies is that in the middle ranges of intelligence the interrelationship between *mental age* and *reading age* holds fairly well, but at extremely high or low mental ages this relationship does not apply. For example, a child of 10 years of age, with a mental age of, say, 13, is much more likely to have a reading age of 12. In other words, one would have a situation in which bright children will be over-represented in a group of under-achievers, and dull children will be under-represented in this group. Yule and others demonstrated this regression effect particularly in the Isle of Wight studies (see also Rutter, Tizard and Whitmore 1970).

Yule has a fact taken up a point made by Crane (1959), criticizing the concept of backwardness and retardation on the grounds of mental age versus chronological age. Instead it is argued that one should develop a predictive variable (score on an IQ test, for example) and a criterion variable (score on reading, for example) and by the use of regression formulae, predict the expected reading age based on the IQ and chronological age of the child. These regression equations are reported by Fransella and Gerver (1965) and have been used extensively by Yule and co-workers. An example illustrates the point. The following regression equation is obtained from Yule (1967) based on a 9-11-year-old population in the Isle of Wight. The equation is based on the interrelationship between a short WISC (Similarities, Vocabulary, Block Design and Object Assembly), and the various Neale Analysis of Reading Ability scores. The example here is of Reading Accuracy. The equation is:

Expected Reading Age = $- 3.87 + (0.93 \times IQ) + (0.68 \times CA)$ (in months)

It should be noted here that 'IQ' refers to the sum of the four Scaled Scores from the short WISC, and CA is the chronological age in months. Assuming 10 years chronological age, a child of IQ equivalent to 104 would have an expected Reading Accuracy score of 9 years 8 months, with an IQ equivalent of 139 a reading age of 11 years 2 months, and with an IQ equivalent of 77 a reading age of 8 years 6 months.

Developing a regression equation is statistically and psychometrically a satisfactory way of calculating a child's reading age based on his intelligence and chronological age. This is the ideal situation, and ought to be undertaken by all psychologists using intelligence tests and attainments. Unfortunately, there are so many situations where it is impossible! This is because the regression equations only apply to the population where the overall correlation between intelligence and reading has been calculated and a regression equation produced for *that population*. This kind of analysis has not been done for many populations; indeed we only have regression equations for Isle of Wight 9, 10 and 11-year-olds, Isle of Wight 14-year-olds, and in the Inner London Education Authority, 10 and 14-year-olds. Regression equations for spelling are even rarer. Applying regression equations to populations or chronological ages outside those given are no more valid, therefore, than making some kind of clinical judgement based on IQ, reading and chronological age. For the interested reader and practising psychologist, regression equations used for various populations, and for various ages, are shown in Appendix 1. The Isle of Wight was chosen for study because it was a population reflecting the demography of the United Kingdom in social, cultural and economic terms, and these regression equations might be used with caution in some circumstances.

The British Ability Scales (BAS) provides further dimensions. The first of these is the provision of T-Score discrepancy tables in the Manual. One subtest of the British Ability Scales is the Word Reading test, (a recognition test of individual words graded in difficulty). The provision of discrepancy tables allows the tester to examine the differences between any sub-ability given in relation to the norms. Based on T-scores (mean 50 standard deviation 19) one can, for the particular age group, find the difference between the T-scores of two abilities, the table providing data at the 5% level of significance. In other words this would enable one to discover whether Word Reading is significantly poorer than, say, Word Definitions (vocabulary) or the reasoning abilities or indeed any other abilities. As these tables are based on national norms, they can be used for a child from any population. This facility is most useful, and enables one to detect whether there is a discrepancy between reading and any other ability or intellectual skill. Unfortunately, the BAS does not provide a spelling or a writing test, so one cannot undertake that analysis.

Another facility in the 1979 BAS are the Expectancy Tables. Here one is able to look at the level of the ability expected from any other ability. For example, one can examine the observed level of, say, verbal reasoning (Similarities) and then see what the expected level of Word Reading might be like. Some examples of this are given in Table 5.6.

Thus the children's reading age based on their verbal reasoning (Similarities) should be somewhat higher than their chronological age, whereas based on their

Table 5.6 Observed and expected Reading Ages from the British Ability Scales

Age groups	8.0–10.11	11.00–13.11
Mean CA	9.8	12.2
Observed BAS Word Reading age	7.7	8.9
Expected BAS Word Reading age		
Based on Similarities	10.0	12.9
Based on Block Design Level	9.9	12.3

(Modified from Thomson, 1982b)

Spatial Imagery as measured by the Block Design it should be around the chronological age. This facility is very useful in clinical practice, although there are some difficulties in the use of the Expectancy Tables. The authors point out that in order to obtain reasonable expectancy tables from smaller samples than would normally be required, they have collapsed age and ability groups. Only mean and standard deviations are available, which may be too coarse for some practical uses. This means that if a child's chronological age falls at the bottom end of the range given for a particular expectancy table (for example 8.0–10.11), one would obtain a somewhat higher than expected reading age. Conversely, a child whose chronological age is at the top level of the age range would obtain a somewhat lower reading age, quite independent of any interrelation between other abilities.

A facility added in the revised manual (Elliott, personal communication and 1983) examines IQ discrepancies. In other words, based on calculations given from the standard errors of differences in the BAS, one can obtain the expected standard score for Word Reading (and Basic Number Skills) given the IQ. This can be transformed into a reading age if required, but the main purpose is to see if the reading score is unusually and reliably below the expected score based on IQ. We now have a way of examining discrepant retardation. For example, in the group data from Thomson (1982b) the Short Form IQ of 96 for the 11.0–13.11 age group gives an expected quotient for Word Reading of 98. The observed Word Reading quotient was 74 (based on calculations from T-score). Computing a Z-score gives -1.8, a score found in less than 1 in 25 children. One would conclude therefore that Word Reading is unusually poor given Short Form IQ. This is a satisfactory method, but the astute reader will note that the Short Form IQ, as mentioned earlier, is computed from Speed of Information Processing, Similarities, Matrices and Recall of Digits. Two of these seem specifically poor in dyslexics (see later). Thus the use of the Short Form IQ in the above may underestimate the level of discrepancy or retardation. However, the manual also provides expected T-scores, predicted from any other. One can therefore predict Word Reading T-scores from the observed (e.g. Similarities score). This is in effect a form of regression and enables one to predict reading age from any other ability and evaluate the discrepancy by Z-score. This is also a very useful facility.

A considerable amount of space has been spent on discussing the interrelationship between intelligence and reading. This is not only important diagnostically and in order to identify appropriate research groups, but has great practical importance. This is because local authorities, in order to provide remedial help for children having learning difficulties, must decide on particular criteria for a child's selection. Resources are limited, and normally they can provide additional help only for children whose difficulties are the most severe. The question then emerges, should this be one year, eighteen months, or two years; retarded in reading and indeed how is one to define retardation with respect to the comments made above? In the Isle of Wight study (Rutter *et al*. 1970), this relates to a little less than 8% of the 9 to 12-year-old population, where a reading retardation of 28 months or more was calculated based on regression equations. This seems a very serious retardation indeed, and in my experience many children who have difficulties that are less severe than this are obviously in need of remedial help. The important point here is the use of the term *retardation*. Children whose reading or spelling is viewed in relation to their *chronological age* may not be given appropriate help and, particularly if highly intelligent, are unable to achieve their full educational potential.

The above describes the first two major functions of intelligence assessment using individual psychological tests which would normally be administered by a psychologist. Tests such as Raven's Matrices, or the English Picture Vocabulary Test are often available and can be used by individuals such as the remedial advisors, speech therapists and others. Raven's Matrices is particularly useful as it provides a measure of non-verbal intelligence and is not loaded against children who have language difficulties. These, plus tests available from the NFER such as in non-verbal reasoning, enable one to rule out slow learning as a reason for the child's learning failure. A word of caution, however. I have sometimes found a discrepancy between my assessment of the child's IQ and the school assessment. On further investigation, it emerged that the intelligence test used in the school was one which required the child to read the questions and write the answers. This is obviously a most inappropriate measure for the dyslexic. Some of the tests available are of this kind and these should be avoided. In addition to the above, appropriate screening tests aimed at identifying learning difficulties can be used. One example of this is the Aston Index, and the appropriate tests in relation to intelligence would be the Goodenough Draw-a-Man and the Aston Vocabulary Test. A detailed example of its use is given later. The advantage of such tests is that they may be used by the classroom teacher.

5.33   Subtest profiles of individual intelligence tests

We now turn to evidence for distinctive profiles of dyslexia in individual intelligence tests, and shall consider WISC initially, as this has been most researched. The first consideration is the overall discrepancy between the Verbal and Performance Scales. A number of studies have reported Verbal/Performance discrepancies in children with reading difficulties, usually that the Verbal IQ is rather lower than Performance IQ. For example, Berger *et al*. (1975) found that the specifically retarded readers in both the Isle of Wight and London studies had Verbal IQ lower than Performance IQ. Other studies reporting a better Performance than Verbal IQs include Graham (1952), Neville (1961), Paterra (1963), McLeod (1965)

Belmont and Birch (1966), Huelsman (1970), Clark (1970) and Warrington (1967). Kinsbourne and Warrington (1963a) found that, on examining children referred for reading difficulties to a clinic, children having Performance greater than Verbal IQs tended to have a linguistic retardation, whereas those having Verbal greater than Performance had some kind of sequential ordering deficit.

Some studies however have found no differences, e.g. Altus (1956), Beck (1968), Lyle and Goyen (1969), Thomson and Grant (1979). Bishop and Butterworth (1980) found in a study on the pre-school version of the Wechsler test (WPPSI) there were no Verbal/Performance discrepancies as predictors of later difficulties. Further, there are serious methodological problems that argue for this lower Verbal score not being accepted at face value. For example, Witelson (1976) selected a group of children who were defined as being of average intelligence if their Performance IQ was 85 or more. She then states that Verbal IQ was lower than Performance. Obviously there will be a greater number of children having Verbal IQs less than 85 as this was not used as a selection criterion. Bishop and Butterworth make similar points in their paper; specifically if one chooses children who have average or average-plus Full Scale IQ, and Verbal intelligence is correlated very highly with reading ability, one will tend to find that children with an average IQ will have compensatingly higher Performance IQs. Which is the valid IQ to use when coming to select the population for comparison of Verbal/Performance distinctions? There are two alternatives here. One is that poor verbal skills (i.e. delay in language development) may give rise to poor reading proficiency. On the other hand, poor reading might give rise to poor verbal intelligence, as the child has not been exposed to written language information to such a great extent. Many of the subtests on the WISC rely heavily on educational elements such as general knowledge and verbal facility which could be acquired through reading.

The differences between Verbal IQs and Performance IQs can also be explained by recourse to the subtest profiles obtained from subtests used in the WISC. Eleven subtests of the WISC are as follows: Information (I)—a general knowledge test; Comprehension (C)—verbal understanding of events; Arithmetic (A)—basic mental arithmetic operations; Similarities (S)—verbal concepts; Vocabulary (V)—defining words, Digit Span (DS)—auditory sequential memory. These comprise the Verbal Scale, given orally. The Performance Scale items are, Picture Completion (Pc)—identifying what is missing from a picture; Picture Arrangement (Pa)—rearranging cartoon pictures to make a story; Block Design (Bd)—arranging blocks to form patterns; Object Assembly (Oa)—placing pieces together to form objects; Coding (Co)—writing in marks against numbers under timed conditions. The reader is referred elsewhere (e.g. Savage 1968, Mittler 1976) for further details of the subtests. There is a remarkable agreement in the literature with respect to the subtest profiles associated with reading difficulties. This is despite the problem of the definition of groups used to examine the subtest profiles, as some of the studies report findings on undefined or poor readers. In some cases these studies look at children who are generally backward, or have difficulties not due to being specifically retarded. Table 5.7 provides a summary of a number of studies looking at subtest profiles of the WISC, from children either defined as being dyslexic, or who appear to have *specific* difficulties on examination of the original research reports. A number of studies which do not have adequately defined groups or which have included children who are generally delayed in reading have been omitted. Many of these studies however produce similar results (see Spache 1976 for a review).

Table 5.7 WISC subtest profiles for specifically retarded readers

	I	C	A	S	V	Ds	Pc	Pa	Bd	Oa	Co
Schiffman 1962	−	=	−	=	=	−	=	=	=	=	−
Schiffman and Clemans 1966	−	=	−	=	=	−	+	+	=	+	=
Klasen 1972	−	=	−	+	=	−	=	=	=	=	−
Bannatyne 1971	−	=	−	=	=	−	+	−	+	=	−
Naidoo 1972	−	+	−	+	−	−	=	=	−	=	−
Thomson and Grant 1979	−	=	−	=	−	−	+	=	=	+	−
McLeod 1965	−	=	−	=	−	−	+	=	=	=	−
Miles and Ellis 1981	−	=	−	+	+	−	=	=	+	=	−
Owen *et al.* 1974	−	=	−	=	=	−	+	=	+	=	−
Beck 1968	=	+	−	=	+	−	=	=	=	=	−
Graham 1952	−	=	−	=	−	=	=	=	=	=	−
Hirst 1960	=	=	−	=	−	−	+	+	=	+	−
Kallos *et al.* 1961	−	=	−	=	=	n/a	=	=	+	=	−
(Boys, Digit Span not given)											

Key   −   subtests found to be lower either intra group, or compared to controls
=   subtests found to be equal either intra group, or compared to controls
+   subtests found to be higher either intra group, or compared to controls

The findings, then, are almost completely consistent in that Information, Arithmetic, Digit Span and Coding are poor in the dyslexic or specifically disabled child, and suggest that there is a profile on the WISC that is associated with dyslexic problems. The implications for this in relation to cognitive abilities will be considered below. Despite the broad agreement in many studies cited it is surprising that this profile (the 'ACID' profile) is not familiar to many educational psychologists. Indeed some writers argue against its use, for example, Tansley and Panckhurst (1981 p. 218) state that '. . . to persist in the search for subtest patterns, in the hope that a definitive dyslexic profile will emerge is to persist in the pursuit of a chimera.' On the contrary, the profile seems quite clear to me.

From the above it begins to emerge just why there might be Verbal/Performance discrepancy. This is not because there is a global difference in these two types of skills, but because three of the subtests described above, namely, Arithmetic, Information and Digit Span, all come from the Verbal Scale. The use of these to compute the Verbal IQ will obviously result in a lower score compared to Performance, where there is only one 'deficit' subtest. An overall linguistic deficiency is not suggested, given the average scores on Comprehension and Similarities.

Bannatyne (1971), based on content analysis of items, postulated four subgroups of clusters of ability on the WISC—Spatial ability (Picture Completion, Block Design, Object Assembly), Sequencing ability (Digit Span, Picture Arrangement and Coding), Conceptualizing ability (Comprehension, Similarities and

Vocabulary) and Acquired knowledge (Information, Arithmetic, Vocabulary). Bannatyne suggested that dyslexic children performed less on well Sequencing ability, and Acquired knowledge, but scored highly on Spatial ability and moderately well on Conceptualizing ability. Rugel (1974) re-analysed the results of several WISC studies for retarded readers in terms of Bannatyne's clusters, and found that Spatial ability was ranked higher for 18 occasions out of 22, Conceptualizing ranked intermediately (14 times) and Sequencing ability ranked lowest (18 times); see also Thomson and Grant (1979).

The British Ability Scales have only been available for a relatively short time compared to the Wechsler Scales. There have been one or two studies examining the BAS with poor readers and dyslexics. Thomson et al. (1981) and Thomson (1982b) found that dyslexics scored significantly less well on Speed of Information Processing, Immediate and Delayed Visual Recall, Recall of Digits, Basic Arithmetic and Word Reading across all the age ranges, when compared to other abilities. Processes involving Speed of Processing and Short-Term Memory were poor, whereas those involving Reasoning, Spatial Imagery and aspects of the Use of Retrieval of Knowledge were found to be average or above average. Examining changes of ability with age it was found that the deficit tasks, such as Recall of Digits, had a growth curve paralleling Word Reading, whereas other abilities, e.g. Similarities (verbal reasoning), were parallel with the norms and chronological age.

Eliott and Tyler (1987) found that, in general, children with specific reading difficulties scored less well on the verbal subtests, but better on the non-verbal subtests, compared to the norm. In their cluster analysis of the BAS profiles, Tyler and Eliott (1988) found three groups. One they labelled 'visual, spatial and linguistic difficulties.' Here children were weaker on Immediate Visual Recall, Recall of Designs, Recall of Digits, Word Definitions and Visualization of Cubes. A second group, labelled 'a sequential processing problem', had the weakest scores in the Speed of Information Processing, Immediate Visual Recall and Recall of Digits. The third group, labelled as 'problems with holistic retrieval of information' had poor performance in Recall of Designs and Word Definitions. All groups naturally had difficulties in reading. The above findings, apart from one or two differences in the Visualization of Cubes and Word Definitions for subgroups, parallel ·the findings of Thomson (1982b) where Short-Term and Speed of Information Processing problems were implicated. Thomson's findings that the Recall of Digits ability parallels closely the Word Reading Ability development suggest some link between these cognitive abilities. This contrasted to the independence of word reading with verbal reasoning scores for the dyslexics.

Although there is not as much research on the BAS, as in the WISC these findings are promising and suggest it is possible to provide some profiles based on the underlying cognitive skills tapped by the BAS.

Another individual test, the Illinois Test of Psycholinguistic Abilities (ITPA), is also worthy of comment here. Again there are a number of studies of the subtest profiles of retarded readers. Spache (1976), in a review of 12 studies, suggests that fairly consistent findings are that Auditory Sequential Memory, Visual Sequential

Memory and Grammatic Closure are tests associated with reading difficulties. In addition, Bannatyne (1971) suggests that Sound Blending and Auditory Closure are associated with dyslexic difficulties. These latter two tests are in fact optional extras in the revised version of the ITPA, and they appear not to have been given in the studies reviewed by Spache. Difficulties showing themselves on the subtest profiles associated with the ITPA are those involving the 'automatic-sequential level' in relation to the constructs of the ITPA. McLeod (1966), in a factor analysis of the ITPA, argues that the grammatic closure, auditory sequential memory and visual sequential memory subtests form a cluster he entitles 'integrative sequencing.'

5.34   Deficits assessed by individual test

The fourth function of an intelligence assessment, it may be recalled, is to provide information in relation to the specific deficits in dyslexic children. As far as the WISC is concerned the situation is not particularly clear. Wechsler himself does not describe what the particular subtests are measuring and one has to consult factor analytical studies or clinical observations. A brief description of the deficit tests is required here. In the Information test the child is asked orally to answer general knowledge questions. The Arithmetic test involves mental arithmetic once the child has gone past the first two or three easy items. Here the child is given the questions orally, and then required to perform the arithmetical operations without recourse to pen or paper; it includes tables, as well as the basic operations. The Digit Span subtest is an auditory sequential memory subtest involving the tester saying a series of numbers at one a second, the child simply having to repeat them. The series of numbers gets longer, ranging from two upwards. There is also a reverse digits task, in which the child has to say the numbers in reverse order. The Coding subtest involves looking at a series of numbers with symbols associated with each number. Below is a series of numbers in which one box underneath is empty. The task for the child is to write in the symbol matching the number under strictly timed conditions.

Cohen (1959) suggests that verbal comprehension is involved in Information, Similarities, Vocabulary, Comprehension and Picture Completion; perception is involved in Block Design and Object Assembly; freedom from distractability in Digit Span and Arithmetic, whereas Coding and Picture Arrangement measure specific skills. These comments are based on factor analysis. This is of limited use, as Arithmetic appears both on the verbal comprehension and freedom from distractability, and saying that Coding, for example, is a specific skill does not tell us much about what it actually is. Rather than looking at factor or cluster analytic studies, it is more useful to look in detail at what the individual subtests might be measuring. Miles and Ellis (1981) argue that the Information subtest relates to reading ability. In other words, anyone who is poor at reading would probably do rather less well on Information, as it relates to obtaining knowledge from reading. This is supported by Bannatyne (1971) and Thomson and Grant (1979), who argue that this acquired knowledge is educationally and culturally biased, reflecting the child's performance at school.

The Arithmetic subtest involves a number of elements, but the one of relevance here is the short-term memory element. Here a child has to remember the problem, and manipulate the numbers in his head, i.e. perform arithmetical operations, including storing the partial results and addenda in short-term memory. Baddeley and Hitch (1974), in discussing working memory, demonstrate quite clearly how an auditorally presented mental arithmetic task increases the short-term memory load drastically, compared to visually presented mental arithmetic tasks. This task obviously demands an additional short-term memory capacity (see Thomson and Wilsher 1979, Ellis and Miles 1981, and Chapter 3). The Arithmetic test is also dependent on scholastic and educational factors. Sequencing difficulties may hinder the ability to learn rote tables, and some studies have indicated that Arithmetic itself in relation to its symbol manipulation aspect is associated with dyslexic problems (Joffe 1981). Ellis and Miles argue that Arithmetic involves encoding, in the sense of translating number symbols into words and holding in mind a number of instructions.

The Digit Span subtest obviously involves short-term and working memory capacities; elements of lexical encoding; the ability to recall separate items of sound which have no meaning as a group; and the ability to remember the specific sequence through time. Poor performances in Digit Span (and Arithmetic) would suggest difficulties in the areas described, requiring remedial techniques to overcome the serial short-term memory difficulties that dyslexic children have—chunking word patterns, and the like (see Chapter 6).

The Coding subtest is a complex one. Miles and Ellis (1981) argue that one of the difficulties in this is that the symbols can be coded in two different kinds of ways. One might be matching a visual pattern; the other matching a visual pattern to *name* pattern. The latter, according to their theory, involves lexical encoding, and will therefore be deficient in dyslexic children. However, Thomson and Grant (1979) argue that Coding embodies a large number of practical skills which underlie verbal and linguistic processes. These include the ability to recognize and memorize symbols at speed, visual and motor coordination, and the capacity to sustain a concentrated attentional effort on a routine task. There are also left/right scanning skills as well as graphic skills. Another important point is that the associations that the child is required to identify are quite arbitrary, and the sequencing irregular. Thus the subtest closely parallels written language, both in its arbitrary and symbolic nature. In addition, of the 9 symbols used, 8 are mirror image or inverted versions (4 pairs).

In relation to some of the other subtests, one might have expected dyslexic children to do less well on Picture Arrangement if there was a sequencing difficulty. However, although there is temporal sequence required here, the conventions of story telling and cartoons are more important. Sometimes dyslexic children place the cards from right to left, but this is scored as correct in the WISC test. Rugel (1974) argues that the Picture Arrangement is not in fact a sequencing test at all, as the pictures are co-present, i.e. laid out in front of the child. This also means that there is no short-term memory involvement either. The fact that most of the studies indicate that dyslexics do not generally score poorly on tests such as Picture Completion, Block Design and Object Assembly suggests that there is no visual perceptual problem *per se*; indeed some writers in fact have argued that dyslexics have rather better spatial skills (Newton, 1974, supported by Bannatyne 1971 and others).

The final comment relates to the Vocabulary subtest. Some studies have found this to be poor in dyslexics. This may relate to a general verbal comprehension difficulty, but my experience leads me to believe that low scores here relate to difficulties in expressing ideas fluently in spoken language. This may be a continuation of late language development, as frequently the children appear to understand what the words are, but cannot explain them fully.

The British Ability Scales are based on a structural model of the intellect and, briefly, postulate five major processes: Speed, Reasoning, Spatial Imagery, Short-Term Memory and Retrieval and Application of Knowledge (see Elliott 1983). Dyslexic children appear to be poor on Short-Term Memory and Speed processes (Thomson 1982b). The speed of Information Processing test consists of a booklet presented to the child, containing five rows of numbers on each page. The task is to cross out the highest number in each row, each page being very strictly timed. Visual Recall involves the child being presented with a card showing 20 drawings of various objects, e.g bottle, scissors, etc. Following each of these objects being named by the tester, the child studies the card for a two-minute period. Immediate Visual Recall is the number of items recalled immediately following the removal of the card, and Delayed Visual Recall is the number of items recalled between 15 and 30 minutes following removal of the card. Recall of Digits is a normal span test, the digits being presented auditorally, one every half second, and being recalled in forward order (unlike some other tests, there are no reverse-digit subtests). Word Reading has been described previously.

The Speed of Information Processing test appears to involve elements of sequential scanning, symbol recognition, and the development and the use of an appropriate strategy. The major difficulty here appears to be aspects of seriation and symbol manipulation. The poor performance on the Recall of Digits test is not surprising; this is a test of auditory sequential memory (see WISC, ITPA). Of further interest is the poor performance of the children on Immediate and Delayed Visual Recall. The term 'Visual Recall' appears to be a misnomer in this case, as the tester names the pictures to be remembered at the outset, a clear invitation to the child to give them their verbal labels. In Thomson's (1982b) study, dyslexic performance on the Recall of Designs was normal suggesting that they do not have any difficulty in visuo-motor memory. The Short-Term Memory tests which are deficient appear to be those involving verbal and visual stimuli, but with a verbal response, i.e. when information is coded phonemically.

It is also of relevance to note the tests in which the dyslexic children did not do poorly. The children did not manifest any deficits in Reasoning or Spatial Imagery. The contrast between their ability in aspects of spoken laguage (as measured by Verbal Fluency and Word Definitions) and their lack of facility with written language reflects the nature of dyslexia. But results such as the apparent lack of deficits in Spatial Imagery appear to give support to arguments such as Vellutino's (1979) that dyslexic children are not deficient in visual perception *per se*, but in aspects of verbal processing appertaining to short-term memory.

Assessment procedures not using individual intelligence tests given by psychologists do not provide subtest profiles. In some cases one can make general comments about differences between non-verbal and verbal intelligence. For example, in the Aston Index the Goodenough Draw-a-Man test has a higher correlation with non-verbal measures of intelligence than the Vocabulary subtest. Children doing poorly on Vocabulary, but well on Draw-a-Man, for example, might well be suspected of having a verbal problem and could be referred for further assessment in this area.

5.4 Attainments

5.41 Delayed attainments in dyslexia

One of the key differences between specifically retarded and backward readers is one of prognosis (see e.g. Yule 1973, and Chapter 1). Table 5.8 presents some of the data from the Isle of Wight study where the children with specific difficulties made less improvement than those who were generally backward and of lower intelligence. An exception to this is the Comprehension score, which confirms the comments made in Chapter 4 on research into reading behaviour in dyslexics.

The dyslexic child's difficulties also become increasingly severe as it gets older. This can be illustrated very well by some data taken from a university clinic (Thomson *et al.* 1980).

Table 5.8 Reading Age scores for specific and general retardates after follow up

Neale Analysis of Reading	Backward readers	Specific retardates
Rate	9.4	8.8
Accuracy	9.4	8.8
Comprehension	9.7	9.4
Spelling (Schonell)	8.5	7.8

(Adapted and represented from original data reported in Yule 1973)

Figure 5.1 shows the improvement over age in the Neale Reading Test for Accuracy, Fluency, Comprehension and the Schonell Spelling Test. Five different age ranges based on 529 children who had been diagnosed as having dyslexic problems are shown. This is a cross-sectional study, not a longitudinal one, but illustrates the above point. For example on Neale Accuracy there is a retardation (from CA) of $1\frac{1}{2}$ years at 9 years old, $3\frac{1}{2}$ years old and 5 years at 15 years old. The children do not 'grow out' of their difficulty.

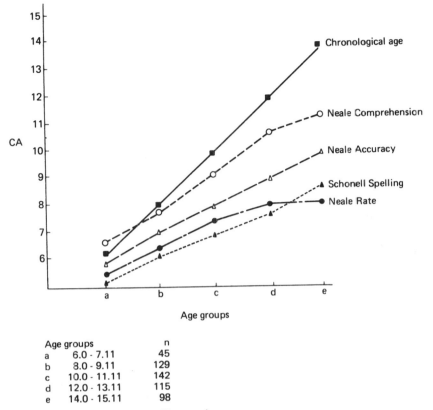

Age groups		n
a	6.0 - 7.11	45
b	8.0 - 9.11	129
c	10.0 - 11.11	142
d	12.0 - 13.11	115
e	14.0 - 15.11	98

Figure 5.1 Reading and spelling against age

5.42 Measuring attainments

One of the most common ways of measuring attainment is a standardized test which enables one to compute a reading and/or spelling age. Tests include single-word recognition skills, e.g. the Schonell Graded Word Reading Test, or Word Reading from the British Ability Scales. These enable a quick and immediate reading age to be obtained in order to make a comparison with the child's chronological age and intelligence. One should also record and note down errors which are made, for example whether the child is able to identify initial blends; whether errors are mainly in vowels and vowel digraphs; reversals and errors of order; mispronunciations; and regular versus irregular word errors. All these have implications for the kind of teaching programme that will be undertaken.

Word recognition tests are, however, rather limited. In some cases the tests are so commonly used (e.g. the Schonell test) that there is some danger of overexposure to the child population (see Yule 1967, for example). The main criticism about word recognition reading tests, however, is that they do not measure reading properly. In other words, they do not measure the child's ability to read in a total linguistic context—this includes predictions based on the knowledge of what the text is about using syntactic and semantic features to aid the decoding of the words. It is therefore recommended that an additional test, involving reading stories, be given. The most useful in the writer's opinion is the Neale Analysis of Reading Ability, which enables one to look at Accuracy, Comprehension and Rate of Reading. The different scores can have important implications as the dyslexic is often quite good at Comprehension, but poor at Reading Accuracy and Reading Rate. The Neale Analysis also has some suggestions for error analysis, including mispronunciations, reversals, and omissions. It is important to record the child's errors—these might be in phonological coding, in misrepresenting the letters by giving them the wrong sounds; omitting whole letters; inappropriate stress; or ignoring punctuation. Even reading tests such as the Neale, in which the child is able to use context clues from stories, have their difficulties. The child is asked to read aloud, and this is not the same as reading to oneself. Moving from a visual input straight to meaning is less likely if phonological or articulatory coding is forced by having to read the words aloud. One or two tests available now involve silent reading and measure comprehension. The difficulty here is that one cannot pin-point the kinds of errors that the child is making. There are many reading tests which can be used, and the reader is advised to consult the National Foundation for Educational Research (NFER) or other publishers' catalogues.

The majority of spelling tests are aimed at providing a spelling age, and invariably are single-word spellings. These include tests like the Schonell Graded Word Spelling Test, or the more recent Vernon Graded Word Spelling Test. As we have commented previously, it is unfortunate that regression equations, expectancy tables and the like have not been calculated for spelling. This makes it very difficult to evaluate the discrepancy between spelling and intelligence, which is a factor in dyslexia. Many dyslexic children, particularly the more intelligent ones, have often overcome early reading difficulties, but spelling and writing remain a very serious problem for them. Focusing on reading alone is to ignore the whole of the syndrome, yet spelling is one of those skills that has been largely ignored until fairly recently in assessment procedures. Tests like the Vernon, and indeed some of the NFER tests, do enable one to compute a spelling quotient which can be compared with the intelligence quotient; and one can say that there is a 20 or 30-point discrepancy between intelligence and spelling, but most of the spelling tests are simply graded words related to age level. There have been one or two attempts to try to systematize spelling errors in terms of the particular sound/symbol correspondence and orthographic rules, for example Nelson (1980). Unfortunately, the number of different sounds actually represented by different symbols (and vice versa) in the English language makes this task rather daunting, and to satisfactorily assess all of them would require spelling tests taking some hours to administer! There are some dictation exercises given in the Aston Teaching Portfolios (Aubrey *et al.* 1982) which include particular spelling patterns and digraphs which could be used diagnostically, as well as for teaching.

Another important attainment is writing. This is even more difficult to evaluate systematically as there are no 'writing age' norms available from the standardized tests. However, I and indeed many other authors (e.g. Cotterell 1970, Newton 1974) suggest that a piece of free writing from the child is almost as valuable diagnostically as many of the other standardized tests. By 'free-writing' one means that the child is invited to write about anything he likes on a plain piece of paper. There are a number of things to note that can be evaluated in a qualitative way; these are listed for convenience (not in order of priority).

1 Does the child initially have any difficulty in thinking up a story or in expressing his ideas in written form? If the child has been talkative, can converse well or has plenty of oral ideas and yet asks 'What shall I write about?', or sits for a long time staring into space, or frowning or thinking, there is obviously some initial difficulty. In some cases one may have to prompt the child and give some kinds of examples of things he could write about.

2 How long does it take the child actually to write his story or piece of writing? If it takes the child 15 to 20 minutes to write one or two lines, this obviously represents a difficulty in written expression compared to a child who reels off a page in about five minutes.

3 Looking at the actual writing style itself is important. Is the general formation of letters mature and commensurate with chronological age? How does the child hold his pen? Is it cramped or tight? Is there an anxious look on the child's face? Do the slopes of letters change from left to right, then from right to left? Is the child unable to maintain a more or less straight line across the page? Does the child start from right to left in his writing?

4 What is the nature of the written material? Is there a discrepancy between what is written and the language the child uses in his oral vocabulary? Is there a stilted and odd syntax, e.g. the omission of function words? Sometimes the child may not notice these omissions on re-reading the text. Does the child use punctuation appropriately, or is it just scattered apparently randomly through the text or not there at all?

5 In spelling does the child use capital letters in inappropriate places, particularly B and D, P and Q and so on? Is the spelling mainly phonetic? Does it fail to follow sound−symbol correspondence? Is it bizarre?

Thus, looking at the child's written versus oral language performance, his motor control, his spelling patterns and general approach to writing provides a good deal of information.

5.43   Error analysis

It is also useful to undertake some kind of informal error analysis of reading, spelling and writing. At one level this could simply involve carefully noting down the particular errors that the child produces, and planning remediation in terms of the particular level to start, e.g. whether to reinforce sound − symbol correspondences, consonant blends, vowel diagraphs or written language rules. Here a kind

Table 5.9 Sample checklist of basic sounds

a	bl x	scr	v	sc(sk)	aw	ir	ace
b x	br x	shr	w	sk	-ay	oa	act
c	-ck	sph	x	sl	ea(e) x	-oe	age
d x	cl	spr	y	sm	éà x	oi	all
e	cr	squ x	z	sn	ee x	oo	ape
f	-ct	str	ch	sp	er	or	ark
g	dr x	thr	sh	st	ew	ou	arm
h	dw	a-e x	th	sw	ie x	ound	art
i	fl	i-e x	wh	tr	igh	ow	ask
j	fr	e-e x	qu x	tw	ai	ow	each x
k	-ft	o-e				-oy	ear x
l	gl	u-e				-ue	east x
m	gr					ur	eat x
n	-mp					-y	ice
o	-nch	ai					oak
p x	-nd	air					oak
q	-ng x	alk					oar
r	nk	ar					oil
s	-nt						old
t	pl x						
u	pr x						

(From Cotterell 1978)

Note: A number of letter combinations, suffixes, etc. are omitted in the example. Items with cross are observed errors.

of 'checklist' of basic sound errors is useful. One such aid is Cotterell's (1978) Checklist of Basic Sounds. Here the child's reading and spelling, whether from a formal test or from classroom assignments, can be observed. Particular error groups can be noted, and used to plan teaching. An example is given in Table 5.9. In this particular example the child appears to have learnt most of the basic sound/symbol correspondences in terms of letter sounds and names. However, he has difficulty in common consonant blends, particularly those that involve voiced/unvoiced distinctions. These blends could usefully be retaught and over-learnt. He also has difficulty in the 'e' sound. He confuses the various representations of this sound in the English language and work in this area will be required. He could usefully be taught one or two simple rules, e.g. 'u' always following 'q', which also appears to be a problem.

The above is a example of just one kind of assessment. Another example of prescriptive or criterion-orientated assessment is from the Aston Teaching Portfolios (Aubrey *et al*. 1982). This attempts to identify difficulties in auditory or visual modality functions, i.e. auditory and visual perception, not vision and hearing *per se*. It includes areas such as short-term memory and sequential skills, the identification of sounds, blending or discrimination. Children are classified as having strength or weakness in a particular channel. The research behind the Portfolios suggested that a combination of auditory and visual teaching techniques is best, with a strength-orientated approach being more effective than a weakness (deficit) orientated approach. Thus if the child has difficulty in auditory recall, discrimination or sound blending, it would be more appropriate to teach him a look/say approach using pictorial aids, diacritical marks, etc. The strength approach gives the child immediate success and achievement, increasing his interest and motivation. At the same time, remediation can be given on the areas of weakness.

A child having *visual* difficulties may confuse letters or words that look similar; may have difficulty in recognizing, remembering or synthesizing the meaning of what is presented visually. He may fail to notice details in words, for example, 'ship/shop', and sometimes has configuration difficulties. He may have difficulty in learning by a look/say approach and the basic phonic methods may be more appropriate in the early stages. A child with *auditory* difficulties will have difficulty in synthesizing sounds into words and analysing the basic sound elements, as well as transferring the learning of sounds to skills of word attack. In general he will experience difficulty in distinguishing contrasts, or in perceiving sound similarities in words. Difficulties in short vowels sounds and initial or final sound similarities are particularly important. The child may learn better through a whole word/sight word approach in the initial stages.

The visual and auditory categories are not mutually exclusive but are a simple way of looking at the child's difficulties. Some children will have both visual and auditory difficulties and in many cases their learning difficulties will be more severe and learning likely to be much slower. Table 5.10 gives further details of this approach.

Another error analysis approach is based on giving the child tasks to investigate particular skills such as a visual versus a phonological strategy. The following description is adapted from Snowling (1982).

If in single-word reading the child reads automatically or quickly the word can be assumed to form part of the individual's sight vocabulary and an estimate of its size can be made. The efficiency of the individual's phonological strategies can be assessed by examining how successfully the words outside of his sight vocabulary can be deciphered. Visual errors (e.g. *sugar* for *saucer, adventure* for *attractive, instruction* for *institution, socialist* for *soloist*) suggest reliance on a visual strategy, whereas phonological errors (e.g. *izland* for *island, angel* for *angle*) suggest reliance on a phonological strategy. Regular (*fresh, treat, dance*) and irregular words (*laugh, glove, biscuit*) can be given to read. Good performance on the former implies grapheme/phoneme correspondence application, or phonological skills. Good performance on irregular words implies good visual or 'direct' reading skills. Another way of examining phonological strategies is to test how well nonsense words can be read, particularly if the phonological structure of the non-word is manipulated so that the point of breakdown of these strategies can be identified, e.g. if monosyllabic non-words can be read, how does the individual manage disyllabic non-words? (e.g. blem (CCVC), tegwop (CVCCVC)).

Snowling cites Frith's (1980a) stage model of spelling as providing a useful framework to analyse errors in dyslexics. Briefly, Frith proposes that unfamiliar words are spelt in three stages:

1 Correct analysis of speech sounds (within the word)

Table 5.10   Reading and spelling error analysis

Reading	Spelling
Auditory channel deficits	
Substitution of sounds.	Omits endings, *ed, s, ing*.
Poor sound blending to make words.	Uses synonyms, *house/home*.
Knows name not sound of letters.	Omits second letter in blends, *fed* for
Mispronounces words, eg. *chimney* as	*fled*, *mid* for *mind*.
chimley.	Substitutes *t/d, f/v, sh/ch* and confuses
Wild guesses where there is no	voiced, unvoiced pairs and high
relationship between words seen and	frequency sounds.
read.	Does not hear subtle differences between
If stuck on word, may not be able to	sounds and leaves out vowels,
sound it out.	*plsh/polish*.
Poor 'phonic' attack.	Identifies beginning or the end of the
Substitutes words *a/the*.	word but not the middle, and this may
Uses synonyms *mummy/mother*.	be missing, for example *md* for *mind*.
	Confuses vowels, *bit* and *bet*.
	Wild guesses, no relationship between
	the sounds and letters representing
	them, and the spelling, *raul/urchins*.
Visual channel deficits	
May invert words or letters.	May visualize the beginning and ending
May reverse words, letters, or phrasing	of the word, omitting the middle,
and word by word reading.	*hapy* for *happy*.
Rate of perception slow.	Spells phonetically, *site/sight* (cannot
Loses place or skips lines and parts.	revisualize).
Adds words which are not there;	Mix capitals and small letters, *cAt*.
occasionally changing the meaning.	Inverts letters *u/n, m/w*.
May omit and read through punctuation,	Reverses letters, words *on/no*.
distorting the meaning.	Gives correct letters in wrong sequence,
Makes guesses or says words that look	*teh/the*.
similar or start in the same way,	
surprise/surface.	
May confuse order, *place/palace*.	

Note: The teaching implications of this kind of analysis will be considered in Chapter 6.

2   Phoneme to grapheme translation
3   Conventionally correct graphemes are selected

Individuals can be described as falling into three groups in spelling. 'Group A' spellers can complete all three stages of the process without difficulty. 'Group B' spellers make phonetic errors, suggesting that they can complete stages 1 and 2 without difficulty. Their phonetic versions (e.g. *addishun* for *addition*) evidence a lack of spelling knowledge (such as *shun* spelled *tion* in a final syllable) which is needed for stage 3 to be completed successfully. 'Group C' spellers produce non-phonetic errors (e.g. *adsun* for *addition*), indicating that they cannot complete stage 2 of the spelling process. Their difficulties could either be in analysing the speech sounds in words or else in phoneme – grapheme translation.

Thus in analysing spelling errors the proportion of phonetic and non-phonetic errors aids the identification of the point of breakdown in the spelling process. The following are suggested ways of obtaining this information.

Assessment of Stage 1 (Analysis of speech stream into sound segments)

1 Segmentation
   (a) Tap out syllables, (con-gra-tu-la-tions).
   (b) Tap out sounds (Tim = /t/ − /i/ − /m/).
   (c) Identify medial sounds (*hop, pick, cub*)

2 Auditory Organization
   For example: 'odd man out' test (see Bradley 1980, Bradley and Bryant 1978)

Initial	SEE	SUN	<u>RAG</u>	SOCK
Medial	MAT	<u>POT</u>	HAT	FAT
Final	WEED	DEED	NEED	<u>PEEL</u>

   Rhyming test. How many words can you think of that rhyme with:
   e.g.   <u>BACK</u>   sack   tack   crack   stack. . . .

3 Articulation
   Examines the segmentation of speech sounds orally, from which spelling can follow. Examples include repeating such words as:

hippopotamus	magnificent
hospital	plimsolls
dominos	electric

Assessment of Stage 2 (Phoneme − grapheme translation)

1 Spelling polysyllabic words
   Individuals may spell single-syllable words phonetically but their powers of phoneme − grapheme translation may break down as the number of syllables in words increases. It is therefore useful to ask them to spell regular words of 2,3 and 4 syllables.
   e.g.: 2 syllables: problem, splendid, thunder
        3 syllables: refreshment, instructed, adventure
        4 syllables: unexpected, conversation, magnificent

2 Spelling non-words
   Occasionally an individual who is primarily a 'phonetic' speller (Group B type) might make a non-phonetic error. This is usually because they think they know the word's spelling and therefore do not adopt the habitual phonological strategy when spelling it. To check the efficiency of phonetic strategies without the interference of spelling knowledge for specific words, the individual can be asked to spell non-words. As in the case of reading, the phonological structure of the non-words can be manipulated.

Assessment of Stage 3 (Spelling knowledge)

If the conventionally correct graphemes to represent phonemes in word spellings are to be selected, extensive knowledge of English spelling conventions is required. Individuals may have poor knowledge of these conventions because of limited reading experience or else because, during reading, they pay little attention to the orthographic structure of words.

1 Checklist of basic spelling patterns allows documentation of those spelling conventions which are known (see above).
2 'Proof reading' task e.g. letter cancellation—crossing out all the e's in:
  (a) She said the green cheese was inedible or
  (b) in alphabet sequences specially prepared to reflect orthographic structure.
3 Morphemic knowledge Spelling performance is improve if spellers know of the morphemic relationship between words, e.g. *sign—signature, condemn—condemnation, hasten—hastily*.
Knowledge of these associations could be tested systematically.

5.5   Perceptual motor and memory skills

Tests such as the WISC and, in particular the BAS, examine aspects of perceptual, motor and memory skills. Tests such as the ITPA, although purporting to measure psycholinguistic skills, do according to various factor analyses (e.g. Burns and Schaaf 1974) measure various kinds of perceptual, motor and memory skills. In addition to these tests, which have been discussed earlier, some procedures have been specifically devised to examine perceptual skills. The Bender Gestalt test, for example, requires the child to copy a series of complex shapes, and difficulties in visuo-motor perception can be identified—a similar test is the Benton Visual Retention Test. Tests for sound discrimination include the Wepman auditory discrimination test in which children are required to indicate whether words are the same or different, and there are many other tests which are commonly used in assessment of the dyslexic, and of children with other learning difficulties. In many cases it is often difficult to know exactly what the tests are measuring, despite their test titles. For example, the Bender Gestalt test may be measuring the ability of the child actually to perceive the shapes in the first instance. The child therefore may make errors not because he cannot draw them, but because he has a severe visual perception difficulty. On the other hand, the child may be able to perceive the shapes perfectly well, but have difficulty in actually copying. This difficulty is a motor one. Similarly, tests such as the Wepman may measure the child's ability to follow careful instructions, or the child's confusion over whether words that rhyme are the same or different, for example.

An alternative way of measuring cognitive skills is to undertake laboratory tasks which have been devised specifically to test particular kinds of encoding, short-term memory, long-term memory or other kinds of behaviours. One could for example envisage procedures used by Thomson and Wilsher (1979), where the subjects were asked to read out a list of numbers presented tachistoscopically as a diagnostic test in terms of processing time. One might administer a Posner-type test as used by Ellis and Miles (1981). (It may be recalled that it was found that dyslexics did less well on a name coding as opposed to a visual coding strategy.) One might present various inter-modality conditions of grapheme/phoneme recognition, such as visual/visual, auditory/visual, visual/auditory and so on, as described by Snowling (1980). There is a vast array of laboratory tasks, described in Chapter 3, which differentiate between dyslexics and controls and seem to pin-point particular areas of cognitive deficit. Unfortunately, many of these are very laborious and time consuming, and are not normatively based. There is still a considerable amount of work to be done in the area of interrelating laboratory and research studies with the assessment procedures used with dyslexic children. One such attempt is Denckla and Rugel's (1976a and b) RAN (Rapid Automatized Naming) test. Here children are simply given a series of pictures or colours and required to give them a name out loud, under strictly timed conditions. They provide norms comparing controls and dyslexic children at various ages. The test was devised in the laboratory, validated on a larger sample of children, and then adapted for diagnostic use in assessment.

5.6   Screening procedures

Screening procedures fall broadly into those that are 'normatively based', and those that are 'criterion oriented'. The former have been developed either for identification of children who are 'at risk' in written language, i.e. children who are likely to be reading and spelling failures later in their school career, or for diagnostic use with those children who have difficulties already. The idea is to pin-point various underlying skills that relate to written language learning in order to suggest areas of diagnosis and remediation. These tests have been validated on samples of children and provide some kind of norm or average with which the child is compared. In the criterion oriented approach, a number of items are given, and it is observed whether the child can do the items and what kind of errors are made. Criterion oriented kinds of tests would include those described by Jordon (1972), Clay (1979), and Aubrey et al. (1982). Normatively based screening procedures include those described by Satz et al. (1978), Silver and Hagin (1972), Silver and Hagin (1975), Newton and Thomson (1976). Those that fall somewhere in between include those described by Slingerland (1971), Miles (1982). The rationale behind many screening procedures is early detection, in order to prevent reading failure by identifying future difficulties. Appropriate first teaching or early remediation would be given. A number of Government reports in the United Kingdom, including the Bullock Report (1975) and the Warnock Report (1978) have stressed the importance of early recognition and identification of learning difficulties.

It is worth considering the distinction between screening and diagnosis. Sometimes screening procedures refer to identifying children with learning problems. This might be a reading or spelling test and the idea is simply to add up the number of children in a particular district who have difficulties, or to identify those for whom further diagnosis is required. Sometimes screening procedures refer to tests given at kindergarten or early in the child's school career in order to *predict* the child's reading, writing and spelling difficulties. The idea here is to identify children who are 'at risk' in acquiring written language. Furthermore, some tests that are labelled screening may refer to tests that are actually diagnostic. These might be test batteries given to children trying to pin-point areas of difficulty in order to plan and suggest remedial techniques which are appropriate for the child. Sometimes a particular screening procedure may have a facility for examining a number of approaches at any given time. However, it is important to bear in mind that there is no neat and commonly agreed description of what screening, diagnosis, reading readiness and other kinds of procedure are.

5.61   Normative screening

Although there may not be a unified concept of the reading process, there is remarkable consistency in the test items which have been used in developing screening tests. Beecher and Goldfluss (quoted by Jansky 1978) reviewed 16 studies that used pre-reading or screening procedures and describe the functions tapped by these 'reading readiness' tests. The most common assessment procedures were: Conceptualization (intelligence); Vocabulary; Letter Knowledge; Auditory Sequential Memory (Digit Span); Visual Discrimination; Visual Memory (often Sequential Memory); and Visuo-Motor Function.

A well researched procedure by Satz and colleagues (1978) is based on a maturational lag theory of dyslexia, specifically that early childhood skills involve mainly visual-perceptual and cross-modal integration skills, whereas skills developing later include language and formal operations. Younger children therefore will tend to have more difficulties in perceptual discrimination of letters and distinctive feature analysis, whereas older children will tend to make more errors on linguistically oriented tasks. Early studies, e.g. Satz and Friel (1973), found that the best predictors of later difficulties in the younger children were finger localization, alphabet recitation and a recognition/discrimination test; and for older children, economic status, grammatic closure (ITPA), a picture vocabulary test and verbal fluency (naming objects under timed conditions). This notion of perceptual discrimination and analysis, i.e. sensory or perceptual/motor/memorial abilities as opposed to comprehension, syntactic and other kinds of linguistic skills, is an attempt to integrate reported difficulties in dyslexia by arguing that they relate to different age levels. In a series of later studies, Satz, Friel *et al.* (1976; Satz, Taylor *et al.* 1978) came up with four major factors which seemed to account for the majority of the variance in the prediction of children's behaviour. Factor 1 (31% of variance) related to sensory, motor and memorial skills, Factor 2 (15% of variance) related to economic status, Factor 3 (13%) related to conceptual ability; and Factor 4 (8%) related to motor dominance and laterality. The criterion used for later success at reading was in some cases the IOTA Word Recognition test, although classroom reading level based on teacher rating was used as well. The results generally suggested that they were able to predict very poor readers and, also, very good readers. The predictions for a 'middle group', i.e. those children who were average in reading or mildly disabled, was much less satisfactory. This however is a weakness with many screening procedures, and relates to the number of false positives and false negatives one is prepared to accept, i.e. children who were predicted to be 'at risk' and who in fact did not turn out to have reading, writing and spelling difficulties, or children who were thought not to be 'at risk' but in fact turned out to have difficulties later on.

Janksy (1978) criticizes Satz's notion of language not being a particularly important element in the early stages of a child's developing reading skills. She argues, observing children with oral difficulties in language, that there are critical linguistic structures which need to be acquired in order for the child to develop written language appropriately. Based on the screening procedures which she and de Hirsch developed (de Hirsch et al. 1966; Jansky and de Hirsch 1972) five major factors were identified: visuo-motor ability; oral language (defining words); pattern matching; pattern memory and oral language—'speech'. Jansky argues that the highest association with reading is oral language, followed by pattern matching and visuo-motor ability, and the highest function associated with spelling is visuo-motor ability, followed by oral language and pattern matching. She also comments that pattern matching and pattern memory were not modality specific, i.e. they cut across all modalities and the common factor appears to be verbal activity. Many of the test items involved assigning names, e.g. picture naming, describing stories and cartoons, and letter naming, as well as awareness of deep linguistic structures in tasks such as sentence repetition. She argues that it is the interaction of perceptual/motor skills and language which is important.

Silver and Hagin (1975) found visual perception discrimination, recall and visuo-motor control to be good predictors of later reading failure. In their SEARCH Test (Silver and Hagin 1976), they stress orientation in time and space as well as temporal sequences. Their test includes measures of visual discrimination; recall of asymmetric figures; visual motor function; auditory discrimination and rote sequencing; articulation; inter-modal dictation; finger gnosis, praxis and left/right discrimination. They report some impressive predictors in identifying children's learning difficulties. For example, they found around 25 to 30% of children had difficulties in spatial and temporal organization at five years old. Based on a cut-off level taking the lowest third of these children, they were able to produce predictors including no false positives in those children having severe difficulties later, 1% false positives having mild difficulties and around 10% false negatives.

The Bangor Dyslexia Test (Miles 1982) is an inventory designed to give 'positive signs', i.e. items that are dyslexic loaded. These include knowledge of left and right (child's and tester's), repeating polysyllabic words, subtraction, tables, saying months of the year, digit span forward and reverse, b/d confusions, and familial incidence of dyslexic difficulties. Based on a simple scoring system of 'dyslexia positive' and 'dyslexia negative' signs Miles presents data showing, for example, that dyslexic 9 to 12-year-olds have a mean of 5.14 dyslexia positive items, whereas control subjects with the same age range had 2.24, a significant difference. Miles also describes the odd strategies used by dyslexics, such as having to start right back at the beginning after making an error in months of the year, or very complex adding exercises to obtain the right answer in simple tables.

Newton and Thomson (1976), in their Aston Index, argue that it is possible to identify an 'at risk' profile, demonstrating lower scores in a group of children on all Index items. This 'at risk' group showed a delay in the development of perceptual skills, the best predictors of later reading difficulty being auditory sequential memory, sound blending and copying names. In relation to the diagnostic or concurrent component of the Index, it was found that vocabulary, visual sequencing, auditory sequencing, sound blending, sound discrimination, laterality and the graphomotor test discriminated between children who were good at reading and spelling and those who were not. Further details of the use of the Aston Index are given in Section 5.7.

Before moving on to criterion oriented tests, it is worth briefly considering the notion of screening for 'at risk/not at risk' children in the population, as this is an important component of screening procedures. In the Aston Index prediction quoted above for example it was found that there were about 5% false positives. There were 19% false negatives, i.e. children who were thought not to be 'at risk' but in fact turned out to have difficulties later on. There are various arguments that can be put forward in relation to which is the most important figure. Benton (1978), for example, argues that any rapid screening instrument cannot detect all the variables involved and therefore a fair number of false negatives are to be expected. He does however suggest that 'danger' comes from the false positives, arguing that this creates self-fulfilling prophecy and labelling. I would disagree with this analysis. It seems more important to identify a greater number of children who are truly 'at risk', and require teaching help, even if it means providing this help for a few who do not need it.

Altering cut-off points will result in a variation in the kinds of error classification. For example, in the research cited above (Thomson *et al.* 1979) on the Aston Index reducing the cut-off points would reduce the number of false negatives down to 1 or 2%; however, this resulted in a much higher proportion of false positives. Some discussion of this area is given by Thomson (1979c) who postulates an approach based on probablistic analysis; specifically, this Bayesian approach develops probabilities of an individual child failing (or alternatively succeeding) in absolute terms, and compares the probabilities to the base rate of reading failure. The stages taken in application of this model are as follows:

1 The establishment of a 'base' rate of reading (or spelling, arithmetic, etc.) failure in the school or area population. This involves monitoring attainments over at least two years if early identification is required;

2 The administration of an appropriate screening test at the age required for identification;

3 A follow-up period to establish criterion and test allocation categories;

4 The establishment of cut-off points on the screening test that gives the highest conditional probabilities for 'success' or 'failure' in the areas being considered;

5 Application of statistical procedures using Bayesian formulae for producing conditional probabilities, for subtests or total test scores as required;

6 Comparison of probabilities with previously established base rates;

7 Consequent use of screening test where probabilities add increased information for local situations.

Stages 1 to 6 may be undertaken over the same period, provided that there is no intervention as a result of initial screening for validation purposes. If intervention takes place at this stage, false 'base-rates' may of course result. Readers may refer to Thomson (1979c) for details and examples of this approach in operation.

5.62 Criterion oriented screening

One aim of the criterion approach is to define clearly some kind of target behaviour e.g. 'able to read Ladybird Book 3' or something more specific like 'able to identify consonant blends'. Having described target objectives one plans teaching based on what the child can or cannot do. There are no implications for underlying deficits, i.e. possible reasons for the child's learning problems. The idea here is to treat the 'symptoms'. Some examples of this are given by Clay (1972), who states that objectives should be:

1 To observe precisely what children are doing and saying;

2 To use tasks that are close to the learning tasks of the classroom (rather than standardized tests);

3 To observe what children have been able to learn (not what they have been unable to do);

4 To discover what reading behaviours they should now be taught from an analysis of performance in reading, not from pictorial or puzzle material, or from normative scores;

5 To shift the child's reading behaviour from less adequate to more adequate responding, by training on reading tasks rather than training visual perception or auditory discrimination as separate activities.

She suggests that a diagnostic survey be carried out with all children who are not making good progress on their sixth birthday. Items would include: Accuracy on book reading (5–10 minutes), Analysis of errors, Integration of skills, Letter identification (5–10 minutes), Concepts about print (5–10 minutes), 'Ready to read' Word Test (2 minutes); Writing vocabulary and Dictation test (Clay 1972). See Clay 1979; Tansley and Panckhurst 1981 for further details.

Other approaches include providing children with various kinds of tasks that relate to the hypothesized visual, motor and perceptual difficulties. Examples of this are the Slingerland (1971) and Jordan (1972) tests. In the latter, for example, test items include visual matching, where the child is required to put a ring round a word in a row which matches the target (a child may be shown 'barn' and required to match that against 'barn', 'pnar' and so on). Similar tasks are given in auditory matching, or the child might be required to identify, then write down the initial letter in a word, or to write down individual letters from memory. Here assessors can use these tests or devise their own assessment procedures. Particularly useful in my experience are items involving writing down from memory letters presented auditorally, identifying initial sounds in words, whether these be as individual letters or letter combinations and, in particular, final blends. Various auditory or visual matching tasks may be appropriate if one is uncertain as to whether the difficulty is mainly auditory or visual. Many of these procedures can be used in initial assessments, but are more useful once remediation has commenced. Some examples of behaviours under various perceptual/motor/memorial headings are given in Table 5.11.

In Chapter 6 we shall be looking at how some of these particular behaviours relate to possible teaching methods.

5.7   Sample reports

This section presents two examples of reports that might be written about children following assessment. One refers to the results of a screening test (the Aston Index) which might be given by a psychologist, speech therapist, teacher, or any other professional involved in learning-disabled children. The other report refers to an assessment based on some screening procedures but mainly involving the British Ability Scales and would normally be given by a psychologist. In both cases, brief recommendations are made in relation to teaching procedures for remediation; however, details of teaching procedures will be picked up in more detail in Chapter 6.

5.7   Sample reports

5.71   Report 1—Aston Index

Richard—CA 8 years 4 months (level 2 of the Index).

The Index is divided into two sections (1) general underlying ability and attainments, and (2) performance items. A summary of the test results can be presented in graphic form based on two profiles obtained from these two sections. These are given as Figures 5.2 and 5.3.

Background
Rating scales in relation to Background Factors indicated that Richard came from a good home where English was the first language and there were no indications of any familial discord or difficulties. Both his hearing (audiometric examination) and his vision had been tested and were found to be within normal limits. Reports from the mother suggest that Richard's developmental milestones were normal

Table 5.11 Examples of criterion oriented observations (from Aston Teaching Portfolio)

Visual discrimination and recall

a   Difficulties in discrimination of sizes, shapes, letters or numbers.
b   Difficulties in recalling direction and orientation of letters and words.
c   Difficulties in retaining letter names and sight words.
d   Lacking attention to structural elements in words, e.g. prefixes and suffixes.

Auditory discrimination

a   Problems in identifying whether a sound is the same or different.
b   Confusion of similar consonants in spelling or reading, for example, $d/t, f/v, b/d, m/n$.
c   Omission of vowels or parts of consonant blends, e.g. *ct* for *cat*, *hp* for *help*, *pan* for *plan*.
d   Mispronunciation of words, *chimley/chimney*.
e   Omission of word endings.
f   Bizarre spelling errors.

Rhyming

a   Difficulties in matching rhyming words in, e.g., *I left my coat in the . . . (house, boat, car)*.
b   Difficulties supplying rhyming words with, e.g., *take, hot, said*.

Memory and sequence

a   Difficulties in following directions, and, e.g., constantly asking for repetitions.
b   Easily distracted by competing stimuli, restless in stories, difficulties in attending to speech.
c   Use of spoonerisms or reversed hyphenated words, *take-over* for *over-take*, *emeny* for *enemy*, *crinimal* for *criminal* and so on.
d   Syllable or letters in wrong order in reading and spelling, *bread/beard*, *felt/left*, etc.
e   Poor serial memory, e.g. days of the week, months of the year, seasons, alphabet, tables.
f   Difficulties in memorizing sequence of sounds long enough to blend them.
g   Difficulties in following or tapping rhythmic patterns.

Auditory and visual integration

a   A child may say one sound or letter, and write another one.
b   Sounding out the wrong letter in reading, although blending correctly.
c   Relying on visual means of recognizing the words, rather than sounding out.

Analysis and synthesis of sounds (also Auditory Memory and Sequencing Ability)

a   Difficulties in blending separate sounds into words or syllables, e.g. *c-a-t*.
b   Difficulties in the identification of separate sounds making up words, i.e. phoneme identification.
c   Omission of initial sounds when asked to blend, e.g. *et* for *pet* and general problems in recognizing that letters in syllables can be given oral sounds.

Syllabification

a   Omission of parts or syllables of words in speech, reading or spelling, e.g. *rember/remember*.
b   The addition of extra syllables or order confusions. *rememberember/remember*.
c   The identification of the number of syllables in a word, when asked to count them or tap them out, i.e. difficulties in tapping a rhythm or beat.

(Adapted from Aubrey *et al.* 1982).

apart from language, which was rather delayed. He did not produce his first single words till around $2\frac{1}{2}$ years, and was referred to a speech therapist when $3\frac{1}{2}$ for phonological and articulation difficulties. He had some treatment for a few months but his language eventually improved and it was felt there were no serious speech or language disorders. Richard himself presented as a boy with no primary emotional difficulties; he related well to other children and although rather anxious and withdrawn in class was not a behaviour problem. His class teacher had moved him to the front of the class as she felt he had difficulty in attending/hearing.

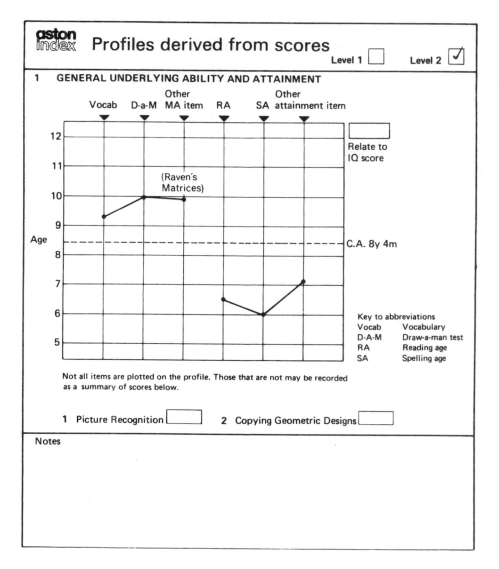

Figure 5.2   Aston Index profile 1

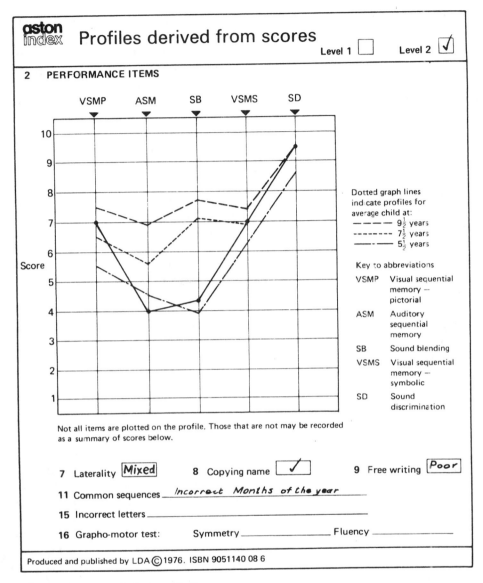

Figure 5.3   Aston Index profile 2

Abilities and attainments

Although Richard scored somewhat lower on the Draw-a-Man test than on Vocabulary, his performance was well above his chronological age. One felt on the Vocabulary test that he understood the words but was unable to express his ideas appropriately. Many of the definitions were rather thin and lacked a 'richness' of linguistic expression. Richard's performance on both these tests suggests that his difficulties were not due to a slow learning or general cognitive difficulty. In general he appeared to be of above average intelligence and it was felt unnecessary to refer him for a full-scale intelligence test at that time.

Richard's reading and spelling were considerably behind his chronological age, at around the $6-6\frac{1}{2}$ year level. He had barely made a start in spelling, being able to spell only a few words correctly on the Schonell Graded Word Spelling test. His reading was somewhat better, but still two years behind his chronological age, and rather more behind his potential ability in relation to his mental age. His reading from a story in an additional test given (NFER test) indicated that his Reading Comprehension was somewhat better as this involved answering questions. The above suggests that Richard had a specific difficulty in reading, writing and spelling.

Richard's reading on the Schonell test was slow and non-fluent, and he lost his place a number of times. He appeared to have no 'phonic attack' skills—although able to sound one or two letters, he could not recognize consonant blends, nor combine letters to form words. Errors included confusion of vowel sounds (e.g. *bak/book*), reversal of letters (e.g. *dun/bun*), omissions (e.g. *fog/frog*), as well as guessing one or two letters and omitting syllables—*sugar/saucer, active/attractive* suggested lack of phonological skills. In spelling, Richard tended to omit letters(e.g. *ht/hat, mid/mind*), as well as incorrect substitutions of sounds (e.g. *goot/good*). Other errors included confusion of letter order (e.g. *form/from*). Free writing was very poor, only a few words completed, with no punctuation, poor writing style for age, and similar spelling errors to the above, including some 'bizarre' attempts.

Performance items

Richard's performance on the Visual Sequential Memory tests, both pictorial and symbolic, was slightly below the norm as given in the Manual, and there do not appear to be any very serious difficulties here. Richard made no orientation errors on the VSMP, his errors here being mainly in order. Richard scored very poorly however on both the Auditory Sequential Memory and Sound Blending. These were well below the norms and indeed well below the level expected for a $7\frac{1}{2}$-year-old. In the case of auditory memory, Richard's performance was at the $5\frac{1}{2}$-year level. Here Richard was unable to retain three digits in reverse, and although occasionally able to remember four or five digits in the forward order, made errors twice in both these conditions. Errors in sound blending included omission of initial sounds (e.g. *egg* for *beg*), confusions of vowels in nonsense blends, (e.g. *dip* for *dup*), as well as attempts from one or two of the sounds in the word, (e.g. *in* for *dinner*). Sound discrimination on the other hand was normal, although Richard made one error (*bit/pit*). The above suggests a difficulty in auditory memory and sound blending, and generally a difficulty in auditory perception, analysis and memory. This does not appear to be a discrimination difficulty, but in more complex aspects of the sound system. Other items, such as mixed laterality, are described on the Profile.

Recommendations

Firstly, it was suggested that Richard be referred for a fuller assessment by the School Psychological Service or the Remedial Advisory Service, particularly in the areas of written language and perceptual/linguistic skills. However the Index results suggested that Richard did have a specific learning problem of a dyslexic type which would need to receive appropriate recognition. This meant recognizing that Richard's difficulties were not due to him being 'stupid' or 'lazy', and that he be given as much opportunity as possible to succeed in other aspects of the school curriculum, such as oral classwork, and in material that did not involve reading, writing and spelling. It was also important that teachers involved with Richard be aware of his difficulties and not have too high an expectation in relation to project work in his writing.

As Richard had barely made a start in some aspects of reading, writing and spelling, it was suggested that teaching be undertaken at this level. The initial sound/symbol correspondences needed to be overtaught and overlearnt. As this was a particular difficulty, he would benefit from help in following his own speech, and here the Edith Norrie letter case (see Chapter 6) was suggested, which might be used to develop speech sound to writing skills. He would need to be gradually introduced to simple blends and building up three-letter words, i.e. consonant-vowel-consonant combinations in spelling.

It was suggested he move from whole to part in learning, emphasizing the sight aspect of reading, (e.g. look-and-say methods), then moving towards the sounds. The teaching techniques would need to go from visual to auditory, including tactile and kinesthetic modalities as aids. As Richard had some confusions of sound/symbol correspondence, it might be useful to undertake procedures identifying sounds at the beginning of words (I-spy games using initial letters sounds, key-words and letter sounds, see for example the Alpha to Omega programme). His severe difficulties in auditory memory suggested that he would benefit from listening to auditory material, e.g. stories on tape, memory games such as *I went to market and bought a . . .*, following verbal commands, using mnemonics and other activities aimed at overcoming auditory memory problems. Richard also would need help later in 'chunking up' spelling and sound patterns. He would need to be overtaught the rules and regulations of the English language system so that he would not be required to remember individual letter combinations, but be able to access whole units. In relation to his sound blending difficulties, sounds in tapes could be put into games, blending could be undertaken with simple words by placing letters on cards and moving the letters appropriately, saying the sounds at the same time.

5.72 Report 2—psychologist's report

The following example of a Psychologist's report is taken from one of the writer's assessments. Name and locality have been changed to ensure confidentiality.

Psychological assessment on:
Name: Mark

Date of Birth: 12.4.71
Chronological age: 11 years
1 month
Date seen: 21.5.82

Psychometric assessment gave the following results:
British Ability Scales
General IQ: 102
Verbal IQ: 102
Visual IQ: 101
Subtest T-Scores Average 50, range 27−73

Speed		Short term Memory	
Speed of Information	44	Immediate Visual Recall	40
		Delayed Visual Recall	40
Reasoning		Recall of Designs	42
Formal Operational Thinking	54	Recall of Digits	41
Similarities	56		
Matrices	61	*Retrieval/Application Knowledge*	
		Word Definitions	49
Spatial Imagery		Word Reading	38
Block Design Level	50		
Block Design Power	51		
Rotation of Letter-Like			
Forms	54		
Visualization of Cubes	53		
Word Reading Age:	8 years 0 months		

Expected Reading Age based on:
Similarities	11 years 8 months
Recall of Digits	9 years 0 months
Word Definition	11 years 1 month

Neale Analysis of Reading Ability
	Yrs	Months
Accuracy	8	8
Rate	8	4
Comprehension	8	5

Vernon Graded Word	Age 8 years 6 months Quotient 85
Spelling Test:	

Free Writing: General performance not commensurate with spoken language ability, poor writing style for age, no punctuation, difficulties in aspects of syntax. Spelling errors included phonetic attempts (e.g. *pratic, practice, cuming, coming*). Occasionally ran separated words together (e.g. *oklok, o'clock, inthe, in the, monng, morning*). Other errors included confusion of vowel sounds (e.g. *forn, fun*) confusions of letter order and consonants (e.g.

presrets, presents). Mark had great difficulty in expressing his ideas fluently in written form, and it took him over 15 minutes to compose 3 or 4 lines of writing.

Aston Index (selected items)

Sound Blending: Some difficulties in blending sounds, e.g. *eat* for *feet*, *but* for *boat*, *bot* for *pot*. Many of these errors suggested difficulties in remembering the whole sequence of sounds, in particular Mark had difficulty in nonsense blends, being unable to represent them at all. This also suggests difficulty in auditory analysis and awareness.

Sound Discrimination: No errors, good performance, no indication of any hearing loss or auditory acuity problems.

Laterality

Right-handed, left-eyed—'cross-lateral'.

Common sequences

Unable to sequence months of year (Confused order).

Knowledge of left and right

Hesitant over own, confused tester's left and right.

Jordan Screening Test: (selected items)

Test 8 (Auditory Perception/Memory)

Difficulties in representing letters given orally (e.g. *tztz* for *tzcb*, *ftijh* for *ftjih*).

Test 11 (Sound Identification/Initial Digraphs)

A good performances in identifying initial digraphs, no errors.

Test 12 (Sound Identification-Final Digraphs)

A fair performance, although some difficulty in more difficult blends, e.g. *og* for *ng* as in *gong*, *lp* for *rp* as in *slurp*. This suggests some difficulty in analysis of final sounds, particularly those acquired later in spoken language.

Bangor Dyslexic Test (selected items)

Polysyllabic words

Some difficulties here, e.g. *perriliminary/preliminary*, *satistical/statistical*

Tables

Confused tables, e.g. had to recite whole table to obtain 6×7.

Subtractions

Occasional difficulty in carrying numbers

Other Indicators

Mark had a little difficulty in some aspects of auditory organization, such as segmentation and identifying the 'odd' sound out. A fair application of phoneme-to-grapheme rules was observed in nonsense-word spelling, and also in grapheme-to-phoneme conversions in nonsense-word reading. He appeared to have greater difficulties in sight or irregular words.

Background Factors

Mark is at present attending Valley School, where he has recently been given some extra help in his maths and reading, which were reported to be poor. Mark attended both the Infant and Primary Departments of the Valley School prior to his current placement, and it was reported early on in his school career that he had difficulties in learning to read, write and spell. At first this was put down to his being generally slow or backward, but currently the teachers are puzzled over his lack of learning as he appears reasonably bright but 'possibly lazy'. There are some adjustment difficulties reported from the School, although these have developed only recently, and he did not have any social adjustment or settling-down problems in his early school career.

Developmental milestones were within normal limits, although Mark was slightly delayed in his language development, and he had some early difficulties in pronunciation. There were no difficulties at the pre-, peri- or post-natal stages, and indeed no evidence of any neurological damage, whether earlier on in life or up to his current development. Both Mark's eyes and ears had been tested and were reported to be within normal limits. There was therefore no reason to suppose that his reading difficulties resulted from any sensory or hearing defects.

Mark himself was very shy and non-communicative at first. He soon settled down however and made good rapport with the tester, but still had some difficulties in verbal communication. This applied particularly to test items where he was asked to describe things in detail, and indeed in many cases appeared to be searching for an appropriate word. This communication difficulty could result in his general ability being underestimated in the school situation. He also presented as a rather introvert and quiet young boy in addition to having a language communication or verbal expression problem, and this kind of general personality style I was sure overlaid some of his learning difficulties (see below). However in general there did not seems to be any primary personality disturbance, emotional problems or other difficulties in this area of development which might account for Mark's reading, writing and spelling problem.

Intelligence and Abilities

The British Ability Scales (BAS) placed Mark in the average range of intelligence. This indicated that any difficulties he may have had did not result from a slow learning potential, nor from general difficulties in spoken language understanding. All things being equal one would have expected Mark to be succeeding fairly well at school, certainly as well as any of his peer group He was a normal and able thinking child, and as such had the same potential to learn as the majority of other children of his age.

There was no discrepancy between Mark's visual and verbal skills in terms of the BAS IQs. This implies that he did not have general difficulty in language. Mark did particularly well on the Reasoning subtests, his IQ equivalent here being 115. These tests are particularly associated with aspects of school learning, and the IQ equivalent placed Mark in the above-average range of intelligence (top 25% of the population). Given some of his specific difficulties, this was perhaps a more realistic estimate of his potential than the general IQ figure, as Mark scored particularly poorly on some of the sub-tests which are used to compute the full-scale IQ (see below). Mark scored in the average range in Spatial Imagery, but very poorly indeed in Short-Term Memory, which was well below average (IQ equivalent 81).

Mark's subtest profile is of some interest and significance. In Speed of Information Processing Mark he scored rather poorly. This test involves elements of left – right serial scanning, grapho-motor skills, but particularly aspects of symbol coding and number identification. This suggests deficits in some of these areas in Mark's case. On the Reasoning subtests, although Mark did rather better on these than the others, as mentioned above, he did somewhat less well on those involving verbal reasoning (Similarities), compared to the non-verbal reasoning (Matrices) in which he scored well above average. In Spatial Imagery tests, those involving three-dimensional and problem-solving ability as well as visualization, Mark did well. His good performance on the Rotation of Letter-Like Forms tests suggests that his problem was not in visuo-spatial representation. The spatial imagery tests coupled with the reasoning tests give a general idea of Mark's overall intellectual potential. However, when we look at the Short-Term Memory abilities, rather specific skills associated with other aspects of school attainments, we notice some problems. In general Mark scored in the below-average range on short-term memory (Immediate and Delayed Visual Recall are not used to compute an IQ, but the Recall of Designs and Recall of Digits are, and this will have tended to result in an underestimate of his Full-Scale Intelligence). In Immediate and Delayed Visual Recall, tests including verbal labelling and the retention of visual/verbal information over time, Mark did rather less well. Also, he scored poorly on Recall of Designs, a test of visual motor memory, which might well relate to problems in remembering materials copied from the blackboard, in copying spellings, and other elements of the written language process. He also scored poorly on Recall of Digits, a test of auditory sequential memory involving the retention of sounds in order, a key feature of early written language learning, particularly spelling. The ability to remember a series of sound patterns, to associate sound with symbol, to internalize the rules and regulations of spelling, and many other tasks appertaining to written language are all associated with short-term memory difficulties. This seemed to be a key area of Mark's problem in reading and spelling. Mark's reading on the BAS was also very poor. Poor performance on short-term memory, particularly Recall of Digits, Immediate and Delayed Visual Recall, as well as on Word Reading test and Speed of Information Processing are typically associated with a dyslexic-type learning difficulty, in my clinical and research experience. It may be seen how closely Mark's profile fits this pattern. From the T-Score Discrepancy Tables, the above subtests were significantly poorer than the other Reasoning, Spatial Imagery and Word Definitions subtests, at the P is less than 0.05 level. In addition, the Recall of Designs was also poorer than the other subtests at the same level. This indicates that these abilities were specifically poor in Mark's case.

In summary Mark's overall abilities were in the average to above-average range, but he had particular difficulties in reading, aspects of short-term memory and symbol processing.

Attainments

Mark's performance on the BAS Word Reading was some three years behind his chronological age. Based on his verbal reasoning abilities (Similarities) one would have expected Mark to be reading rather above his chronological age. There was thus a discrepancy between Mark's overall intelligence and his reading performance. On the Word Reading Test, a test of word recognition, Mark's performance was characterized by a number of visually orientated errors such as confusions of letter order and omissions (e.g. *deal* for *idea, flavour* for *favour*). Other errors included mispronunciations, (e.g. *fin* for *thin*, *earo* for *error*). He also made further confusions of letter order (e.g. *cafl* for *calf, bread* for *beard*).

When Mark was able to use context clues in reading from a story, as in the Neale Analysis, his reading was somewhat better; however the Accuracy age was over two years retarded from his chronological age. Reading errors included problems in relation to visual analysis (e.g. *voice* for *choice, finishing* for *fishing, disgusting* for *discussing*). In addition, Mark also made errors of letter order (e.g. *thre* for *theatre*). It was noticeable that Mark's Reading Comprehension was rather poor. This contrasted with his overall verbal abilities—he appeared to be spending a good deal of time trying to decode what the word was saying, and missed out on the meaning. Reading is after all about communicating ideas, and this particular component of his reading would also require a good deal of attention and remedial help.

Some of Mark's strategies in relation to comprehension also led him into difficulties. He tended to guess from context or from one or two letters for example, *because he was unusually clothed* instead of *because he wore unusual clothes*; this did not change the meaning of the sentence. Occasionally however this attempt to guess one or two letters and provide appropriate words in context led to problems, for example, *the torches scorched the hardwood*, instead of *their torches searched the darkness*.

Reading Rate was also very poor, and it is important to recognize that Mark would require a much longer time to read stories and, for example, set texts relating to class work even if they were within his Reading Accuracy ability. This would make reading a very slow, laborious and difficult process for him. In general his reading fluency was some $2\frac{1}{2}$ years behind his chronological age.

Mark's spelling was also considerably retarded from his chronological age. Spelling errors suggested, as did his reading, some problems in the visual analysis area. He seemed to be able to perceive the sound patterns correctly, and spell phonetically, but he had problems in 'revisualization', i.e. in seeing what a spelling pattern looked like and recognizing that it was wrong, and remembering the visual representation of the letters. This also implies that he had problems in remembering and internalizing spelling patterns. Spelling errors here included phonetic attempts, such as *honney* for *honey, ofice* for *office, reson* for *reason, strate* for *straight*, where he was failing to apply appropriate spelling rules but getting the sound patterns correct. Mark occasionally made confusions of sound order, suggesting difficulties in written symbol association, and auditory analysis (e.g. *rold* for *royal, shorthely* for *shovel*), as well as confusions of vowel sounds (e.g. *thom* for *thumb*). Some of these auditory difficulties were manifested in his Sound Blending performance, which again was rather poor in many ways for a child of 11.

Opinion
The discrepancy between Mark's intellectual abilities or intelligence and his written

language performance, his profile on the British Ability Scales, his reading and spelling errors, his late language development, confusion of left and right directions, and other aspects of his test profile suggest a learning problem described by many as being of a dyslexic type. The relevant points made in earlier chapters may be summarized as follows.

This problem is a specific difficulty with reading, writing and spelling. It is a particular category of reading difficulty, independent of many of the other factors which can effect written language attainment, for example, intelligence, socio-cultural background, emotional difficulties. It should not be viewed as a 'disease' or 'defect', but rather an individual difference in learning style not predisposing some children to acquire our written language system easily. This specific difficulty with written language is often associated with the perceptual and motor skills outlined above.

Mark's particular difficulties appeared to be associated with aspects of short-term memory problems, a typical feature of the above syndrome, but specifically in aspects of visual perception. This does not imply that he could not 'see', but rather that he had difficulty in letter-order perception, and in internalizing what spelling patterns look like. In addition, however, he did have the the occasional difficulty in aspects of auditory memory, and auditory analysis, particularly in phonemic perception or segmentation, i.e. blending and chunking words up into whole units. Whatever label one wants to give to Mark's difficulties however, the implications seem fairly clear.

Recommendations

The next two years were going to be crucial in Mark's school career, in my opinion. It was important for his reading and spelling to be improved considerably and to approximately match his age level by the time he transferred to secondary school. If he is was to achieve his potential, attain qualifications appropriate to himself and indeed to obtain an appropriate job it was important for a good deal of intensive remedial work to be undertaken over the following two or three years.

An initial recommendation was for Mark's difficulty to be recognized. This implies understanding that his learning problem was not because he was 'thick' or 'lazy' and recognizing that he would have severe difficulty in expressing his ideas fluently in written form, in reading material appropriate to his age level, and indeed would become increasingly demotivated and uninterested in school work as he found it more and more difficult. It should be borne in mind that children with written language problems confront their own failure every day, as most tasks in school require one to read, write and spell. In Mark's case, his problem was overlain with a communication difficulty and a rather introvert personality, making it all the more important to provide appropriate success, and for him to be involved in classwork and oral work as much as possible.

As well as recognition of his problem, Mark required some intensive remedial work. Providing more reading, writing and spelling was not enough; the programme had to be specifically geared to his individual needs. This implied some kind of structured programme, i.e. involving the overlearning and overteaching of the written language system, and a careful consideration of rules, regulations and spelling patterns starting at a level just below his current attainments to give him immediate success, and to build very carefully and cumulatively on this structure. Some examples of this kind of approach are given in the Alpha to Omega programme by (Hornsby and Shear), or the Gill Cotterell phonic reference cards.

He would need particular components of programmes aimed at circumventing his difficulties, for example chunking-out spelling patterns into whole units to overcome his short-term memory problems, and encouraging the use of phonic analysis and blending skills, as these seemed to be rather better than visual analysis skills in his case. A good source of ideas is the Aston Teaching Portfolios, which give a number of games, remedial procedures and written language work.

Another recommendation was that the teaching programme be multi-sensory. This implies linking the sound with the symbol and with the writing/motor kines-thetic equivalent, e.g. using the Fernald Tracing technique. In particular this might be used for learning whole words, words that he required for everyday or frequent use, such as in science or particular classroom situations. He would also benefit from some kind of adaptation of the multi-sensory learning programme, such as the Hickey Language Training Course or something based on the Gillingham and Stillman programme. He would also need some work on comprehension. In the early stages this might involve a good deal of verbal and oral discussion about stories and the world in general, to try to bring Mark's verbal abilities much more to the fore. He needed to be able to express his ideas much more fluently before he could start to write about them. However, he would also need to do some work on reading comprehension, and on written language expression and planning.

It was impossible to describe a very detailed teaching programme in such a rela-tively short report. It was most important for Mark to receive some help from a teacher familiar and experienced in helping children with a specific learning or dyslexic type problem. From talking to Mark's parents it appeared that the best plan of action at the moment was to continue with the remedial help that Mark was receiving from the local authority at that time, but to arrange for a specialist teacher to be brought in, either peripatetically, or for Mark to attend a local centre. I suggested that this report be forwarded to the Headteacher and the class teacher who were involved with Mark. If however the local authority was not able to provide appropriate help Mark would certainly benefit from the teaching programme undertaken at [centre]. If this was the course of action contemplated, it was suggested that the [centre] be contacted over the summer, in order that Mark could attend at the beginning of the school year in September.

Whatever the course of action, it was important for this to be discussed with the Headteacher and with the local authority officers such as the remedial teacher or psychologist.

6

Remediation: evaluation and assessment

This chapter will examine the relationship between assessment and remediation, and look at how one evaluates remediation. We shall present some general comments in this area as well as some specific examples of evaluation studies.

6.1 The relationship between assessment and remediation

Having examined the process of assessment and diagnosis in Chapter 5 it is worth at this point making some comments about the relationship between assessment and remediation. Assessment is not merely a sterile process of putting on a label, but should have implications for teaching.

Assessment is important for remediation in that it aids diagnosis, deciding on the level of teaching, matching task to learner and placement of the child.

1 Diagnosis: Many critics of the notion of an assessment to diagnose an individual as having a dyslexic problem argue that using the label dyslexia has no implications for teaching. Rather to the contrary, my view is that this diagnosis has very important implications. The first of these is that the child's learning failure is not due to something else, for example 'slow learning'. This indicates that the kinds of teaching procedures used for slow learners and generally backward readers are not particularly appropriate for the child. In other words a general language programme in order to improve conceptual and cognitive development is inappropriate. Expectations are going to be somewhat different—the intelligent child may well be able to learn quite complex rules and regulations of the written language and there might be quite a sophisticated use of aspects of spoken language. Dyslexia also implies that there will be a gap between the child's ability to read certain books and his *understanding* of the books. He may need intellectually more challenging kinds of material. Also implied is that the child will be able to understand much more that goes on in the classroom, and that there will be a particular gap between this and his written language expression. The overall curriculum for the child should be at his chronological or intellectual level. The diagnostic aspects also imply that the child does not have a sensory difficulty. The teaching programmes aimed at the deaf or the partially sighted child are also not appropriate. This may seem an obvious point, but from the writer's experience it is quite common for people trying to help the dyslexic child to make the assumption that there is some kind of sensory learning problem. They might, for example, make the child sit in the front so that he can hear better, or so that he can see the blackboard better—this being the sole extra remediation given.

Another very important point is that a diagnosis of dyslexia implies that diffi- culties do not result primarily from an emotional problem, or from a personality defect. This is perhaps the most common erroneous kind of treatment given to the dyslexic child. Here the child may attend a local centre where he is given 'therapy'. This may well alleviate some of their secondary emotional symptoms, but does not tackle the cause, and is an inappropriate way to help the dyslexic. Another implica- tion from diagnosis is that the child's difficulties are not due to lack of experience in the learning process, poor teaching or lack of opportunity to learn. The teaching programme should not just be 'more of the same'. What often happens is that the child is given a greater number of spelling lists to learn, additional reading assign- ments, more reading with the teacher, or a lot more writing. This will not enable the dyslexic child to learn unless linked to a structured programme—the dyslexic has not failed due to lack of opportunity.

As well as remedial programmes that are excluded by virtue of describing a child as being dyslexic, the diagnosis also implies that a particular type of teach- ing programme should be undertaken. This teaching programme should follow the principles which we have outlined, be structured, sequential, cumulative and multi-sensory.

2   *The 'level' of teaching programme:* Another important component of assessment is to decide which particular level of teaching programme to commence at for the individual child. This might be in terms of relating reading material to interest and ability. A very bright child, for example, would need to do a lot of oral project work, might be expected to take certain elements of a teaching programme much more quickly than a child that is intellectually less capable. However the level referred to here is the particular access point of a structured programme. The implication is that one is teaching the rules and regulations of the written language system in a very systematic way, and one wants to know whereabouts to start. Ideally this needs to be just below the child's current attainment level to obtain immediate success, and to build up very gradually. As well as requiring some general notion as to the child's overall level in terms of reading and spelling ages, one needs to know the kinds of particular spelling or reading errors which the child makes in relation to a particular level of programme. For example, one might want to start with individual letter-sound correspondences, or consonant blends, vowel digraphs, prefixes, or complex spelling patterns and rules.

3   *Matching task to learner:* Assessment enables a delineation of the child's specific weakness whether in short-term memory, motor coordination, visual per- ception, blending or sound discrimination. This enables the emphasis of the pro- gramme to match the child's needs. Remediation can follow the particular child's

specific area of weakness or strength. For example, if he has a difficulty in copying and visual motor memory, one might want to provide some basic copying exercises; in relation to written language work, to provide margins and lines to write through; encourage him to remember spelling patterns by following his own speech; tracing and so on. Conversely if the child had a difficulty in auditory memory one would want to stress the importance of chunking-up spelling patterns into whole units, rather than discrete elements (for example str + ing rather than six sounds—$s + t + r + i + n + g$. If the child had a very severe blending problem, or omitted important letters in words, or was unaware of sound patterns in general, one might want to suggest following his own speech sounds much more systematically by the use of, say, the Edith Norrie letter case (see Figure 7.1), or by various tracing techniques. When using a multi-sensory procedure one would want to find out whether weaknesses occurred in tracing, or in auditory or visual memory. This would have implications for emphases on the multi-sensory programme; for example, trying to overcome a phonological coding weakness by tracing, or using a simultaneous oral spelling technique in order to make the child aware of the relationship between sound and symbol in terms of motor and auditory organization.

4   Placement of the child: A final point is the appropriate placement of the child. This is important in a number of ways. While, in ideal circumstances, the dyslexic benefits from a one-to-one situation, especially in the early stages, this may well be impracticable due to resource and situational variables. It is important therefore to place a child in an appropriate group of children having similar learning problems. This does not necessarily imply matching children of the same age level, but matching them in terms of their attainment level. Sometimes this can give rise to difficulties in respect of, for example, an older child of 13 with an attainment age of 7, with children who are 9 with similar attainment ages. But in general it is best to place children together who are undertaking a similar kind of teaching programme. This is so that each can be provided with as much individual attention as possible, and the teacher does not have to worry about switching material between children. Another important mode of matching is in relation to the child's intellectual level. It is often very useful to place children who are rather brighter together. We thus have a number of criteria for placing children in an appropriate group—chronological age, attainment age, particular specific difficulties (and consequent emphasis on teaching programmes), and intelligence—and we have not even touched on other areas which may be important such as interest level, particular school, sex, and so on. Finding an appropriate group may be a difficult task, but an assessment is needed if one is to make any attempt at appropriate grouping.

Having made some comments in the assessment one can also draw parallels between the sort of difficulties found and the kinds of remedial techniques required. Table 6.1 presents some examples. We shall return to this table when we examine the diagnostic teaching procedures in the Aston Portfolio (see Section 7.41). We shall also refer specifically to the ideas of teaching given in the above, particularly in Chapter 7.

Table 6.1 Matching diagnosis to classroom procedures

Diagnosis	Procedures
Short-term memory weakness	Chunking of letters; letter phonogram units; over-learning mnemonics
Visual–motor deficits	Writing patterns; copying exercises; margins; following speech and phonic approach; use of word processor; tracing
Blending difficulties	Follow speech; Edith Norrie letter case; teach through visual (re-visualization, looking for letter patterns, cut out letters put together; tape recordings)
Sound discrimination problems	Sound matching; speech therapy; pairs of words, similar sounds; nonsense words
Phonological (auditory memory phonemic awareness) difficulties	Multi-sensory; tracing; SOS; orthography – syllables, blends
Visual channel problems	Auditory approach train visual skills – phonic analysis, blending, regular orthography
Auditory channel problems	Visual approach, train auditory; whole word re-visualization

6.2 Evaluating remediation

This section will examine the evaluation of remedial procedures by looking at some of the methodological problems concerned, followed by some general research findings and then some specific case studies from the author's own school.

Although much of the published research relates to teaching methods in general and although there is not as much as one would hope for in relation to help for the *dyslexic* individual, it is still important to review some of this work, particularly in relation to some of the negative findings on teaching underlying perceptual and motor skills, in the hope that this will improve reading, writing and spelling performance. According to Gittelman and Feingold (1983) 'no teaching programme has been shown to induce significant improvement in the reading ability of children with learning disorders' (see also Gittelman, in press). This startling conclusion is not based on the assumption that one cannot help children with learning difficulties, but that *proving* the efficacy of instruction is difficult. This is due to statistical and research design artefacts, which we shall now review.

6.21 Methodological problems

One specific artefact is that of regression. This is not regression in relation to the intercorrelations between reading and intelligence, but an effect called *regression to the mean*. Regression to the mean is a tendency for any individual who scores very differently to the norm, whether it be below average or above average, to produce scores on re-testing that are closer to the mean. In other words if a child scores well below average on reading in the first test, the child's performance, on average, will tend to be closer to the norm on the second re-test even if there is no intervention or remediation. This is a very important factor in test/re-test research, yet it is ignored by many researchers—or at least reported so badly that one is unable to see how it was controlled. Associated with regression effects are considerations of the tests themselves. In some cases tests reported have dubious or unknown reliability. Even those that are reliable will have a given standard error of measurement. Psychometrically this is simply a measure of how much the test varies in relation to the 'true' scores of the individual. Each test itself has built-in error due to the construction of the test, the way that it is administered, the inter-subject variations and all kinds of other possible factors (see e.g. Cronbach 1979). This takes us into psychometric arguments which are beyond the scope of this book, but it is well worth remembering the considerable variation in test performance, and that an apparent improvement may be well within the test error.

Another very important problem is that of teacher attitude. This can affect the results in a number of ways. Perhaps the most important is the 'Hawthorne Effect'. Generally anything which is new, involving additional attention given to subjects by enthusiastic teachers, would tend to result in an improved performance. This effect applies not only to teaching but also industrial training—and indeed, this is where the initial description arose. It is very difficult to see how one can control this effect, particularly as most of the individuals actually teaching the programmes have either been involved in developing them, or are trying to demonstrate that these programmes do in fact work. One could control this effect by providing a control group with a new teaching programme, taught by enthusiastic teachers, which was deliberately selected to be inappropriate. This is an ethically dubious procedure, and it would be exceedingly difficult to develop in terms of motivating the teachers to be enthusiastic about it!

In relation to the school, or the remediation situation itself, another important variable is the teacher who is actually undertaking the programme. There will also be a difference between the teacher who has actually developed the programme himself, a teacher who has been 'converted' and is tremendously enthusiastic, a teacher who is trying it out as a last resort, and a teacher who has been told to do this by the Headteacher because it is part of a research programme! In addition there will be personality interactions between teacher and child, as well as other more subtle variables in relation to school learning.

In relation to research design, it is amazing how many studies do not have control groups. Some claim that they use the subjects as their own control, i.e. they examine the development of improvement above and beyond normal or chronological age improvements. This latter may well result in improvement being demonstrated, but this cannot indicate which particular aspect of the child's experience has resulted in that improvement. It could be attending a particular resource centre, getting on well with that particular set of teachers, coming out of school, or having a teacher visit the school and therefore feeling much more important. In other words one is not able to say whether it is the remedial programme, unless one has control groups who are similar in every kind of way apart from the particular experimental variable—the teaching technique.

Furthermore, many studies do not randomly assign children to treatment groups. (Gittelman and Feingold, 1983, could find only two studies doing this.) This means that one must identify, for example, a group of 50 dyslexic children, and then assign 25 to a treatment group and 25 to no treatment. This is not often done, mainly due to the problems in relation to the ethics of the situation. If one believes that one of the teaching programmes will work, it is very difficult to justify not giving this programme to any child that appears to need it. In other cases the treatment groups and controls are not equivalent and differ on attainment, reading, spelling, writing, chronological age, type of school, or home background. It is impossible to match on every variable, but at least partial correlations, or a multifactorial analysis, needs to be undertaken. Another problem is in deciding what particular standard to measure improvement by. Often the assumption is that children's attainment age should match their chronological age, and that a gain of one year's reading in one year's chronology is average. However, as we have seen, this assumption cannot be made in relation to high and low levels of intelligence. One might argue that if dyslexic children started off at chronological age 10 with a reading age of 7, and at 13 had a reading age of 10, they would in fact be doing quite well, because they would have maintained their chronological age improvement. In absolute terms, of course, they are still three years retarded. Also we have problems in relation to maturational lag theory, i.e. a possible late development of perception, motor skills or language. This might imply that one would expect the dyslexic child to improve very quickly, as he was somewhat older. In fact much of the research on reading improvement suggests that the later you provide remedial help the more difficult it is to overcome a learning problem.

In addition to the above, Myers and Hammill (1976) mention the following as being particularly poorly controlled in studies that they review: experimental or treatment groups apparently out-performing the control groups, due to the control group getting worse, rather than due to the improvement of the experimental group; too few subjects and length of programme being far too short for appropriate analysis; teacher/pupil ratio differing between groups—the treatment groups having more attention; no information as to how many actual hours teaching the children had; those who were believing in the material, or producing the method, being involved in the evaluation and training; and up to 20% of the children between the pre- and post-tests 'disappearing'. The latter might be due to drop-out owing to moving, and so on, but in most cases it is just reported without comment. Myers and Hammill also argue that inappropriate comparisons between controls are made. For example in the treatment method group the differences between the pre- and post-tests might be significant, and the differences between the control group pre- and post-test not significant. This is interpreted to show that the treatment had a desired effect. However a *further* analysis is necessary—that of comparing the experimental or treatment group's post-test with the control group's post-test, bearing in mind that both groups are supposed to be equivalent in performance initially and similar in every other kind of way, apart from that fact that one was going to receive the programme and the other was not. This is the important comparison, not the treatment or experimental group within itself. If one does not do this one cannot reject the 'null hypothesis' (that there is no difference between treatment and non-treatment groups).

We shall see later that it is possible to evaluate the development of attainment in dyslexics. We shall do this by computing achievement ratios, based on the number of months' attainment improvement in a year (see also Section 5.41 on attainments). However, it is worth considering here the statistical and development problems in using achievement ratios. One is that being a year behind in reading at 8 years is a greater retardation than being a year behind at 12 years. Similar improvement ratios may reflect some different degrees of achievement. In addition children may often develop rapidly, followed by a plateau. Bearing these caveats in mind the improvement ratio will be presented later on. They have the advantage of comparing children receiving help with a 'control' group of dyslexics not receiving help.

Considering the above, it is not surprising that people are daunted by undertaking such research. However this is not to say that no remedial techniques work with dyslexic children, only to say that they cannot be absolutely proved to work. Most individuals working with dyslexic and other learning disabled children have absolutely no doubt at all that the teaching programmes they provide do actually help the children! The research reviewed below should be not be assumed to be free from any of the inaccuracies and problems that have been outlined above. It is merely illustrative of the kinds of research that has been done.

6.22   General research findings

One idea in remediation is that one can take some basic factor such as directional perceptual difficulty, or a visuo-motor integration problem, and by providing appropriate training procedures such as copying shapes, visual discrimination, matching sounds to taps or tactile presentation, one can remediate this basic difficulty. Reading, writing and spelling processes will thus improve. This idea has been quite common and is still widely used by many practitioners today. Some of these approaches (e.g. Frostig 1961) have useful concepts, e.g. finding the child's strengths and weaknesses using psychometric tests, and by using the strengths to give success, training areas of weaknesses. However the problem lies in the way in which these strengths and weaknesses are assessed and then remediated. For example using the Frostig Test of Visual Perception one might, on the basis of this, suggest activities in finding shapes in pictures, or improving speed of recognizing flash cards. The initial assumptions are based on correlated deficits—a correlation between visual memory for designs and reading. Sometimes, standardization of measures is a problem, in particular with low reliability. For example the Illinois Test of Psycholinguistic Ability is quoted by Frostig as being a very appropriate test to use to identify a particular learning weakness, but the subtests of ITPA vary in reliability from 0.21 to 0.89 (Ysseldyke and Salvia 1974). Another assumption here might be that separate factors are in fact being measured, and using examples from the ITPA again, Carroll, J. (1972) argues that the ITPA measured three factors—verbal comprehension, immediate memory span and auditory visual processing. This is not to suggest that the use of the ITPA is of no value, but merely to illustrate its inappropriateness in identifying underlying deficits in reading, writing and spelling. The assumption is that one will find Grammatic Closure difficulties for example, which one would then remediate by using grammatic closure tasks in the training procedure. The important point is that one might well identify a learning problem by using a subtest such as the Grammatic Closure subtest, but then that one would remediate this difficulty within written language itself. This is the crucial difference between the approach reviewed here and the ones we shall examine in later sections.

In remediation of visual perceptual factors Hammill (1972) reviewed 25 educational experiments and found 23 studies in which a treatment groups, on being given material such as suggested by the Frostig Tests, showed no difference in relation to *reading* improvement compared to a control group. The telling point here is that many of the studies showed an increase in performance on the Frostig Test. In other words the child is doing better at visual perception, visual discrimination and visual motor skills, but not better at reading, writing and spelling.

A similar underlying factors approach is undertaken by Delacato (1963). Put simply, this approach suggests that one can train the brain by a series of neurological patterning exercises involving crawling, creeping and moving limbs in a strict and controlled fashion. This is claimed to develop cerebral lateralization and therefore results in an improvement of reading and spelling skills. There is considerable controversy over this method. Robbins (1966) found no difference between control groups that were given unpatterned exercises and those that were given the Delacato exercises—no improvement in written language or laterality. O'Donnell and Eisenson (1969) compared the Delacato programme with physical activity and found no differences on reading test or indeed lateral dominance after 20 weeks of training. Hallahan and Cruickshank (1973) reviewed a number of studies in which they examined different dependent variables such as sensory and motor functions, laterality, directionality, visual motor functions, memory, academic achievements and language functions. In a review of 31 studies on the Frostig techniques they described two-thirds of these showing no effect and 7% showing mixed results. They concluded that there was overwhelming evidence for the lack of influence on reading readiness, achievement or cognitive growth. Examining the motor development programmes such as Kephart and Barsch they again reviewed 31 studies and found 80% showed a negative effect, and around 10% only minimal effects. In a review of the Delacato methods they described 14 studies, only 5 of which provided evidence of improvement on academic achievement and laterality—these were undertaken by Delacato at his Institute and criticized by Robbins (1966) and others in relation to research methodology (see also Myers and Hammill 1976).

In relation to remedial teaching Collins (1961) found that children given group remedial teaching made considerable gains compared to controls who were not given teaching, but there were no differences after re-testing 2½ years later. This is quite a common finding in relation to remediation, for example Cashdan and Pumfrey (1969) found regression after 2 years (regression in the sense of 'doing worse', in this case), and great variation in improvement (between 8 months to 3 years reading age in a 6-month period). Chazan (1967), in a review of a number of studies, found that there were substantial short-term gains, but in the longer term there were very few gains. However Carroll, J. (1972) in his review found that there were improvements in reading as well as in social adjustment. Cashdan *et al*. (1971) examined over 1000 retarded readers who were given remedial teaching for one or two sessions for 11 months. The mean gain was 21 months. The individuals who did not respond appeared to have specific reading difficulties or dyslexic-type learning problems, although most of this research was directed at children who were failing for a variety of reasons and examines the efficiency of remedial teaching in general. This general teaching approach is 'more of the same', and perhaps not as specific as the kinds of techniques we shall be describing later.

Lovell *et al*. (1962) compared children who obtained individual help through a remedial centre to those who were given small-group help at school by a peripatetic teacher. In general the first group made greater reading gains, an effect which was maintained after a 2 to 3-year gap. Chansky (1963) examined the effects of remediation in dyslexics between 8 and 14 years, and found the improvement for remedial teaching was negatively correlated with age. In other words the older the children were, the more difficult it was to obtain an increase in their reading and spelling ages. Vernon (1971) points out that this may be largely due to motivational problems rather than to an underlining entrenchment of a cognitive deficit. In other words when the children are older they have an increased experience of failure, frustration and disappointment in relation to their school career. Guthrie *et al*. (1978) in a review of 15 studies, concluded that the major factor in improvement was tutoring ratio. If there was a 1 to 3 pupil/teacher ratio the average improvement was 3.7 years in a one-year period of instruction; if it was more than 1 to 4, the improvement fell to 1.7 per year. Factors such as the method, the training of the tutor or the age of entry to the programme were not as important.

Vernon (1971) argues that dyslexia is very resistant to remedial teaching, and that even in adulthood individuals may still be poor spellers. We have already seen that there is a differential prognosis between dyslexic or specific reading disabled children and those who are generally backward; indeed this is one of the definitions put forward by Yule and Rutter (1976) for specific reading disorder. In their study they found that children with specific reading difficulties lost ground compared to children who were generally backward in reading (of lower intelligence). Both groups were 33 months behind chronological age at 10 years, but the retardates were a *further* 6 months behind the backward group on retest. This underlines the fact that one cannot assume that bright children will catch up in reading, writing and spelling.

A recent study by Hornsby and Miles (1980) compared three centres specializing in giving help to dyslexic children. The particular techniques used in these centres will be described later, mainly involving structured multi-sensory techniques.

Although they use subjects as their own control, they argue that they can calculate reading gains by comparing the ratio of reading improvement to chronological age. Scores over 1 would therefore be gains. In most cases the centres they compared either had individual or very small group teaching. They argue that gains made by the children were real and not just 'keeping up with the clock', i.e. maintaining a level of chronological/reading age. In reading, the children's ratio prior to teaching had been 0.53, i.e. gradually getting worse as they got older, and now the ratio was 1.91. In spelling the ratio had been 0.32 and now was 1.95. They found that 85% of the children gained more than unity. They also comment, and this is a most important point, that the children had previously obtained specialized remedial help at school. There was no indifference to the children, mainly uncertainty as to what to do in order to help them appropriately. This study was aware of the 'Hawthorne effect', and commented concerning it, but claimed that this could not have been the case as the children came from caring families and school backgrounds. This seems a very unsatisfactory way of controlling for this particular effect. However it is invidious to select this particular piece of work for criticism of this nature as it could be aimed at any of the other studies which are reported here. This study is reported in more detail because it relates particularly to examining the teaching of dyslexic children with specialized techniques. Hornsby and Miles also comment on the importance of phonetic principles in teaching, this being common to all three teaching programmes. Gittelman and Feingold (1983), in a carefully controlled study, with random assignment to experimental and control groups, support this contention. They found that children with specific reading difficulties improved with reading instruction emphasizing phonetic decoding, compared with those receiving non-specific treatments such as motivational reinforcement. The improvement in reading was maintained after 2-month and 8-month follow-up periods.

In relation to multi-sensory techniques, Shevill (1978) argues that tactile learning improves alphabet recognition, serial ordering and learning distinctive features of letters—the latter transcribing word patterns by sound and shape. Linn and Ryan (1968) examined teaching first-graders names and sounds by tracing and vocalizing, as opposed to visual studying. Those given multi-sensory training improved the most. Fernald (1943), Orton (1937), and Rawson (1968) all describe various kinds of tracing or multi-sensory methods, claiming great success in helping dyslexic children. Bradley (1981) examined the notion of multi-sensory and tracing techniques in spelling. Here reading-retarded children were given a written word; a child names it then writes it from memory, saying the letter names at the same time. Next the child names the word again, and checks that he has written it correctly, he then practises the word for six days. This is an adapted version of 'simultaneous oral spelling' described initially by Gillingham and Stillman (see below). The difference here is that the child uses a word in his own vocabulary.

Bradley found that children using this 'SOS' technique had an 84% success rate, whereas those who did not use a writing technique (i.e. just simply visual and auditory inputs) had only a 37% success rate, and those not taught did considerably less well. In an additional experiment the child repeats the name of the whole word, but does not name individual letters. She found that a simultaneous oral spelling of letters was rather better, and argued that it was not just the motor movement, i.e. not the actual tracing procedure itself that was important, but relating the motor movement to a sound pattern. She suggests that it is the organization of motor patterns providing a one-to-one relationship between the sound and written symbol which aided discrimination, recall and subsequent organization, and provided help in verbal labels.

Another series of studies undertaken by Hulme (1981a and b) also provides experimental evidence for the efficacy of tracing or multi-sensory techniques. This study in particular is interesting in applying experimental psychology techniques to remedial methods. This surely is the best way to demonstrate that particular techniques and teaching methods are useful. In other words rather than try to demonstrate increased reading over the whole range of the child's behaviours one pin-points, very specifically and in great detail, some particular behaviour which relates to reading, writing and spelling learning, and examines that in the laboratory. Hulme's study involved letter naming and learning visual/verbal paired associates in various tracing tasks. He argues that the tracing supports a phonological code, i.e. there is a kinesthetic memory trace which aids the phonological memory trace. This takes place in short-term memory. The interesting finding here is that when verbal material was used, tracing technique improved the performance of the reading retardates, but *not* the normals. When using non-verbal stimuli both groups improved. The control group presumably had adequate phonological memory coding and did not benefit in the verbal condition. This illustrates quite clearly that there are differences required in teaching techniques between dyslexics and other children who are poor at reading for different reasons. Hulme argues for a distinctive motor memory trace improving visual recognition. Another interesting finding was that there was an interaction between these various performances when the delay between presentation of stimuli and testing was varied. If this was short (15 seconds) there was little improvement, but if there was a longer delay (1 minute 30 seconds), there was an improvement. Hulme argues that this suggests that the motor memory traces are more durable. He also suggests that the reading retardates rely too much on a visual rather than on a verbal code.

Another area of research is in the teaching of 'subtypes' of dyslexia by various means. Batemann (1966) found no interaction between modality presentation and modality of learning of words, and Gittelman (1984) argues that simple modality presentation does not readily generalize to remediation. However, other studies have been more specific. For example Aubrey *et al.* (1982) (see also Hicks and Murgatroyd 1981) divided dyslexics into various subtypes of learning difficulty (auditory and visual problems). The important feature to note here is that the subtypes were based on reading, writing and spelling performance, and not on an assumed deficit resulting from experimental work.

For one group of children with auditory problems various teaching methods were employed which emphasized the visual skills, another similar group had rather more emphasis on auditory skills, and another group had a combination of visual and auditory techniques. Children with auditory *and* visual problems were given multi-sensory kinds of learning. There were a number of different groups of children who were given six hours teaching per week (two hours for three days). The teachers undertaking the programme were rotated to control for teacher effect. They also had a control group of children who had been given various non-specific kinds of remedial techniques. They found that a combined approach was more effective where one used the strengths of the child. They found improvement in all children compared to the control group, apart from those children who had auditory problems and who had been given a programme based on auditory techniques. It was concluded that one should emphasize the strengths of the child in teaching and remediate specific weaknesses.

Thomson (1988, 1989b) has undertaken a number of evaluation studies. In one study Thomson (1988) looked at the spelling of non-words and attempted to evaluate the phonological and orthographic skills appertaining to sound/symbol association. Non-words can only be read by a phonetic as opposed to a look-and-say strategy. The development of these skills in a group of children who have received remediation over a 2 year period was compared to development in children who had not received remediation. It was found that the non-treatment group had greater difficulty in using phonological skills to decode non-words. Those who had received remediation had much better phonological skills. However, these skills were still weak when compared to control groups. Thomson also examined the use of simultaneous oral spelling and multi-sensory technique in the teaching of spelling (see later). This was compared to the visual inspection of words and it was found that the use of a simultaneous oral spelling technique was advantageous. It was concluded that some cognitive deficits could be overcome in dyslexics. Phonological coding, phonemic awareness and alphabetic skills could specifically be helped. However, non-lexical phonological spelling was particularly resistant, whereas lexical alphabetical skills could be improved considerably. In addition, help over phonemic awareness using kinesthetic coding can improve spelling. In a further study (Thomson 1989b) on the spelling of regular and irregular words, Thomson concluded that there appears to be an alphabetic 'barrier' in the reading and spelling of regular words, which can be overcome around the reading age of 8 years. This seems to provide a platform for a relative 'take-off' in aspects of written language learning. However, the irregularities of written language were much more difficult to remediate.

6.23   Some evaluation studies

Some detailed examples are now given to illustrate the evaluation of teaching. These studies are taken from some aspects of monitoring and evaluating at East Court School for dyslexics. Some of the studies have been reported in Thomson (1989c).

Our observations of children attending a specialist school for dyslexics is that their learning strategies change, as a result not only of developing age, but also of the particular teaching input they receive. It may seem an obvious point, but a child's ability to decode sounds/symbol correspondence, to undertake an analysis of sounds within words (phonemic awareness) and other skills which are focused on by theoretical studies will depend on whether the child has received a phonetic teaching programme. Children in our first year, for example, are taught how to analyse long and short vowel sounds, how to recognize common letter patterns, how to use rhyming to help them spell word families and so on. In evaluating attainments we followed up children over a 5 year period (1983–88). Children's attainments were monitored using the British Ability Scales Word Reading, the Neale Analysis of Reading Ability and the Vernon Graded Word Spelling. Their performance in reading when they entered the school was compared with their performance when leaving school. The general teaching programme used was as described in Chapter 7.

Before summarizing these results, it is worth examining what is normally expected from dyslexics. Typically, if the child has not received a lot of extra help, the dyslexic will be two or more years behind chronological age (CA) in reading and spelling attainments. (This of course begs the question of expected attainment age taking into account intelligence; if a child is well above average intelligence one would expect an above average CA attainment.) If not given help, the dyslexic child's attainments fall further and further behind so that what was a 2 year retardation at 8 years of age, can be a 5 year retardation at 13 years of age. The reader is referred to Chapter 5 (Section 5.41) and Figure 5.1 (p. 165) to illustrate this point.

It may be seen from Figure 5.1 that the Reading Accuracy of the dyslexic becomes relatively weaker as he or she gets older – attainment lags behind. The same applies to spelling, although attainment here is even lower than for reading. Thus the aim of teaching is to stop this widening gap and try to catch up with the average performance. In many cases, particularly spelling, the dyslexic will never reach the 'norm'. One hopes to make reading 'fluent' and spelling 'competent' for examinations and adult needs.

Improvement is often in a series of 'plateaus' (no improvement at all), followed by sudden 'spurts' as things 'click' in the child's skills. Conversely a sudden initial 'spurt' is followed by a period of marking time as the child consolidates what is learnt.

The result may be looked at as an achievement ratio, i.e. the attainments achieved during a 12 month period. Thus 12 months of reading in 12 chronological months gives an improvement ratio of 1.00. Anything over 1.00 is a 'better than expected' improvement for the non-dyslexic. Based on the data in Figure 5.1 the dyslexic's typical improvement ratio is 0.40 in Reading Accuracy (an improvement of only about 5 months in a 12 month period). In spelling, the ratio from Figure 5.1 is 0.27 (about 3 months in 12) and indicates relatively worsening retardation. We would wish to better these ratios to stop this widening gap between age and attainment. An achievement ratio in excess of 1.00 would begin the 'catching up' process. These improvement ratios apply to groups of children; the individual often has variable development as described earlier.

We can also look at mean (average) improvement. The mean attainments are shown for the children on entering the school and then on leaving. Table 6.2 shows improvement ratios and means.

Table 6.2   Mean reading and spelling attainment at entry and on leaving East Court (*n* = 87)

	Entering school	Leaving school	Improvement ratio
Chronological age	10; 9	12; 10	—
Word reading age	8; 7	12; 5	1.84
Reading accuracy age	8; 2	11; 6	1.60
Reading comprehension age	9; 0	12; 0	1.44
Spelling age	7; 10	11; 4	1.68

The results show that the children are not only doing better than dyslexics not given help, but are bettering the 'norm', and catching up.

In word reading (recognizing individual words), the children are almost up to their age level. In reading from a story (Neale Accuracy) the level is well above everyday competence. The same applied to reading comprehension, although this is always less of a difficulty for dyslexics. (The problem, by and large, is in de-coding, not understanding, what is read.) Spelling is greatly improved to be competent for everyday use.

It should be noted that the somewhat lower scores on the Neale Accuracy compared to the BAS test is due to the ceiling effects of the Neale Accuracy test which is at a maximum of 13;0 years. The BAS Word Reading has a ceiling of 14+. Also any mispronunciations count as errors in the Neale Accuracy test. Slight inaccuracies, although they may not alter the understanding of a text, are penalized.

The above data are encouraging in that it suggests that dyslexic difficulties, given appropriate help, can be remediated. In the case of reading one can bring levels up to everyday competence, and certainly spelling to a level that can be understood in essay writing and in day-to-day use.

A particular difficulty is in spelling syllables. This might reflect weaknesses the dyslexics have in short-term memory (they may forget the later syllables), or reflect poor application of grapheme/phoneme skills.

As part of these evaluation studies a number of examinations of the spelling and reading of syllables was undertaken. Basically, it was found that, as expected, dyslexics had greater difficulty with multi-syllable words (see Thomson 1989b). As the number of syllables increased the children found them increasingly difficult to spell, both for those who had had remedial help and for controls. When looking at children's spelling of syllables over time, it was found that as their spelling ages increased they were better at spelling two syllable words, but that the dyslexics have a much slower development of syllabification skills. Presented below is a study examining the specific training of syllable skills.

The complete annual intake at our school was chosen (20 children). They were divided randomly into 10 controls and 10 training group children (mean CA 9;8, mean SA 6;11).

All the children were given regular one, two and three syllable words to spell, e.g. 'fresh, grin, spade, inside, nutmeg, lemonade, astonish'. Ten words from each category were given as a pre-test, and the same test given after a training period of 2 weeks.

The procedure for the training was to teach by 'syllable analysis'. This involves teaching the children that words in English can be divided into six basic syllable types: open, closed, vowel-consonant 'e', vowel diagraph, consonant 'le', and 'r' combination syllables. This is as described in Chapter 7, Section 7.5. Children were encouraged to tap out words into their beats or units, and to recognize how many beats there are in a given word. They were then taught how to divide the words up into syllables and to assign them to one of the above six categories of classification. Particular attention was paid to the pronunciation of vowels and consequent syllable units.

The control group was given the same words but asked to look at them and then simply copy them and read them (with prompting if necessary). Table 6.3 shows the result of the tests before and after the 2 week training period. The results show that both groups are nearly at the ceiling level for one syllable words, but that the syllable analysis training significantly helped the treatment group for two and three syllable words.

Table 6.3   Mean scores for spelling multi-syllable words by training group taught syllable analysis and controls

Syllable length	Training group (n = 10) (Maximum score = 10)		Controls (n = 10)	
	Pre-test	Post-test	Pre-test	Post-test
One	8.8	9.1	9.1	8.9
Two	6.2	8.7*	5.9	6.3
Three	2.9	6.8†	3.2	3.4

* Difference between pre- and post-significant at $P<0.05$.
† Difference between pre- and post-significant at $P<0.01$.
Other differences not significant.

The particular techniques of syllable analysis using the categorization of syllables based on vowels can help two or three syllable spelling of regular words. Presumably this technique aids problems of phonological analysis, and focuses on the importance of studying quite specific teaching techniques for specific subskills.

The two case studies above are presented in some detail, in order to give the reader some idea of how teaching programmes can go hand in hand with evaluation and research. Further studies have been reported in Thomson (1989c) and are available from East Court. These include the evaluation of self-esteem, a further examination of the simultaneous oral spelling component compared to a control group of spelling age-matched children, and a number of others which are on-going.

7

Remediation: principles and techniques

7.1 General principles of remediation

Blank (1978) argues that teaching a dyslexic is very different to teaching blind, deaf or other children with communication or learning problems. In some cases one very often teaches a completely new system of communication, such as Braille or sign language. The dyslexic child, however, must be taught precisely what is difficult for him. Although we can attempt to circumvent particular deficits by teaching in a different kind of a way, in the final analysis the child will need skills such as applying phonological rules if he is to read, write and spell appropriately. There is a limit, for example, to what can be achieved by purely visual methods; one must get to grips with sounds eventually.

Johnson (1978) suggests that there are several terms of reference in devising a teaching programme. One is broadly psycholinguistic—in other words assuming that there are input, integrative or mediation processing and output problems. Disturbances may be based on any of these particular aspects, and also involve any modality, such as visual or auditory. Another approach might be verbal versus non-verbal or auditory versus visual learning. In information processing terms, one could postulate a hierachy of experience, e.g. talking about sensation, then perception, then imagery and internal representation, or symbolization, conceptualization. The particular frame of reference one has gives rise to the particular kind of techniques that one describes. Vellutino (1979), for example, is using the information processing approach in his description of dyslexia. He describes the importance of attention to acoustic and visual features, whether these be training for phonemic segmentation and awareness, in sound symbol associations in natural language, and finally in respect to accessing higher-order language components. Others, such as Johnson and Myklebust (1967), argue that visual dyslexics require a phonic kind of teaching programme, and the auditory dyslexic requires a whole-word method. They argue that one emphasizes strengths, to provide immediate success in areas within the child's grasp but also provides some kind of additional remediation or training programmes to improve deficits.

Teaching approaches will, therefore, differ depending on the initial frame of reference used. Sometimes the same terms are used to describe different kinds of approaches. For example, the word multi-sensory may apply to the Gillingham-Stillman or the Fernald Programmes, yet, as we shall see, these are different in some important ways. Similarly, a so-called 'phonic approach' might suggest that the individual has to analyse the sounds into the constituent parts and then blend them together. Alternatively some kind of 'synthesis' may be emphasized. The rules used to describe orthography may be explicit (i.e. taught), or implicit (i.e. based on structured experience). Nevertheless it soon becomes apparent that there are close agreements between various writers in relation to the principles that should be used for the dyslexic child. Many of these go back to Rawson (1975), where it is argued that the programme should be structured, sequential, cumulative and thorough. These particular words are also re-echoed in the British Dyslexia Association publication (1981) called *Teaching the Dyslexic*, which was produced by the Education Sub-Committee.

The notion of *structure* suggests that there should an organized and coherent presentation of the written language system. In other words, written language should be taught in a way that makes sense to the individual, and is based on an overview of the written language skills required, rather than bits and pieces taken at random. The idea of structure also implies the systematic teaching of the rules, regularities and orthography of the written language system. Normally this is started at a level just below the child's present attainment to give immediate success, and ranges from basic sound/symbol correspondences, through consonants and vowel digraphs, to suffix rules, all taught in a systematic and related fashion. The idea of a *sequential* programme implies that there is a gradual disclosure of sounds, letter combinations and orthography of the written language system. This should be a *cumulative* programme. The implication here is that there is a gradual build-up of the written language learning process. The rules, regulations, and so on are not taught in isolation. One teaches consonant blends after teaching a consonant; one teaches the prefix *dis* after one has taught the short vowel sound in a closed syllable; one teaches the vowel *e* before learning about vowel digraph combinations. *Thoroughness* encapsulates the above, and argues that one should make sure that each stage is fully learnt before going on to the next stage.

Although authors differ slightly in their emphasis, most agree that some form of multi-sensory learning is required. Multi-sensory learning involves the integration of visual, auditory, tactile or kinesthetic modes, as in associating letters with sounds and in writing. Again, most writers agree that remediation should be 'phonically' based, using 'phonetic' principles. This implies the association of word patterns and sounds with the letters, digraphs, blends or syllables. The way that this is actually taught of course varies, but it is implied that a child will eventually have to learn a phonological route to reading, although it is not always expressed in that way. A further agreed component of teaching a dyslexic is the idea of overlearning and overteaching. Due to attentional, memorial and other difficulties, the dyslexic will need the same material presented over and over again using different modalities and tasks. He will not deduce or 'catch' the rules unless they are continually reinforced. In connection with this, it is often observed (to the irritation of some teachers who do not understand the dyslexic problem), that an item taught one day will be forgotten the next. The idea of overlearning and overteaching implies that one has to present the technique in different ways to keep the child's motivation and interest in the learning task. Sampson (1976), in her summary of teaching principles for the dyslexic taken from Johnson and Myklebust (1967), Kirk and Kirk (1971), Jordon (1972), Bannatyne (1971) and Newton and Thomson (1975), states these principles as (1) an individual approach (not necessarily individual teaching, but attempting to examine the child's specific difficulties and provide an appropriate teaching programme aimed at that individual child, (2) some kind of multi-sensory technique, (3) overlearning of structure, the rules and regulations of the written language system, (4) teaching to the strengths and remediating deficits.

A last, but by no means least, principle is that teaching should be sympathetic. This implies providing the children with self-esteem, in letting them know that one understands the nature of their difficulty, and helping to circumvent some of the secondary emotional problems arising from the written language difficulty itself. The teaching should also be enjoyable. This may not be an easy task, as the children have, in some cases, many years of failure and difficulty in struggling with written language script. They confront their own failure every day, and to expect them to enjoy to read, write and spell is like expecting someone to enjoy doing a task which he finds totally difficult and boring. The ability to make the work interesting is one of the most important skills for the teacher, and will require a considerable rapport and mutual respect between pupil and teacher. This brings us to examine an important consideration in teaching, that of appropriate attitudes to the child.

It is important to recognize that the child will often become frustrated due to his inability to express his ideas in written form, or read books of interest to him, and will have had to work considerably harder than others to achieve the same attainment level. Remedial work should be 'accepting' and patience is required. Progress will be slow, so that continual encouragement and praise will be needed. Sometimes the child will manifest secondary anxiety difficulties such as withdrawing, becoming aggressive, indulging in attention seeking behaviours or 'acting out'. The recognition of the child's difficulties, and discussion with him about his problems, coupled with sympathetic understanding and appropriate help often dramatically improves general adjustment difficulties. In addition the dyslexic can be inconsistent in performance, getting a spelling right one day and wrong the next. In many cases the child has to work slowly because of his difficulties, and is always under pressure of time; this can result in getting tired much more quickly than other children, as much greater concentration is required.

The following are specific suggestions for classroom situations:

1 Let the child know you are interested in him, and willing to help him. He is unsure of himself and concerned about your reactions.
2 Set standards for his work in concrete terms he can understand. Know that error-free work might be beyond his grasp. Help him work on one area of improvement at a time.
3 Give him individual attention as frequently as possible. Let him know he may ask questions about work he does not understand.

4   Make sure he understands assignments; he often will not. Break a lesson down into its parts and check, step by step, his understanding of it.

5   New information must be given to him more than once because of his problems with distractability, short-term memory, and sometimes poor attention span.

6   He may need more practice than the usual student to master a new skill.

7   He will need help in relating new concepts to past experience.

8   Give him time: to organize his thoughts, to complete his work. If the time pressure is off, he will be less anxious and better able to let you know what he knows. Extra time includes copying from the blackboard and taking notes!

9   If he has a reading disability he may well need to have someone read part of his material to him, and to take tests orally. When he reads for information, he will have to read books that are at his reading ability level. Remember he has a disability just as real as the blind child who is not expected to receive information from the usual printed page. Some children may well be able to read a passage correctly out loud and yet may not get the sense of the text.

10   If he has a spelling problem, try to grade papers for content, separate from spelling errors. Do not expect him to study the same number of spelling words as a non-handicapped child. In respect to this, try to avoid giving long lists of spelling words to learn, especially different spelling patterns. Also try to avoid correcting all the mistakes in written work; sometimes it is very discouraging to see a page full of words crossed out with a red pen or equivalent with 'sp' written next to it!

11   Consider testing him on his knowledge, without the mechanical handicaps of poor reading, writing, spelling and organizational ability. He could be tested orally or dictate answers to a tape recorder or volunteer.

12   Be aware it will take him longer to complete homework assignments than the majority of his classmates. He needs time to develop skills and to relax. Perhaps a lighter homework load is in order, for example shorter essays, or underline the main points to be learnt.

13   Try to put positive comments on his papers, as well as commenting on where he needs to improve. Praise and encourage wherever possible.

14   Be aware of the need to build his self-esteem. Give him opportunities to make contributions within the class. Avoid comparing him with others in a negative way, or making fun of his difficulties; also avoid making the dyslexic read aloud in public if he is unwilling to do so. It is worth finding out something that the child is particularly good at, and build his self-esteem by encouragement and success.

15   Consider grading him on his own effort and progress rather than rating him with others in the class. Feelings of success often lead to success: failure breeds failure.

16   Allow him to learn any way he can, using any tools available: fact tables, matrix charts, small calculators, tape recorders. These are tools for learning, just as hearing aids and eye-glasses are.

Aubrey *et al.* (1982), stress the importance of overlearning in the classroom, and that at least a third of the remedial session should be devoted to revision of earlier work. New material should be presented frequently and in a number of ways. Learning appears to be optimal after the stages: recognition, recall, relearning, and recall. The learned material should be presented in a variety of situations so that the child can generalize his knowledge: tests of one (or at most two) rules not long lists of mixed spellings on the same test occasion, dictation; or in reading-matter, news-papers, journals, comics. They suggest that the remedial session should take place in the morning when the child is most responsive, with shorter follow-up sessions in the afternoon. Activities should be novel, so that the child is not taught by methods on which he has previously failed; and should be changed frequently, so that the child does not become bored and de-motivated. In planning the session, the initial part should involve activities on which the child should achieve 80–90% success, since this will act as a powerful motivator for the rest of the lesson, and the learning task should be divided into small units, so that the child can feel he has mastered a skill. Occasionally some form of reward may be necessary. The successful reader derives intrinsic reinforcement from the reading task. The retarded reader may need a system of bonus points or additional encouragement from the teacher. Group activities can have a strong motivational factor, providing that the children are roughly matched on attainment and developmental levels.

They also argue that remedial help should refer to the precise skill to be learned, rather than to an assumed gross deficit. Thus *b/d* confusions may well be a product of directional confusion, but it is more productive if the child is trained specifically on *b/d* discriminations, rather than on general directions. The child's active involvement in the learning process is stressed, as is immediate feedback and rein-forcement of correct attempts.

Another important consideration is of course the organization of a remedial unit within a school and the particular approaches to take overall. Some basic questions are whether there should be an integrated day, i.e. specialist teaching in conjunction with the main timetable (perhaps during an English lesson) or whether children should work with a withdrawal system, and if so how often? This will of course depend on the child to some extent, and on what the 'target' population is. Is one looking for intense help for short periods or continuing support over a long period of time if a child is severely handicapped? Very often children who have experienced failure at school need a special base or centre. This is a place where the child is not threatened with the possibility of failure. It is also important to build on success. This implies teaching specific skills in a hierarchical order, building up from something the child can do into a learning situation. One should not make assumptions about what a child might know and also not be surprised when the child fails at what the teacher may think is a very basic task for their chronological age and intelligence.

Consideration should also be given to appropriate training for staff. It is not enough to have staff trained in 'remedial' education. They will need to be trained specifically in helping the dyslexic. There are specific training courses for this purpose, some run by the independent sector, such as the Dyslexia

Institute or the Helen Arkell Centre. Others are run by organizations such as the British Dyslexia Association, and there is now an RSA validated diploma course, which is run at a number of centres. Increasingly LEAs are also developing training courses. Most of these courses tend to be over a 1 year period, usually on a day release basis.

Once one begins to help the child there are a number of techniques which we shall examine later, but in general one can look at the learning processes in a series of stages, Table 7.1 shows an example of this and is taken from the author's colleague at East Court, Bill Watkins.

Table 7.1 The teacher's role

1 Accept the child, 'warts and all' strengths and weaknesses Non-judgemental Welcome him/her as a person, give time to breathe, relax Organize 150%		'Earthing'
2 No failure at first Success through endeavour Develop trust Strengthen trust Enjoying the experience	Fun	'Hooking'
3 Issue challenge Competition against self, peers, groups Consolidation		'Challenge'

A major problem for dyslexics is also organization and it is crucial to provide them with this organization in stages. Later on one can take supports away and encourage a child to stand on his or her own two feet. This organization relates to both physical situations, such as looking after clothes and belongings, but also relates to time keeping and planning of work. In our written language work at East Court all our children have a similar structure in their English folders to work from and this is shown in Table 7.2.

Another point of discussion is the best way to group for teaching dyslexics. Some people argue that the one-to-one method is the best. At East Court we find that small groups provide a useful source of enjoyment and interaction among peer groups. Of course all the children have similar difficulties and it is easier to carry out, but it also allows for some gentle competition later on as the children become more proficient and enjoy spreading their wings. All our children are organized into groups of five or six for written language work, but in addition they have a one-to-one, or two-to-one, staff tutorial during the course of a week. In addition there are other written language-oriented lessons during the school week, including handwriting, reading workshop, library periods, typing periods and 'extra English' which includes more phonics for the

Table 7.2   The Blue File: English organization at East Court School

An A4 ring clip folder with subject dividers as follows:
  Star check
  Spelling lists
  Spelling rules
  Spelling tests
  Composition
  Phonics
  Grammar
  Writing
  Reading workshop
  Computer/word processing
  Tutorials
  Vocabulary
  Comprehension
  Private dictionary

younger ones and more traditional English, such as literature, for the older children. Of course, the situation would be different if one is taking children out on a sessional basis.

In summary, we can look at some of the general principles based on research findings as follows.

Research shows that dyslexics *do* improve with:

- Small group (or one-to-one) teaching.
- As early identification and help as possible.
- Understanding and encouragement.
- Multi-sensory techniques – tracing, sound–symbol associations and simultaneous oral spelling.
- A structured approach based on established phonetic principles.
- Matching task to learner, i.e. individualizing instruction based on careful assessment.
- Teaching to strengths and remediating weakness where appropriate.
- Mnemonics and 'concrete' aids.
- Help in organization.
- Constructive, supportive, exciting classroom experiences.

Dyslexics *do not* improve with:

- Unspecific remedial methods, i.e. 'more' reading, spelling.
- Extra attention and psychotherapy alone.
- Being left to 'grow out of it'.
- Training visual or auditory perception alone (unless within written language itself).
- 'Patterning' or other 'neurological' exercises to develop laterality.
- Punishment or 'threats'.
- Inappropriate labelling, e.g. 'thick', stupid, lazy, maladjusted etc.

7.2   Structured written language programmes

A structured programme means a cumulative one. In other words one would start (depending on the child's particular level) with letters, sound/symbol correspondences moving on to blends, regular words, then polysyllabic words, and syllable division. There are many examples of detailed phonic and structured programmes, and a few examples based on some UK teaching methods for the dyslexic are described here. It is impossible to present these in any great detail, as they are very thorough indeed, and the reader is referred to the actual programmes. What is important is that whatever particular structure is chosen, it should be adhered to closely. The teacher should be aware of the structures and have at his fingertips the appropriate examples of rules, patterns and order of teaching.

7.21   Alpha to Omega programme

A widely used programme in this country is the Alpha to Omega (Hornsby and Shear 1976), which provides the teacher with a very detailed and structured written language learning programme. The authors advocate starting with consonants, and emphasize that these should be taught in the order in which they claim is the order of acquisition in spoken language (i.e. *b,p,m,w,h* and then *d,t,n,g,k,m,g*; *f,s,z*; *v,th,sh,l,ch*, *a ;y,q,u,r,th,ks,or*, and finally consonant blends.) They also point out some of the interrelationships between vowels and their formations in articulation, and describe the programme as based upon a linguistic approach in relation to its syntactic expectations. The order of teaching is alphabet sounds, followed by consonant digraphs, then vowels, consonants blends, various individual letter combinations such as *w* and its associated rules, long vowels, rules of soft *c* and *g*, consonant trigrams, vowel digraphs, suffixing and syllabification. A summary of the programme follows (taken from the programme itself).

Stage 1
This stage deals with monosyllablic words, except where prefixes and suffixes can be added without changing the spelling of the 'root' word. The vowels are mostly short vowels, or one and two phoneme words ending in a vowel; open syllable words and the vowel will, therefore, be long. For example:

a	be	he	me	she	the	we
no	so	go	to	do		
I	by	my				

Also used are 'lengthening *e*' long vowels, which re-open the syllable:

cake   these   ripe   hope   tune

Stage 2
This stage also deals with monosyllablic words, but now we add prefixes and suffixes where the final spelling of the 'root' word does change. Here we also discover the other ways of getting long vowels.

Stage 3

This stage deals with polysyllabic words; the peculiarities of final syllables and open and closed syllables are gone into more thoroughly.

Prefixes and suffixes

A prefix is a morpheme placed in front of a word to change or extend its meaning. A suffix is a morpheme placed after a word to change its meaning or grammatical function.

Those it is felt must be mastered are:

Prefixes			*Suffixes*		
	be	de	ed	er	est
en	mis	in	ing	ous	able
re	to	un	ly	s	ment
ad	dis	pre	y	age	ful

More advanced prefixes and suffixes are introduced later, or form part of some rule being taught.

Games and exercises can be devised to help the pupil become familiar with the concept of suffixing and prefixing. Even quite young pupils can be shown the concept using a familiar word, e.g.:

root word—'do'; add prefix, 'un' = 'undo' i.e. change meaning
root word—'do'; add suffix, 'ing' = 'doing' i.e. change grammatical sense.

Other devices such as Flashcards with the root word, suffix or prefix can be incorporated into games and exercises. Understanding prefixes and suffixes will also aid reading comprehension in later lessons.

7.22   Bangor Teaching Programme

Another example of the structured teaching of the written language system is the Bangor Teaching Programme (Miles and Miles 1975, Miles 1970 and Miles, E. 1982). The current teaching programme recommends a number of reading schemes using phonic teaching methods and argues that an overall look-and-say method is not suitable. The approach is flexible, but suggests that one commences with consonants and vowels, particularly emphasizing the structure of words to the child. This is followed by simple plurals, *w* and *l* words, single vowels, long vowels, vowel digraphs, the *c* and *g* rules, various combinations of spelling patterns, irregular words, doubling silent letters, various odd combinations such as 'ch', /k/, and suffixes. An example of the approach follows.

Long vowels: (a) Long vowels with -e

After the regular short vowels one normally moves on to long vowels. These involve the use of two vowels, either (i) separated by a consonant, as in *game*, or (ii) together, as in *meat*.

(i) In the former case, the addition of an *e* to each of the five vowels has the effect of lengthening the sound, which becomes the same as the name of the letter. It should be noted, however, that -e-e is rare and is best left until the more common -ee- and -ea- words have been studied. However, the column can be drawn, and possibly the word *these* and/or names like *Pete* and *Steve* fitted in for demonstration. (ii) When the same pairs of vowels (viz -ae, -ee,-ie, -oe and -ue) are together at the end of a word, with no consonant intervening, there is the same long sound as (i). It may therefore be worthwhile eventually to add words of this kind in the child's book at the bottom of the page (e.g. *see, pie, hoe, due*, etc.) in the appropriate column.

Sample 'page 2' (long vowels with -e)
(i) Separated

a-e	e-e	i-e	o-e	u-e
game	these	ride	bone	tune
cage	Pete	mice	note	rule
bake		(w)rite	rose	cube
		like		

(ii) Together at the end

-ee	-ie	-oe	-ue
see	die	toe	blue
tree	tie	doe	glue
	lie	hoe	due
	pie		

The above illustrates the complexity of some of these programmes. Teachers need to be aware of all the ins and outs of the written language system. The Bangor programme recommends that one write out the structure and the spelling patterns in book form. In other words the child has an exercise book, the pages of which are reserved for particular groups of vowels, vowel digraphs and so on.

7.23   Helen Arkell Centre Programme

The use of the Edith Norrie letter case has already been mentioned as part of this programme, but a structured approach is used also, for example, Pollock (1978), commences with short vowels including clue cards (*apple, egg, igloo, orange* and *umbrella*). This then goes on to, for example, doubling consonants, long vowels, silent *e*, the soft *g* rules, suffixing, (*le, able*, etc.), trigrams (e.g. *dge, tch*), more complex suffixing and plurals. There is an interesting section on the origins of language. An example taken from this programme is also given below.

DGE
After a short vowel put *d* before *ge* (double *g* would be hard.)

badge	edge	ridge	dodge	fudge
cadge	hedge	bridge	lodger	judge
Madge	ledge	fridge	podgy	nudge

Mnemonic: The bad badger is sitting on the edge of a ledge eating fudge.

N.B. (i) No *d* is needed if another consonant is present: *plunge, bulge*
(ii) The *a* is long in *nge*—words: *range, stranger, change, danger.*

Exceptions occur in multisyllabic words ending in *-age* and *-ege*:

cottage	village	college
garage	allege	
garbage	sacrilege	

The illustration, of which there are a number of very amusing ones, is unfortunately omitted from the above.

7.24   Hickey Programme

Another example of a structured and systematic approach is the Hickey Programme (1977) used by the Dyslexia Institute. Some examples, taken from the middle level difficulty of this dyslexia training course, are given below. How these particular patterns are taught in this programme will be described in more detail later.

The dyslexic child will not learn the written language system unless it is specifically taught and he is made aware of grapheme/phoneme structure. This is a problem for the dyslexic child as it is this precise area which is difficult for him. There is no real way round this difficulty, although one should attempt to make the system less 'orthographic' and more 'ideographic'—in other words, provide mediational clues, e.g. a spelling or word pattern which the child can access immediately. One is trying to syllabify the written language, to overcome short-term memory problems in the individual letter combinations, to aid sound-blending and to provide some kind of immediate awareness to the child in his reading and spell-

Table 7.3   Examples of material from dyslexia training course

On card	Clue-word	Sound	Irregular word
or	stork	(or)	
ea	seat	(e)	
ar	car	(ar)	quarter, warm
ai	tail	(a)	straight
oa	loaf	(o)	
ou	house	(ow)	could, would should
ow	crow	(o)	
	sow	(ow)	

Hickey advocates using cards with clue words; the above shows examples of the letters on cards, with the example clue word given, the sound and irregular words.

ing. If the child does not need to search for the individual letters that represent sounds, then he may have immediate access to an overall sound, symbol pattern or representation. It is unfortunate that this representation must be made explicit for the child, and children find this difficult (indeed many adults comment they find spelling rules not particularly accessible). Nevertheless it is unavoidable if the child is to read, write and spell appropriately.

Remedial work can also be hard work for teacher and pupil, as written language needs to be taught in a very thorough way, and the danger is in making the whole lesson or learning situation tedious and boring. It is imperative (and no easy task!) to make the learning interesting, and in different ways, so that the child does not feel that he is doing the same thing with no gain. It is therefore important to provide the child with small stages, so that he can see how he is progressing and intersperse this rather formal teaching with games, enjoyable reading, and the occasional break for breathing space. The latter might occur in a 40-minute period—even if the teacher only has two or three of these with a given child per week, and sees them as being very precious.

There are two methods of using a structured programme. One could take the particular programme and follow it from start to finish, using the particular teaching methods described and suggested in the programme. This is a perfectly acceptable way of going about the teaching, particularly for a teacher who is only beginning to help dyslexic children, and who may be uncertain about the written language system itself. These schemes are a tremendous source of confidence for the teacher. But as the teacher becomes more familiar and experienced with the written language structure and teaching programmes, they could be then used in a more flexible manner. They can provide a basic source for teacher and pupil, and can be dipped into appropriately.

7.25   Writing approach

A particularly flexible approach is described by Cotterell (1978 and 1981) as 'a writing approach'. This method is also advocated by Newton and Thomson (1975), and in addition can form the basis for diary writing (see Section 7.1). This idea simply suggests that one teaches the structure taken from the child's own written language learning. The argument is that one can provide appropriate context, appropriate interest, and follow the child's own language development. Initially one would get a child to undertake a piece of free writing, a short essay, or any other written work. The teacher then takes one, or at the most two, spelling/word patterns from the child's writing, and isolates that as the particular material to be learnt. For example, it might be *ai* saying /a/ in the middle of words, a suffixing rule, or one letter of the alphabet. This is then looked at in any one of the structures, such as the Alpha to Omega Programme, the Cotterell Phonic Reference Cards, or Bangor Programme. The child would have his own filing index system, and this spelling pattern or rule would be entered into it. The child and teacher, perhaps taking turns, might think up words that illustrate or represent that particular spelling or word pattern—these will then be written down. Then they will be checked against the structure source, and other words as examples also read, and, if appropriate, entered into the child's own filing system. Two or three of these words will then be taken by the child and incorporated into his own sentence. This will be read back to the teacher, and if necessary a corrected version written. The particular pattern needs then to be reinforced in a number of ways, by making a game out of identifying the pattern, finding it in a magazine, putting a big ring around it, or reading it in a story (a reading scheme which has a similar structure to that being used is useful here). Cotterell suggests that one can illustrate the story or the spelling pattern by putting it in different colours, for example drawing a big picture of a foot, illustrating an *oo* sound with various words representing it written and illustrated.

The proceeding section has incorporated the notion of structure, sequence and a cumulative programme in respect of the general principles which we outlined in Section 7.1. An additional element often described as being important by teachers of dyslexic children is that of a multi-sensory programme, and it is to this that we turn to next.

7.3   Multi-sensory teaching

Two of the early proponents of multi-sensory techniques were Gillingham and Stillman (1969, this refers to the 5th edition of their work; there are earlier editions going back to the 1930s). Essentially these multi-sensory techniques involve a phonic programme. The basis is the learning of 'phonograms' i.e. basic sound units which may be made up of single letters or letter combinations. Some of the techniques that we have already described are 'multi-sensory', in the sense that they involve relating speech to visual symbols; but here we are concerned specifically with the notion of the interrelationship between auditory, visual and kinesthetic or tactile modalities. Many multi-sensory techniques are based on the Orton (1937) theories, particularly the pioneering programme of Gillingham and Stillman. The concepts behind the methods are that if there is a weakness in a particular modality, whether this is auditory or visual, one can teach through another modality, i.e. teach to strengths; that the integration of the various senses can provide additional routes for the child's written language learnings and that all the senses working together are essential for the development of appropriate written language skills. The approach has been criticized in relation to theoretical background, on the grounds that one is overloading the child's senses in some kind of way. However we have already seen some current and recent work examining the possible underlining mechanisms in relation to multi-sensory technique (see Hulme 1981 a and b, Bradley 1981 and p. 190 above). Vernon (1971) comments that written language involves the appreciation of phoneme sequences, relating them to printed letter sequences, and synthesizing these to form word sounds. In other words grasping the correlation between spatially extended letter sequences and temporally ordered phoneme sequences.

7.31   Gillingham/Stillman Programme

In the Gillingham/Stillman Programme one commences with letters, then letter blends, analysis of blends and letters, followed by phonic analysis of regular words, polysyllabic words, with particular importance attached to syllable division. However an additional component of these techniques is sometimes called the VAKT method. This refers to Visual, Auditory, Kinesthetic and Tactile interrelationships. Here emphasis is placed not only on the child following its own speech, but also on relating the visual symbols to sound, and representing them in the way they are formed in writing. The idea is to train all of these modalities so that there is automatic production in writing, spelling and reading, whether it is visual-to-auditory transmission, or sound-to-motor programming. A good example of a particular technique which is a key element of these programmes is the simultaneous oral spelling (SOS) technique. Typically, the teacher says the word, and the child then repeats the word, reinforcing the sound and the auditory component. Next the child names the letters. This important component provides additional reinforcement to the child that letters can have both a name and a sound but, more importantly, reinforces the serial, sequential aspect of letter combinations, providing awareness of the detailed letter structure of words. (There is some minor disagreement about this particular notion of teaching letter names, e.g. the Bangor Programme does not teach letter names as such, but their sounds.) Following repetition and the naming of the letters, the child then writes the word, naming each letter as he writes. This is important in relation to translating the sound into a written equivalent, and as a motor, tactile or kinesthetic programme. Naming each letter is also important in relation to mapping out the correspondences. The child then repeats the word, by reading it, i.e. the visual to auditory component. This also helps train auditory recall of sequence.

Multi-sensory techniques encourage careful systematic observation of words, involving necessary left-right directions and providing immediate feed-back for errors. The Gillingham and Stillmann technique involves learning phonograms by eight linkages. These are as follows (taken from the 5th edition):

Linkage 1
A card with a letter is presented: pupil looks while teacher gives the name of the letter; pupil repeats. Once the name is known the procedure is repeated but now the teacher gives, and the pupil repeats, the sound of the letter (visual-auditory: auditory-kinesthetic).

Linkage 2
The letter is made by teacher. Its orientation, where to start in writing, and the direction of movement are discussed; pupil then traces over the letter, copies, writes it from memory and then with eyes averted (visual-kinesthetic: kinesthetic-visual).

Linkage 3
The letter is shown; pupil names; teacher may move pupil's hand passively to form letter (visual-auditory: kinesthetic-auditory).

Linkage 4
Teacher dictates the letter name: pupil writes (auditory-kinesthetic: auditory-visual).

Linkage 5
The letter is presented: pupil gives its sound (visual-auditory). This is the important linkage for reading.

Linkage 6
Teacher gives the name of phonogram: pupil gives its sound (auditory-auditory).

Linkage 7
Teacher gives the sound, pupil gives the name of the phonogram (auditory-auditory). This is the important linkage for oral spelling.

Linkage 8
Teacher gives the sound, pupil writes it (sometimes with eyes averted) and gives the name (auditory-kinesthetic: auditory-visual). This is the important linkage for written spelling.

There are a number of basic drills which are aimed at reinforcing these links. As a detailed example of multi-sensory techniques we shall turn now to the British adaptation of this programme undertaken by Hickey (1977). This is widely used in the UK, particularly by the Dyslexia Institute, an organization having a number of assessment and teaching branches throughout the country.

7.32   Language training course

The following is a description of the teaching programme, adapted from parts of the manual. It should be pointed out that this is only a sample; the programme is very detailed and structured, and indeed it is recommended by Hickey that the teacher undertake a specialized course in its use. The course is based on the teaching of phonograms or sound/symbol pattern(s) in a systematic way. This would start off, for example, with individual letters by use of clue words and sound. Some examples follow.

Multi-sensory Learning for Reading and Writing
The aim is for the learner to acquire, for permanent automatic response, the name-sound-shape of phonograms and an ability to put them in correct sequential order. His visual, auditory, tactile-kinesthetic and oral-kinesthetic perceptual systems must interact sufficiently to make learning so secure that he can produce any aspect of the phonograms when needed whether for reading or spelling. For example,

when he is given:

(a) the name of the letter, he must be able to recall the clueword, the sound, the appearance of the symbol for reading and the feel of the shape for writing;
(b) the sound, he must be able to recall the clueword, the appearance of the symbol for reading, the name for spelling and the shape for writing;
(c) the writing shape, he must be able to recall the name, clueword, sound and relate it to the printed shape for reading;
(d) the clueword, he must be able to recall sound, name and shape of the letter for reading, writing and spelling.

The Reading Pack consists of 84 cards, each with a phonogram (a symbol representing a spoken sound) printed in lower-case letters. At the bottom right-hand corner of the card is its capital form in a small type size, acting as a reminder to the pupil that capitals behave in the same way as the lower-case letters for sound-blending. On the reverse of the card is a picture of the clue to the sound of the phonogram, the 'clueword' and the representation of the sound. The written form of the sound should become familiar to the pupil as he progresses. For example, the letter *i* which is the first letter in the language training course is represented by the picture of an igloo, the clueword *igloo* and the sound (i) which is heard at the beginning of the clueword. It is not necessary for the pupil to be able to read the cluewords; they are clues to the spelling choices. Vowel cards are recognized by two bars across the top. The cards are self-corrective. They are introduced one at a time and the pack is gradually completed. As each card is added, the learner's reading skills are built up and his knowledge of the English language broadens. The routine practice for using the Reading and Spelling Packs needs to be studied carefully by the teacher. Expertise will come with use. The Reading Pack should be used by the learner alone for practice at least once a day whenever he has a spare moment. When he is with his teacher he should handle his own cards under observation so that correct responses are checked and maintained.

When the teacher presents a new card, he should go through the Introduction to a Phonogram and Stimulus Response Routine (SRR). The learner working alone or under observation picks up the first card in the pack, sees the phonogram, says the clueword and sound 'igloo' (i) iron (i), turns the card over and places it face down, checks by the picture/s that his response is correct and looks at the next card. If he has made a mistake he looks at the phonogram again, repeats the clueword and sound and places the card at the back of the pack so that he can re-read it. He must have an awareness of the need to increase his speed. When revising with the teacher, if the learner gives an incorrect response to a phonogram, clueword and/or sound, the teacher may have to repeat the SRR until secure. The pupil should be encouraged to make a note of the phonograms he finds difficult to remember and when presenting himself for a lesson to tell his teacher; alternatively, he can separate them from the pack so that revision is concentrated on them.

With each phonogram, the learner has multi-sensory practice for reading:

Visual	he looks at the letter *i*
Kinesthetic	uses his spatial ability to see the letter is alone on the card, its direction, the relationship of its parts and figure-ground,
Auditory	listens to himself giving the clueword and sound (i) for the letter *i*,
Oral-Kinesthetic	repeats and relates the clueword to the sound and feels the position of his teeth, tongue and lips in reproducing it.

The Spelling Pack consists of 50 cards whose purpose is to present the written sounds so that the learner can listen to them and spell them, if necessary in their several possible ways. The teaching procedures are as follows.

Teacher or	Learner: eyes averted
learner	Listens to the sound (i)
reads the	Repeats the sound (i)
sound aloud	Spells the sound by naming the letters *i,y*
	Writes the letter(s), naming each one just before writing.

Later, he may add the irregular spellings *igh* and *ie* to the (i) card, noting their correct positions.

The pupil has multi-sensory practice for spelling.

Auditory	he listens to a sound,
Oral	speaks the sound aloud, links it to the name(s) of the letters in its possible different spellings,
Kinesthetic	uses movement to write correctly the spelling alternatives naming each before writing,
Visual	sees the spellings he has written and learns their different positions in words or their order of probability in words.

Further procedures are described for spelling, and the above example is mainly concerned with learning basic sound/symbol correspondence or individual letters. The same kind of approach would be undertaken with more sophisticated spelling patterns, suffixes or blends. Another important component is syllabification. This teaches various kinds of patterns, such as vowel/consonant/vowel or *vc/cv, v/cc* and so on. Indeed the child is encouraged by exercises to learn the forms of short and long vowels in respect to syllables, and this particular aspect of written language is made explicit.

7.33   Fernald tracing

We have mentioned in passing the Fernald Tracing Technique. This is also a multi-sensory learning programme, and is similar at first glance to the ones we have described above. However the difference with the Fernald Tracing Technique is that it is essentially a modified look-and-say method. The additional element is the tracing involved. Here the child learns a whole word, rather than any kind of phonic analysis and synthesis of the word. The Fernald Tracing Technique is particularly useful when teaching words which are irregular or new words that need to be learnt quickly, and is also very useful for words which are required frequently but cause difficulty. A detailed description of the Fernald Tracing Technique now follows, taken from Myers and Hammill (1976) and Cotterell (personal communication).

Although the system is referred to as kinesthetic, it is really a Look, Say and Do method. Phonics are not involved. In practice the method is slow, but it provides a method of whole-word learning for the child to whom 'sounds' mean little.

Procedure
Stage I
(a) The word required is written for the child, regardless of length, with a wax crayon in blackboard size print on a strip of paper $2\frac{1}{2} \times 12$ inches.
(b) With finger contact, the child traces over the word, saying each part of the word aloud as naturally as possible as he does so. He repeats this as many times as is necessary until he is able to write the word on a scrap of rough paper, saying it, without looking at the original copy. (If he looks to and fro, he breaks the word up into small meaningless units.)
(c) The word should always be written as a whole unit from the beginning. In the case of interruption or error it should be started again.
(d) When the word has been written correctly in rough, it is written in the story, under a picture, etc., the child saying it quietly as he writes it.
(e) Several words can be taught in this manner, and the child can start to make his own book about anything of interest to him. Working through high interest is an important feature of this method and motivates the child.
(f) Whatever he writes should be typed out by the teacher so that it is read back in print the next day.
(g) A word file is needed to hold a child's words. This should be alphabetically indexed (an old shoe box makes an excellent word file). In filing his words, he learns to identify the initial letter of a word and it is excellent training for later use of a dictionary.
(h) Words learnt should always be used in context so that they are experienced in meaningful groups.
(i) The amount of tracing necessary per word depends on the child and the length of the word being learnt.

Stage II
This is the same as Stage I but tracing is no longer necessary. After a certain period the child can learn a new word simply by looking at it, saying it over to himself as he looks and writing it without looking at the copy, again saying each part of the word as he writes it. As his vocabulary builds up, his 'stories' become longer. He should always read back what he has written afterwards, and the 'printed copy' next day. When vocalizing a word it should not be a stilted, distorted sounding-out of letters and syllables so that the word is lost in the process. It takes a little practice to get the

connections established between the articulation of the word and the hand movement. The child should stop tracing when he seems able to learn without it and it should be dropped gradually. First there is a decrease in the number of tracings, and then certain words are learnt without it. The average tracing period is about two months, but ranges from one to eight months. No attempt should be made to simplify the content written. It is of more interest to the child to write and read fairly difficult material at his level of understanding. He delights in learning difficult words if he has always known failure. He gradually builds up a reading vocabulary of commonly used words and of words connected with particular subjects. As he progresses, his curiosity is aroused and he wants to know more. A desire to read is created. When tracing is no longer necessary, a small word file or alphabetical pocket notebook can be substituted for this larger file. The teacher now writes the word in ordinary writing for the child and he learns it by looking at it, saying it and writing it.

Stage III

The child learns directly from the printed word without having it written for him. He merely looks at it and says it to himself before writing it. Now the child should want to read books. He is allowed to read what he wishes and is told words he does not know. After reading, the new words should be gone over and learnt. They should be checked for retention later.

See Miccinati (1979) for further suggestions concerning this method.

The above are specific techniques from particular programmes. In general the approach here is to try and link various senses, particularly using kinesthetic, or motor memory, programmes to aid the weak phonological or auditory coding memory that dyslexic children have. We have found a form of multi-sensory learning and spelling to be particularly helpful, and indeed have undertaken some studies (see Thomson 1988, 1989a) showing the efficacy of these methods over visual inspection. Our version of simultaneous oral spelling involves each child having a word list. This might be individual words that they make errors with in their essays, it might be a particular word family or pattern that we are trying to teach, it might be selected words, e.g. words having simple consonant blends at the beginning followed by a vowel and a consonant, or they may be irregular words. The children work in pairs, as follows: child A will have child B's word list. Child A will read the first word out aloud, child B will repeat it, and he will say the individual letters by name, one by one. He will then repeat the word again, and write it down saying each letter as he writes it, followed by reading the word that he has written. If the whole procedure is correct then child A puts a tick against that particular word. This routine is repeated with about 10 words every day in the first 5 minutes of the English lesson. Each of the 10 words is given in this fashion for 2 weeks making 10 working days. If the child has 10 ticks that word is deemed to be 'learnt' and put into a private dictionary. Of course that word will have to come up again and again as dyslexics will invariably forget it at a later date! If there are any crosses that word is then put into the next 2 week word list.

7.4   Matching task to learner

We have already briefly made comments concerning attempts to match teaching programmes to particular subtypes of dyslexia. Johnson and Myklebust (1967) and Johnson (1978) suggest that the visual dyslexic is taught by a 'synthetic phonic' method. Synthetic here refers to the construction of words and units from their constituent parts. It is suggested that there should be no learning of letter names, but that one learns individual sounds which are then blended together to form words and in turn these words form sentences. Sight words are taught only in context and there might be some additional exercises in visual perception. It is emphasized by many remediators that this should be with the printed word itself, and not through the visual perception exercises which we briefly described and criticized in the earlier part of this chapter. The auditory dyslexics, on the other hand, need more help in retrieving letter names, in sequencing and blending, and particularly in techniques involving rhyme and syllabification. They will be taught using a whole word/story method, particularly matching pictures and objects to the printed word. Function words need to be taught in context, and there will be some additional training in auditory analysis and synthesis, particularly in sound similarities. Phonic rules will need to be taught very carefully. There will also be emphasis on syllable units and multi-sensory techniques such as the Fernald Tracing (see previous section).

Every dyslexic child does not have exactly the same kind of programme. It is important to identify the child's strengths and weaknesses and to develop an individualized programme matched to his own skills. One of the fundamental rationales behind this is the need to match written language to the child's particular mode of perception or learning style. Some general ideas are given in a series of booklets published by the Helen Arkell Dyslexia Centre (Pollock 1974, Waller 1974, Pollock and Waller 1978). For example, Waller suggests that in examining handwriting problems, one should focus on which particular element is at fault—whether it is in general motor control, formation of letters, speed of writing, inappropriate tensions or hand-grip, size of individual letters, or crossings out. One would then encourage the child to study his own writing, and pick out his own faults, by giving him examples of various different kinds of difficulties. Then one could look at posture, grip, paper angle, and so on. She also points out that writing can be formed from six basic shapes: viz | — / \ ( )

It is also worth noting in the context of handwriting that a cursive script is recommended for the dyslexic. This is common to many different programmes (see the Hickey Programme, Bangor Programme, Aston Portfolios). It is essential for teachers concerned to liaise closely, as there are many different writing techniques and it is important not to confuse the child. Indeed some practitioners hold very closely to the particular writing programme that they are teaching, and there can be quite serious disagreements over this element.

Another example of a particular weakness might be a child having sequencing or orientation difficulties. Pollock and Waller (1970), argue that one needs to provide exercises for the days of the week, months of the year and other serial learning.

They also suggest laying out the alphabet in sequence, a technique also recommended by Hickey. This involves having, for example, upper-case letters carved out of wood (also aiding tactile identification according to Hickey) and putting them into a semi-circle around the child. Various exercises can then be undertaken, e.g. picking out letters after /h/, reciting them or picking them out to form words. In addition Pollock and Waller recommend the use of maps, from very simple to complex, for example, asking a child to make up a story describing movements around an island, to imagine what it might be like looking down from a hill, to describe the scenery, and later on to use map references.

These are some general items and ideas which relate task to learner by examining the child's particular difficulties. Another approach to matching task to learner is to examine in some detail the child's learning strategies and undertake a 'task analysis'. In the UK this approach has essentially drawn upon behavioural psychology, and is used increasingly by educational psychologists in terms of their way of conceptualizing the learning process. The idea is atheoretical, in the sense that one does not necessarily describe the child as being dyslexic, and one does not necessarily use a particular teaching technique because one believes that this is overcoming a particular deficit. The child's errors are examined and a hierachy of objectives is drawn up. This idea of objectives is particularly important, as one must define at every point the next stage. This might simply be teaching letter—sound correspondence or it might be recognizing a whole word. A detailed example

Table 7.4   Resources for subtypes of dyslexia

Type of problem	Remediation approaches

Auditory problem
  Teaching through visual modality with
    training of auditory skills
	Whole word approach
	Breakthrough to Literacy
	Lyn Wendon Pictogram System
	Dragon Pirates
	Griffen Pirates
	Reading Games
	Stott Programmed Kit
	Auditory Training by use of e.g.
	    Language Master Sound Sense etc.

Visual problems
  Teaching through auditory modality
    with training of visual skills
	Phonic approach
	Language in Action
	Royal Road Readers
	Stott Programmed Reading Kit
	Phonic Games
	Visual training e.g. Frostig

Visual and auditory problems
  Strengthening of all sensory pathways by
    using visual, auditory kinesthetic and
    tactile modalities.
	Multi-sensory approaches e.g. Fernald
	    tracing plus recent derivations

(From Hicks and Murgatroyd 1981.)

can be found in Myers and Hammill (1976).

A final approach to the aim of matching tasks to the learner is to examine the child's particular perceptual, memorial or other skills. This can be done psychometrically or by analysis of reading and spelling. Both of these approaches are described in Chapter 5, along with some very general guidelines to programmes given by Hicks and Murgatroyd (1981), as summarized in Table 7.4.

7.41   Aston Teaching Portfolio

To make some of the above more concrete, we shall take as an example the case given in Chapter 5, involving the assessment of a child with the Aston Index, and we shall examine a possible programme resulting from this assessment. It is recommended at this point that the reader returns to this case and reviews the descriptions of the child's difficulties.

It will be recalled that 'Richard' had a severe reading and spelling difficulty. There were some basic difficulties in sound–symbol correspondences and one would start a remedial programme at that level. This might include, perhaps, use of the Edith Norrie Letter Case, or one of the structured programmes. However an early stage would involve the teaching of consonant blends followed by vowel digraphs in the kinds of ways outlined under structure previously. (Indeed the assumption will be made in talking about matching task to learner that the general remedial strategies that we have outlined earlier will be incorporated, i.e. some kind of multi-sensory programme involving systematic structured overteaching.) Richard had auditory difficulties in particular. He had difficulty in phonic analysis or in applying any kind of 'phonic attack', in syllabification, or realizing the appropriate sound/symbol correspondence in letter combinations. He also had great difficulties in sound blending, both in his reading and also on the Aston Index Test. Further problems were in auditory sequential memory. Reading and Spelling errors suggested serious auditory confusion, particularly illustrated by his occasional difficulties in following his own speech sounds. Therefore two specific areas for help in Richard's case would be in auditory discrimination and sound blending, the following being a few examples of activities taken from the Aston Teaching Portfolio.

Auditory discrimination: Activities

Sound Matching. Ask the child to make a sustained sound, e.g. /n,r,f/ and continue making it while the teacher makes other sounds. The child stops as soon as he hears the teacher make the identical sound. Say a sound, ask the child to memorize it and raise his hand when he hears the teacher say it in a series of sounds. Use speech therapy methods to help child distinguish between similar sounds; e.g. watch his own lips and tongue (through a mirror), or another person's, as words are spoken. Show the child pictures of people saying different sounds; e.g. /p,w,l/; the child then imitates. Ask the child to listen to words either on tape or face-to-face, then choose a picture to go with them. Then use written words. Read out a few words with the same initial or final sound, saying, e.g., 'Do these words start or end with the same sound'? e.g. *sun / slid / set* or *end / mad / lid*. Then say three words with different initial or final sounds and ask the same question, e.g. *man / met / not*. Read out pairs of words either with the same or different initial or final sound; the child must say whether the words are the same or different, e.g. *pit/bit, beg/peg, no/on*. Then get the child to listen to two words on tape, either similar or the same, and either find the correct matching pair on a worksheet, or say whether the pair are the same or different. Use the child's visual strengths to improve auditory discrimination, e.g. give him a card with three words with the same initial, medial or final sound and ask him to underline the similar sound (e.g. *cut/call/candle*.) Then say the words and ask the child if he can hear the similarities. Have child match flashcards with similar initial, medial and final sound (saying the words first). To help discrimination of short vowel sounds, ask the child to draw a line from a picture to the correct vowel sound he hears (see SRA Workbooks). Use nonsense phrases or sentences for oral or written work, with same initial, medial, final sounds. e.g. *Jolly Jumping Jane* (for a child's name in class), *Feel free to feed the sheep* (These can be used with Language Master cards, or tape recorder and worksheet).

Sound Blending (Reinforce through visual or kinesthetic channels).
The pushing together of clay and sandpaper letters will help the child see how sounds go together through physical blending.

1 Blending: begin with simple words with sustained consonants, e.g. *led*. Place the letters an inch apart. Take the *l*, say it, and move it simultaneously towards the *e*, then move both towards *d*, saying sounds while moving them together. Ask child to repeat. (Later, use consonant blend units.)
OR: (as an alternative to 1):
Place the letters together and say *led*, then take *d* away. What is left? Repeat with other similar words, e.g. *red, wed, fed*, etc. However, if this method fails, the alternative method of blending the vowel to the final sound first could be used if it is preferred.

2 Let the child listen to the teacher say the word slowly, then note down on paper a mark for each separate sound unit (syllable). The child can then look at the printed word to check if it is correct. Start with simple words first, e.g. *cat*, then ones with consonant or vowel blends.

3 As above, but the child selects the appropriate letter or blend, made in wood or cardboard, for each separate sound unit of the words.

4 Child listens to the separate sound of the word, e.g. *m-a-n* on tape, then selects the matching word from array of worksheets, e.g. *can/man/hat/cat*.

5 Using cut-out letters, ask the child to select letters to make *bat* (they are read out separately), then get the child to remove *b*, put in *c* and read the word. It is good for the child to see a physical change in the word, when dissected, and then relate this to the auditory pattern.

6 Using cut-out letters and letter-blends, make a word for the child, e.g. *cat*, then separate it into *ca-t*; then put the parts together again, until the child can blend them. Make other similar words with a different set of letters (e.g. *fat*,

mat, pat) and line them up for the child to see similarities. Play games with this combination.

The activities described are only a few of those given, and sound discrimination and blending are only two examples of activities for Richard. The Aston Portfolio provides an additional source of teaching diagnosis to help match task to learner. By teaching diagnosis it is meant that one can, during the course of teaching, give activities to the child which can pin-point a particular problem. Some examples of these activities from the Assessment Check Lists in the Portfolio are given in Table 7.5.

Table 7.5   Examples of diagnostic teaching procedures from Aston Portfolio

Reading

Visual

Letters
1   Have the child select letter in row that matches the first letter:
    a: a o e d   G: G C O D   p; d d p q
    j: i j t y   R: B P R F   m: w m v u
2   Have the child draw line from lower case to upper case letter for each letter of alphabet.
    eg   a   D
            b   C
            c   B
            d   A etc
3   Have the child ring in red phonic pattern(s) in each word:
    eg   strip   train   coat   tie   meat   day   etc.

Advanced reading skills
CLOZE tests
23   Have the child complete sentences when presented orally.
24   Semantic cues:
    (i) John went to the lake to ——— (swim, fish, walk)
    (ii) A cat has four ——— (hands, legs, dogs)
    Stages:
    (a) Present the words to choose from: (swim, fish, walk)
    (b) Present initial letter of word: (s or f)
    (c) Later give written CLOZE tests:
    (i) with words supplied;
    (ii) without words supplied
25   Syntactic cues:
    (i) I am ——— to the shop (go going, went)
    (ii) My mother ——— driving her car (liked, liking, likes)

Spelling

Auditory-visual
12   Have the child write down letter forms from dictation both for names and sounds (capitals and lower case) of letters.
13   Have the child repeat and then write the following series:
    (a) sounds: b h n v a g m u
                  d i p a e k r x
    (b) phrases: The good boy   A red ball   The tin box
    (c) sentences: John went to the shop   Ann is going to play

Table 7.5 *continued*

14   Have the child write down the letters (from dictation) for each consonant/vowel/more difficult blend.

15   Test the child on Basic Sight Vocabulary list, giving about ten words at a time.

16   Have the child analyse these words into their separate sound components before writing them:

strain (str-ai-n)   feet (f-ee-t)

baby (ba-by)   institution (in-sti-tu-tion)

Also observe during spelling test.

17   When the child has written the above words (in 16) have him look at each word and blend the sound units back into the complete word to check the spelling.

18   Have the child write the word that rhymes with the initial one — from the following list presented visually:

man;   can   hat   mab   train;   mate   rain   trade
let;   net   pen   tell   sing;   sink   wind   thing

The advantage of this kind of programme is its flexibility; one may take out and adapt appropriate ideas and materials for the individual child's learning problem both from initial assessment and, as a child progresses in the learning situation, during remediation. The disadvantage of course is that one may be omitting a general structured approach, and the child may become rather lost in bits of materials. However, there is no reason why the activities cannot be used in addition to the child undertaking one of the more formal programmes that we have already described.

7.5   Phonetic teaching

A crucial element in teaching the dyslexic is to take a phonic approach to learning. This is of course teaching the particular area which is difficult for them. However, it is necessary if the dyslexic is to get over the 'alphabetic barrier'. Educational approaches such as reading for meaning, language development or psycholinguistic approaches all founder in the case of the dyslexic because the basic mechanical reading is weak.

The early stages of teaching phonics to dyslexics involve areas of weakness in phonemic awareness and segmentation. Many dyslexics have great difficulty in recognizing individual component parts of letters, particularly the vowel sounds. The alphabet has to be taught by sounds and letter names initially, and many routines developed to help children classify and recognize sounds within words. One common example might be asking a child to put CVC words under appropriate vowel headings, or to recognize commonalities in words, both by visual inspection or rhyme and by blending and producing new words through just changing one or two letters. Classification of sounds of all kinds is particularly useful. One example linked to a spelling rule might be that of the sound /k/ at the end of words. Here if there is a short vowel sound /k/ it is spelt 'ck', as in 'lick', if there is a long vowel sound it is spelt 'ke' (the magic 'e' pattern', as in 'like'. The letters '-ck' and '-ke' can be put into two columns at the top of the paper, the child is given words to listen to and must decide whether the vowel is short or long, and is then required to put the word under the right heading. This technique of organizing and classifying sounds can be used in many different ways in many different language structures. It is also important to relate teaching in class to reinforcement worksheets, of which there are many sources.

Even quite early on, particularly with more intelligent dyslexics, we find it useful to help them analyse sounds by teaching some rudimentary phonetics. This involves recognizing that words can be spelt the way they sound but also that many other words are not spelt as they sound. We often teach the children 'sound pictures'. This is a representation of the sound of a word, which may be different to its spelling. We also teach the use of breves and macrons to sound out the vowels. Table 7.6 shows some examples of these. It is also important to stress the inter-relationship between written language and the speech system.

Table 7.6 Some examples of 'sound pictures' and diacritical marks

Sound pictures ·	Spelling
(ā)	a as in cake
(ū)	u as in cup
(răt)	rat
(bīt)	bite
(bōt)	boat
(ĭn'vīte)	invite

Although spoken language is communicated by voice the task for written language learning is to translate the printed word into its spoken equivalent and vice versa. We have found that visual-to-sound coding is a particular problem for dyslexic children, as are aspects of relevant spoken language matters, such as segmentation and linguistic awareness (see Chapters 3 and 4). An important point here is that the teacher needs to have a good knowledge of the structure of spoken and written language systems. This is particularly important when it comes to teaching a child the rules and regulations of spelling, writing and reading patterns. It is not appropriate for the dyslexic child to be taught individual sight words on their own. The child needs to generalize orthographic structure, for example understand that the sound /p/ in *put* can be generalized to words such as *pat*, *pit*, *pot*, and so on. A good deal of written language is in fact based on the closed pattern, found in the above example, i.e. *p-t*. Joos (1966) argues that individual letter combinations need to be enclosed and embedded in context if they are to be useful.

One of the first stages in remediation is thus to examine the relationship between written and spoken language. Techniques here are similar to some speech therapy exercises and programmes. The first stage is to make the child aware of his own speech and sound system. Hamilton-Fairley (1976) suggests that the child can be instructed to listen and attend, and to watch the speaker closely, particularly his lips and tongue, as well as noting non-verbal cues. In other words one is drawing attention to the communication process right from its preliminary stages, before one even gets to written language learning. In order to provide some help in diffi-culties in memory and sound perception, another suggestion is that the child be asked to recall sequences, for example to pick out the order of noises made with a whistle, a rattle, and a bell; to tap out rhythms, pick out objects in a particular order, or carry out instructions. Hamilton-Fairley (1976) recommends five stages in the discrimination of sounds which are needed for written language. (i) The therapist or teacher shall give examples of the sound on it own, (ii) the child should differentiate that sound amongst others, (e.g. k/t), (iii) the child should use the sound in nonsense words in initial and final position, with reinforcement and guidance from the teacher, (iv) the child should use the sound in real words, and (v) the teacher or therapist should say words incorrectly to and try to get the child to notice the correct and incorrect version. The important point is for the child to be made constantly aware of his spoken language and its consequent translation to the written language system. One could point out the difference between voiced and unvoiced sounds, with the teaching following the normal course of phonological development.

A very useful technique in the early stages, and indeed even as reinforcement for the adult dyslexic or child who is progressing well, is the Edith Norrie Letter Case (see Figure 6.1). This is used extensively by, and is available from, the Helen Arkell Dyslexia Centre. It is a multi-sensory technique, building individual letters into words by following the spoken sound sequence from a letter case. The child is required to pick out appropriate letters. The important aim of this particular piece of apparatus is to make the child consciously aware of his own speech process. Indeed there is a small mirror for this purpose, in which the child is encouraged to

LIP			TIP				BACK		
2 *M* 6 *m*	2 *B* 6 *b*	2 *N* 10 *n*	2 *D* 10 *d*	2 *T* 12 t	1 th	2 *G* 8 *g*	6 *ng*	2 Q 6 q
2 V 6 *v*	2 P 6 p	2 *R* 10 *r*	2 *L* 10 *l*	2 S 10 s	2 C 8 c	2 C 8 c	2 Q 6 q	ck
2 *W* 10 *w*	2 F 6 f	2 *Z* 6 *z*	2 *J* 6 *j*	1 sh	1 ch	2 X 4 x	2 H 6 h	
2 wh	2 **A** 12 **a**	2 **E** 18 **e**	6 **I** 10 **i**	2 **O** 12 **o**	2 **U** 8 **u**	2 **Y̶** 10 y	6 1 2	Mirror

Key: Bold letters for vowels; Y has a line through it to indicate use as vowel (e.g. *fly*)
Voiced letters – italic – m, b, v, w, n, j, g, d, r, l, z, ng.

Figure 7.1   The Edith Norrie Letter Case

look at his own lips, tongue, position of mouth, and so on, when forming the various sounds. In addition there is colour-coding of voiced/non-voiced sounds, and for vowels. This enables the child to build up words in which there must be at least one red letter (i.e. vowel). The letters are also categorized in relation to articulation. A description of the Letter Case follows, including one or two ideas for its use from the Helen Arkell Centre.

The letters are arranged phonetically not alphabetically. The vowels are in the five middle boxes at the bottom of the case and each one is red. Children should learn that there must be at least one 'red letter' in every word, and one in every syllable; 'y' sounds as a vowel and is in the same row. The consonants are divided into 'The Lip Sound Family'; a 'Tip of the Tongue Family'; and a 'Back of the Throat Family'. This enables the child to narrow down the range of letters to choose from. By means of a small mirror the pupil learns whether sounds are produced by his lips, tip of the tongue or the back of the throat.

Starting with phonetically regular words and short sentences the pupil spells out the sentence from the box and is allowed as much time as he likes to sort out difficult words. He reads it through looking for mistakes, and the teacher may supply more clues to help him correct them, e.g. 'Say that word again and look at your lips in the mirror' or 'How many syllables are there in that word, and how many red letters have you?' When the sentence is correct, including capital letters and punctuation, it is copied out, the pupil being able to pay attention to the formation of the letters. The sentence can be covered up and written from memory, then checked for corrections by the child. Later the letters can be removed when a couple of words have been studied so that there is no control check. Memory is being trained. Later on the letters need only be used for difficult words, which are best used in context.

The apparatus is particularly useful for children who are failing to follow their own speech sounds, or have serious auditory confusions. For children who are doing reasonably well in written language after teaching, sometimes the occasional word for which they are confused can be built up using the Letter Case. Cotterell (1970) for example suggests the use of the Letter Case with those having spelling errors such as omission (*belog* for *belong, sak* for *sank*), as well as omissions in initial consonant blends (*tay* for *tray*), and weak auditory discrimination (*crig* for *grip*), or vowel confusion (*nat* for *net*). The technique helps teach basic sound symbol correspondence links, as well as building up simple words that are phonetically regular.

However the written language system is not always regular and goes beyond a simple sound/symbol component. Word patterns tend to be open at vowels, closed at consonants, and one might describe a *phonogram unit* as a closed syllable (grapheme) beginning with a vowel, yet producing the same sound. An example might be *an* which might be used to produce a longer unit such as *and*, which in turn might be used in words such as *sand, stand, mandate* and so on. This generates some kind of phonetic stability and coding generability in the written language. This of course applies particularly to regular sound/symbol correspondence rules. The important point here however is that although different language patterns may produce many meanings, there are some regular and easily identifiable units. This structure will need to be taught explicitly.

It is not possible within the context of this book to go into all examples of teaching phonics. Suffice it to say that an important component is the overlearning requirement, and therefore a great deal of resources in terms of phonic worksheets, reinforcement exercises. Creative teaching is needed to make a difficult task enjoyable!

As well as the so-called phonic approach, dyslexics will need a good deal of help on the spelling rules. Common ones are the suffix rules. One of these is what is called the 111 rule, i.e. with words with one syllable, one vowel, one consonant, double the consonant if the suffix begins with a vowel; thus swim becomes swimming, but clamp becomes clamping, and spoon becomes spooning. There are many other examples of these spelling rules. There are also numerous guides, for example when /l/, /s/ and /f/ are at the end of one syllable words, double up the end letter, and so on. These need to be reinforced every so often. There are always exceptions, of course, but we are trying to introduce the idea that the majority of written language is regular. Many children like these rules and they can be taught systematically and accessed when appropriate. The difficult trick is to get the child to utilize his knowledge of spelling rules when writing essays, as opposed to in an exercise. There are also some useful mnemonics for difficult words that children may have to learn, e.g. 'eat apples up' for the 'eau' in beautiful or 'never eat cheese eat salmon sandwiches and remain young' for 'necessary'. It is fun for children to develop their own mnemonics.

For irregular word spelling it is difficult to pick out rules and follow common spelling patterns. Here the simultaneous oral spelling mentioned earlier is quite useful, but sometimes one must expect the irregular words to come later in the child's written language development.

As far as multi-syllable words are concerned—a severe difficulty for dyslexics as we have seen in earlier research—it is quite useful to undertake syllable analysis. This is particularly useful when the words are regular multi-syllable words. Syllable analysis involves analysing words into their 'beats'. In the initial stages children tap out the words into their syllables. A useful clue is that all syllables in English contain a vowel and syllables can sometimes be felt by putting your hand underneath your chin. When your chin moves down this is a syllable! Children can learn to beat out the rhythm of syllables. The next stage is to examine the vowels and see whether they are long or short and undertake analysis based on the six types of syllable. Initially, we introduce only the open, closed and magic 'e' syllable and then go on to the other three types which are more complicated. Children can then read words and analyse them into their syllable types, classifying them as shown in Table 7.7. They can then be encouraged to spell them out syllable by syllable in the words, work out what kind of syllable it is and write the appropriate spelling pattern for it. We find that this technique is very helpful for learning to read unfamiliar yet long words, both for confidence and developing sophisticated word attack skills. It is also

Table 7.7 Six types of syllables*

Syllable type
1 The <u>O</u>pen syllable (o)   <u>me</u> <u>no</u> <u>o</u>'pen <u>cry</u>'ing <u>fi</u>'nal The vowel is open at the end of the syllable, often says its name
2 The <u>C</u>losed syllable (c)   <u>in</u> <u>lost</u> o'<u>pen</u> cry'<u>ing</u> fi'<u>nal</u> The vowel is closed by one or more consonants; says its sound
3 The <u>VCE</u> or magic 'c' syllable (vce)   <u>ice</u> <u>wine</u> <u>scrape</u> re'<u>bate</u> dis'<u>place</u>   (suffix: drop 'e '- <u>biting</u>) The vowel has been opened by the magic 'e', says its name
4 The <u>-le</u> or consonant -le syllable (-le)   ta'<u>ble</u> pad'<u>dle</u> stee'<u>ple</u> (suffix drop 'e' strug'gl'ing)
5 The <u>DIPHTHONG</u> or DIGRAPH ('dippy') syllable (dip)   <u>wait</u> <u>snow</u> au'gust main'<u>tain</u> de'<u>stroy</u>'ing
6 The <u>R COMBINATION</u> SYLLABLE (rc)   <u>ford</u> <u>bird</u> de'<u>ter</u>'mine <u>cur</u>'tain A vowel combined with an 'r'. The vowel comes first – ar, ir, ur etc.

Some examples of syllable analysis

o rc	dip c	o rc c vce
a'corn	spoon'ful '	re'or'gan'ize
c rc o c	c vce	c -le
trans'for'ma'tion	stag'nate	crum'ble

* Each example of the syllable for the syllable types is underlined.

very helpful for spelling. Table 7.7 shows the six kinds of syllable, with example words analysed into their syllable types. This system is based on Steere *et al.* (1971).

In addition to phonics it is, of course, crucial to develop the written language skills of comprehension and understanding. This implies that reading for meaning and enjoyment needs to be continued. There are many books and sources of materials for the teacher and this is something that one needs to be aware of in teaching dyslexics. Particularly important is a good source of 'high/low' readers, i.e. readers who have a high interest level but low reading ages. This is particularly important for children in the 11, 12 and upward age range. Other useful books are those which present phonic exercises in an unusual way. Good examples are the adventure game formats, such as *Word Quest* or *Book of Letters* (Thomson 1985, 1989a).

7.6 Essay writing

One of the major difficulties which a dyslexic has to deal with is having many ideas in the mind, but being unable to express these appropriately on paper. A good deal of time is spent at East Court, particularly in the final year with children aged 12 and 13 years, in developing essay techniques. Of crucial importance is helping the dyslexic organize his or her thoughts and providing the appropriate structure. An early introduction is made to the notion of 'thought plans', one particularly useful approach being the notion of key words. Table 7.8 presents one way of approaching this and it is often discussed as a way to begin an essay topic with the children.

Table 7.8 Thought plans

Key words

1 Brainstorm – think of <u>anything</u> to do with the topic. Write down key word

2 List key words – write down key words in order of importance
  Reject irrelevant words

3 Organize words – mark off into paragraphs

4 Clothe words – put words into sentences and fill out

Another way of organizing ideas and essays is to develop them graphically by linking up boxes. This is particularly useful with children who are doing flow diagrams in computer work. Figure 7.2 shows examples of this, based on the essay title 'The hunter' and shows some ways that one can organize some ideas in two different ways using either flow diagrams or spreading root.

Because of the difficulties in organizing sequences and getting the order of ideas right we usually opt for a linear plan with children. It is quite useful to aim for a target number of pages that a child will write, and give a timed session in writing for 1 minute. See how many lines have been written in that time and then calculate how long it will take them to write one, two or three pages. Children are very surprised just how much time they do have, even including time for planning and thinking. By the time they leave us our children are writing three page essays within an hour, which is no mean achievement for a dyslexic. We insist that every child undertakes a plan. In a three page essay they divide their plan into three pages. Each page is then divided into paragraphs (say three or four paragraphs per page). Each paragraph must have a key word associated with it, and then that paragraph or key word linked to a number of ideas, either further key words or sentences. The essay must then be written by following that plan, including those key words or ideas which are linked to the plan. There is usually a line written down from start to finish. Figure 7.3 gives you an example of a model plan, the essay title being 'The wreck on the Goodwin sands'.

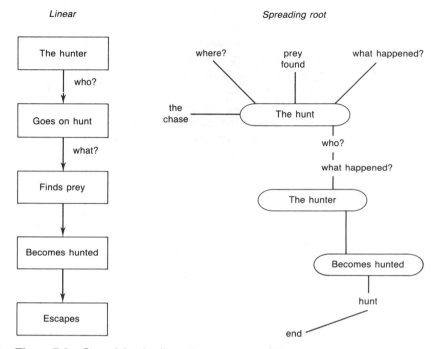

Figure 7.2   Organizing by flow diagram or spreading root for the essay title 'The hunter'

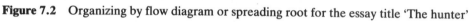

Page	Paragraph		Sentence plan
		Start	
1	1	Introduction	Set sail, the ship (description), coaster left Ramsgate, Nov. 15, stormy day, cargo
	2	Storm	Storm, dark clouds, rain, wind, waves, lightning strike, navigation out of order
	3	Wrecked	Low tide, pushed onto sands, ship broken up, self rescue, all safe
2	4	The wreck	Find old wreck on sands, tide coming in, climb mast, fear, flash back to good times
	5	Tide in	Cling to mast, see ship go by, signal, don't see you
	6	Tide out	Explore wreck, find skeleton, find gold
3	7	Ghost	Head sound, see 'ghost', really wind blowing skeleton with telescope
	8	Rescue	Sun comes out, dries wood, use glass from telescope, made fire, see helicopter
	9	Take off	Winched up, have share in gold, a tale to tell
		End	

Figure 7.3   A model plan for the essay title 'The wreck on the Goodwin sands'

Paragraph	(Page 1)
	Start
1	What is capital punishment and for what offences?
2	In what countries is capital punishment still used? Give brief examples
3	What is the situation in the UK? Brief history
	(Page 2)
4	Introduction to arguments: for/against

5	Deterrent:
	    examples to others
	    make you think twice
	    police/terrorists

6	Punishment: revenge by society
7	Stops offenders doing it again. Early release from prison
	(Page 3)

8	Do deterrents work?
	    evidence of history
	    why people murder

9	Mistaken conviction
10	Rehabilitation/insane people
11	Uncivilized: religion
12	Sum up arguments: own opinion

Figure 7.4   Essay plan for 'Capital punishment'

Another example may be in a discussion essay. Figure 7.4 shows an example of a 12 paragraph plan for an essay on 'Capital punishment'. Typically this would involve a discussion in class, and then the class would all think about the paragraphs and put them in order; after this they would produce their own plan.

Linking with computer programming planning is, as mentioned previously, particularly useful in organizing linear plans; this is also useful in undertaking activities, e.g. a linear plan can be created for putting records on a record player, or for making a cup of tea. Again, this helps with organizing thought processes and the sequence of events. Similarly, computer programs such as 'Story writer' (ESM), or others which enable stories to be built up in a sequential linear way are also useful if linked at the early stages of development of the essay plans.

Naturally, getting the order of events right, thinking of the plot and having sequential plans are not the whole story. One wants writing to be rich and create an interesting and vivid description. This of course implies teaching simile and

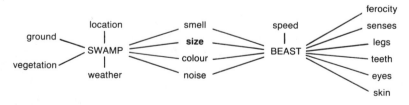

Figure 7.5   Descriptions of the 'swamp beast'

Use adjectives	Set scene	Description
Alternative words, e.g. hot, boiling, burning, frying, sizzling, scorching, dehydrating, scalding, sweaty	Enter desert	Heat Sand Wind Distance
	Encounter	Colour Vileness, Shape, horror Smell
	Storm	Clouds, flood Cold, rain, sand
	Salvation	Hot again Oasis, cool, green

Figure 7.6   Description, based on an essay 'In a desert'

metaphor, but also introducing how to describe things. Again, one might use thought plans here. Figure 7.5 gives an example of how one might use key elements to attach descriptions to. This is actually taken from an essay about a 'swamp beast' and some similar 'pegs' can be used to describe 'swamp' and 'beast' as illustrated in the figure.

It is not just enough to give vivid descriptions; one needs to discuss how one can do this. Figure 7.6 shows another example that is based on an essay 'In a desert'. Here one needs to introduce alternative adjectives as well as setting the scenes: entering the desert, encountering the lizard (this was part of the essay story) and possibly a desert storm.

It is particularly useful to have tutorials with older children to discuss their essays. This means going through it with them, discussing punctuation, giving them follow-up exercises in punctuation and essay work, and, in addition, correcting spellings and, according to their errors, short comments on spelling rules. One could give them a simultaneous oral spelling task to learn irregular words. This feedback needs to be given as soon as possible so that the child does not forget the content of his or her essay. Also helpful is linking it to word processor work for corrections and fair copy (see later).

7.7   The older dyslexic

7.71   General points

Although the main focus of this book has been on children, we should bear in mind that the notion 'developmental' can refer from before birth right through to death. Indeed developmental psychology looks not only at the child but also at the problems of old age, as this is all part of human development. We have made one or two comments about the older dyslexic, particularly in terms of the increasing gap between reading, spelling and chronological age, and given a case history. As far as remediation is concerned the older dyslexic will require the same kind of teaching programme. The difficulty is devising a programme at an appropriate conceptual, emotional and social level for the older individual. In many cases the level of reading may enable the person to read only very simple and childish books. This is clearly inappropriate for the older person, particularly the teenager who may feel that it is beneath his dignity. It is important therefore to obtain story materials which are at the relevant interest level, and indeed where spelling patterns and reading skills are at a controlled level. Unfortunately these are very rare because many of the books with controlled reading levels use simple conceptual or linguistic structures. They are aimed mainly at those who are very slow learners, but not dyslexic. What is needed is a series of books with appropriate content, concept and interest, as well as controlled reading and spelling age (see for example a review by Lulham 1981).

A number of adult literacy schemes do in fact recognize dyslexia as one sub-component of the learning problems besetting adults, and may have specialist teachers specifically trained for that purpose. Other areas unfortunately do not differentiate between types of reading difficulty. Each individual is given a volunteer tutor and the dyslexic adult may make very little progress in the early stages. Many adults who are picked up by adult literacy schemes are those who have perhaps had little opportunity to learn to read and with a few signposts and someone reading with them, they learn very quickly. The dyslexic adult will need just as much systematic overteaching and specialized provision as has been described already in this chapter.

Other important elements for the older dyslexic concern social and occupational needs. In many cases the adult dyslexic has not achieved a qualification appropriate to his own intellectual or skill potential. This may be because firms require English GCSEs, or that he needs to take an entrance exam, or that he cannot undertake a study programme at whatever level in order to achieve the qualifications they require for a particular job. This is, of course, a very important and overwhelming tragedy in itself, but is often exacerbated by the individual's experience while at work. In many cases he will hide his disabilities in reading, writing and spelling in order to prevent being mocked by his peers, and indeed there are many stories of individuals who have been exposed to just that kind of misunderstanding. Lack of written language skills may bar promotion, and will have obvious effects on the person's ability to perform aspects of the job, whether this be in filling in forms, writing reports, or performing similar tasks. There are many other areas in which a dyslexic handicap can affect a person's job; for example, needing to use a calculator, or to have a set of 'tables' for arithmetic. An interesting example is given by Gerhardt (cited by Newton 1974). Gerhardt, as a psychologist, was invited to investigate the apparently large number of accidents or incidents that were associated with particular pilots in the Air Force. He found that many of the individuals who were having a higher number of incidents were poor readers and spellers, and in addition they often confused left and right directions. This had disastrous consequences, as one might imagine, when having to make decisions very quickly, i.e. whether to perform a left or right action following an instrument reading. Similarly, Helen Arkell (1974) comments that she even now confuses and forgets telephone numbers, and occasionally will find herself on the wrong bus having misread the numbers.

However it is beyond the scope of this book to outline in any detail the continuing difficulties facing the dyslexic adult, or indeed to describe detailed teaching programmes adapted for the adult (see for example Gauntlett 1980). But some comments in respect to examinations are relevant here.

7.72   Examinations

As well as the basic difficulties facing the dyslexic individual in written language, one of the most daunting prospects is examinations. Examinations are important in their own right but also the dyslexic individual finds certain qualifications difficult to obtain, such as GCSE for vocational training courses, or other forms of higher education. Examinations in particular demand a high level of written language skills. In reading before the examination, the individual will find that lack of reading fluency and accuracy will make it difficult for him to obtain information from set text books. This means that it will take longer for him to acquire knowledge, and in many cases to read at a level appropriate for the forthcoming examination. Even if the individual has overcome the basic reading accuracy difficulties, fluency and comprehension may lag behind somewhat, and meaning may get lost due to difficulty in the actual 'techniques' of reading. This is particularly frustrating where 'skimming' is needed for the great amount of literature to be surveyed in higher education. In many cases, the dyslexic individual reports that he has to read material two or three times—once for reading accuracy, a second time to obtain some kind of comprehension, and a third time to try to remember the material. Reading will also obviously affect examination performance. The individual will be handicapped when it comes to reading questions, particularly those that require a considerable amount of interpretation, such as English Language or Literature. Spelling will also present a major difficulty as very poor spelling will give a false impression of retarded scholarship—the reader focuses on the spelling errors and does not observe the actual content in respect to understanding, or knowledge of subject matter. This is important in terms of general written language but particularly in more technical subjects. Not only do spelling errors make a very poor impression on the examiner, but will also slow down the rate of work output due to the constant checking required by the examinee.

As well as spelling and reading, other more subtle written language difficulties present themselves. These include inappropriate punctuation, and poor grammatical structure, which combine to give the impression of a less able student. Finally, the obvious lack of fluency in writing will handicap the individual considerably. This inability to organize one's thoughts in written language is one of the greatest problems for the older dyslexic. It results in a tremendous gap between oral comprehension and its written form, that will apply to writing essays, reports and projects, as well as in the examination itself.

In higher education one sometimes gets a piece of writing more typical of an 8-year-old from a very able Engineering or Physics student. This incompatibility between thinking power and effective problem-solving, on the one hand, and immature spelling and writing, on the other, is a source of great frustration to the able student. Even worse, it can result in a potentially very able student being refused entry to a higher education course. An interesting observation is the success intelligent dyslexics have in subjects such as geology, biology, engineering/technical drawing, pharmacy, art, photography or geography, if support and understanding are given by the institution to reading and writing difficulties. Such topics would appear to reflect the 'spatial' nature of the skills involved (as opposed to sequential, symbolic systems like written language). Often familial skills reflect these occupations, e.g. engineering, surgery, draughtsmanship, design, athletics, and architecture.

In preparing for examination it is essential to select examination topics with great care. This applies to GCSE, 'A' level and Institute examinations, where time must be spent on considering a collection of five or six of the best probabilities. This will entail discussion with the headteacher and subject teachers, as the combination of subjects chosen might not be the traditional or usual one for a particular school. It has been found, for example, that in some comprehensive schools where children begin to specialize in the third year, they are placed in 'courses' from which subsequent change is difficult. Parents of dyslexics should be particularly aware of this probability so that early discussion can be held with the school. It is hoped of course that wherever possible the difficulties in English Language (which present a very special problem for the dyslexic) have been recognized earlier in the school career and some intensive remedial teaching provided. This recognition and special help, together with a report from a qualified authority, will help here. Although one would advise individuals to avoid subjects which require a tremendous amout of written language and are very 'literacy' based, this is sometimes unavoidable due to the tremendous interest an individual has in a particular subject. English Language, however, is often a requirement for acceptance on training courses, or further education. This presents an invidious difficulty to many dyslexics. Many examation boards will provide allowance for some exams (see below) but are reluctant to make allowance for English Language, their argument being that spelling, writing, syntax and so on are all part of the English Language component. It is sometimes possible to obtain a waiver for English Language in some Higher Education courses, if one can provide evidence for dyslexic difficulties, but in many cases the individuals are resigned to having to take English Language GCSE a number of times.

After selecting the topics with the above criteria in mind, the examinee will need to develop strategies for the actual undertaking of the examination. In the initial stages (preferably at least a year before the actual event), it is important that cooperation is maintained between school, parent and possible relevant authorities. The first step is to check the particular Examination Board's attitude to written language difficulties. This establishes what kind of allowance it is prepared to make, and in what subject areas. Ideally this checking should be done through the school, which may be able to advise on alternative Boards. In some school situations, however, where there appears to be a lack of sympathy for this specific difficulty, it may be up to the parent to instigate enquiries as to the possible attitudes of Examination Boards. A survey of the Examination Boards' attitudes to the dyslexic is available from the Dyslexia Institute and from the School Psychological Service of ILEA. However, in many cases it is not possible to know in detail what allowances exams boards will make and what attitudes they have. This is because they are autonomous bodies.

The next stage is to obtain reports from a local authority or agency specializing in dyslexic problems. This report can be submited to the Examination Board prior to the examination answer scripts. The report should be as recent as possible, and should normally be sent by the school or the college or authority where the individual is studying. In addition to a report from an independent specialist, a report from the school is also helpful. This should indicate that the individual has a good ability in the subject area, has produced good projects in oral work and in the class, and in the opinion of the teacher, is a candidate who would normally pass and do well in the examinations, were it not for his written language difficulties.

There are certain important aspects to the report which are worth considering. It is not enough simply to obtain a report saying that an individual is dyslexic. This may not be accepted by the Examination Board—one reason being that some Examination Boards do not fully understand the implications of 'being dyslexic'. Further information is required if they are to make a fairer assessment of the allowance that is to be made for that individual. Exam Boards have standards to maintain and are particularly concerned that an 'excuse' for poor ability in the subject is not used, or that the individual just does not happen to be particularly good at essay-writing as opposed to having a specific learning problem. Typically, they require a report from a psychologist with some kind of reliable measure of intelligence. This is particularly important, as it will indicate that the individual's problems are not due to low ability.

As well as an objective measure of general intelligence, the report should include some measure of current reading, writing and spelling performance. This is important also for the kind of recommendations that should be made to the Exam Board. For example, if the individual is hardly able to write or spell at all, and has very severe reading difficulties, one might want to recommend an amanuensis. However, if the problem is less severe, involving difficulty in expressing ideas fluently in written form, one might want to recommend simply that allowance be made for spelling, punctuation, graphic style, and marking for content or knowledge of the subject matter.

The following are comments for the examination itself:

1 Specific preparation for examinations can take place at least a year before the actual event. This preparation could take the form of practice in short, weekly sessions, in writing answers relevant to the subject being studied. One needs therefore to obtain copies of previous examination papers. One question per week can be chosen, and a 'model' answer prepared. A teacher (or parent/friend) can go through the answer, checking obvious things (punctuation, capitals, spelling, sentence structure, etc.), discussing the answer and fostering care of fluency in

expressing ideas. This provides an opportunity to find the relevant content of the subject in question. Another exercise is timing the answer, as during the examination it is important to allow only a limited time for each question, and it is essential to answer the correct number of questions.

2   Develop appropriate study techniques (see Wilsher 1979).

3   The following strategies for answering questions might be addressed to the student:

(a) Read the question 3 times!

(i)   To check the actual words and ensure correct reading.

(ii)   To read it for understanding: 'what does it say'.

(iii) To read it finally for what question/problem it is posing: 'what does it ask'.

(b) After being quite sure of what it asks, jot down quickly on spare paper all the words, names, ideas (and dates) associated or linked with the question. Anything at all that can be remembered connected with the topic can be jotted down. Once one or two words are down on rough paper, these in turn will suggest more associated thinking, until between 10 and 30 words are on the rough paper.

(c) Next, 'order' these words into some hierarchy of importance, writing them as a list, with the most important idea or name, etc., first. Develop the ability to make a meaningful 'sequence' of ideas, names, examples, etc., perhaps in their importance to the subject or the steps and stages of the problem. But first, just a list of key-words.

(d) Begin the answer by rephrasing the question in some way, as an introductory sentence. Writing has now commenced on the answer paper! Take key-word 'one' and 'clothe' it in a simple sentence or two. Try and write a 'link' sentence to key-word two, and so on. It is useful to prepare a few typical 'link' sentences to use in answers.

(e) When the words have been exhausted, write a 'summing up' sentence or two, a conclusion or a short discussion. This will require reading through what has been already written.

(f) Read through the completed answer, correcting any errors, omissions, etc., that are noticed.

(g) Do not attempt to write too lengthy discursive essays. Use diagrams, flow-charts, graphs or block designs whenever possible. Concentrate on: making a plan, and writing short, clear sentences which relate directly to the question. Then read the question again; and read the answer so far; finally write a concluding, summing-up sentence.

4   These strategies can be practised on questions some time well before the examination. These practice answers can form very good revision material if they are kept. Begin by writing short answers. Time the answer and, spending 10 minutes or so initially, gradually make your answers longer. Aim to bring the plan and writing within 35 minutes. It is essential to read the whole paper through first and choose the easiest question for the first answer. Be sure to answer the correct number of questions. This means taking time for at least some writing on the questions that appear more difficult, or less interesting, but which must be answered to complete the requirement.

5   When the examination day arrives, the candidate should be more confident after a year or so experience of this kind. He will have accustomed himself to his 'examination strategy' and will know that he will be able to sit down and tackle the questions immediately.

7.8   Computer-assisted learning and word processing

There has been a great deal of interest and development in the area of micro-computers and education in recent years. Government interest and sponsorship for computing in schools is rapidly expanding. In many cases, however, the software is not so well developed. In particular, there is a need for the systematic development of suitable programs for remedial work, including dyslexics. There are signs of this, for example, a recent competition produced a number of entries for programs concerned with dyslexia, some written by dyslexic children themselves (Osman 1982). As this field is so new one can make only general comments based on anecdotal evidence (e.g. Horan 1981) and our experience at East Court. Computer-assisted learning and the use of micro-processors with children can not be accepted uncritically as a new curriculum development. In order to develop appropriate applications, particularly with learning disabled groups, an examination of advantages and disadvantages over more conventional procedures is necessary. Although based on teaching experience rather than research, the following features seem relevant:

Advantages

Provides new motivation in a 'failed' task.

Provides essential overlearning

Response to the child is immediate providing reinforcement.

The child dictates the pace of learning.

The computer is non-judgemental and predictable.

Use of keyboard can help graphic difficulties.

Learning to program may aid sequential thinking.

Written language structure may be stored and accessed easily.

Disadvantages

The auditory component of written language is difficult to program properly.

Multi-sensory teaching is not available at present.

The computer has limited reaction and program modification to child's error.

Reading teletext and instructions can be difficult for dyslexics.

'Therapeutic' teaching involving human contact is missing.

These advantages are rather general and do not, as yet, include new teaching procedures suited to the medium. The disadvantages are due to current programming and hardware limitations. Some recommendations for future research and development including computerizing existing structured programs, and the development of multi-sensory activities, especially the auditory component of written language. There is considerable scope for the development of more sophisticated 'reactive' or teaching programs, as well as for programs in assessment and diagnosis. In using computers basic questions include which system to use in terms of educational software available, its compatability with other computers and development potential. This requires advice from specialist teachers.

There are basically two ways in which one can use computers. The first uses computers as a separate entity: children go to a computer department for computer studies. The problems here are that subjects tend to be 'blocked' and therefore there is a lack of integration between this and other areas of the curriculum. It also gives computers an air of 'mystique' which means that only certain children or staff can use them. An advantage is that it may be easier to set up a unit like this and involves less staff training and costs. It also may mean less time and travel in moving computers about. The second use is where computers are integrated and are equally important and dovetail other subjects. The advantage is that the computers become relevant for day-to-day use and are just another 'tool' or educational resource. There is also immediate access and use when required. The difficulties can be that one needs a major staff/child training in the basics of computer use. It can be expensive and one needs to re-think one's teaching to use a computer and work round it. We tend to favour both approaches at the school. We are lucky enough to have a computer room with seven computer systems; but we also have our English or written language classrooms each equipped with a printer, computer monitor and word processing facilities. In addition our maths and science rooms have computers and printers. We therefore have 14 computers for less than 60 children. It is an important part of our curriculum (see later).

7.81   Use of computers in written language: a case example

This section describes the uses of computers in written language; by way of example, the use of computers at East Court, a specialist school for dyslexics, is described.

Resources

Hardware   East Court has 15 BBC computers and monitors, with 5 printers. All of these are equipped with disk drive which enables fast loading and increased storage of data. Seven of the computers are situated in the computer room, with a printer. Each of the four English rooms has a computer and printer. The science room and the two maths rooms also have computers. Our office has a computer with extended memory and a daisy wheel printer and other peripherals.

Software   In addition each computer is fitted with a word processing chip (View) and a Logo chip. We have many English/phonic programs, and also a number of adventure games which are used for English. Other programs are used for maths, geography, science. As well we have disks full of 'arcade' games.

Curriculum

All children at East Court have at least one lesson each week of computer studies. The older children have two lessons each week and the computer room can be booked up for other subjects. For example the English classes typically use the computer room once a week for adventure games, word processing or other relevant programs. In addition work is undertaken in the English and maths classrooms on the computer, when appropriate. A detailed curriculum follows.

Computer studies   The term 'computing' covers a wide range of areas and disciplines. At East Court we do not concentrate on any one specific area, but instead introduce the pupils to a variety of tasks during their time with us. The children are introduced to the idea of computing systems; how to load and access programs and simple computer applications. Simulation and adventure programs demonstrate computer usage, and the older children learn to program and develop their own procedures.

All children are taught word processing applications (see detailed curriculum under English). Logo, a computer language particularly useful for our age group of children, is also used, particularly 'Turtle Graphics'.

We use a wide variety of software both in 'computer time' and within the 'normal' classroom situation. We have approximately 300 maths programs (not all of which are considered 'work' by our pupils), approximately 150 English programs and about 200 miscellaneous subjects.

English   The computers in English are used mainly in three ways: word processing, adventure games, and spelling/reading reinforcement activities.

Written language activities   A number of programs are used for the overlearning essential with dyslexic pupils. These range from practice drill programs, including ones that we have devised ourselves and include programs which teach particular spelling rules. Typically children may be taught particular spelling patterns in class and then, to reinforce an exercise, in a worksheet and also on a computer.

In addition, a computer can be used in planning essays, e.g. using the Storywriter program, and in aiding reading. There are a number of programs which produce the so-called 'cloze' procedures. A popular program we use is 'Copywrite' (ESM), which enables us to make text on screen; the child has to recreate this text, using guesses from context. Each English classroom has a number of disks containing these English programs.

Adventure games   A number of adventure games are used. Typically for each English year adventure games are used, such as 'Flowers of Crystal', 'Dragon World', 'Grannies Garden'. These provide useful reading practice, aid structured and sequential thinking and provide a useful spur for creative writing. In addition, to solve the adventure games the child must make notes and enter in responses that are correctly spelt!

Word processing   Word processing is an important component of the curriculum at East Court. Our children are taught typing to match the keyboard skills that are required for word processing, and the following is a detailed curriculum.

Children are taught basic *skills* in using word processing, supplemented by *activites* to develop these skills. Word processing is linked to both the English and computer studies curricula, although the word processing is seen increasingly to pervade all areas of the curriculum.

Objectives for children leaving East Court

1 To be familiar with the concept(s) of word processing systems.
2 To be familiar with keyboard layouts and have basic typing skills, such as paper loading, positioning, line spacing, and correct fingering.
3 To be able to load, save, print out and access both 'Folio' and 'View' as examples of word processing systems.
4 To use word processing for simple editing, planning and structuring of the written word.
5 To be aware of, and have used in some cases, application of word processing (e.g. developing of work sheets, writing letters, standardized addresses etc.).

Skills and activities   Skills are hierarchical. Activities are linked to other curriculum work (especially English but not exclusively).

Skills	*Activities*
1 Familiarity with computing system. Using disk and word processing system, saving, loading, and writing text on screen	Writing brief sentences on screen, or doing phonic exercises on screen
2 Write and simple editing, use of delete, addition, insertion	Changing spellings. Adding words/sentences to prepared texts. Preparing 'cloze' procedures and (later on) punctuation exercises on prepared texts
3 Writing and printing, using file-names. Storing text, printing hard copy, using printers (simple commands)	Printing out short stories/poems. Fair copy of 'Star' work. Keeping own disk/data
4 Searching through documents. Finding sections for editing	Finding target words/sentences in texts
5 Splitting/joining lines	Adding/deleting sentences to texts

Skills contd.	*Activities contd.*
6 Screen modes 'wrap around' screen and printout	Examining texts in different modes
7 Formating, justifying	'Tidying up' a text
8 Presentation, layout Highlighting, printer codes Type of print	Simple changing layout of texts, changing typefaces of texts
9 Shifting paragraphs, re-structuring text, use of markers	Moving key words about, re-ordering sentences/paragraphs, expanding, developing ideas of text
10 Systematic spelling errors	Change in text
11 Tabulation	Re-tabulate/organize text

Mathematics The maths department has disks containing tables, games, puzzles, problems, tests, at various levels of difficulty. Computerized records of each pupil's progress are also kept.

The programs cover such topics as number patterns, place value, problem solving, logic, coordinates, vectors, geometry, decimals, fractions, and percentages. The levels range from 'Derrick the spider, who helps with band of 10', to 'Governing Britain and devising a Budget', or equating fractions, decimals etc.

These programs reinforce a class topic in a visual, colourful and often a comical way. Thus the learning process becomes fun rather than a chore.

Whilst some children work on these self-correcting programs, a teacher is able to give another child individual attention.

Games Of course computers are always available for the children in their off-duty times for 'Space Invaders', other adventure games, personal word processing, personal letters and as a hobby for them to use. The children may book their free time to play computer games. There is always a waiting list!

7.82   Logo

Most computers used in schools have BASIC language as the medium for interaction and programming the computer. However another language, Logo, is seen to be a particularly useful programming language for children. Most program languages require quite a high level of literacy. Logo is useful in the sense that it is a much more direct programming language. The commands are put in directly to the computer which then performs some action. One should not confuse Logo as just being 'Turtle Graphics', i.e. creating pictures either on screen or with a 'Turtle' drawing on the floor. It also has its 'list processing' which can produce work on poetry and grammar with dyslexics. We find Logo useful with dyslexics as it provides a bridge between the concrete and the abstract, i.e. it tends to make programming much more 'real life' as opposed to symbolic. The latter can be difficult for dyslexics. There is an immediate response in the computer and it can aid logical and sequencing skills in the dyslexic. As far as mathematics is concerned, problems with angles, distance, and numbers can be helped as can left/right skills. The reader can look at some of the British Dyslexia Association booklets for further details (see below).

7.83   British Dyslexia Association computer subcommittee

The British Dyslexia Association has a computer subcommittee which has a lot of information concerning the use of computers with dyslexics. The writer was chairman of the committee at one time, and it has produced booklets entitled *General Guidelines, Use of Word Processing* and *Use of Logo*, as well as a regular software bulletin.

The software bulletin gives details of programs reviewed by members of the committee, or those using the programs with dyslexic subjects.

Finally, here are some 'do's' and 'don'ts' from Jean Hutchins, currently the Chairman of the Committee.

Do
- Choose programs to reinforce skills.
- Know the child and the program.
- Enough hints to assure success.
- Read aloud from screen and things entered (= multi-sensory).
- Keep record of program used – repeat or next stage?
- Pupils to compete against themselves rather than against others.
- Programs where you can enter words.

Don't
- Use incorrect spelling to correct.
- Anagrams or jumbled letters.
- Hangman programs.
- Wrong interest level.
- Boring programs.
- Lots of reading but little interaction.
- Visual approaches: meat, bear, head in one list.
- Non-corrective (do not show answers) programs.

7.9   Role of the parent in remediation

It is assumed in our educational system that the responsibility for teaching lies with the teacher rather than the parent. In the case of a child with a learning problem, that a specialist provide remediation. This may be a teacher, psychologist, speech therapist, or other person involved with learning-disabled children. This emphasis is unfortunate, in some ways, as the parents can be a tremendous source of aid to the child. There are a number of guides and descriptions for the role that the parent can have as teacher, and also in helping the child with specific learning problems (see, for example, *The Dyslexia Review Parent Supplement* 1982). It is not the intention here to review the series of activities which might be useful, but to make some fairly general statements.

Perhaps the most important role for the parent of a dyslexic child is in terms of emotional and social support. The child should know that his parents understand the nature of his learning problem. This will often require some kind of explanation to the child of his dyslexic difficulties—whether this is actually giving the child the label dyslexia to use, or a general explanation. The important message to get over is that it is recognized by all concerned that the child is not stupid and that he may have been working very hard to achieve his current level of reading, writing and spelling performance. It is also important to communicate to the child that one will continue to love him, despite the fact he may not be succeeding particularly well at school. It is sometimes the case that parental anxiety can often exacerbate the situation, making the child become more and more worried, and creating greater secondary emotional difficulties. This worry can also be counterproductive in the sense of making the child not want to succeed. This is because the child secretly 'knows' that he cannot succeed, and yet as it seems so important to his parents he is frightened to try because he might fail. A corollary is that the parents should make it quite clear to the child that although he may have a learning difficulty he *can* succeed. The success might require some considerable work, but his problem is understood and he is going to be helped in a special kind of way in order to overcome the difficulty. Ironically it is sometimes the parents who have had similar difficulties themselves, who have suffered greatly at school, that are often the most anxious and tend to put on the greatest pressure. This is understandable because they do not want the child to fail and undergo the same kind of misery, but this anxiety needs to be recognized by such parents and their own early problems shared with the child.

In relation to other members of the family, it is obviously very inappropriate and unhelpful to compare the dyslexic child unfavourably with a child who is succeeding. This is particularly the case if a child who is doing well at school is younger, and can read and spell better than the older child. This can give rise to all kinds of inter-sibling rivalries leading to quite serious aggression. It is important here to pinpoint some particular area where the dyslexic child excels. While obviously not comparing the non-dyslexic child too unfavourably, it is worth reminding the children that they are individuals and have their own particular skills.

It is important to build up the child's self-esteem at every level. This can be undertaken by unconditional positive regard for the child, particularly when he is feeling low or a 'failure'. Also one needs to reinforce learning, reading and writing skill development when this occurs. Parents need to change their criteria somewhat here, and will need to know where the child has reached in his own written language skills, so that if there is improvement in his development this is what should receive the praise and reward. One has to be careful here—this does not imply that every single thing the child does is praised. Children soon recognize that they are being 'patronized' in this kind of way; praise, reward and 'gold star' treatment follow from good work, but within the child's own particular framework.

Another problem for parents is to recognize the other learning problems associated with dyslexia. This implies confusions in times of the day, in where things have been left, in following instructions, and sometimes in clumsiness. This requires a great deal of patience but is just as important as understanding the written language learning difficulties.

Parents may also have a teaching role. This depends very much on the particular relationship the parents and children have; sometimes it is completely impossible for parents to help the children as there is such an anxious or fraught situation that either parents or children lose their temper very quickly! Occasionally some kind of work can be undertaken at home, bearing in mind that dyslexic children have to work exceptionally hard at school, and for them to have to do an extra two hours when they return from school is very unfair. The child needs time to relax, to do something else and to switch off completely from the very daunting task of written language learning. If the parent does want to help the child in some kind of way, it is recommended that careful liaison be maintained with the teacher(s).

One useful activity is a piece of free writing. This might take the form of a daily diary, in which in the initial stages only two or three lines are actually written. Ideal is a small autograph book in which the child writes two or three lines of material, then the parent writes a corrected version on an additional piece of paper. This version can then be copied into the autograph book opposite the original and the child can read it through with the parent. This needs to follow the child's own interests, of course, but provides a daily experience in expressing ideas in written form, as well as in spelling. One (at most two) spelling errors can be isolated, and then a spelling pattern, or rule, can be written on a special card filing index which is the child's own property. This can then take the format described under the writing approach to reading (Section 6.6.4). It is also important (even for the somewhat older child, where one would normally expect this to be seen as 'babyish') to have a regular 5 or 10 minute session of reading every evening. This might involve either the child reading aloud to the parent, or perhaps the parent reading to the child with the text being followed. This would be from the child's own choice of literature. This not only provides useful additional interest and understanding that reading is in fact quite an enjoyable task, but it provides listening skills in respect of the prosody of spoken language, as in many cases the child's actual reading level may prevent him from obtaining access to a book of appropriate interest, motivational or intellectual level. It may also be useful for the parent to encourage the use of a typewriter. This may overcome any motor control difficulties, as well as being a useful skill for later life. Indeed the professional appearance of a typescript can be a powerful incentive to write.

There are a number of games and activities that can help. These include, for the child with pre-literacy skills, joining dot-to-dot pictures; an involvement of sequential and motor skills such as painting and tracing, snap, for development of visual discrimination, 'Simon says', 'Hokey-Kokey' (identification of left-right body image), and so on. Word games can also provide incidental learning as their purpose is not always apparent. These include Junior Scrabble, Lexicon, Hang-Man, Eye Spy, words within words, Crosswords and any word puzzles. Travel and party games can also aid memory functions. These might include the learning of limericks and rhymes, production of as many rhyming words as possible, rumour games, Kim's Game, or 'I went to the shop and bought a' (an item is added by each player). Indeed by careful choice of games and activities the parent can easily provide appropriate 'training' or reinforcement for the basic perceptual/memory skills which seem to underlie dyslexia.

Appendix

Regression equations for IQ, CA and Attainment
Some regression equations for predicting expected reading age based on chronological age and intelligence taken from various sources. The items to be entered into the equation vary, although they may be given the generic term 'IQ,' etc. This may lead to confusion and erroneous reading ages. Consequently the items have been explained in some detail.

1 *Yule et al., 1974* Equations used for Isle of Wight, and Inner
London samples for 10-year-olds.

Reading Accuracy $= 75.33 + (1.11 \times IQ)$
Reading Comprehension $= 77.06 + (1.16 \times IQ)$
This gives the expected Neale test scores *in months*. The IQ used is the short form of the WISC (Similarities, Vocabulary, Block Design, Object Assembly).
NB *Sum of the 4 scaled scores should be entered in the equation*.

2 *Yule, 1967* Ages 9 − 11 yrs, based on Isle of Wight.

Rate $= 28.45 + (0.96 \times IQ) + (0.41 \times CA)$
Accuracy $= 3.87 + (0.93 \times IQ) + (0.68 \times CA)$
Comprehension $= 23.44 + (1.15 \times IQ) + (0.79 \times CA)$
This gives the expected Neale scores *in months*. The CA (Chronological age) above should be entered *in months*, and IQ in short form of WISC, but: NB *the sum of the 4 scaled scores* should be entered in the equations.

3 *Fransella and Gerver, 1965* Based on a London clinic population
6 − 9yrs − $8.44 + (0.98 \times CA) + (0.085 \times IQ)$
10 − 12yrs − $7.68 + (0.64 \times CA) + (0.117 \times IQ)$
13 − 15yrs − $10.86 + (0.72 \times CA) + (0.114 \times IQ)$
The above give the expected Schonell graded word reading scores, in years.
The chronological age entered should be in *years and months*, and the 'IQ' refers to the WISC verbal scale *IQ figure*.

4 *Savage and O'Connor, 1966* Based on Northumberland population,
age range 6.9 − 7.9yrs

Expected RQ (reading quotient) $= 30.84 + (0.653 \times IQ)$
This gives a Watt's sentence reading *quotient*, and IQ to be entered is the *IQ figure* for the Otis Mental Ability test.

5 *Yule, Landsdown and Urbanavicz, 1982*Based on a 'primary school population'. For age ranges 6 − 12yrs

Neale Accuracy	=	$-38.86 + (0.63 \times FSIQ) + (0.78 \times Age)$
Neale Comprehension	=	$-50.88 + (0.69 \times FSIQ) + (0.83 \times Age)$
Vernon Spelling	=	$25.66 + (0.59 \times FSIQ) + (0.11 \times Age)$
Vernon Mathematics	=	$22.54 + (0.69 \times FSIQ) + (0.04 \times Age)$

This gives scores in months. FSIQ is Full Scale WISC *IQ figure*. Age is chronological age *in months*.

References

AARON, P.G. 1978: Dyslexia, an imbalance in cerebral information processing strategies. *Perceptual and Motor Skills* 47, 699–706.

ABIGAIL, E.R. and JOHNSON, E.G. 1976: Ear and hand dominance and their relationship with reading retardation. *Perceptual and Motor Skills* 43, 1031–6.

ADLER-GRINBERG, D. and STARK, L. 1978: Eye movements, scan paths and dyslexia. *American Journal of Optometry and Physiological Optics*, 55, 557–70.

ALTUS, G.T. 1956: A WISC profile for retarded readers. *Journal of Consulting Psychology* 20, 155–6.

ALWITT, L.T. 1963: Decay of immediate memory for visually presented digits among non-readers and readers. *Journal of Educational Psychology* 54, 3, 144–8.

AMAN, M.G. 1978: Drugs, Learning and the Psychotherapies. In Werry, J. (ed.), *Paediatric Psychopharmacology: The Use of Behaviour Modifying Drugs in Children*. New York: Brummer.

—— 1980: Psychotropic drugs and learning problems—a selective review. *Journal of Learning Disabilities* 13, 36–46.

AMAN, M.G. and WERRY, J.S. 1982: Methylphamidate and diazepam in some reading retardation. *Journal of Academic Child Psychiatry* 21, 31–7.

ANNETT, M. 1967: The binomial distribution of right, mixed and left handedness. *Quarterly Journal of Experimental Psychology* 19, 327–33.

ANOPOLLE, L. 1967: Visual training and reading performance. *Journal of Reading* 10, 372–83.

ARKELL, H. 1974: *Dyslexia: Introduction—A Dyslexic's Eye View*. London: Helen Arkell Dyslexia Centre.

AUBREY, C., EAVES, J., HICKS, C. and NEWTON, M.J. 1982: *The Aston Portfolio*. Wisbech: Learning Development Aids.

BACKMAN, J.E., MAMEN, M. and FERGUSON, H.B. 1984: Reading level design: conceptual and methodological issues in reading research. *Psychological Bulletin* 96, 560–8.

BADCOCK, D., and LOVEGROVE, W. 1981: The effects of contrast, stimulus duration, and spatial frequency on visual persistence in normal and specifically disabled readers. In Bouma,H. Kolers, P.A. and Wrolstad, M.(eds.), *Processing of Visible Language*.

BADDELEY, A. 1976: *The Psychology of Memory*. Milton Keynes: Open University.

—— 1979: Working memory and reading. In Bouma, H. Kolers, P.A. and Wrolstad, M. (eds.), *Processing of Visible Language*. Proceedings of Conference at Institute of Perception Research, IPO, Eindhoven.

BADDELEY, A. and HITCH, G. 1974: Working Memory. In Bouma, G.H. (ed.), *The Psychology of Learning and Motivation* 8, 47–90. New York: Academic Press.

BADDELEY, A., ELLIS, N., MILES, T. and LEWIS, M. 1982: Developmental and acquired dyslexia: a comparison. *Cognition* 11, 185–99.

BAKKER, D.J. 1967: Temporal order, meaningfulness and reading ability. *Perceptual and Motor Skills* 24, 1027–30.

—— 1970 a: Temporal order perception and reading retardation. In Bakker, D.J. and Satz, P. (eds.), *Specific Reading Disability: Advances in Theory and Method*. Rotterdam: Rotterdam University Press.

—— 1970 b: Ear asymmetry with monaural stimulation. Relation to lateral dominance and lateral awareness. *Neuropsychologia* 8, 103–17.

—— 1972: Temporal order in disturbed reading—developmental and neuropsychological aspects in normal and reading-retarded children. Rotterdam: Rotterdam University Press.

—— 1973: Hemispheric specialisation and stages in the learning to read process. *Bulletin of the Orton Society* 23, 15–27.

—— 1976: Perceptual asymmetries and reading proficiency. Amsterdam: *Paedologisch Institut Research Report* No. 2.

BAKKER, D.J. and SCHROOTS, H.J. 1981: Temporal order in normal and disturbed reading. In Pavlides, G. and Miles, T. (eds.), *Dyslexia Research and its Applications to Education*. Chichester: J. Wiley.

BAKKER, D.J., SMINK, T. and REITMA, P. 1973: Ear dominance and reading ability. *Cortex* 9, 301–12.

BAKKER, D.J., TENNISSEN, J. and BOSCH, J. 1976: Development of laterality-reading patterns. In Knights,R.M. and Bakker, D.J. (eds.), *The Neuropsychology of Learning Disorders: Theoretical Approaches*. Baltimore: University Park Press.

BAKWIN, H. 1973: Reading disability in twins. *Developmental Medicine and Child Neurology* 15, 184–7.

BALOW, B. RUBIN, R. and ROSEN, M.S. 1976: Prenatal events as precursors of reading disability. *Reading Research Quarterly* 11, 36–71.

BANNATYNE, A.D. 1971: *Language, Reading and Learning Disabilities*. Springfield, Ill.: Thomas.

BARLOW, I.H. 1963: Lateral dominance characteristics and reading achievement in the first grade. *Journal of Psychology* 55, 323–8.

BARNARD, A., COMBER, S. and THOMSON, M.E. 1983: *Pre-school Screening: Review and Case Study*. University of Aston: Occasional Papers, Educational Enquiry.

BARON, J. 1977: Mechanisms for pronouncing printed words: Use and acquisition. In La Berge, D. and Samuels, S.J. (eds.), *Basic Processes in Reading: Perception and Comprehension*. Hillsdale, N J: Lawrence Erlbaum Associates.

BARRETT, T.C. 1965: The relationship between measures of prereading visual discrimination and first-grade achievement: A review of the literature. *Reading Research Quarterly* 1, 51–78.

BARRON, R. W. 1980: Visual and Phonological Strategies in Reading and Spelling. In Frith, U. (ed.), *Cognitive Processes in Spelling*. London: Academic Press.

BARRY, C. 1981: Hemisphere asymmetry in lexical access and phonological encoding. *Neuropsychologia* 19, 3, 473–7.

BATEMAN, B.D. 1966: Learning disorders. *Journal of Educational Research* 5, 36.

BATTLE, J. 1981: *Culture Free S. E. I.* Windsor: NFER

BEAUMONT, J.G. 1982: *An Introduction to Neuropsychology*. London: Grant McIntyre.

BEAUMONT, J.G. and RUGG, M.D. 1978: Neuropsychology laterality of functions and dyslexia. *Dyslexia Review* 1–1, 18–22.

BEAUMONT, J.G., THOMSON, M.E. and RUGG, M. 1981: An intrahemispheric integration deficit in dyslexia. *Current Psychological Research* 1, 185–9.

BECK, F. 1968: Performance of retarded readers on parts of the WISC. In Robinson,H. and Smith, H.K.(eds.), *Clinical Studies in Reading, 111.* Chicago: University of Chicago Press.

BEERY, J. 1967: Matching of auditory and visual stimuli by average and retarded readers. *Child Development* 38, 827–33.

BELMONT, L. and BIRCH, H.G. 1965: Lateral dominance, lateral awareness and reading disability. *Child Development* 36, 59–71.

—— 1966: The intellectual profile of retarded readers. *Perceptual and Motor Skills* 22, 787–816.

BENDER, L.A., 1965: *Psychopathology of Children with Organic Brain Disorders.* Springfield, Ill.: Thomas.

—— 1957: Specific disability as a maturational lag. *Bulletin of the Orton Society* 7, 9–18.

BENSON, D.F. and GESCHWIND, N. 1969: The alexias. In Vinken, P.J. and Bruyn, G.W. (eds.), *Handbook of Clinical Neurology* vol. 4, 112–40. Amsterdam: North-Holland.

—— 1970: Developmental Gerstmann Syndrome. *Neurology* 20, 293–8.

BENTON, A.L. 1962: Dyslexia in relation to form perception and directional sense. In Money, J. (ed.), *Reading Disability: Progress and Research Needs in Dyslexia.* Baltimore: Johns Hopkins University Press.

—— 1975: Developmental dyslexia; Neurological aspects. In Friedlander, W.J. (ed.), *Advances in Neurology*, vol. 7. New York: Raven Press.

—— 1978 Some conclusions about dyslexia. In Benton, A. and Pearl, D. (eds.), *Dyslexia and Appraisal of Current Knowledge.* New York: Oxford University Press.

BENTON, A.L. and BIRD, J.W. 1963: The EEG and reading disability. *American Journal of Orthopsychiatry* 33, 529–31.

BEREITER, C. and ENGLEMAN, S. 1966: *Teaching Disadvantaged Children in the Preschool.* Englewood Cliffs, NJ: Prentice-Hall.

BERGER, M., YULE, W. and RUTTER, M. 1975: Attainment and adjustment in two geographical areas 11. The Prevalence of specific reading retardation. *British Journal of Educational Psychology* 126, 510–19.

BERKO, J. 1958: The child's learning of English morphology. *Word* 14, 150–77.

BERLIN, R. 1872: *Eine besondere Art der Wortblindheit* (Dyslexia). Wiesbaden.

BERLIN, C.I. and MCNEIL, M.R. 1976: Dichotic listening. In Lass, N.J.(ed.), *Contempory Issues in Experimental Phonetics.* New York: Academic Press.

BIRCH, H. 1962: Dyslexia and Maturation of visual function. In Money, J. (ed.), *Reading Disability: Progress and Research Needs in Dyslexia.* Baltimore: Johns Hopkins University Press.

BIRCH, H. and BELMONT, L. 1964: Auditory-visual integration in normal and retarded readers. *American Journal of Orthopsychiatry* 34, 852–61.

BIRCH, H. and LEFFORD, A. 1963: Intersensory development in children. *Monographs of the Society for Research in Child Development* 25, 5 (Whole No. 89).

BISHOP, D.V.M. and BUTTERWORTH, G.E. 1980: Verbal-performance discrepancies: relationship to birth risk and specific reading retardation. *Cortex* 16, 375–89.

BLANK, M. 1968: Cognitive processes in auditory discrimination in normal and retarded readers. *Child Development* 39, 1091–101.

—— 1978: Review of Vellutino's 'Towards Understanding'. In Benton, A. and Pearl, D. (eds.), *Dyslexia: An Appraisal of Current Knowledge.* New York: Oxford University Press.

BLANK, M. and BRIDGER, W.H. 1964: Cross-modal transfer in nursery school children. *Journal of Comparative and Physiological Psychology* 58, 227–82.

—— 1966: Deficiencies in verbal labelling in retarded readers. *American Journal of Orthopsychiatry* 36, 840–47.

BLANK, W., WEIDER, S. and BRIDGER, W. 1968: Verbal deficiencies in abstract thinking in early reading retardation. *American Journal of Orthopsychiatry* 38, 823–34.

BODER, E. 1970: Developmental dyslexia: A new diagnostic approach based on the identification of three subtypes. *Journal of School Health* 40, 289–90.

—— 1971 a: Developmental dyslexia: A diagnostic screening procedure based on three characteristic patterns of reading and spelling. In Bateman, B. (ed.), *Learning Disorders*. Seattle: Special Child Publications.

—— 1971 b: Developmental dyslexia: prevailing diagnostic concepts and a new diagnostic approach. In Myklebust, H. (ed.), *Progress in Learning Disabilities*, vol. II, 293–321. New York: Grune & Stratton.

—— 1973: Developmental Dyslexia: a diagnostic approach based on three atypical reading patterns. *Developmental Medicine and Child Neurology* 15, 663–87.

BOUMA, H. and LEGEIN, C. 1977: Foveal and parafoveal recognition of letters and words by dyslexics and by average readers. *Neurolopsychologia* 15, 69–80.

—— 1980: Dyslexia: A specific recoding deficit? An analysis of response latencies for letters and words in dyslectics and in average readers. *Neuropsychologia* 18, 285–98.

BRADLEY, L. 1980: *Assessing Reading Difficulties*. London: Heinemann Educational.

—— 1981: The organisation of motor patterns for spelling: an effective remedial strategy for backward readers. *Developmental Medicine and Child Neurology* 23, 83–91.

BRADLEY, L. and BRYANT, P.E. 1978: Difficulties in auditory organisation as a possible cause of reading backwardness. *Nature* 271, 746–7.

—— 1981: Visual memory and phonological skills in reading and spelling backwardness. *Psychological Research* 43, 2, 193–200.

BRANAT, J. and ROSEN, J.J. 1980: Auditory Phonemic perception in dyslexia: categorised identification and discrimination of stop consonants. *Brain and Language* 9, 2.

BRANCH, C. MILNER, B. and RASMUSSEN, J. 1964: Intracarotid sodium amytal for the lateralization of cerebral dominance. *Journal of Neurosurgery* 21, 399–405.

British Dyslexia Association 1981: *Teaching the Dyslexic*, London BDA Publication.

BRITTAIN, M.M. 1970: Inflectional performance and early reading achievement. *Reading Research Quarterly* 6, 1, 34–48.

BROWN, B., HAEGERSTROM–PORTNOY, G., ADAMS, A., YINGLING, C., GALIN, P., HERRON, J. and MARCUS, B. 1983: Predictive eye movements do not discriminate between dyslexic and control children. *Neuropsychologia* 21, 121–8.

BRUCE, D.J. 1964: Analysis of word sounds by young children. *British Journal of Educational Psychology* 34, 158–69.

BRYANT, P.E. 1968: Comments on the design of developmental studies of crossmodal matching and cross-modal transfer. *Cortex* 4, 127–8.

—— 1975: Cross modal developments and reading. In Duane, D. and Rawson, M. E. (eds.), *Reading, Perception and Language*. Baltimore: York.

BRYANT, P.E. and BRADLEY, L. 1980: Why children sometimes write words which they do not read. In Frith, U. (ed.), *Cognitive Processes in Spelling*. London: Academic Press.

BRYANT, P.E. 1988: Review of cognitive analysis of dyslexia by P. Seymour. *British Journal of Developmental Psychology* 6, 109–111. ·

BRYANT, P. and BRADLEY, L. 1985: *Children's Reading Problems*. Oxford: Blackwell.

BRYANT, P.E. and GOSWAMI, U. 1986: The strengths and weaknesses of the reading level design: A comment on Backman, Mamen and Ferguson. *Psychological Bulletin* 100, 101–3.

BRYDEN, M.P. 1970: Laterality effects in dichotic listening: Relations with handedness and reading disability in children. *Neuropsychologia* 8, 443–50.

—— 1972: Auditory- visual and sequential-spatial matching in relation to reading ability. *Child Development* 43, 824–32.

BUDOFF, M. and QUINLAN, D. 1964: Reading problems as related to efficiency of visual and oral learning in the primary grades. *Journal of Educational Psychology* 55, 247–52.

BUFFERY, A.W. 1976: Sex differences in the neuropsychological development of verbal and spatial skills. In Knights, R. M. and Bakker, D.J. (eds.), *The Neuropsychology of Learning Disorders*. Baltimore University of York Press.

BUFFERY, A.W. and GRAY, J.A. 1972: Sex differences in the development of spatial and linguistic skills. In Ounsted, C. and Taylor, D.C. (eds.), *Gender Differences: Their Ontogeny and Significance*. London: Churchill Livingstone.

Bullock Report. Department of Education and Science 1975: *A language for life*. London: HMSO

BURNS, E. and SCHAAF, S. 1974: The validity of the ITPA Composite Psycholinguistic Age and Psycholinguistic quotient scores. *Psychology in Schools* 11, 3, 308–9.

BYRNE, B. 1981: Reading disability, linguistic access and short term memory: Comments prompted by Jorm's review of developmental dyslexia. *Australian Journal of Psychology* 33, 1, 83–95.

CALFEE, R.C. 1977: Assessment of independent reading skills: Basic research and practical applications. In Reber, A.S. and Scarborough, D.L. (eds.), *Towards a Psychology of Reading*. Hillside, NJ: Lawrence Erlbaum Associates.

CAPALAN, B.M. 1977: Cerebral lateralisation, cognitive strategy and reading disability. Doctoral Dissertation, 381916B, University of New York.

CARROLL, H.C. 1972: The remedial teaching of reading: An evaluation. *Remedial Education* 7, 1, 10–15.

CARROLL, J. 1972: Review of ITPA. In Buros, O. (ed.), *Seventh Mental Measurements Year Book*, New Jersey: Gryphon.

CASHDAN, A. and PUMFREY, P.D. 1969: Some effects of remedial teaching of reading. *Educational Research* 11, 138.

CASHDAN, A., PUMFREY, P.D. and LUNZER, E.A. 1971: Children receiving remedial treatment in reading. *Educational Research* 13, 1, 98, 105.

CATALDO, S. and ELLIS, N. 1988: Interactions in the development of spelling, reading and phonological skills. *Journal of Research in Reading,* Autumn

CELDRIC, 1970: *One Million Children*. Toronto Commission on Emotional and Learning disorders in children.

CERMAK, L.S., GILDBERG, J., CERMAK, S.C. and DRAKE, C. 1980: The short-term memory ability of children with learning disabilities. *Journal of Learning Disabilities* 13, 1, 25–9.

CHANSKY, N.M. 1963: Age, IQ and improvement of reading. *Journal of Educational Research* 56, 439.

CHASTY, H.T. 1979: Functional asymmetry of the brain in normal children and dyslexics. *Dyslexia Review* 2–1, 9–12.

CHASTY, H.T. 1981: Dyslexia: spreading word effectively. *Times Educational Supplement,* 13th November.

CHAZAN, M. 1967: The effects of remedial teaching in reading: a review of research. *Remedial Education* 2, 1, 4–12.

CHILDS, B., FINUCCI, J.M. and PRESTON, M.S. 1978: A medical genetics approach to the study of reading disability. In Benton, A. and Pearl, D. (eds.), *Dyslexia: An Appraisal of Current Knowledge*. New York: Oxford University Press.

CHOMSKY, C. 1972: Stages in language development and reading exposure. *Harvard Educational Review* 42, 1–33.

CIOFFI, S. and KANDEL, G.C. 1979: Laterality of stereognostic accuracy of children for words, shapes and bigrams: a sex difference for bigrams. *Science* 204, 1432–3.

CIUFFREDA, K.J., BAHILL, A.T., KENYON, R.V. and STARK, L. 1976: Eye movements during reading: case reports. *American Journal of Optometry and Physiological Optics* 53, 384–95.

CLARK, M.M. 1970: *Reading Difficulties in School*. Harmondsworth: Penguin.

—— 1976: *Young Fluent Readers*. London: Heinemann Educational Books.

CLAY, M.M. 1972 and 1979: *The Early Detection of Reading Difficulties: A diagnostic survey*. Auckland, NZ: Heinemann Educational Books.

CLAY, M. and IMLACH, R.H. 1971: Juncture, pitch and stress as reading behaviour variables. *Journal of Verbal Learning and Verbal Behaviour* 10, 133–9.

CLEMENTS, S.D. and PETERS, J.E. 1962: Minimal brain dysfunction in the school age child. *Archives of General Psychiatry* 6, 185.

CLIFTON-EVEREST, I.M. 1976: Dyslexia: Is there a disorder of visual perception? *Neuropsychologia* 14, 491–94.

COHEN, J. 1959: Factoral structure of the WISC at age 7–10, 10–16 and 13–16. *Journal of Consulting Psychology* 23, 285–99.

COHEN, J. 1976: Learning disabilities and conditioned brain activity. In Karrer, R. (ed.), *Developmental Psychophysiology*, Springfield, Ill.: Thomas.

—— 1977: Cerebral evoked response asymmetry in dyslexic children. *Physiology* 14, 89.

—— 1980: Cerebral evoked responses in dyslexic children. *Progress in Brain Research* 54, 503–6.

COHEN, J. and WALTER, W.G. 1966: The interaction of responses in the brain to semantic stimuli. *Psychophysiology* 2, 187–96.

COHEN, R. 1961: Delayed acquisition of reading writing abilities in children. *Archives of Neurology* 4, 153–64.

COHEN, R.L. and NETLEY, C. 1978: Cognitive deficits, learning disabilities and WISC-performance consistency. *Developmental Psychiatry* 14, 6.

—— 1981: Short term memory deficits in reading disabled children, in the absence of opportunity for rehearsal strategies. *Intelligence* 5, 69–76.

COLEMAN, R.I. and DEUTSCH, C.P. 1964: Lateral dominance and right-left discrimination: a comparison of normal and retarded readers. *Perceptual and Motor Skills* 19, 43–50

COLEMAN, J.C. and RASOF, B. 1963: Intellectual factors in learning disorders. *Perceptual and Motor Skills* 16, 139–52.

COLLINS, J.E. 1961: *The Effects of Remedial Education*. University of Birmingham Educational Monograph no. 4.

COLTHEART, M. 1978: Lexical access in simple reading tasks. In Underwood, G. (ed.), *Strategies of Information Processing*. London: Academic Press.

—— 1980: Reading, phonological recording and deep dyslexia. In Coltheart, M., Patterson, K. and Marshall, J. (eds.), *Deep Dyslexia*. London: Routledge & Kegan Paul.

—— 1982: *The psychologistic analysis of acquired dyslexia*. Paper presented to Royal Academy seminar.

COLTHEART, M., PATTERSON, K. and MARSHALL, J. (eds.) 1980: *Deep Dyslexia*. London: Routledge & Kegan Paul.

CONNORS, C.K. 1970: Cortical visual evoked response in children with learning disorders. *Psychophysiology* 7, 418–28.

CONNORS, C.K. 1978: Critical Review of Hughes 1978. In Benton, A. and Pearl, D. (eds.), *Dyslexia; An Appraisal of Current Knowledge*. New York: Oxford University Press.

CONRAD, R. 1964: Acoustic confusions in immediate memory. *British Journal of Psychology* 5, 75–84.

—— 1965: Order error in immediate recall of sequences. *Journal of Verbal Learning and Verbal Behaviour* 4, 161–9.

COOPERSMITH, S. 1966: Studies in self esteem. *Scientific American*, February, 128–36.

CORAH, N.L. and POWELL, B.J. 1963: A factor analytic study of the Frostig test of visual perception. *Perceptual and Motor Skills* 16, 59–63.

CORAH, N., PANISTER, A., STERN, J. and THURSTON, D. 1965: Effects of perinatal anoxia after 7 years. *Psychological Monographs* 79, (3) 596–9.

CORBOLLIS, M.C. and BEALE, I.L. 1976: *The Psychology of Left and Right*. Hillsdale, NJ: Lawrence Erlbaum Associates.

CORCELLE, L., ROZIER, J., DEDIEU, E., VINCENT, J.D. and FAURE, L. 1968: Variations of cortical evoked potentials according to the modality of sensory stimulation in dyslexic children. *Review of Laryngoscopy* (Bordeaux) 89, 458–68.

CORKIN, S. 1974: Serial-ordering deficits in inferior readers. *Neuropsychologia* 12, 347–54.

CORWIN, B.J. 1967: The relationship between reading achievement and performance on individual ability tests. *Journal School Psychology* 5, 156–7.

COTTERELL, G. 1970: Teaching the dyslexic. In Franklin, A. and Naidoo, S. (eds.), *the Assessment and Teaching of the Dyslexic Child*. London: Invalid Children's Aid Association.

—— 1978: *Checklist of Basic Sounds and Phonic Reference Cards*. Wisbech: Learning Development Aids.

—— 1981: Helping the bad speller: suggestions for helping the dyslexic child. *Dyslexia Review, Parent Handbook*.

COX, F.N. 1970: *Psychological Assessment for Remedial Teaching*. Victoria: SLD Association of Victoria.

CRANE, A.R. 1959: An historical critical account of the accomplishment quotient idea. *British Journal of Educational Psychology* 29, 252–9.

CRITCHLEY, M. 1967: Some observations upon developmental dyslexia. *Modern Trends in Neurology* 4, 135–44.

—— 1970: *The Dyslexic Child*. Springfield, Ill: Thomas.

CRITCHLEY, M. and CRITCHLEY, E. 1978: *Dyslexia Defined*. London: Heinemann Medical Books.

CROMER, R.F. 1980: Spontaneous spelling by language-disordered children. In Frith, U. (ed.), *Cognitive Processes in Spelling*. London: Academic Press.

CRONBACH, L. 1979: *Essentials of Psychological Testing* (5th edn.) New York: Harper & Row.

CROSBY, R.M. 1968: *Reading and the Dyslexic Child*. London: Souvenir Press.

CROXEN, M.E. and LYTTON, H. 1971: Reading disability and difficulties in finger localization and right-left discrimination. *Developmental Psychology* 5, 256–62.

CROWTHER, G. 1982: Dyslexia. *Education*, 20th August, 143

CRUICKSHANK, W.M. 1968: The problems of delayed recognition and its correction. In Keeney, A.H. and Keeney, V.T. (eds.), *Dyslexia: Diagnosis and Treatment of Reading Disorders*. St Louis: C.V. Mosby.

CRYSTAL, D. 1980: *Introduction to Language Pathology*. London: Arnold.

CURRY, L, ROSS, R., and CALFEE, R.C. 1973: *Components of Visual Matching Skills in Pre-readers*. Paper presented to American Psychological Association.

CURTIS-JENKINS, G.H. 1979: The identification of children with learning problems in general practice. *Journal of Royal College of General Practitioners*. 29, 647–51.

DALBY, J.T. 1979: Deficit or delay: Neuropsychological models of developmental dyslexia. *Journal of Special Education* 13, 240–62.

DARBY, R. 1974: Ear asymmetry phenomenon in dyslexic and normal children. Unpublished master's thesis, University of Florida.

DAVIE, R., BUTLER, N. and GOLDSTEIN, H. 1972: *From Birth to Death*. London: Penguin.

DECKER, S.N. and DEFRIES, J.C. 1980: Cognitive abilities in families with reading disabled children. *Journal of Learning Disabilities* 13, 9, 53–7.

—— 1981: Cognitive ability profiles in families of reading disabled children. *Developmental Medicine and Child Neurology* 23, 217–27.

DEJERINE, J. 1871: Sur un cas de eccite verbale avec agraphis, suivi d' autopsia. *Mem. Social Biology* 3, 197–201

DEHAAS, A. 1972: *Oor dominantie bij LUM-Kindren*. Doctoral thesis, Amsterdam, Free University.

DE HIRSCH, K., JANSKY, J. and LANGFORD, W. 1966: *Predicting Reading Failure*. New York: Harper & Row.

DELACATO, C.H. 1963: *The diagnosis and treatment of speech and reading problems*. Springfield, Ill.: Thomas.

DENCKLA, M.B. 1972: Color-naming defects in dyslexic boys. *Cortex* 8, 164–76.

—— 1977 a: Minimal brain dysfunction and dyslexia: beyond diagnosis by exclusion. In Blaw, M. E., Raipin, I. and Kinsbourne, M. (eds.), *Topics in Child Neurology*. New York: Spectrum Publications.

—— 1977 b: The neurological basis of reading disability. In Roswell, F.G. and Natchez, G. (eds.), *Reading Disability: A Human Approach to Learning*. New York: Basic Books.

—— 1978: Review of Hughes in Benton, A. and Pearl, D., *Dyslexia: an Appraisal of Current Knowledge*. New York: Oxford University Press.

DENCKLA, M.B. and RUDEL, R. 1976 a: Naming of pictured objects by dyslexic and other learning disabled children. *Brain and Language* 3, 1–15.

—— 1976 b: Rapid 'automatized' naming RAN: Dyslexia differentiated from other learning disabilities. *Neuropsychologia* 14, 471–9.

DENCKLA, M., RUDEL, R. and BROMAN, M. 1981: Tests that discriminate between dyslexics and other learning disabled boys. *Brain and Language* 13, 118–29.

DEUTSCH, C.P. 1964: Auditory discrimination and learning: Social factors. *Merril-Palmer Quarterly* 10, 277–96.

DEUTSCH, M. 1963: The disadvantaged child and the learning process. In Passow, A.H. (ed.), *Education in Depressed Areas*. New York: Teachers College, Columbia University.

—— 1965: The role of social class in language development and cognition *American Journal of Orthopsychiatry* 35, 78–88.

DIMOND, C. and BEAUMONT, G. 1976: *Hemisphere Function in the Human Brain*. London: Elek.

DIMOND, S. and BROUWERS, E.Y. 1976: Improvement of human memory through the use of drugs. *Psychopharmacology* 49, 307–9.

DIVISION OF EDUCATION AND CHILD PSYCHOLOGY 1983: Specific Learning Difficulties. *Occasional Papers* 7, 3.

DOEHRING, D.G. 1968: *Patterns of Impairment in Specific Reading Disability*. Bloomington: Indiana University Press.

—— 1972: Ear asymmetry in the discrimination of monoaural tonal sequences. *Canadian Journal Psychology*. 26, 106–10.

—— 1976: Evaluation of two models of reading disability. In Knights, R.M. and Bakker, D.J. (eds.) *The Neuropsychology of Learning Disorders*. Baltimore: University Park Press.

—— 1978: The tangled web of behavioural research on developmental dyslexia. In Benton,

A. and Pearl, D. (eds.), *Dyslexia: An Appraisal of Current Knowledge*. New York: Oxford University Press.

DOEHRING, D.G. and HOSHKO, IM. 1977: Classification of reading problems by the Q-techniques of factor analysis. *Cortex* 13, 281–94.

DOEHRING, D.G. and LIBMAN, R. 1974: Signal detection analysis of auditory sequence discrimination in children. *Perceptual and Motor Skills* 38, 163–9.

DONALDSON, M. 1979: *Childrens' Minds*. London: Fontana.

DONE, D.J. and MILES, J.K. 1978: Learning, memory and dyslexia. *Dyslexia Review* 1, 2, 13–14.

DORMAN, M.F., CUTTING, J.E. and RAPHAEL, L.J. 1975: Perception of temporal order in vowel sequences with and without formant transitions. *Journal of Experimental Psychology, Human Perception and Performance* 104, 121–9.

DOSSETOR, D.R. and PAPAIOANNON, T.C. 1975: Dyslexia and eye movements. *Language and Speech* 18, 312–17.

DOUGLAS, J.W., ROSS, J.M. and SIMPSON, M.R. 1968: All our future. *National Survey Health and Development*. London: Davies.

DOUGLAS, V.I. 1980: Treatment and training approaches to hyperactivity: establishing internal and external control. In Whalen, C.K. and Henker, B. (ed.), *Hyperactive Children: The Social Ecology of Identification and Treatment*. New York: Academic Press.

DRAGE, J., KENNEDY, C., BERENDES, H., SCHWARZ, B. and WEISS, W. 1966: The Apgar score as an index of infant morbidity. *Developmental Medicine and Child Neurology* 8, 141–8.

DRASDO, N. 1972: The ophthalmic correlates of reading disability. *British Optical Association* 97–106.

DUNLOP, D.B., DUNLOP, P. and FENELON, B. 1973: Visual analysis in children with reading disability: The results of new techniques of examination. *Cortex 9*, 227–36.

DUNLOP, P. 1972: Dyslexia, the orthoptic approach. *Australian Orthoptic Journal* 12, 16–20.

DYKMAN, R.A. (1980): Psychotropic drugs and learning problems. *Journal of Learning Disabilities* 6, 10.

DYKMAN, R.A., ACKERMAN, P.T., CLEMENTS, S.D. and PETERS, J.E., 1971: Specific learning disabilities: an attentional deficit syndrome. In Myklebust, H.R. (ed.), *Progress in Learning Disabilities* vol. II, 56–93. New York: Grune & Stratton.

DYKSTRA, R. 1966: Auditory discrimination abilities and beginning reading achievement. *Reading Research Quarterly* 1, 3, 5–34.

EAKIN, S. and DOUGLAS, V.I. 1971: Automatization and oral reading problems in children. *Journal of Learning Disabilities* 4, 31–8.

EDWARDS, R.P., ALLEY, C.R., and SNIDER, W. 1971: Academic achievement and minimal brain dysfunction. *Journal of Learning Disabilities* 4, 134–8.

EIMAS, P.D., SIQUELAND, E.R., JUSZYCK, P. and VIGORITO, J. 1971: Speech perception in infants. *Science* 171, 303–6.

EISENBERG, L. 1966: The epidemiology of reading retardation and a program for preventive intervention. In Money, J. (ed.), *The Disabled Reader: Education of the Dyslexic Child*. Baltimore: Johns Hopkins University Press.

—— 1967: Clinical considerations in the psychiatric evaluation of intelligence. In Zubin, J. and Jervis, G.A. (eds.), *Psychopathology of Mental Development*, New York: Grune & Stratton, 502–13.

—— 1978: Definition of dyslexia: implications and policy. In Benton, A. and Pearl, D. (eds.), *Dyslexia: An Appraisal of Current Knowledge*. New York: Oxford University Press.

EISENSON, A. 1972: *Aphasia in Children*. London: Harper & Row.

ELKIND, D.A., HORN, J. and SCHNEIDER, G. 1965: Modified word recognition reading achievement and perceptual de-centralization. *Journal of Genetic Psychology*, 107, 235–51.

ELLIOTT, C. 1983: *British Ability Scales, Handbook and Technical Manual*. Windsor: NFER/Nelson.

ELLIOTT, C.D. and PEARSON, L.C. 1980: The British Ability Scales: a flexible approach to individual assessment. *Association of Educational Psychologists Journal* 5, 3, 71–8.

ELLIS, A.W. 1979: Developmental and acquired dyslexia; some observations on Jorm. *Cognition* 7, 413–20.

ELLIS, N. 1980: *Functional Analysis of Reading and Short-term Memory in Dyslexic Children*. Doctoral Thesis, University of Wales, Bangor.

—— 1981 a: Visual and name coding in dyslexic children. *Psychological Research* 43, 2, 201–19.

—— 1981 b: Information processing views of developmental dyslexia I and II. *Dyslexia Review* 4, 1, 15–21.

—— 1981 c: Information processing views of developmental dyslexia III, IV *Dyslexia Review* 4, 2, 10–16.

ELLIS, H. 1988: The development of literacy and short-term memory. In Morris P.E. and Sykes R.N. (eds.), *Practical Aspects of Memory 11*. Chichester: Wiley

ELLIS, N. and LARGE, B. 1988: The early stages of reading. A longitudinal study. *Applied Cognitive Psychology* 2, 47–76.

ELLIS, N. and MILES, T. 1978: Visual information processing in dyslexic children. In Gruneberg, M., Morris, P. and Sykes, R. (eds.), *Practical Aspects of Memory*. London: Academic Press.

—— 1981: A lexical coding deficiency 1. In Pavlides, G. and Miles, T. (eds.), *Dyslexia Research*. Chichester: Wiley.

ELLIS, N.C., BADDELEY, A.P., MILES, T.R., and LEWIS, M. Limitations in reading ability and short term memory span, cited by Ellis and Miles (1981).

ELLIOTT, C.D. and TYLER, S. 1987: Learning disabilities and intelligence test results: a principal components analysis of the British Ability Scales. *British Journal of Psychology* 78, 325–33.

ELTERMAN, R.D., ABEL, C.A., DAROFF, R.B. DELL'OSSO, L.F. and BORNSTEIN, J.L. 1980: Eye movement patterns in dyslexic children. *Journal of Learning Disabilities* 13, 1, 16–21.

ERIKSON, C.W. and COLLINS, J.F. 1968: Sensory traces versus the psychological movement in the temporal organization of form. *Journal of Experimental Psychology* 77, 376–82.

ERLENMEYER, L. 1879: Die Schrift, Grundzüge ihrer Physiologie and ihrer Pathologie. Stuttgart, cited in Critchley, M. (ed.), *Mirror-writing*. London: Kegan Paul 1928.

ESKENAZI, B. and DIAMOND, S. 1983: Visual exploration of non-verbal material by dyslexic children. *Cortex* 19, 353–70.

ESTES, W.K. 1972: An associative basis for coding and organization in memory. In Melton, A.W. and Martin, E. (eds.), *Coding Processes in Human Memory*. Washington, D C: Wintons.

FARR, J.E. and LEIGH, J. 1972: Factors associated with reading failure. *Social Science and Medicine* 6, 241–51.

FARNHAM-DIGGORY, S. 1972: The development of equivalence system. In Farnham-Diggory S. (ed.), *Information Processing in Children*. New York: Academic Press.

—— 1978: *Learning Disabilities*. London: Fontana/Open Books.

FARNHAM-DIGGORY, S. and GREGG, L.W. 1975: Short term memory function in young readers. *Journal of Experimental Child Psychology* 19, 2, 279–98.

FAURE, J.M.A., ROZIER, J., BENSCH, C., VINCENT, J.D., CORCELLE, L. and PORTMANN, M. 1968:

Potentiels associatifs evoqués par des stimulations combinées auditives et visuelles chez l'enfant amblyope fonctionnel strabique et chex l'enfant dyslexique. *Revue Neurologique* 118, 502–12.

FELTON, R.H. and CAMPBELL, S.K. 1985: Reliability and validity of a test of reading disability sub-types. *Annals of Dyslexia* 35.

FERNALD, G.M. 1943: *Remedial Techniques in the Basic Subjects*. New York: McGraw-Hill.

FESTINGER, L. 1972: *Eye Movement Disorders in Dyslexia*. New York: School for Social Research, ERIC Documents ED 074 691.

FILDES, L.G. 1921: A psychological inquiry into the nature of the condition known as congenital word-blindness. *Brain* 44, 286–307.

FINLAYSON, M.A.J. and REITAN, R.M. 1976: Tactile-perceptual functioning in relation to intellectual, cognitive and reading skills in younger and older normal children. *Developmental Medicine and Child Neurology* 18, 442–6.

FINNEGAN, D.S. 1979: Auditory skills and word-calling ability. *Academic Therapy* 14, 3, 299–312.

FINUCCI, J.M. 1978: Genetic considerations in dyslexia, in Mykelbust, H.R. (ed.), *Progress in Learning Disabilities*. New York: Grune & Stratton.

FINUCCI, J.M., GUTHRIE, J.T., CHILDS, A.L., ABBEY, H. and CHILDS, B. 1976: The genetics of specific reading disability. *Annals of Human Genetics* 40, 1–23.

FIRTH, I. 1972: *Components of Reading Disability*. Doctoral dissertation, University of New South Wales.

FISH, J.R. 1979: Developments in the provision for children with specific learning difficulties. *Dyslexia Review* 2, 2, 1–2.

FISHER, J.H. 1910: Congenital work blindness. *Transcribe, Opthalmological Society* UK. JD, 216–25.

FISHER, E. 1980: Backwardness in reading and linguistic/memory deficits. *First Language* 1, 3, 3, 223–6.

FISHER, D.F. and FRANKFURTER, A. 1977: Normal and disabled readers can locate and identify letters: Where's the perceptual deficit? *Journal of Reading Behaviour* 9, 1, 31–43.

FLAX, N. 1969: Visual function in dyslexia. *American Journal of Optometry* 45, 574–86.

—— 1970: The contribution of visual problems to learning disability. *Journal of the American Optometric Association* 41, 10.

FLETCHER, J.M. and SATZ, P. 1979: Unitary deficit hypothesis of reading disabilities; Has Vellutino led us astray? *Journal of Learning Disabilities* 12, 3, 155–9.

FLETCHER, J.M., SATZ, P. and SCHOLES, R.J. 1981: Developmental changes in the linguistic performance correlates or reading achievement. *Brain and Language* 13, 78–90.

FLETCHER, P. and GARMAN, M. (eds.) 1979: *Language Acquisition*. Cambridge: Cambridge University Press.

FOX, F.J., ORR, R.R. and ROURKE, B.O. 1975: Shortcomings of the standard optometric visual analysis for the diagnosis of reading problems. *Canadian Journal of Optometry* 37, 57–61.

FOX, B. and ROUTH, D. 1980: Phonemic analysis and reading disability in children. *Journal of Psycholinguistic Research* 9, 2, 115–19.

FRANSELLA, F. and GERVER, D. 1965: Multiple regression equations for predicting reading age from chronological age and WISC verbal IQ. *British Journal of Educational Psychology* 25, 80–9.

FRASER, E. 1959: *Home Environment and the School*. London: University of London Press.

FREDMAN, G. and STEVENSON, J. 1988: Reading processes in specific reading retarded and reading backward 13 years olds. *British Journal of Developmental Psychology* 6, 97–109.

FRIES, C.E. 1962: *Linguistics and Reading*. New York: Holt, Rinehart & Winston.

FRITH, U. 1980 a: Unexpected spelling problems. In Frith, U. (ed.), *Cognitive Processes in Spelling*. London: Academic Press.

—— 1980 b: *Cognitive Processes in Spelling*. London: Academic Press.

—— 1981: Experimental approaches in developmental dyslexia: an introduction. *Psychological Research* 43, 2, 97–109.

—— 1985: Beneath the surface of developmental dyslexia. In Marshall, J.C. Patterson, K.E. and Coltheart, M. (eds.), *Surface Dyslexia in Adults and Children*. London: Routledge & Kegan Paul.

FRITH, U. and FRITH, C.D. 1980: *Relationships between Reading and Dyslexia*. Baltimore: University Park Press.

FROSTIG, M. 1961: *The Marianne Frostig Development Test of Visual Perception*. Palo Alto: Consulting Psychologists Press.

FROSTIG, M. and HORNE, D. 1964: *The Frostig Program for the Development of Visual Perception*. Chicago: Folett.

FRY, M.A., JOHNSON, C.S. and MUEHL, S. 1970: Oral language production in relation to reading achievement among select second graders. In Bakker, D.J. and Satz, P. (eds.), *Specific Reading Disability: Advances in Theory and Method*. Rotterdam: Rotterdam University Press.

FURNESS, E.L. 1956: Perspectives on reversal tendencies. *Elementary English* 33, 38–41.

FURTH, H. G. and PUFALL, P.B. 1965: Visual and auditory sequence learning in hearing-impaired children. *Journal of Speech Hearing Research* 9, 441–9.

GADDES, W. 1976: Learning disabilities: prevalence estimates and the need for definition. In Knights, R. and Bakker, D.J. (eds.), *The Neuropsychology of Learning Disorders*. Baltimore: University Park Press.

GALBURDA, A.M. and KEMPER, T.L. 1979: Cytoarchitectonic abnormalities in developmental dyslexia: a case study. *Annals of Neurology* 6, 94–100.

GALIFRADT-GRANJON, J. 1952: Le Probleme de l'organisation spatiale dans les dyslexies d'evolution. In Nanent, N. (ed.), *L'Apprentissage de la lecture et ses troubles*. Paris: Presses Universitaires de France.

GASCON, G. and GOODGLASS, H. 1970: Reading retardation and the information content of stimuli in paired associate learning. *Cortex* 9, 417–29.

GAUNTLETT, D. 1980: Thought plans: a strategy for the dyslexic student. *Dyslexia Review* 3, 1, 18–21.

GAZZANIGA, M.S. 1970: *The Bisected Brain*. New York: Appleton.

GELB, I.J. 1952: *A Study of Writing*. Chicago: University of Chicago Press.

GESCHWIND, N. 1962: The anatomy of acquired disorders of reading. In Money, J. (ed.), *Reading Disability: Progress and Research Needs in Dyslexia,* Baltimore: Johns Hopkins University Press.

—— 1974: *Selected papers on Language and the Brain*. Boston Studies in the Philosophy of Science 16. Boston: Rerdal.

—— 1982: *Biological Foundations of Dyslexia*. Paper presented to BPS Cognitive Psychology Section conference in Dyslexia, Manchester, February.

GETMAN, G., KANE, E.R., HALLGREN, M.R. and MCKEE, F. 1964: *The Physiology of Reading Readiness*. Minneapolis: PASS.

GHENT, L. 1961: Form and its orientation: A child's-eye view. *American Journal of Psychology* 74, 177–90.

GIBSON, E.J. 1968. Learning to read. In Endler, N.S., Boutler, L.R. and Osser, H. (eds.), *Contemporary Issues in Developmental Psychology*. New York: Holt, Rinehart & Winston.

—— 1970: The ontogeny of reading. *American Psychologist* 25, 136–43.

—— 1971: Perceptual learning and the theory of word perception. *Cognitive Psychology* 2, 351–68.

GIBSON, E.J. and LEVIN, H. 1975: *The Psychology of Reading*. Cambridge, Mass.: The MIT Press.

GILBERT, L.C. 1953: Functional motor efficiency of the eyes and its relation to reading. *University of California Publications in Education* 11, 159–231.

GILLINGHAM, A. and STILLMAN, B.W. 1969: *Remedial Training for Children with Specific Disability in Reading, Spelling and Penmanship*. 5th edn. Cambridge, Mass: Educational Publishing Co.

GITTELMAN, R. 1984: Treatment of reading disorders. In Rutter, M. (ed.), *Behavioural Syndromes of Brain Dysfunction in Childhood*. New York: Guildford Press.

GITTELMAN, R. KLEIN, R., and KLEIN, D.F. 1976: Methyl phenidate effects in learning disabilities. *Archives of General Psychiatry* 33, 655–64.

GITTELMAN, R. and FEINGOLD, I. 1983: Children with reading disorders 1, Efficacy of reading remediation. *Journal of Child Psychology and Psychiatry* 24, 2, 169–93.

GITTELMAN, R., KLEIN, D.F. and FEINGOLD, I. 1983: Children with reading disorders II. Effects of methyl phenidate in combination with reading remediation. *Journal of Child Psychology and Psychiatry* 24, 2, 193–213.

GLEITMAN, L.R. and ROZIN, P. 1977: The structure and acquisition of reading, 1: Relations between orthographies and the structure of language. In Reber, A.S. and Scarborough, D.L. (eds.), *Toward a Psychology of Reading*. The proceedings of the CUNY conferences. New York: Wiley.

GOETZINGER, C.P., DIRKS, D.D., and BAER, C.J. 1960: Auditory discrimination and visual perception in good and poor readers. *Annals of Otalaryngology, Rhinology, and Laryngology* 69, 121–36.

GOINS, J.T. 1958: *Visual Perceptual Abilities and Early Reading Progress*. Supplementary Educational Monographs no. 87, University of Chicago.

GOLDBERG, H.K. and ARNOTT, W. 1970: Ocular motility in learning disabilities. *Journal of Learning Disabilities* 3, 160–6.

GOLDBERG, H. and SCHIFFMAN, G. 1972: *Dyslexia: Problems of Reading Disabilities*. New York: Grune & Stratton.

GOLDSTEIN, M.N. 1974: Auditory agnosia for speech (pure word deafness). *Brain and Language* 1, 195–204.

GOLINKOFF, R.M. and ROSINSKI, R.R. 1976: Decoding, semantic processing, and reading comprehension skill. *Child Development* 47, 252–8.

GOODMAN, K.S. 1969: Analysis of reading miscues: applied psycholinguistics. *Reading Research Quarterly* 5, 9–30.

GORDON, H.W. 1980: Cognitive asymmetry in dyslexic families. *Neuropsychologica* 18, 645–56.

GOYEN, J.D. and LYLE, J. 1973: Short-term memory and visual discrimination in retarded readers. *Perceptual and Motor Skills* 36, 403–8.

GRAHAM, E.E. 1952: Wechsler-Bellvue and WISC Scattergrams of unsuccessful readers. *Journal of Consulting Psychology* 16, 268–71.

GREEN, J.B. 1961: Association of behaviour disorder with an EEG focus in children without seizures. *Neurology* 11, 337–44.

GRIFFEN, D.C., WALTON, H.N. and IVES, V. 1974: Saccades as related to reading disorders. *Journal of Learning Disabilities* 7, 310–16.

GRIFFITHS, A.N. 1977: The WISC as a diagnostic-remedial tool for dyslexia. *Academic Therapy* 12, 4, 401–9.

GRIFFITHS, P. 1972P *Developmental Dysphasia: An Introduction*. London: Invalid Children's Aid Association.

GROENENDALL, H.A. and BAKKER, D.J. 1971: The part played by mediation processes in the retention of temporal sequences by two reading groups. *Human Development* 14, 62–70.

GROFF, P. 1975: Reading ability and auditory discrimination: are they related? *Reading Teacher* 28: 742–7.

—— 1979: Reading ability and auditory discrimination: a further consideration. *Academic Therapy* 14, 3, 313–19.

GROSS, K. and ROTHENBERG, S. 1979: Developmental dyslexia; research methods and inferences. *Neuropsychologica* 16, 704–9.

GROSS, K. ROTHENBERG, S., SCHOTTENFELD, M., DRAKE, C. 1979: Duration thresholds for letter identification in left and right visual fields for normal and reading disabled children. *Neuropsychologica* 16, 709–15.

GRUBER, E. 1962: Reading ability, binocular coordination and the ophthalmograph. *Archives Opthalmology* 67, 280–8.

GUBBAY, S.S., ELLIS, E., WALTON, J.N., and COURT, S.D. 1965: Clumsy children. *Brain* 88, 295.

GUILDFORD, J.P. 1956: *Fundamental Statistics in Psychology and Education*. New York: McGraw-Hill.

GULLIFORD, R. 1969: *Backwardness and Educational Failure*. Slough: NFER.

GUTHRIE, J.T. 1973: Reading comprehension and syntactic responses in good and poor readers. *Journal of Educational Psychology* 65, 3, 294–9.

GUTHRIE, J., SEIFERT, M. and KLUNIE, L. 1978: Clues from research on programs for poor readers. In Samuels, S. (ed.), *What Research has to Say About Reading Instruction*. Newark: International Reading Association.

HABER, R.N. and STANDING, L.G. 1969: Direct measures of short-term visual storage. *Quarterly Journal of Experimental Psychology* 21, 43, 54.

HAGGARD, M. 1973: Abbreviation of consonants in English pre-and post-vocalic clusters. *Journal of Phonetics* 1, 9–24.

HALL, J., EWING, A., TINZMAN, M. and WILSON, K. 1981: Phonetic coding in dyslexics and normal readers. *Bulletin of Psychonomic Society* 17, 4, 177–8.

HALLAHAN, D.P. and CRUICKSHANK, W.M. 1973: *Psychoeducational Foundations of Learning Disabilities*. Englewood Cliffs, NJ: Prentice-Hall.

HALLGREN, B. 1950: Specific dyslexia (congenital word blindness): a classical and genetic study. *Acta Psychiatra et Neurologica Scandinavia*, supplement 65.

HAMILTON-FAIRLEY, D. 1976: *Speech-Therapy and the Dyslexic*. London: Helen Arkell Dyslexia Centre.

HAMMILL, D.D. 1972: The resource room model in special education. *Journal of Special Education* 6, 349–54.

HAMMILL, D.D. and LARSEN, S. 1974: Relationship of selected auditory perceptual skills and reading ability. *Journal of Learning Disabilities* 7, 429–36.

HANLEY, J. and SKLAR, B. 1976: Electroencephalic correlates of developmental reading dyslexics: computer analysis of recordings from normal and dyslexic children. In Leisman, G. (ed.), *Basic Visual Process and Learning Disability*, 212–43. Springfield, Ill.: Thomas.

HANSON, D. and RODGERS, T.S. 1968: An exploration of psycholinguistic units in initial reading. In Goodman, K.S. (ed.), *The Psycholinguistic Nature of the Reading Process*. Detroit: Wayne State University Press.

HARBER, J.F. 1980: Auditory perception and reading: another look. *Learning Disabilities Quarterly* 3, 19–25.

HARDY, W.G. 1965: On language disorders in children: a reorganisation of thinking. *Journal of Speech and Hearing Disabilities 8:* 3–16.

HARDY, M. 1973: *Development of Beginning Reading Skills: Recent Findings in Reading and Related Skills*, Proceedings of UKRA conference, London: Ward Lock.

HARDYCK, C. 1977: Laterality and intellectual ability: a just not noticeable difference. *British Journal of Educational Psychology* 43, 305–11.

HARDYCK, C. and PETRINOVITCH, C.F. 1977: Left handedness. *Psychological Bulletin* 84, 385–404.

HARRIS, A.J. 1957: Lateral dominance, directional confusion and reading disability. *The Journal of Psychology* 44, 283–94.

―― 1979: Lateral dominance and reading disability. *Journal of Learning Disabilities* 12, 5, 339–43.

HART, S. and FAGG, R. 1976: Left-handed children. *Where* 178, 196–9.

HARTLAGE, L.C. and HARTLAGE, P.L. 1977: Relationships between neurological behavioural and academic variables. *Journal of Clinical Child Psychology* 6, 52–63.

HARTLAGE, L.C. and GREEN, J.B. 1973: The EEG as a predictor of intellective and academic performance. *Journal of Learning Disabilities* 6, 239–42.

HEALY, A.F. 1974: Separating item from order information in short-term memory. *Journal of Verbal Learning and Verbal Behavior* 13, 644–55.

―― 1975: Coding of temporal-spatial patterns in short-term memory. *Journal of Verbal Learning and Verbal Behavior* 14, 481–95.

―― 1977: Pattern coding of spatial order information in short-term memory. *Journal of Verbal Learning and Verbal Behavior* 16, 419–37.

HECAEN, H. and DE AJURIAGUERRA, J. 1964: *Left-Handednes, Manual Superiority and Cerebral Dominance*. Translated by E. Ponder. New York: Grune & Stratton.

HEIMAN, J.R. and ROSS, A.U. 1974: Saccadic eye movements and reading difficulties. *Journal of Abnormal Child Psychology* 2, 53–61.

HEILMAN, K.M., ROTHI, L., CAMPANELLA, D. and WOLFSON, S. 1979: Wernickes and global asphasia without alexia. *Archives of Neurology* 36, 129–33.

HELVESTON, E.M., BILLIPS, W.C. and WEBER, J.C. 1970: Controlling eye dominant hemisphere relationships as a factor in reading ability. *American Journal of Ophthalmology* 70, 90–100.

HENRY, A. 1975: Specific difficulties in reading. *Remedial Education* 10, 2, 81–5.

HERMANN, K. 1959: *Reading Disability: a Medical Study of Word-Blindness and Related Handicaps*. Copenhagen: Munksgaard.

HERON, W. 1957: Perception as a function of retinal locus and attention. *American Journal of Psychology* 70, 38–48.

HICKEY, C. 1977: *Dyslexia: Language Training Course for Teachers and Learners*. Available from Dyslexia Institute, Staines.

HICKS, C. 1980: The ITPA visual sequential memory task: An alternative interpretation and its implications for good and poor readers. *British Journal of Educational Psychology* 50, 16–25.

―― 1981: B/D confusions in dyslexia. *Journal of Research in Reading* 4, 21–28

HICKS, C. and MURGATROYD, S. 1981: Helping the dyslexic child. *Counsellor* 3, 3, 11–22.

HINSHELWOOD, J. 1900: Congenital word-blindness. *Lancet* 1, 1506–8.

—— 1917: *Congenital Word-Blindness*. London: H.K. Lewis.

HIRST, L. 1960: The usefulness of a two-way analysis of WISC subtests in the diagnosis of remedial reading problems. *Journal of Experimental Education* 29, 153–60.

HOCKETT, C.F. 1963: The problems of universals in language. In Greenberg, J.H. (ed.), *Universals of language*. Cambridge, Mass.: The MIT Press.

HOLMES, J.M. 1973: *Dyslexia: A Neurolinguistic Study of Traumatic and Developmental Disorders of Reading*. Ph.D. Thesis, University of Edinburgh.

HOLMES, J.M. 1978: Regression and reading breakdown. In Caramazz, A. and Zurif, E. (eds.), *Language Acquisition and Language Breakdown*, Baltimore: Johns Hopkins University Press.

HOLMES, D.L. and PEPER, R.J. 1977: An evaluation of the use of spelling error in the diagnosis of reading disabilities. *Child Development* 48, 1708–11.

HORAN, P. 1981: *The Use of Computer Programs with Dyslexic Children*. MSc thesis. University of Aston.

HORNSBY, B. and SHEAR, F. 1976: *Alpha to Omega*. London: Heinemann.

HORNSBY, B. and MILES, T.R. 1980: The effects of a dyslexia-centred teaching programme. *British Journal of Educational Psychology* 50, 236–42.

HUELSMAN, C.R. 1970: The WISC subtest syndrome for disabled readers. *Perceptual and Motor Skills* 30, 535–50.

HUEY, E.B. 1908: *The Psychology and Pedagogy of Reading*. Reprint 1968: Cambridge, Mass.: The MIT Press.

HUGHES, J.R. 1971: Electroencephalography and learning disabilities. In Myklebust, H.R. (ed.), *Progress in Learning Disabilities* vol. 2. New York: Grune & Stratton.

—— 1976: Biochemical and electroencephalographic correlates of learning disabilities. In Knights, R.M. and Bakker, D.J. (eds.), *Neuropsychology of Learning Disorders: Theoretical Approaches*. Baltimore: University Park Press.

—— 1978: Electo-encephalographic and neurophysiological studies in dyslexia. In Benton, A., and Pearl, D. (eds.), *Dyslexia: An Appraisal of Current Knowledge*. New York: Oxford University Press.

HUGHES, J.R. and PARK, G.E. 1968: The EEG in dyslexia. In Kellaway, P. and Petersen, I. (eds.), *Clinical Electroencephalography of Children* 307–27. Stockholm: Almquist and Wiksell.

HUTTENLOCHER, J. 1967 a: Discrimination of figure orientation: Effects of relative position. *Journal of Comparative and Physiological Psychology* 63, 359–61.

—— 1967 b: Children's ability to order and orient objects. *Child Development* 38, 1169–76.

HULME, C. 1981 a: The effects of manual training on memory in normal and retarded readers: some implications for multi-sensory teaching. *Psychological Research* 43, 2, 178–93.

—— 1981 b: *Reading Retardation and Multi-Sensory Teaching*. London: Routledge & Kegan Paul.

INGRAM, T.T.S. 1964: The nature of dyslexia. In Young, F.A. and Lindsley, D.B. (eds.), *Early Experience and Visual Information Processing in Perceptual and Reading Disorders*. Washington, DC.: National Academy of Sciences.

—— 1969: Developmental disorders of speech. In Vivian, P. and Brain, G. W. (eds.), *Handbook of Clinical Neurology* 4, Amsterdam: North Holland.

—— 1976 a: Speech disorders in childhood. In Lenneberg, E.H. and Lenneberg, E. (eds.), *Foundations of Language Development*, vol 2. New York: Academic Press.

INGRAM, D. 1976 b: *Phonological Disability in Children*. London: Arnold.

INGRAM, T.T.S., MASON, A.W. and BLACKBURN, 1970: A retrospective study of 82 children with reading disability. *Developmental Medicine and Child Neurology* 12, 271–81.

INGRAM, T.T.S. and REID, J.F. 1966: Developmental dysphasia observed in a department of child psychiatry. *Archives of Disorders of Childhood* 31, 162–72.

JAKSOBSEN, R., FANT, C., and HALLE, M. 1963: *Preliminaries to Speech Analysis: The Distinctive Features and their Correlates*. Cambridge, Mass.: The MIT Press.

JANSKY, J. 1978: A critical review of some developmental and predictive precursors of reading disabilities. In Benton, A.C. and Pearl, D. (eds.), *Dyslexia: An Appraisal of Current Knowledge*. New York: Oxford University Press.

JANSKY, J. and DE HIRSCH, K. 1972: *Preventing Reading Failure no. 1. Prediction, Diagnosis, Intervention*. New York: Harper & Row.

JOFFE, L. 1981: *Mathematical Difficulties and Dyslexia* Ph. D. thesis, University of Aston.

JOHNSON, D.J. 1978: Remedial approaches and dyslexia. In Benton, A. and Pearl, D. (eds.), *Dyslexia: An Appraisal of Current Knowledge*. New York: Oxford University Press.

JOHNSON, D., and MYKLEBUST, H. 1967: *Learning Disabilities Educational Principles and Practices*. New York: Grune & Stratton.

JOHNSON, D.J. and HOOK, P.E. 1978: Reading disabilities: problems of rule acquisition and linguistic awareness. In Myklebust, H. (ed.), *Progress in Learning Disabilities* IV. New York: Grune & Stratton.

JONES, B. 1974: Cross-modal matching by retarded and normal readers. *Bulletin of the Psychonomic Society* 3, 3A, 163–5.

JOOS, L.W. 1966: Linguistics for the dyslexic. In Money, J. (ed.), *The Disabled Reader*. Baltimore: Johns Hopkins University Press.

JORDAN, D.R. 1972: *Dyslexia in the Classroom*. Columbus, Ohio: Merrill.

JORDON, S.H. 1979: High frequency deafness in dyslexic children, Unpublished undergraduate project, Applied Psychology Department, University of Aston.

JORM, A.F. 1977: Effect of word imagery on reading performance as a function of reader ability. *Journal of Educational Psychology* 69, 46–54.

—— 1978: Reading process in dyslexia. *Cortex* 2, 3.

—— 1979 a: The cognitive and neurological basis of developmental dyslexia; a theoretical framework and review. *Cognition* 7, 19–33.

—— 1979 b: The nature of reading deficit in developmental dyslexia: A reply to Ellis. *Cognition* 7, 421–33.

—— 1981: Children with reading and spelling retardation: Functioning of whole word and correspondence rule mechanisms. *Journal of Child Psychology and Psychiatry* 22, 171–8.

JORM, A.F., SHARE, D.L., MACLEAN, R. and MATTHEWS, R. 1986: Cognitive factors at school entry predictive of specific reading retardation and general reading backwardness, also behaviour problems in specific reading retarded and general reading backward children: a longitudinal study. *Journal of Child Psychology and Psychiatry* 27, 33–43.

KALLOS, G., GRABOW, J. and GUARINO, E. 1961: The WISC profile of disabled readers. *Personnel and Guidance Journal* 39, 476–8.

KAHN, D. and BIRCH, H.G. 1968: Development of auditory-visual integration and reading achievement. *Perceptual and Motor Skills* 27, 459–68.

KAMIL, M.L. and RUDEGEAIR, R.E. 1972: Methodological improvements in the assessment of phonological discrimination in children, *Child Development* 43, 1087–91.

KARPOVA, S.N. 1955: Awareness of word composition of speech in the pre-school child. *Voprosy Psikhologii* 4, 43–4 (trans).

KASS, C.E. 1962: *Some Psychological Correlates of Severe Reading Disorders*. Ph. D. thesis, University of Illinois, Urbana.

KATZ, L. and WICKLUND, D. 1971: Word scanning rates for good and poor readers. *Journal of Educational Psychology* 62, 138–40.

—— 1972: Letter scanning rate for good and poor readers in grades two and six. *Journal of Educational Psychology* 63, 363–67.

KATZ, P.A. and DEUTSCH, M. 1967: *The Relationship of Auditory and Visual Functioning to Reading Achievement in Disadvantaged Children*. Paper presented to the Society for Research in Child Development, New York.

KAVANAGH, J.F. and MATTINGLY, I.G. 1972: *Language by Ear and by Eye*. Cambridge, Mass.: The MIT Press.

KAWI, A.A. and PASAMANICK, B.P. 1958: Association of factors of pregnancy with reading disorders in childhood. *Journal of the American Medical Association* 166, 1420–3.

—— 1959: *Prenatal and Perinatal Factors in the Development of Childhood Reading Disorders*. Monographs of the Society for Research in Child Development 24.

KEEFE, B. 1976: A comparison of laterality between normal and dyslexic readers. *ERIC* document ED 135168.

KEEFE, B. and SWINNEY, D. 1979: On the relationship of hemispheric specialisation and developmental dyslexia. *Cortex* 15, 3, 471–81.

KEENEY, A.H. and KEENEY, V.T. 1968: *Dyslexia Diagnosis and Treatment of Reading Disorders*. St Louis: C.V. Mosby.

KELLMER-PRINGLE, M.L., BUTLER, N.R. and DAVIE, R. 1966: *11,000 Seven Year Olds, Studies in Child Development*. London: Longmans.

KENDALL, J.R. and HOOD, J. 1979: Investigating the relationship between comprehension and word recognition: oral reading analysis of children with comprehension or word recognition disabilities. *Journal of Reading Behavior* 1, 1, 41–8.

KEOGH, B.K. 1965 b: The Bender Gestalt as a predictive and diagnostic test of reading performance. *Journal of Consulting Psychology* 29, 83–4.

KEPHART, N. 1960: *The Slow Learner in the Classroom*. Columbus, Ohio: Charles E. Merrill.

KERR, J. 1897: School hygiene in its mental, moral and physical aspects. *Journal of the Royal Statistical Society* 60, 613–80.

KERSHNER, J.R. 1977: Cerebral dominance in disabled readers, good readers, and gifted children. *Child Development* 48, 61–7.

KIMURA, D. 1961: Cerebral dominance and the perception of verbal stimuli. *Canadian Psychologist* 15, 166–71.

—— 1963: Speech lateralization in young children as determined by an auditory test. *Journal of Comparative and Physiological Psychology* 56, 899.

—— 1967: Functional asymmetry of the brain in dichotic listening. *Cortex* 3, 163–78.

—— 1975: Cerebral dominance for speech. In Tower, D.B. (ed.), *The Nervous System vol 3: Human communication and its disorders*. New York: Raven Press.

KINSBOURNE, M. 1973: Minimal brain dysfunction as a neurodevelopmental lag. *Annals of the New York Academy of Sciences* 205, 268–73.

—— 1976: Looking and listening strategies and beginning reading. In Guthrie, J.T. (ed.), *Aspects of Reading Acquisition*, 141–61. Baltimore: Johns Hopkins University Press.

—— 1976: The criteria of cerebral dominance. In Rieber (ed.), *The Neuropsychology of Language*. London: Plenum Press.

KINSBOURNE, M. and HISCOCK, M. 1978: Cerebral lateralisation and cognitive development. In Chall, J. and Mively, A. (eds.), *Education and the Brain*. Chicago: University of Chicago Press.

KINSBOURNE, M. and WARRINGTON, E.K. 1963 a: Developmental factors in reading and writing backwardness. *British Journal of Psychology* 54, 145–56.

—— 1963 b: The developmental Gerstmann syndrome. *Archives of Neurology* 8, 490–501.

—— 1966: Developmental factors in reading and writing backwardness. In Money, J. (ed.), *The Disabled Reader*. Baltimore: Johns Hopkins University Press.

KIRK, S.A. and KIRK, W.D. 1971: *Psycholinguistic Learning Disabilities; Diagnosis and Remediation*. Urbana: University of Illinois Press.

KIRK, S.A. and MCCARTHY, J.J. 1968: *The Illinois Test of Psycholinguistic Abilities*. Urbana: University of Illinois Press.

KLASEN, E. 1972: *The Syndrome of Specific Dyslexia*. Baltimore: University Park Press.

KLERMAN, G.M. 1975: Speech recording in reading. *Journal of Verbal Learning and Behaviour* 14, 323–39.

KLINE, C.L. 1972: The adolescents with learning problems: How long must they wait? *Journal of Learning Disabilities* 5, 127–44.

KNABE, G., MISSBERGER, V. and SCHMIEDEBERT, J. 1970: Die Arbeit mit einer Gruppe begabter less-rechtschreib-schwacher Kinder in Köln (ein vorläufiges Modell zur Diskussion fortgeschrittenen Sondererziehungssystemen in den heutigen and zukunftigen Schulen). *Praxis der Kinderpsychologie* 19, 170–84.

KNOX, C. and KIMURA, D. 1970: Cerebral processing of nonverbal sounds in boys and girls. *Neuropsychologia* 8, 227–37.

KOLERS, P.A. 1970: Three stages of reading. In Levin, H. and Williams, J.P. (eds.), *Basic Studies in Reading*. New York: Basic Books.

—— 1975: Pattern-analyzing disability in poor readers. *Developmental Psychology* 11, 3, 282–90.

KOLSON, C.V. and KALUGER, G. 1963: *Clinical Aspects of Remedial Reading*. Springfield Ill.: Thomson.

KOOI, K.A. 1972: Letter to the editor. *Psychophysiology* 9, 154.

KOOS, E. 1964: Manifestations of cerebral dominance and reading retardation in primary grade school. *Journal of Genetic Psychology* 104, 155–65.

KOPPITZ, E.M. 1958: The Bender Gestalt Test and learning disturbances in young children. *Journal of Clinical Psychology* 14, 292.

—— 1973: Visual aural digit span test performance of boys with emotional and learning problems. *Journal of Clinical Psychology* 29, 263–6.

—— 1975: Bender gestalt test, visual aural digit span test and reading achievement. *Journal of Learning Disabilities* 8, 3, 154–8.

KORNMANN, R., BRAUCH, L., HILS, U., RIEMER, C. and SCHWENDER, V. 1974: Präferenz und Leistungs Dominanz der Hände bei lernbehinderten Sonderschülern, Lagasthenikern und Grundschülern. *Zeitschrift für Heilpädagogik* 25, 147–56.

KRACKE, I. 1975: Perception of rhythm sequences by receptive aphasic and deaf children. *British Journal of Disorders of Communication* 10, 43–51.

KUCERA, O., MATEJCEK, Z., and LANGMEIER, J. 1963: Some observations on dyslexia in children in Czechoslovakia. *American Journal of Orthopsychiatry* 33, 448.

KUSSMAUL, A. 1877: Disturbance of speech. In von Ziemssen, H. (ed.), *Clycopaedia of the Practice of Medicine* vol. 14. Translated by J.A. McCreery. New York: William Wood.

KYOSTIO, O.K. 1980: Is learning to read easy in a language in which the graphemephoneme correspondences are regular. In Kavanagh, J.F. and Venezky, R. (eds.), *Orthography Reading and Dyslexia*. Baltimore: University Park Press.

LABOV, W. 1967: Some sources of reading problems for Negro speakers of non-standard English. In Frazier, A. (ed.), *New Directions in Elementary English*. Champaign, Ill.:

National Council of Teachers of English.

LANYON, R.M. 1974: An experimental investigation into the relevance of auditory discrimination and articulatory skills for spelling and achievement in children. In Wade, B. and Wedell, K., *Spelling-Task and Learner.* Birmingham: Education Review Publication.

LAWSON, L. 1968: Opthalmological factors in learning disabilities. In Myklebust, H.R. (ed.), *Progress in Learning Disabilities*, vol 1. New York: Grune & Stratton.

LEAVELL, V. and BECK, H. 1959: Ability of retarded readers to recognise symbols in association with lateral dominance. *Peabody Journal of Education* 37, 7–13.

LEFFORD, A., BIRCH, H.G. and GREEN, G. 1974: The perceptual and cognitive bases for finger localization and selective finger movements in preschool children. *Child Development* 45, 335–43.

LEFTON, L.A., LAHEY, B.B. and STAGG, D.I. 1978: Eye movements in reading disabled and normal children, a study of systems and strategies. *Journal of Learning Disabilities* 1, 22–31.

LEGEIN, CH. and BOUMA, H. 1981: Visual recognition experiments in dyslexia. In Pavlides, G. and Miles, T. (eds.), *Dyslexia Research and Application to* Education. Chichester: Wiley.

LEISMAN, G. and SCHWARTZ, J. 1976: Ocular-motor variables in reading disorders. In Knights, R.M. and Bakker, D.J. (eds.), *Neuropsychology of Learning Disorders: Theoretical Approaches.* Baltimore: University Park Press.

LEISMAN, G. and ASHKENAZI 1980: Aetiological factors in dyslexia IV. Cerebral hemispheres are functionally equivalent. *Neuroscience* II, 157–64.

LEONG, C.K. 1976: Lateralization in severely disabled readers in relation to functional cerebral development and synthesis of information. In Knights, R.M. and Bakker, D.J. (eds.), *Neuropsychology of Learning Disorders: Theoretical Approaches.* Baltimore: University Park Press.

—— 1980: Laterality and reading proficiency in children. *Reading Research Quarterly* 15, 2, 188–202.

LESERVRE, N. 1964: *Etude electo-oculographic comparée d'enfant normaux et d'enfant dyslexique.* Doctoral dissertation, University of Paris.

LESLIE, L. 1980: Mediation or production deficiency in disabled readers? *Perceptual and Motor Skills* 50, 519–30.

LEVY, B.A. 1970: Reading: speech and meaning processes. *Journal of Verbal Learning and Verbal behaviour* 14, 304–16.

—— 1978: Speech processing during reading. In Lesgold, A. and Pellegrino, S., *Cognitive Psychology and Instruction.* New York: Plenum Press.

LEVY, J. 1969: Possible basis for the evolution of lateral specialisations of the human brain. *Nature* 234, 614–15.

LEWITTER, F.I., DEFRIES, J. and ELSTON, R. 1980: Genetic models of reading disability. *Behaviour Genetics* 10, 1, 9–31.

LENNEBERG, E.H. 1967: *The Biological Foundations of Language.* Cambridge, Mass.: The MIT Press.

LIBERMAN, I.Y. 1971: Basic research in speech and lateralization of language: Some implications for reading disability. *Bulletin of the Orton Society* 21, 71–81.

LIBERMAN, I.Y., SHANKWEILER, P., LIBERMAN, A.M., FOWLER, P.L. and FISCHER, F.W. 1976: Phonètic segmentation and the beginner reader. In Reber, A.S. and Scarborough, D. (eds.), *Reading; Theory, and Practice.* New York: Erlbaum.

LIBERMAN, I., LIBERMAN, A., MATTINGLY, I. and SHANKWEILER, P. 1980: Orthography and the beginning reader. In Kavenagh, J. and Venezky, R. (eds.), *Orthography Reading and*

Dyslexia. Baltimore: University Park Press.

LIBERMAN, I.Y. and SHANKWEILER, D. 1978: Speech, the alphabet and teaching to read. In Resnick, L. and Weaver, P. (eds.), *Theory and Practice of Early Reading*. New York: Wiley.

LIBERMAN, I.Y., SHANKWEILER, D., FISCHER, F.W. and CARTER, B. 1974: Explicit syllable and phoneme segmentation in the young child. *Journal of Experimental Child Psychology* 18, 201–12.

LIBERMAN, I.Y., SHANKWEILER, D., LIBERMAN, A.M., FOWLER, C. and FISCHER, F.W. 1977: Phonetic segmentation and recoding in the beginning reader. In Reber, A.S. and Scarborough, D. (eds.), *Towards a Psychology of Reading*. The Proceedings of the CUNY Conferences. Hillsdale, NJ: Lawrence Erlbaum Associates.

LIBERMAN, I.Y., SHANKWEILER, D., ORLANDO, C., HARRIS, K.S. and BERTI, F.B. 1971: Letter confusion and reversals of sequence in the beginning reader: implications for Orton's theory of developmental dyslexia. *Cortex* 7, 127–42.

LINDER, R. and FILLMAN, H.T. 1970: Auditory and visual performance of slow readers. *The Reading Teacher* 24, 17–22.

LINDGREN, N. 1965: Theoretical models of speech perception and language. *IEEE Spectrum* 2, no. 4.

LINN, J.R. and RYAN, T.J. 1968: The multi-sensory motor method of teaching reading. *Journal of Experimental Education* 36, 57–9.

LOBAN, W. 1963: *The Language of Elementary School Children*. NCTE Research Report no. 1. Urbana, Ill: National Council of Teachers of English.

LOVE, A.D. and CAMPBELL, R.A. 1965: Temporal discrimination in aphasoid and normal children. *Journal of Speech, Hearing Research* 8, 313–14.

LOVEGROVE, W., BILLING, G. and SLAGHUIZ, W. 1978: Processing of visual contour orientation information in normal and reading disabled children. *Cortex* 14, 268–78.

LOVEGROVE, W.J., HEDDLE, M. and SLAGHUIZ, W. 1980: Reading disability: spatial frequency specific deficits in visual information store. *Neuropsychologia* 18, 118–15.

LOVELL, K. and GORTON, A. 1968: Some differences between backward and normal readers of average intelligence. *British Journal of Educational Psychology* 38, 240–8.

LOVELL, K., GRAY, E.A. and OLIVER, D.E. 1964: A further study of some cognitive and other disabilities in backward readers of average non-verbal reasoning scores. *British Journal of Educational Psychology* 34, 275–9.

LOVELL, K., JOHNSON, E. and PLATTS, D. 1962: A summary of a study of the reading ages of children who had been given remedial teaching. *British Journal of Educational Psychology* 32, 66.

LOVELL, K., SHAPTON, D., and WARREN, N.S. 1964: A study of some cognitive and other disabilities in backward readers of average intelligence as assessed by non-verbal test. *British Journal of Educational Psychology* 34, 58–64.

LOVELL, K., and WOOLSEY, M.E. 1964: Reading disability, non-verbal reasoning and social class. *Educational Research* 6, 226.

LUBERT, N. 1981: Auditory perceptual impairments in children with specific language difficulties: A review of the literature. *Journal of Speech and Hearing Disorders* 46, 3–9.

LULHAM, M. 1981: *Books for Dyslexics*. London: Helen Arkell Dyslexia Centre.

LYLE, J.G. 1968: Performance of retarded readers on the memory for designs tests. *Perceptual and Motor Skills* 26, 851–4.

—— 1969: Reading retardation and reversal tendency: A factorial study. *Child Development* 40, 832–43.

—— 1970: Certain antenatal, perinatal and developmental variables and reading retardation in middle class boys. *Child Development* 41, 481–91.

LYLE, J.G. and GOYEN, J. 1968: Visual recognition, developmental lag, and strephosymbolia in reading retardation. *Journal of Abnormal Psychology* 73, 25–9.

—— 1969: Performance of retarded readers on the WISC and educational tests. *Journal of Abnormal Psychology* 74, 105–12.

—— 1975: Effect of speed of exposure and difficulty of discrimination on visual recognition of retarded readers. *Journal of Abnormal Psychology* 8, 673–6.

LYON, R. 1977: Auditory perceptual training: The state of the art. *Journal of Learning Disabilities* 10, 564–72.

MCBURNEY, A.K. and DUNN, A.G. 1976: Handedness, footedness, eyedness: A prospective study with special reference to the development of speech and language skills. In Knights, R.M. and Bakker, D.J. (eds.), *The Neuropsychology of Learning Disorders*. Baltimore: University Park Press.

MCCLERN, G.E. 1978: Review of dyslexia: genetic aspects. In Benton, A. and Pearl, D. (eds.), *Dyslexia, An Appraisal of Current Knowledge. New York*: Oxford University Press.

MCDONALD, A. 1964: Research for the classroom, reading potential, appraisal or prediction. *Journal of Reading* 8, 115–9.

MCGEE, R., WILLIAMS, S., SHARE, D.L., ANDERSON, J. and SILVA, P.A. 1986: The relationship between specific reading retardation, general reading backwardness and behavioural problems in a large sample of Dunedin boys: a longitudinal study from five to eleven years. *Journal of Child Psychology and Psychiatry* 27, 597–611.

MCGRADY, H.J. and OLSON, D.A. 1970: Visual and auditory learning processes in normal children and children with specific learning disabilities. *Exceptional Children* 36, 8, 581–91.

MCKEEVER, W.F. and HULING, M.D. 1970: Lateral dominance in tachistoscopic word recognition of children at two levels of ability. *Quarterly Journal of Experimental Psychology* 22, 600–4.

MCKEEVER, W.F. and VAN DEVENTER, A.D. 1975: Dyslexic adolescents: evidence of impaired visual and auditory language processing associated with normal lateralization and visual responsivity. *Cortex* 11, 361–78.

MCLEOD, J. 1965: A comparison of WISC subject scores of preadolescent successful and unsuccessful readers. *Australian Journal of Educational Psychology* 17, 220–8.

—— 1966: Dyslexia in young children: a factorial study with special reference to the ITPA. *IREC Papers in Education*, University of Illinois.

MCNINCH, G. and RICHMOND M. 1972: Auditory perceptual tasks as predictors of first grade reading success. *Perceptual and Motor Skills* 35, 7–13.

MCRARE, R. and WARREN, S.A. 1978: Inadequate and adequate readers performance on a dichotic listening task. *Perceptual and Motor Skills* 46, 709–10.

MACCOBY, E.E. and JACKLIN, A.N. 1974: *The Psychology of Sex Differences*. Stanford, California: Stanford University Press.

MACKWORTH, J.F. 1971: Some models of the reading process: Learners and skilled readers. In Kling, M., Davis, E.B. and Geyer, J.J. (eds.), *The Literature of Research in Reading with Emphasis on Models Project no. 2* Cornell University: US Office of Education No. 0–9030.

—— 1972: Some models of the reading process: Learners and skilled readers. *Reading Research Quarterly* 7, 701–33.

MAISTO, A. and SIPE, S. 1980: An examination of encoding and retrieval processes in reading disabled children. *Journal of Experimental Child Psychology* 30, 223–30.

MAKITA, K. 1968: The rarity of reading disability in Japanese children. *American Journal of Orthopsychiatry* 38, 599–614.

—— 1974: Dyslexia and orthography. In Moyle, D. (ed.), *Reading: What of the Future?* London: Ward Lock Educational.

MALMQUIST, E. 1958: *Factors Related to Reading Disabilities in Five Grades of Elementary School*. Stockholm: Almquist & Wiksell.

MANN, V.A., LIBERMAN, I.Y. and SHANKWEILER, D. 1980: Children's memory for sentences and word strings in relation to reading ability. *Memory and Cognition* 8, 4, 329–35.

MANZO, A.V. 1977: Dyslexia as a specific psycho-neurosis. *Journal of Reading Behaviour* 9, 3, 305–8.

MARCEL, T. 1980: Phonological awareness and phonological representation: Investigation of a specific spelling problem. In Frith, U. (ed.), *Cognitive Processes in Spelling*. London: Academic Press.

MARCEL, T., KATZ, K. and SMITH, M. 1974: Laterality and reading proficiency *Neuropsychologia* 12, 131–9.

MARCEL, T. and RAJAN, P. 1975: Lateral specialization for recognition of words and faces in good and poor readers. *Neuropsychologia* 13, 489–97.

MARK, L.S., SHANKWEILER, D., LIBERMAN, I.Y. and FOWLER, C.A. 1977: Phonetic recoding and reading difficulty in beginning readers. *Memory and Cognition* 5, 623–9.

MARSHALL, J.C. 1982: *Developmental and Acquired Dyslexia, Some Parallels*. Paper presented to 'Focus on Dyslexia Conference', Egham Dyslexia Institute/British Dyslexia Association.

MARSHALL, J.C. and NEWCOMBE, F. 1973: Patterns of paralexia: A psycholinguistic approach. *Journal of Psycholinguistic Research* 2, 175–99.

MARTIN, J.G. 1972: Rhythmic (hierarchical) versus serial structure in speech and other behaviour. *Psychological Research* 79, 487–509.

MASLAND, R.L. 1968: Some neurological processes underlying language. *Annals of Otology, Rhinology and Laryngology* 77, 787–804.

—— 1981: Neurological aspects of dyslexia. In Pavlides, G. and Miles, T. (eds.), *Dyslexia Research and its Applications to Education*. Chichester: Wiley.

MASLOW, P., FROSTIG, M., LEFEVER, D. and WHITTLESEY, J.R. 1963: The Marianne Frostig Developmental Test of visual perception 1963 Standardisation. *Perceptual and Motor Skills* 19, 463–99.

MATTHEWS, B.A. and SEYMOUR, C.M. 1981: The performance of learning disabled children on tests of auditory discrimination. *Journal of Learning Disabilities* 14, 1, 9–11.

MATTINGLY, I.G. 1972: Reading, the linguistic process, and linguistic awareness. In Kavanagh, J.F. and Mattingly, I.G. (eds.), *Language by Ear and Eye*. Cambridge, Mass.: The MIT Press.

MATTIS, S., FRENCH, J.H. and RAPIN, I. 1975: Dyslexia in children and young adults: Three independent neuropsychological syndromes. *Developmental Medicine and Child Neurology* 17, 150–63.

MATTIS, S. 1978: A working hypothesis that works. In Benton, A. and Pearl, D. (eds.), *Dyslexia, an Appraisal of Current Knowledge*. New York: Oxford University Press.

MENYUK, P. 1971: *The Acquistion and Development of Language*, New York: Prentice-Hall

MESSER, S. 1967: Implicit phonology in children. *Journal of Verbal Learning and Verbal Behaviour* 6, 609–13.

MICCINATI, J. 1979: The Fernald Tracing Technique: modifications increase the probability of success. *Journal of Learning Disabilities* 13, 3.

MILES, E. 1982: *The Bangor Teaching Programme*. Wales, Bangor Dyslexia Unit.

MILES, T. 1970: *On Helping the Dyslexic Child.* London: Methuen.

—— 1974: *Understanding Dyslexia.* London: Priory Press.

—— 1982: *Dyslexia: The Pattern of Difficulties.* St Albans: Granada.

MILES, T. and ELLIS, N. 1981: A lexical encoding deficiency I and II. Experimental evidence and classical observations. In Pavlidis, G. and Miles, T. (eds.), *Dyslexia Research and its Application to Education.* Chichester; Wiley.

MILES, T.R. and HASLUM, M.N. 1986: Dyslexia: Anomaly or normal variation *Annals of Dyslexia,* 36.

MILES, T.R. and MILES, E. 1975: *More Help for the Dyslexic Child.* London: Methuen.

MILES, T. R. and WHEELER, T.J. 1974: Towards a new theory of dyslexia. *Dyslexia Review* 11, 9–11.

MILLER, G. 1967: The magic number 7 plus or minus 2. In Miller, G. (ed.), *The Psychology of Communication.* Harmondsworth: Penguin.

MILLER, G.A. 1969: The organization of lexical memory; Are word associations sufficient? In Talland, G.A. and Waugh, N.C. (eds.), *The Pathology of Memory.* New York: Academic Press.

MILNER, B. 1962: Laterality effects in audition. In Mountcastle, V.B. (ed.), *Interhemispheric Relations and Cerebral Dominance.* Baltimore: Johns Hopkins University Press.

—— 1971: Interhemispheric differences in the localization of psychological processes in man. *British Medical Bulletin* 27, 272–7.

MITTLER, P. 1976: *The Psychological Assessment of Mental and Physical Handicaps.* London: Methuen.

MONEY, J. 1966: On learning and not learning to read. In Money, J. (ed.), *The Disabled Reader: Education of the Dyslexic Child.* Baltimore: Johns Hopkins University Press.

MONSEES, E.K. 1961: Aphasia in children. *Journal of Speech and Hearing Disorders* 26, 23–86.

MONTGOMERY, D. 1981: Do dyslexics have difficulty accessing articulatory information? *Psychological Research* 43, 2, 235–45.

MORANT, C. 1904: Code of regulations for public elementary schools. Cd. 2074, 1–3 cited by Van Der Eyken, W. (1973), *Education, The Child and Society* Harmondsworth: Penguin.

MORENCY, A., WEPMAN, J. and HASS, S.K. 1970: Developmental speech inaccuracy and speech therapy in the early school years. *Elementary School Journal* 70, 219–24.

MOREHEAD, D.M. 1971: Processing of phonological sequences by young children and adults. *Child Development* 42, 279–89.

MORGAN, W.P. 1896: A case of congenital word-blindness. *British Medical Journal* 11, 378.

MORRIS, R. 1966: *Standards and Progress in Reading.* Slough: NFER

MORTON, J. 1977: *Perception and Memory in Cognitive Psychology Memory* (Pt. 1) 0303,3, Unit 13–15, Milton Keynes: Open University Press.

—— 1979: Word recognition. In Morton, J. and Marshall, J.C. (eds.), *Psycholinguistics Series 2: Structures and Processes.* London: Elek.

—— 1980: The logogen model and orthographic structure. In Frith, U. (ed.), *Cognitive Processes in Spelling.* London: Academic Press.

—— 1987: An information processing account of reading acquisition. *Paper to 'From Neurons to Reading' Symposium,* June, Florence.

MORTON, J. and PATTERSON, K. 1980: A new attempt at an interpretation, or an attempt at a new interpretation. In Coltheart, M., Patterson, K. and Marshall, J.C. (eds.), *Deep Dyslexia.* London: Routledge & Kegan Paul.

MORRISON, F.J., GIODANI, B. and NAGY, J. 1977: Reading disability: An information processing analysis, *Science* 196, 77–9.

MOSKOWITZ, B.A. 1973: On the status of vowel shift in English. In Moore, T.E. (ed.), *Cognitive Development and the Acquisition of Language*. New York: Academic Press.

MOSCOVITCH, M. 1977: The development of lateralisation of language functions and its relation to cognitive and linguistic development. In Segalowitz, S.J. and Gruber, F.A. (eds.), *Language Development and Neurological Theory*. New York: Academic Press.

MOSELEY, D.V. 1972: Children who find reading and spelling difficult. In Brennan, W.K. (ed.) *Aspects of Remedial Education*. London: Longman.

MOSSE, H.Z. and DANIELS, C.R. 1959: Linear dyslexia. *American Journal of Psychotherapy* 13, 826–41.

MOTFESE, D.L., FREEMAN, R.B. and PALERMO, D.S. 1975: The ontogeny of brain lateralisation for speech and non speech stimuli, *Brain and Language* 2, 356–68.

MUEHL, S. and FORELL, E.R. 1973: A follow-up study of disabled readers: variables related to high school reading performance. *Reading Research Quarterly* 9, 110–23.

MUEHL, S., KNOTT, J.R. and BENTON, A.L. 1965: EEG abnormality and psychological test performance in reading disability. *Cortex* 1, 434–40.

MUEHL, S. and KREMENAK, S. 1966: Ability to match information within and between auditory and visual sense modalities and subsequent reading achievement. *Journal of Educational Psychology* 57, 230–9.

MURDOCH, B.D. 1974: Changes in the electroencephalogram in minimal cerebral dysfunction. Controlled study over 8 months. *South African Medical Journal* 48, 606–10.

MYERS, P.I. and HAMMILL, D.D. 1976: *Methods for Learning Disorders* (2nd edn,) New York: Wiley.

MYKLEBUST, H.R. and JOHNSON, D.J. 1962: Dyslexia in children. *Exceptional Children* 29, 14–25.

MYKLEBUST, H.R. and BOSHES, B. 1969: *Final Report Minimal Brain Damage in Children*. Washington DC: Dept. of Health, Education and Welfare.

MYKLEBUST, H.R. (ed.) 1978: *Progress in Learning Disabilities* vol IV. New York: Grune & Stratton.

NAIDOO, S. 1972: *Specific Dyslexia*. London: Pitman.

NELSON, H.E. 1974: The etiology of specific spelling disabilities- a neuropsychologist's approach. In Wade, B. and Wedell, K. (eds.), *Spelling Task and Learner*. Birmingham: Educational Review Occasional Publication No. 5.

—— 1980: Analysis of spelling errors in normal and dyslexic children. In Frith, U. (ed.), *Cognitive Processes in Spelling*. London: Academic Press.

NELSON, H.E. and WARRINGTON, E.K. 1974: Developmental spelling retardation and its relation to other cognitive abilities. *British Journal of Psychology* 65, 265–74.

—— 1976: Developmental spelling retardation. In Knights, R.M. and Bakker, D.J. (eds.), *The Neuropsychology of Learning Disorders—Theoretical Approaches*. Baltimore: University Park Press

—— 1980: An investigation of memory functions in dyslexic children. *British Journal of Psychology* 71, 487–503.

NEVILLE, D. 1961: A comparison of WISC patterns of male retarded and non-retarded readers. *Journal of Educational Research* 54, 195.

NEWELL, D. and RUGEL, P. 1981: Hemisphere specialisation in normal and disabled readers. *Journal of Learning Disabilities* 14, 5, 296–77.

NEWSON, J. and NEWSON, E. 1965: Patterns & Infant love. Harmondsworth: Penguin.

NEWTON, M. 1970: A neuro-psychological investigation into dyslexia. In Franklin, A.W. and Naidoo, S. (eds.), *Assessment and Teaching of Dyslexic Children*. London: ICAA.

—— 1974: *Dyslexia: Towards Diagnosis*. Unpublished Ph.D. thesis, University of Aston.

NEWTON, M.J. and THOMSON, M.E. 1975: *Dyslexia: A Guide for Teachers and Parents*. London: University of London Press.

—— 1976: *The Aston Index: A Screening Procedure for Written Language Difficulties*. Wisbech: Learning Development Aids.

NEWTON, M.J., THOMSON, M.E. and RICHARDS, I. (eds.), 1979: *Reading in Dyslexia*. Wisbech: Learning Development Aids.

NICHOLS, A.S. 1947: *To Optometry this 1946 Yearbook*. Published by the author in USA.

NIELSEN, H.H. and RINGE, K. 1969: Visuo-perceptive and visuo-motor performance of children with reading disabilities. *Scandinavian Journal of Psychology* 10, 225–31.

NOBLE, J. 1968: Paradoxical interlocular transfer of mirror-image discrimination in the optic chiasm sectioned monkey. *Brain Research* 10, 127–51.

NODINE, C.F. and LANG, N.J. 1971: Development of visual scanning strategies for differentiating words. *Developmental Psychology* 5, 221–32.

NOELKER, R.W. and SCHUMSKY, P.A. 1973: Memory for sequence, form and position as related to the identification of reading retardation. *Journal of Educational Psychology* 64, 22–5.

NORMAN, D.A. 1976: *Memory and Attention: An Introduction to Human Information Processing*. New York: Wiley.

OAKLAND, T.D. 1969: Auditory discrimination and socio-economic status on correlates of reading ability. *Journal of Learning Disabilities* 2, 324–9.

OBRZAT, J.E. 1979: Dichotic listening and bisensory memory in qualitatively dyslexic readers. *Journal of Learning Disabilities* 12, 5, 304–13.

O'CONNOR, N. and HERMELIN, B. 1978: *Seeing and Hearing in Time and Space*. London: Academic Press.

O'DONNELL, P.A. and EISENSON, J. 1969: Delacato training for reading and achievement and visual-motor integration. *Journal of Learning Disabilities* 2, 441–50.

OHLSON, E.L. 1978: *Identification of specific learning disabilities*. Chicago, Ill.: Research Press.

OLSON, A.V. and JOHNSON, G.I. 1970: Structure and predictive value of the Frostig Developmental Test of visual perception in Grades 1 and 3. *Journal of Special Education* 41, 1, 49.

OLSON, D.R. and BAKER, N.E. 1969: Children's recall of spatial orientation of objects. *The Journal of Genetic Psychology* 114, 273–81.

OLSON, M.E. 1973: Laterality differences in tachistoscopic word recognition in normal and delayed readers in elementary school. *Neuropsychologia* 11, 343–50.

OLSON, R., KLIEGEL, R. and DAVIDSON, F. 1983: Dyslexics and normal readers' eye movements. *Journal of Experimental Psychology, Human Perception and Performance* 9, 816–25.

OLSON, R.K., KLIEGEL, R., DAVIDSON, B.J. and DAVIES, S.E. 1984: Development of phonetic memory in disabled and normal readers. *Journal of Experimental Child Psychology* 37, 187–206.

OPCS *Population Trends* 1981. London: HMSO.

ORNSTEIN, R. 1975: *The Psychology of Consciousness*. Harmondsworth: Penguin.

ORTON, S.T. 1925: Word-blindness in school children. *Archives of Neurology and Psychiatry* 14, 581–615.

—— 1937: *Reading, Writing and Speech Problems in Children*. London: Chapman Hall.

OSGOOD, C.E. and MIRON, M.S. (eds.) 1963: *Approaches to the Study of Aphasia*. Urbana, Ill.: University of Illinois Press.

OSMAN, C. 1982: Computer program competition. *Sunday Times Magazine*, October.

OTTO, W. 1961: The acquisition of retention of paired associates by good, average and poor readers. *Journal of Educational Psychology* 52, 241–8.

OWEN, F.W., ADAMS, P.A., FORREST, T., STOLZ, L.M. and FISHER, S. 1971: *Learning Disorders in Children: Sibling Studies*. Monographs of the Society for Research in Child Development, 36, no. 4.

—— 1978: Dyslexia—genetic aspects. In Benton, A.I. and Pearl, D. (eds.), *Dyslexia, an Appraisal of Current Knowledge*. New York: Oxford University Press.

PARASKAVOPOULOS, J.N. and KIRK, S. 1969: *The Development and Psychometric Characteristics of the Revised Illinois Test of Psycholinguistic Abilities*. Urbana, Ill.: University of Illinois Press.

PARK, G.E. and SCHNEIDER, K.A. 1975: Thyroid function in relation to dyslexia (reading failures). *Journal of Reading Behaviour* 7, 197–9.

PATERRA, M.C. 1963: A study of thirty three WISC scattergrams of retarded readers. *Elementary English* 40, 394.

PATTERSON, K. 1981: Neuropsychological approaches to the study of reading. *British Journal of Psychology* 72, 151–74.

PATTERSON, K. and PARCEL, A.J. 1977: Aphasia, dyslexia and the phonological coding of written words. *Quarterly Journal of Experimental Psychology* 29, 307–18.

PAVLIDES, G.TH. 1978: The dyslexic's erratic eye movements. *Dyslexia Review* 1, 1.

—— 1981: Sequencing, eye movements and the early objective diagnosis of dyslexia. In Pavlides, G.Th. and Miles, T. (eds.), *Dyslexia: Research and its Applications to Dyslexia*. Chichester: Wiley.

PAVLIDES, G. and FISHER, D. (eds.) 1986: *Dyslexia: its neuropsychology and treatment*. Chichester: Wiley.

PERFETTI, C.A. and GOLDMAN, S. R. 1976: Discourse memory and reading comprehension skill. *Journal of Verbal Learning and Verbal Behaviour* 14, 33–42.

PERFETTI, C.A., BELL, L.C., HOGABOAM, T.W. and GOLDMAN, S.R. 1977: *Verbal Processing Speed and Reading Skill*. Paper presented at the Psychonomics Society. Washington, DC.

PERFETTI, C.A. and LESGOLD, A.M. 1978: Discourse comprehension and sources of individual differences. In Just, M.A. and Carpenter, P.A. (eds.), *Cognitive Processes in Comprehension*. Hillsdale, NJ: Lawrence Erlbaum Associates.

PERIN, D. 1981: Spelling, reading and adult literacy. *Psychological Research* 43, 2, 245–55.

PERLO, P. and RAK, T. 1971: Developmental dyslexia in adults. *Neurology* 21, 21, 12233–5.

PFLAUM, S. 1980: The predictability of oral reading behaviours on comprehension in learning disabled and normal readers. *Journal of Reading Behaviour* 12, 3, 231–3.

PIERRE, C. 1974: *Analyse de comprehension de la lecture chez de garçons de l'enseignement primasive normal age de 9 a 12 ans*. Brussels: Institut Libre Marie Haps.

PIROZZOLO, F.J. and RAYNER, K. 1977: Hemispheric specialization in reading and word recognition. *Brain and Language* 4, 248–61.

—— 1978: The neural control of eye movements in acquired and developmental reading disorders. In Avakiam-Whitaker, H. and Whitaker, H.A. (eds.), *Advances in Neurolinguistics and Psycholinguistics*. New York: Academic Press.

POLLOCK, J. 1974: *Dyslexia: The Problem of Spelling*. London: Helen Arkell Dyslexia Centre.

—— 1978: *Signposts to Spelling*: London: Heinemann Educational Books.

POLLOCK, J. and WALLER, E. 1978: *The Problems of Orientation and Sequence.* London: Helen Arkell Dyslexia Centre.

POND, D.A. 1967: Communication disorders in brain-damaged children. *Proceedings of Royal Society of Medicine* 60, 343–8.

POPPEN, R., STARK, J., EISENSON, J. FORREST, T. and WERTHESIN, G. 1969: Visual sequencing performance of aphasic children. *Journal of Speech and Hearing Research* 12, 288–300.

PORAC, C., and COREN, S. 1976: The dominant eye. *Psychological Bulletin* 83, 880–97.

POSNER, M.I., LEWIS, J.L. and CONRAD, C. 1972: Component processes in reading: A performance analysis. In Kavanagh, J.F. and Mattingly, I.G. (eds.), *Language by Ear and by Eye.* Cambridge, Mass.: The MIT Press.

PRESTON, M., GUTHRIE, J.T. and CHILDS, B. 1974: Visual evoked response in normal and disabled readers. *Psychophysiology* 11, 452–7.

PRESTON, M.S., GUTHRIE, J.T., KIRCH, I., GERTMAN, D. and CHILDS, B. 1977: VERS in normal and disabled readers. *Psychophysiology* 14, 8–14.

PUMFREY, P.D. and NAYLOR, J. 1978: The alleviation of psycho-linguistic deficits and some effects on the reading attainments of poor readers. *Journal of Research in Reading* 1, 2, 87–107.

RABINOVITCH, R.D. 1959: Reading and learning disabilities. In Arieti, S. (ed.), *American Handbook of Psychiatry.* New York: Basic Books.

—— 1968: Reading problems in children: Definitions and classification. In Keeney, A. and Keeney, V. (eds.), *Dyslexia: Diagnosis and Treatment of Reading Disorders.* St Louis: C.V. Mosby.

RABINOVITCH, R.D., DREW, A.L., DE JONG, R.N., INGRAM, W. and WITHEY, C.I. 1964: A research approach to reading retardation. *Public Association for Research in Nervous and Mental Diseases* 34, 363.

RAPIN, I. and WILSON, B.C. 1978: Children with developmental language disability: Neurological aspects and assessment. In Wyke, M. (ed.), *Developmental Aphasia.* London: Academic Press.

RASMUSSEN, J. and MILNER, B. 1975: Clinical and surgical studies of the cerebral speech areas in man. In Zulch, K.J., Creutzfeldt, O. and Galbraith, G.C. (eds.), *Fifth Symposium on Cerebral Lateralisation.* Heidelberg: Springer-Verlag.

RAVENETTE, A.T. 1961: Vocabulary level and reading attainment. *British Journal of Educational Psychology* 31, 96–103.

—— 1968: *Dimensions of Reading Difficulties.* Oxford: Pergamon.

RAWSON, M.B. 1968: *Developmental Language Disability.* Baltimore: Johns Hopkins University Press

—— 1975: Developmental dyslexia: educational treatments and results. In Duane, D.D. and Rawson, M.B. (eds.), *Reading, Perception and Language.* Baltimore: York Press.

RAY, W.J., MORELL, M., FREDIANI, A.W. and TUCKER, D.M. 1976: Sex differences and lateral specialisation of hemisphere functioning. *Neuropsychologia* 14, 391–4.

REBERT, C.S. and WEXLER, B.N. 1977: EEG lateralisation as a function of task and language disorder in children. *Electroencephalography and Clinical Neurophysiology* 42, 722–3.

READER, J.C. 1967: Lateralized finger agnosia and reading achievement at ages 6 and 10. *Child Development* 38, 213–20.

—— 1968: The ability deficits of good and poor readers. *Journal of Learning Disabilities* 2, 134, 9.

REHAB. 1974: *People with Dyslexia: Report of Working Party.* London: British Council for the rehabilitation of the disabled.

REITAN, R.M. 1966: A research program on the psychological effects of brain lesions in human beings. In Ellis, N.R. (ed.), *International Review of Research in Mental Retardation* vol. 1. New York: Academic Press.

RICHARDSON, E., DI BENEDETTON, B. and BRADLEY, C.M. 1977: The relationship of sound blending to reading achievement. *Review of Educational Research* 47, 319–34.

RICHMAN, L. and KITCHELL, M. 1981: Hyperlexia as a variant of developmental language disorder. *Brain and Language* 12, 203–12.

ROBBINS, M.P. 1966: A study of the validity of Delacato's theory of neurological organisation. *Exceptional Children* 32, 517–23.

RODGERS, B. 1983: The identification and prevalence of specific reading retardation. *British Journal of Educational Psychology* 53, 369–73.

ROEBECK, M.C. and WILSON, J.A. 1974: *Psychology of Reading*. New York: Wiley.

ROBINSON, M. E. and SCHWARTZ, L.B. 1973: Visuo-motor skills and reading ability: a longitudinal study. *Developmental Medicine and Child Neurology* 15, 281–6.

ROE, M.C. 1965: *Survey into progress of maladjusted pupils*. Report for Inner London Education Authority.

ROGERS, D.C. 1969: *Memory Abilities in Retarded Readers in Reinforcement and Non-Reinforcement Conditions*. Doctoral thesis, University of Toronto.

ROSENTHAL, J.H. 1973: Self esteem in dyslexic children. *Academic Therapy* 9, 1, 27–39.

ROSENZWEIG, M.R. 1954: Cortical correlates of auditory localization and of related perceptual phenomena. *Journal of Comparative and Physiological Psychology* 47, 269–76.

ROSNER, J. 1972: *The development and validation of an individualized perceptual skills curriculum*. Learning Research and Development Center, University of Pittsburgh.

ROURKE, B.P. 1976 a: Issues in the neuropsychological assessment of children with learning disabilities. *Canadian Psychological Review* 17, 89–102.

—— 1976 b: Reading retardation in children: developmental lag or deficit? In Knights, R.M. and Bakker, D.J. (eds.), *Neuropsychology of Learning Disorders: Theoretical Approaches*. Baltimore: University Park Press.

—— 1978: Neuropsychological research in reading retardation: a review. In Benton, A. and Pearl, D. (eds.), *Dyslexia: An Appraisal of Current Knowledge*. New York: Oxford University Press.

ROURKE, B.P., DIETRICH, D.M. and YOUNG, G.C. 1973: Significance of WISC verbal performance discrepancies for younger children with learning disabilities. *Perceptual and Motor Skills* 36, 275–82.

ROZIN, P. and GLEITMAN, L.R. 1977: The structure and acquisition of reading II: The reading process and the acquisition of the alphabetic principle. In Reber, A.S. and Scarborough, D.L. (eds.), *Towards a Psychology of Reading*. Hillsdale, NJ: Lawrence Erlbaum Associates.

ROZIN, P., POVITSKY, S. and SOTSKY, R. 1981: American children with reading problems can easily learn to read English represented by Chinese characters. *Science* 171, 1264–7.

RUBENSTEIN, H., LEWIS, S.S. and RUBENSTEIN, M.A. 1971: Evidence for phonetic recording in visual word recognition. *Journal of Verbal Learning and Verbal Behaviour* 10, 647–57.

RUBINO, C.A. and MINDEN, H.A. 1973: An analysis of eye movements in children with a reading disability. *Cortex* 9, 217–20.

RUDEL, R.G. 1978: Neuroplasticity: Implications for development and education. In Chall, J.S. and Mirsky, A.F. (eds.), *Education and the Brain*. Urbana: University of Chicago Press.

RUDEL, R.G., DENCKLA, M.B. and SPALTEN, E. 1974: The functional asymmetry of Braille letter learning in normal sighted children. *Neurology* 24, 733–8.

—— 1976: Paired associated learning of Morse code and Braille letter names by dyslexic and normal children. *Cortex* 12, 61–70

RUDEL, R.G. and TEUBER, H.L. 1963: Discrimination of direction of line in children. *Journal of Comparative and Physiological Psychology* 56, 892–8.

RUGEL, R.P. 1974: WISC sub-test scores of disabled readers. *Journal of Learning Disabilities* 7, 48–55.

RUTTER, M. 1969: The concept of dyslexia. In Wolff, P. and MacKeith, R.C. (eds.), *Planning for Better Learning*. Developmental Medicine 33. London: Heinemann.

—— 1978: Prevalence and types of dyslexia. In Benton, A. and Pearl, D. (eds.), *Dyslexia: An Appraisal of Current Knowledge*. New York: Oxford University Press.

—— 1979: *Maternal Deprivation Revisited*. Harmondsworth: Penguin.

RUTTER, M., GRAHAM, P. and BIRCH, H.G. 1966: Inter-relations between the choreiform syndrome, reading disability and psychiatric disorder in children of 8–11 years. *Developmental Medicine and Child Neurology* 8, 149–59.

RUTTER, M., TIZARD, J. and WHITMORE, K. 1970: *Education, Health and Behaviour*. London: Longman.

RUTTER, M. and YULE, W. 1973: Specific reading retardation. In Mann, L. and Sabatino, D. (eds.), *The First Review of Special Education*, Philadelphia: Burntwood Farms.

SABATINO, D.A. 1973: Auditory perception: development, assessment and intervention. In Mann, L. and Sabatino, D. (eds.), *The First Review of Special Education*. Philadelphia: Burntwood Farms.

SAKAMOTO, T. and MAKITA, K. 1973: Japan, In Downing, J. (ed.), *Comparative Reading*. New York: Macmillan.

SAMPSON, O. 1976: Fifty years of dyslexia: a review of the literature 1925–1975, II *Practice Research in Education* 15, 39–53.

SAPIR, S.G. and WILSON, B. 1979: *A professional's guide to working with the learning disabled child*. New York: Brunner/Mazel.

SATTERFIELD, J.H., LESSER, L.I., SAUL, R.E. and CANTWELL, D.P. 1973: EEG aspects in the diagnosis and treatment of minimal brain dysfunction. In de la Cruz, F.E., Fox, B.H. and Robert, R.H. (eds.), *Minimal Brain Dsyfunction. Annals of the New York Academy of Sciences* 205, 274–82.

SATZ, P. 1976: Cerebral dominance and reading disability: an old problem revisited. In Knights, R. and Bakker, D.J. (eds.), *The Neuropsychiatry of Learning Disorders: Theoretical Approaches*. Baltimore: University Park Press.

SATZ, P. and FRIEL, J. 1973: Some predictive antecedents of specific reading disability: a preliminary one-year follow-up. In Satz, P. and Ross, J.J. (eds.), *The Disabled Learner: Early Detection and Intervention* Rotterdam: Rotterdam University Press, 78–98.

SATZ, P., FRIEL, J. and RUDEGEAIR, F. 1974: Some predictive antecedents of specific reading disability: A two- three- and four-year follow-up. *The Hyman Blumberg Symposium of Research in Early Childhood Education*. Baltimore: Johns Hopkins University Press.

—— 1976: Some predictive antecedents of specific reading disability: A two-, three-, and four-year follow-up. In Guthrie, J.T., (ed.), *Aspects of Reading Acquistion*. Baltimore: Johns Hopkins University Press.

SATZ, P., RARDIN, D. and ROSS, J. 1971: An evaluation of a theory of specific developmental dyslexia. *Child Development* 42, 2009–21.

SATZ, P. and SPARROW, S.S. 1970: Specific developmental dyslexia: a theoretical formulatio In Bakker, D.J. and Satz, P. (eds.), *Specific Reading Disability: Advances in The and Method*. Rotterdam: Rotterdam University Press.

SATZ, P., TAYLOR, H.G., FRIEL, J. and FLETCHER, J.M. 1978: Some developmental and predictive precursors of reading disabilities: A six year follow-up. In Benton, A.L. and Pearl, D. (eds.), *Dyslexia: An Appraisal of Current Knowledge*. New York: Oxford University Press, 313–48.

SATZ, R. and VAN NOSTRAND, G.K. 1973: Developmental dyslexia: an evaluation of a theory. In Satz, P. and Ross, J. (eds.), *The Disabled Learner: Early Detection and Intervention*. Rotterdam: Rotterdam University Press.

SAVAGE, D. 1968: *The Psychological Assessment of the Child*. Harmondsworth: Penguin.

SAVAGE, R.D. and O' CONNOR, D. 1966: The assessment of reading and arithmetic retardation in school. *British Journal of Educational Psychology* 34, 317–18.

SAVIN, H.B. 1972: What the child knows about speech when he starts to learn to read. In Kavanagh, J.F. and Mattingly, I.G. (eds.), *Language by Ear and Eye*. Cambridge, Mass.: The MIT Press, 319–36.

SAVIN, H.B. and BEVER, T.G. 1970: The nonperceptual reality of the phoneme. *Journal of Verbal Learning and Verbal Behaviour* 9, 297–302.

SCARR-SALAPTEC, S. 1975: Genetics and the development of intelligence. In *Review of Child Development Research* vol 4. Chicago: University of Chicago Press.

SCHAIN, R.J. 1972: *Neurology of Childhood Learning Disorders*. Baltimore: Williams & Wilkins.

SCHEERER-NEUMAN, G. 1978: A functional analysis of reading disability: the utilization of intraword redundancy by good and poor readers. In Lesgold, A. and Pellegrino, J., *Cognitive Psychology and Instruction*. New York: Plenum Press.

—— 1981: The utilization of intraword structure in poor readers: experimental evidence and a training programme. *Psychological Research* 43, 2, 155–79.

SHEVILL, H. 1978: Tactile learning and reading failure. In Myklebust, H. (ed.), *Progress in Learning Disabilities* IV. New York: Grune & Stratton.

SCHIFFMAN, G. 1962: Dyslexia as an educational phenomenon: its recognition and treatment. In Money, J. (ed.), *Reading Disability: Progress and Research Needs in Dyslexia*. Baltimore: Johns Hopkins University Press.

SCHIFFMANN, G. and CLEMMENS, D. 1966: *Learning Disorders vol. II* Seattle: Helmuth, Special Childrens Publication.

SCHULMAN, J. and LEVITON, A. 1978: Reading disabilities: An epidemiological approach. In Myklebust, H. (ed.), *Progress in Learning Disabilities IV*. New York: Grune & Stratton.

SCHWARTZ, M.F., SAFFRAN, E.M. and MARIN, O.S. 1980: Fractionating the reading process in dementia, evidence for word specific print-to-sound associations. In Coltheart, M., Patterson, K. and Marshall, J.C. (eds.), *Deep Dyslexia*. London: Routledge & Kegan Paul.

SEGALOWITZ, S.J. and GRUBER, T.A. (eds.) 1972: *Language Development and Neurological Theory*. New York: Academic Press.

SENF, G.M. 1969: Development of immediate memory for bisensory stimuli in normal children and children with learning disorders. *Developmental Psychology* 6, 28, Pt 2.

SENF, G.M. and FRESHBACH, S. 1970: Development of bisensory memory in culturally deprived dyslexic, and normal readers. *Journal of Educational Psychology* 61, 461–70.

SENF, G.M. and FREUNDL, P.C. 1971: Memory and attention factors in specific learning disabilities. *Journal of Learning Disabilities* 4, 94–106.

—— 1972: Sequential auditory and visual memory in learning disabled children. *Proceedings of the Annual Convention of the American Psychological Association* 7, 511–12.

SEYMOUR, P.H.K. 1986: *Cognitive Analysis of Dyslexia*. London: Routledge and Kegan Paul.

SEYMOUR, P. and MCGREGOR, C.J. 1982: *Characteristics of developmentally dyslexic readers*. Paper presented to BPS Cognitive Psychology Section on Dyslexia, Manchester, March.

SEYMOUR, P.H. and PORPODAS, C.D. 1978: Coding of spelling in normal and dyslexic subjects. In Gruneberg, M. and Morris, P. (eds.), *Practical Aspects of Memory*. London: Academic Press.

—— 1980: Lexical and non-lexical processing of spelling in developmental dyslexia. In Frith, U. (ed.), *Cognitive Processes in Spelling*. London: Academic Press.

SHAKESPEARE, R. 1975: Severely Subnormal Children. In Mittler, P. (ed.), *The Psychological Assessment of Mental and Physical Handicap*. London: Methuen.

SHALLICE, T. and WARRINGTON, E.K. 1980: Single and multiple component central dyslexic syndromes. In Colthear, M., Patterson, K. and Marshall, J.C. (eds.), *Deep Dyslexia*. London: Routledge & Kegan Paul.

SHANKWEILER, D. 1963: A study of developmental dyslexia. *Neuropsychologia* 1, 267–86.

SHANKWEILER, D. and STUDDERT-KENNEDY, M.A. 1975: A continuum of lateralization for speech perception? *Brain and Language* 2, 212–25.

SHANKWEILER, D. and LIBERMAN, A.M. 1972: Misreading; a search for causes. In Kavanagh, J.F. and Mattingly, I.G. (eds.), *Language by Ear and by Eye*. Cambridge, Mass: The MIT Press.

SHANKWEILER, D. and LIBERMAN, I.Y. 1976: Exploring the relations between reading and speech. In Knights, R.M. and Bakker, D.J. (eds.), *Neuropsychology of Learning Disorders: Theoretical Approaches*. Baltimore: University Park Press.

—— 1978: Reading behaviour in dyslexia: is there a distinctive pattern? *Bulletin of the Orton Society* 28, 114–23.

SHANKWEILER, D., LIBERMAN, I.Y., MARK, L.S., FOWLER, C.A. and FISCHER, F.W. 1979: The speech code and learning to read. *Journal of Experimental Psychology Human Learning and Memory* 5, 531–45.

SHARE, D.L., MCGEE, R., MCKENSIE, D., WILLIAMS, S. and SILVA, P. 1987: Further evidence relating to the distinction between specific reading retardation and general reading backwardness. *British Journal of Developmental Psychology*, 5, 35–45.

SHEARER, E. 1968: Physical skills and reading backwardness. *Educational Research* 10, 3, 197–206.

SHRINER, T.H., HOLLOWAY, M.S. and DANILOFF, R.G. 1969: The relationship between articulatory deficits and syntax in speech defective children. *Journal of Speech Hearing Research* 12, 319–25.

SILVER, A.A. 1968: Diagnostic considerations in children with reading disability. In Natchez, L. (ed.), *Children with Reading Problems*. New York: Basic Books.

SILVER, A.A. and HAGIN, R. 1960: Specific reading disability: Delineation of the syndrome and relationship to cerebral dominance. *Comparative Psychiatry* 1, 2, 126–34.

—— 1964: Specific reading disability: follow-up studies. *American Journal of Orthopsychiatry* 34, 95–102.

—— 1970: Visual perception in children with reading disabilities. In Young, F.A. and Lindsley, D.B. (eds.), *Early Experience and Visual Information Processing in Perceptual and Reading Disorders*. Washington: National Academy of Sciences.

—— 1972: Profile of a first grade: A basis for preventive psychiatry. *Journal of American Academy of Child Psychiatry* 11, 645–74.

—— 1975: *Search: a Scanning Instrument for the Identification of Potential Learning ability: Experimental Edition*. New York: New York University Medical Center.

—— 1976: *Search*. New York: Walker Educational Book Corp.

SILVER, L.B. 1971: A proposed view on the etiology of the neurological learning disability syndrome. *Journal of Learning Disabilities* 4, 132–4

SIMON, A. and WARD, L. 1978: Further doubts about the Frostig Test of Visual Perception. *Remedial Education* 13, 4, 200–3.

SINGER, J.E., WESTPHAL, M. and NISWANDER, K.R. 1968: Sex differences in the incidence of neonatal abnormalities and abnormal performance in early childhood. *Child Development* 39, 103–12.

SKLAR, B., HANLEY, J. and SIMMONS, W.W. 1972: An EEG experiment aimed toward identifying dyslexic children. *Nature* 241, 414–16.

—— 1973: A computer analysis of EEG spectral signatures from normal and dyslexic children. *Institute of Electronics and Electrical Engineering Transactions of Biomedical Engineering* 20, 20–6.

SLADEN, B.K. 1971: Inheritance of dyslexia. *Bulletin of the Orton Society* 31, 30–9.

SLINGERLAND, B.H. 1971: *A Multisensory Approach to Language Arts for Specific Language Disability Children*. Cambridge, Mass.: Educational Publishing Service.

SMITH, F. 1971: *Understanding Reading: A Psycholinguistic Analysis of Reading and Learning to Read*. New York: Holt, Rinehart & Winston.

—— 1973: *Psycholinguistics and Reading*. New York: Holt, Rinehart & Winston.

SMITH, M. and RAMUNAS, S. 1971: Elimination of visual field effect by use of a single report technique: evidence for order of report artifact. *Journal of Experimental Psychology* 87, 23–8.

SMITH, P.A. and MARX, R.W. 1971: The factor structure of the revised edition of the Illinois Test of Psycholinguistic Abilities. *Psychology in Schools* 8, 349–56.

SNOWLING, M.J. 1980: The development of grapheme-phoneme correspondences in normal and dyslexic readers. *Journal of Experimental Child Psychology* 29, 294–305.

—— 1981 a: Phonemic deficits in developmental dyslexia. *Psychological Research* 43, 2, 219–35.

—— 1981 b: *The Spelling of Nasal Clusters by Dyslexic and Normal Children*. Paper presented to 3rd Conference of Simplified Spelling Society, Edinburgh, July.

—— 1982: The assessment of reading and spelling strategies. *Dyslexia Review* 5, 1.

—— 1983: The comparison of acquired and developmental disorders of reading: a discussion. *Cognition*.

—— 1987: *Dyslexia: A cognitive developmental perspective*. Oxford, Blackwell.

SNOWLING, M.J., GOULANDRIS, N., BOWLEY, M. and HOWELL, P. 1986: Segmentation and speech perception in relation to reading skill: a developmental analysis. *Journal of Experimental Child Psychology* 41, 489–507.

SOBOTKA, R. and MAY, J.G. 1977: Visual evoked potentials and reaction time in normal and dyslexic children. *Psychophysiology* 14, 18–24.

SOMMERS, R.K. and TAYLOR, M.L. 1972: Cerebral speech dominance in language disordered and normal children. *Cortex* 8, 224, 32.

SPACHE, G.D. 1976: Investigating the issues of reading disabilities. Cambridge Mass: Allyn & Bacon.

SPARROW, S. 1969: Reading disability and laterality. *Proceedings of the 77th Annual Convention of American Psychological Society* 673–9.

SPARROW, S. and SATZ, P. 1970: Dyslexia, laterality, and neuropsychological development. In Bakker, D.F. and Satz, P. (eds.), *Specific Reading Disability: Advances in Theory and*

Method. Rotterdam: Rotterdam University Press.

SPERLING, G. 1960: The information available in brief visual presentations. *Psychological Monographs. General and Applied* 74, 1, 29.

—— 1963: A model for visual memory tasks. *Human Factors* 5, 19–31.

SPERRY, R.W. 1964: The great cerebral commissure. *Scientific American* 210, 42–52.

SPOEHR, K.T. and SMITH, E.E. 1973: The role of syllables in perceptual processing. *Cognitive Psychology* 5, 71–89.

SPREEN, O. 1978: The dyslexias: A discussion of neurobehavioural research. In Benton, A. and Pearl, D. (eds.), *Dyslexia: An Appraisal of Current Knowledge*. New York: Oxford University Press.

SPRING, C. 1976: Encoding speed and memory span in dyslexic children. *The Journal of Special Education* 10, 1, 35–40.

SPRING, C. and CAPPS, C. 1974: Encoding speed, rehearsal, and probed recall of dyslexic boys. *Journal of Educational Psychology* 66, 780–6.

STANLEY, G. 1975: Visual memory processes in dyslexia. In Deutsch, D. and Deutsch, J.A. (eds.), *Short-term Memory*. New York: Academic Press.

—— 1976: The processing of digits by children with specific reading disability (dyslexia). *British Journal of Educational Psychology* 46, 81–4.

STANLEY, G. and HALL, R. 1973: Short-term visual information processing in dyslexics. *Child Development* 44, 841–4.

STANLEY, G. and MALLOY, M. 1975: Retinal and visual information storage. *Acta Psychologica* 39, 283–8.

STANLEY, G. and WATSON, M. 1980: Comparison of writing and drawing performance of dyslexic boys. *Perceptual and Motor Skills* 51, 776–8.

STANLEY, G., SMITH, G. and HOWELL, E. 1983: Eye movements and sequential tracking in dyslexic and control children. *British Journal of Psychology* 74, 181–7.

STEERE, A., PECK, C. and KAHN, L. 1971: *Solving Language Difficulties*. Cambridge, Mass.: Educators Publishing Service Inc.,

STEIN, J.F. and FOWLER, S. 1981: Diagnosis of dyslexia by means of a new indicator of eye dominance. *British Journal of Ophthalmology* 66, 5, 322–6.

STEINHEISER, R. and GUTHRIE, J.T. 1974: Scanning times through prose and word strings for various targets by normal and disabled readers. *Perceptual and Motor Skills* 39, 931–8.

STEINHEISER, F. and GUTHRIE, J. 1978: Reading ability and efficiency of graph-phonemic encoding. *Journal of Genetic Psychology* 99, 281–91.

STERRITT, G.M. and RUDNICK, M. 1966: Auditory and visual rhythm perception in relation to reading ability in fourth-grade boys. *Perceptual and Motor Skills* 22, 859–64.

STEVENS, D.A. 1967: Presumed minimal brain dysfunction in children. *Archives of General Psychiatry* 16, 281–5.

STEVENSON, H.W., PARKER, T., WILKINSON, A., HEGION, A. and FISH, E. 1976: Longitudinal study of individual differences in cognitive development and scholastic achievement. *Journal of Educational Psychology* 68, 377–400.

STEVENSON, J., GRAHAM, P., FREDMAN, G. and McLOUGHLIN, V. 1987: A twin study on genetic influences on reading and spelling ability and disability. *Journal of Child Psychology and Psychiatry* 28, 229–49.

STOTT, D.H. 1958: *Unsettled Children and their Families*. London: University of London Press.

STRAG, G.A. 1972: Comparative behavioural rating of parents with severe mentally retard[ed] special learning disability and normal children. *Journal of Learning Disabiliti[es]*

52–6.

STUDDERT-KENNEDY, M. and SHANKWEILER, D.P. 1970: Hemispheric specialisation for speech perception. *Journal of Acoustical Society of America* 48, 579–94.

SUPRAMANIAM, S. and AUDLEY, R.J. 1976: *The Role of Naming Difficulties in Reading Backwardness*. Paper presented at the British Association Annual Conference, London.

SUTHERLAND, N.S. 1957: Visual discrimination of orientation by Octopus. *British Journal of Psychology* 48, 55–71.

SYMMES, J.S. and RAPOPORT, J.L. 1972: Unexpected reading failure. *American Journal of Orthopsychiatry* 42, 1, 82–91.

TALLAL, P. 1976: Auditory perceptual factors in language and learning disorders. In Knights, R.M. and Bakker, D. (eds.), *The Neuropsychology of Learning Disorders*. Baltimore: University Park Press.

—— 1980: Auditory temporal perception, phonics and reading disabilities in children. *Brain and Language* 9, 182, 98.

—— 1981: Language disabilities in children: Perceptual correlates. *International Journal of Pediatric Otorhinolaryngology* 3, 1–13.

TALLAL, P. and PIERCY, M. 1974: Developmental aphasia: Rate of auditory processing and selective impairment of consonant perception. *Neuropsychologia* 12, 83–93.

TANSLEY, P. and PANCKHURST, J. 1981: *Children with Specific Learning Disabilities*. NFER Report. Slough: NFER/Nelson.

TARNOPOL, L. and TARNOPOL, E. 1976: *Reading Disabilities; An International Perspective*. Baltimore: University Park Press.

TAYLOR, D.C. 1969: Differential rates of cerebral maturation between sexes and between hemispheres. *The Lancet* 2, 140–2.

TAYLOR, L.B. 1962: *Perception of digits to right and left ears in children with learning difficulties*. Paper to meeting of Canadian Psychological Association, Hamilton, Canada.

TAYLOR, S.E., FRANCKENPOHL, H. and PETTE, S.L. 1960: Grade level norms for components of fundamental reading skill. *EDC Information Research Bulletin 3*. New York: Education Development Labs.

TEMPLE, C.M. 1986: Developmental dysgraphias. *Quarterly Journal of Experimental Psychology* 38A, 77–110.

THOMSON, M.E. 1975: Laterality and reading: a research note. *British Journal of Educational Psychology* 45, 317–21.

—— 1976: Laterality effects in dyslexics and controls using verbal dichotic listening tasks. *Neuropsychologia* 14, 243–6.

—— 1977: The Aston Index; A classroom screening test for written language difficulties. *Journal of British Association for Teachers of the Deaf*. 1, 4.

—— 1977: *Individual Differences in the Acquisition of Written Language: An Integrated Model and its Implications for Dyslexia*. PhD Thesis, University of Aston.

—— 1978 a: A psycholinguistic analysis of reading errors made by dyslexic and normal readers. *Journal of Research in Reading* 1, 1, 7–20.

—— 1978 b: *Stress reaction to dyslexia*. Paper to the International Conference on the Child under Stress, Monte Carlo, 15–21, October.

—— 1979 a: Identifying the dyslexic child. *Dyslexic Review* 18, 12–14.

—— 1979 b: The nature of written language. In Newton, M.J., Thomson, M.E., and Richards, I.R., *Readings in Dyslexia: A Study Text to Accompany the Aston Index*. Wisbech: Learning Development Aids.

—— 1979 c: A Bayesian model for the identification of the disabled reader. In Newton, M.J., Thomson, M.E. and Richards, I.R., *Reading in Dyslexia: A Study Text to Accompany the Aston Index*. Wisbech: Learning Development Aids.

—— 1979 d: Featural dependancies and the use of sequential redundancy in the visual identification of words in dyslexics and controls. In Newton, M.J., Thomson, M.E. and Richards, I.R., *Readings in Dyslexia: A study text to accompany the Aston Index*. Wisbech: Learning Development Aids.

—— 1979 e: The Aston Intervention Programme. In Raggett, M., Tutt, C. and Raggett, P. (eds.), *Assessment and Testing of Reading: Problems and Practice*. London: Ward Lock Educational.

—— 1980: *The development of written language skills in dyslexic children: a reading and spelling error analysis*. Paper presented to British Psychological Society, Developmental Section, Annual Conference, Edinburgh, September.

—— 1981: An analysis of spelling errors in dyslexic children. *First Language* ii, 141–50.

—— 1982 a: Assessing the intelligence of the dyslexic child. *British Psychological Society Bulletin* 35, 94–6.

—— 1982 b: The assessment of children with specific reading difficulties (dyslexia) using the British Ability Scales. *British Journal of Psychology* 73, 461–78.

—— 1982 c: Written and spoken language difficulties in children with specific learning disorders. *Australian Journal of Remedial Education* 14, 182–4.

—— 1982 d: *Reading and spelling errors in dyslexic children: delayed or deviant?* Paper to BPS Cognitive Psychology section conference on dyslexia; Manchester, March.

—— 1982 e: *Problems in the Psychological Assessment of Dyslexics*. Focus on Dyslexia Conference BDA/Dyslexia Institute, Egham, April.

—— 1985: *Word Quest: A spelling adventure game*. Wisbech: Learning Development Aids.

—— 1988: Preliminary findings concerning the effects of specialised teaching on dyslexic children. *Applied Cognitive Psychology* 2, 19–33.

—— 1989a: *The Book of Letters*. Wisbech: Learning Development Aids.

—— 1989b: Teaching programmes for children with specific learning difficulties: Implications for teachers. In Elliott C. and Pumfrey P. (eds.), *Primary School Pupils' Reading and Spelling Difficulties*. London: Falmer Press (in press).

—— 1989c: Teaching the Dyslexic Child: Some evaluation studies to be published as Proceedings of Bath International Conference on Dyslexia. *British Dyslexia Association* in press.

THOMSON, M.E. and HARTLEY, G.M. 1980: A study of self-concept in dyslexic children. *Academic Therapy* 16, 1, 19–36.

THOMSON, M.E., HICKS, C. and WILSHER, C. 1980: Specific written language difficulty in children: a clinical and factorial description. Unpublished Paper, University of Aston.

THOMSON, M.E., HICKS, C., JOFFE, L. and WILSHER, C. 1981: The use of the British Ability Scales amongst children with dyslexia. *Dyslexia Review* 4, 2, 18–22.

THOMSON, M.E. and GRANT, S.E. 1979: The WISC subtest profiles of the dyslexic child. In Newton, M.J., Thomson, M.E. and Richards, I.R., *Readings in Dyslexia: A Study Text to Accompany the Aston Index*. Wisbech: Learning Development Aids.

THOMSON, M.E. and NEWTON, M.J. 1979: A concurrent validity study of the Aston Index. In Newton, M.J., Thomson, M.E. and Richards, I.R., *Readings in Dyslexia: A Study to Accompany the Aston Index*. Wisbech: Learning Development Aids.

THOMSON, M.E., NEWTON, M.J. and RICHARDS, I. 1979: The Aston Index as a predic written language difficulties: A Longitudinal study. In Newton, M.J., Thomson, and Richards, I.R., *Readings in Dyslexia: A Study Text to Accompany the Aston Index*. Wisbech: Learning Development Aids.

THOMSON, M.E. and WILSHER, C. 1979: Some aspects of memory in dyslexics and controls. In Gruneberg, M., Morris, P. and Sykes, R. (eds.), *Practical Aspects of Memory*. London: Academic Press.

THOMPSON, B.B. 1963: A longitudinal study of auditory discrimination. *Journal of Educational Research* 56, 376–8.

TINKER, K.J. 1965: The role of laterality in reading disability. In Figurel, J.A. (ed.), *Reading and Enquiry*. Newark, Delaware: International Reading Association.

TINKER, M.A. 1958: Recent studies of eye movements in reading. *Psychological Bulletin* 55, 215–31.

—— 1965: *Bases for Effective Reading*. Minneapolis: University of Minnesota Press.

Tizard Report, Dept. of Education and Science 1972: *Report of the Advisory Committee on Handicapped Children*. London: HMSO.

TIZARD, J. 1974: The epidemiology of handicapping conditions of educational concern. In Pringle, M. and Varma, V. (eds.), *Advances in Educational Psychology*. London: University of London Press.

TORGESON, J.K. 1977: Memorization process in reading disabled children. *Journal of Educational Psychology* 69, 571–8.

TORGESEN, J. and GOLDMAN, T. 1977: Verbal rehearsal and short term memory in reading disabled children. *Child Development* 48, 1, 56–60.

TORRES, F. and AYERS, F.W. 1968: Evaluation of the electroencephalogram of dyslexic children. *Electroencephalography and Clinical Neurophysiology* 24, 281–94.

TRIESCHMAN, R.B. 1968: Undifferentiated handedness and perceptual development in children with reading problems. *Perceptual and Motor Skills* 27, 1123–34.

TUCKER, D.M. 1976: Sex differences in hemispheric specialisation for synthetic visuospatial functions. *Neuropsychologia* 14, 447–54.

TYLER, S. and ELLIOTT, C.D. 1988: Cognitive profiles of groups of poor readers and dyslexic children on the British Ability Scales. *British Journal of Psychology* 79, 493–509.

TZENG, O. and HUNG, D. 1980: Reading in a nonalphabetic writing system. In Kavanagh, J.F. and Venesky, R.L. (eds.) *Orthography Reading and Dyslexia*. Baltimore: University Park Press.

UNDERWOOD, G. (ed.) 1978: *Strategies of Information Processing*. London: Academic Press.

VALTIN, R. 1970: *Legasthenie Theorien und Untersuchungen*. Weinheim: Beltz.

—— 1973: *Report of research on dyslexia in children*. Paper to Annual Convention of IRA, Denver, ERIC Document.

VANDE VOORT, L. and SENF, G.M. 1973: Audiovisual integration in retarded readers. *Journal of Learning Disabilities* 6, 170–9.

VANDE VOORT, L., SENF, G.M. and BENTON, A L. 1972: Development of audiovisual integration in normal and retarded readers. *Child Development* 44, 1260–72.

VAN DER WESSEL, A. and ZEGER, F.E. 1985: Reading retardation revisited. *British Journal of Developmental Psychology* 3, 3–19.

VAN DUYNE, H.J. and BAKKER, D.J. 1976: *The development of ear asymmetry related to coding processes in memory in children*. Paper presented at the meeting of the International Neuropsychological Society, Toronto.

VELLUTINO, F.R. 1978: Toward an understanding of dyslexia: Psychological factors in specific reading disability. In Benton, A. and Pearl, D. (eds.), *Dyslexia: An Appraisal of*

Current Knowledge. New York: Oxford University Press.

—— 1979: *Dyslexia—Theory and Research*. Cambridge, Mass.: The MIT Press.

VELLUTINO, F.R., BENTLEY, W. and PHILLIPS, F. 1978: Inter- versus intra-hemispheric learning in disabled and normal readers. *Developmental Medicine and Child Neurology* 20, 71–80.

VELLUTINO, F.R., DESETTO, L. and STEGER, J.A. 1972: Categorical judgement and the Wepman Test of auditory discrimination. *Journal of Speech and Hearing Disorders* 37, 2, 252–7.

VELLUTINO, F.R., HARDING, C.J., PHILLIPS, F. and STEGER, J.A. 1975: Differential transfer in poor and normal readers. *Journal of Genetic Psychology* 126, 3–18.

VELLUTINO, F.R., PRUZEK, R., STEGER, J.A. and MESHOULAM, U. 1973: Immediate visual recall in poor and normal readers as a function of orthographic-linguistic familiarity. *Cortex* 9, 368–84.

VELLUTINO, F.R., SMITH, H., STEGER, J.A. and KAMAN, M. 1975: Reading disability: Age differences and the perceptual deficit hypothesis. *Child Development* 46, 487–93.

VELLUTINO, F.R., STEGER, J.A. and KANDEL, G. 1972: Reading disability: An investigation of the perceptual deficit hypothesis. *Cortex* 8, 106–18.

VELLUTINO, F.R., STEGER, J.A., KAMAN, M. and DESETTO, L. 1975: Visual form perception in deficient and normal readers as a function of age and orthographic linguistic familiarity. *Cortex* 11, 22–30.

VELLUTINO, F.R., STEGER, J.A., DESETTO, L. and PHILLIPS, F. 1975: Immediate and delayed recognition of visual stimuli in poor and normal readers. *Journal of Experimental Child Psychology* 19, 223–32.

VELLUTINO, F.R., STEGER, J.A. and PRUZEK, R. 1973: Inter- versus intrasensory deficit in paired associated learning in poor and normal readers. *Canadian Journal of Behavioural Science* 5, 2, 111–23.

VELLUTINO, F.R., STEGER, B.M., MOYER, S.C., HARDING, C.J. and NILES, J.A. 1977: Has the perceptual deficit hypothesis led us astray? *Journal of Learning Disabilities* 10, 6, 375–85.

VENEZKY, R.L. 1970: *The Structure of English Orthography*. The Hague: Mouton.

VERNON, M.D. 1971: *Reading and its Difficulties*. Cambridge: Cambridge University Press.

—— 1977 a: Varieties of deficiency in the reading processes. *Harvard Educational Review* 37, 396–410.

—— 1977 b: Deficiencies in Dyslexia. *Dyslexia Review* 17, 4–8.

—— 1978: Neuropsychological laterality of function: Comment on Beaumont and Rugg. *Dyslexia Review* 1–2, 10–11.

—— 1979: Variability in reading retardation. *British Journal of Psychology* 70, 1, 7–16.

VINGILIS, E., BLAKE, J. and THEODOR, L. 1977: Recognitions vs recall of visually vs acoustically confusable letter matrices. *Memory and Cognition* 5, 146–50.

VOGEL, S.A. 1974: Syntactic abilities in normal and dyslexic children. *Journal of Learning Disabilities* 7, 2, 103–9

VOGEL, J.M. 1980: Limitations on children's short-term memory for left-right orientation. *Journal of Experimental child Psychology* 30, 473–95.

WADDINGTON, C.H. 1957: *The Strategy of Genes*. London: Allen & Unwin.

WALLER, E. 1978: *The Problems of Handwriting*. London: Helen Arkell Dyslexia Centre.

WALLER, T.G. 1976: Children's recognition memory for written sentences; a comparison of good and poor readers. *Child Development* 47, 90–5.

WALTON, D. 1975: The relationship between short-term memory capacity and intermediate reading skills. *Cambridge Journal of Education* 5, 3, 125–30.

Warnock Report. Committee of Enquiry into Education of Handicapped Children, 1978, *Special Education Needs*. London: HMSO.

WARREN, R.M. 1971: Identification times for phonemic components of graded complexity and for spelling of speech. *Perception and Psychophysics* 9, 345–49.

WARRINGTON, E.K. 1967: The incidence of verbal disability associated with retardation in reading. *Neuropsychologia* 5, 175–9.

WEBER, R.M. 1968: The study of oral reading errors: A survey of the literature. *Reading Research Quarterly* 4, 1, 98–119.

—— 1970: First grader's use of grammatical context in reading. In Levin, H. and Williams, V.P. (eds.), *Basic Studies in Reading*. New York: Basic Books.

WEBER, R. (ed.) 1974: *Handbook of Learning Disabilities*. London: University of London Press.

WECHSLER, D. 1946: *The Wechsler Intelligence Scale for Children* (revised edition 1977). Windsor: NFER/New York: Psychological Corporation.

WECHSLER, D. and HAGIN, R.A. 1964: The problem of axial rotation in reading disability. *Perceptual and Motor Skills* 19, 319–26.

WEDELL, K. 1977: Perceptual deficiency and specific reading retardation. *Journal of Child Psychology and Psychiatry* 18, 191–4.

WEDELL, K. 1987: Specific Learning Disabilities in the United Kingdom. A perspective. *Paedoperisse,* Monograph on Learning Disabilities. 1.1, 17–29.

WEIGL, E. and FRADIS, A. 1977: The transcoding process in patients with agraphia to dictation. *Brain and Language* 4, 11–12.

WEINER, M. and CROMER, W. 1967: Reading and reading difficulty: A conceptual analysis. *Harvard Educational Review* 37, 620–43.

WEINER, J., BARNSLEY, R.H. and RABINOVITCH, M.S. 1970: Serial order ability in good and poor readers. *Canadian Journal of Behavioural Science* 2, 116–23.

WEINSTEIN, R. and RABINOVITCH, M.S. 1971: Sentence structure and retention in good and poor readers. *Journal of Educational Psychology* 62, 25–30.

WEPMAN, J.M. 1960: Auditory discrimination, speech, and reading. *The Elementary School Journal* 9, 325–33.

—— 1961: The interrelationships of hearing, speech, and reading. *The Reading Teacher* 14, 245–7.

WHEELER, T. 1978: Dyslexia: The problem of definition. *Dyslexia Review* 1, 1, 13–15.

WHEELER, T.J., WATKINS, E.J. and MCLAUGHLIN, S.P. 1977: Reading retardation and cross-laterality in relation to short term information processing tasks. *British Journal of Educational Psychology* 47, 126–31.

WHEELER, T. and WATKINS, E.J. 1979: A review of symptomology. *Dyslexia Review* 2, 1, 12–16.

WHITE, M. 1973: Does cerebral dominance offer a sufficient explanation for laterality differences in tachistoscopic recognition? *Perceptual and Motor Skills* 36, 479–85.

WHORF, B. 1956: Linguistics as an exact science. In Carroll, J.B. (ed.), *Language, Thought and Reality*. Cambridge, Mass.: The MIT Press, 220–32.

WIIG, E.H. and ROACH, M.A. 1975: Immediate recall of semantically varied sentences by learning disabled adolescents. *Perceptual and Motor Skills* 40, 119–24.

WIIG, E.H., SEMEL, M.S. and CROUSE, M.B. 1973: The use of English morphology by high-risk and learning disabled children. *Journal of Learning Disabilities* 6, 457–65.

WILSHER, C.R. 1978 a: Is dyslexia a disease? *Quarterly Journal of Birmingham Medical and Dental School* 65, 13–15.

—— 1978 b: *Increased verbal learning in dyslexic control subjects using Piracetam (UCB6215)*. AP Report 87, University of Aston.

—— 1979: Study techniques for the dyslexic undertaking examinations. *Dyslexia Review* 2, 2, 13–15.

—— 1980: Piracetam treatment for specific language difficulties: a discussion. *Dyslexia Review* 3, 1, 8–9.

—— 1981: *Psychological Investigation of Hemisphere Function and Dyslexia using Pharmaceutical Intervention*. PhD thesis: University of Aston: Birmingham.

WILSHER, C.R., ATKINS, G. and MANFIELD, P. 1979: Piracetam as an aid to learning in dyslexia: Preliminary report. *Psychopharmacologia* 65, 107–9.

WING. A.M. and BADDELEY, A.D. 1980: Spelling errors in handwriting: a corpus and distributional analysis. In Frith, U. (ed.) *Cognitive Processes in Spelling*. London: Academic Press.

WINTERS, J.J., GERJUOY, I.R., CROWN, P. and GORRELL, R. 1967: Eye movements and verbal reports in tachistoscopic recognition by normals and retardates. *Child Development* 38, 1193–9.

WITELSON, D.F. 1976: Abnormal right hemisphere specialization in developmental dyslexia. In Knights, R.M. and Bakker, D.J. (eds.), *The Neuropsychology of Learning Disorders*. Baltimore: University Park Press.

WITELSON, S. 1977: Developmental dyslexia: two right hemispheres and none left. *Science* 195, 309–11.

WITELSON, S.F. and PALLIE, W. 1973: Left hemisphere specialisation of language in the newborn: neuro-anatomical evidence of asymmetry. *Brain* 96, 641–6.

WITELSON, S.F. and RABINOVITCH, M.S. 1972: Hemispheric speech lateralisation in children with auditory-linguistic deficits. *Cortex* 8, 412–26.

WRIGHT, L.S. 1974: Conduct problem or learning disability. *Journal of Special Education* 8, 4, 331–6.

WYKE, M.A. (ed.) 1978: *Developmental Dysphasia*. London: Academic Press.

YENI-KOMSHIAN, G.H., ISENBERG, S. and GOLDBERG, H. 1975: Cerebral dominance and reading disability, left visual field deficit in poor readers. *Neuropsychologia* 13, 18, 83–94.

YOUNG, A.W. and ELLIS, A.W. 1981: Asymmetry of cerebral hemispheric function in normal and poor readers. *Psychological Bulletin* 89, 1, 183–900.

YSSELDYKE, J. and SALVIA 1974: Diagnostic-prescriptive teaching: two models. *Exceptional Children* 41, 3, 181–5.

YULE, W. 1967: Predicting reading ages on Neale Analysis of reading ability. *British Journal of Educational Psychology* 37, 252–5.

—— 1973: Differential prognosis of reading backwardness and specific reading retardation. *British Journal of Educational Psychology* 43, 244–8.

YULE, W., RUTTER, M., BERGER, M. and THOMPSON, J. 1974: Over and under achievement in reading: distribution in the general population. *British Journal of Educational Psychology* 44, 1, 1–12.

YULE, W. and RUTTER, M. 1976: Epidemiology and social implications of specific reading retardation. In Knights, R.M. and Bakker, D.J. (eds.), *The Neuropsychology of Learning Disorders*. Baltimore: University Park Press.

YULE, W., LANDSDOWN, R. and URBANOWITZ, M. 1982: Predicting educational attainment for WISC (R). *British Journal of Clinical Psychology* 21, 1, 43–7.

ZAHALKOVA, M., URZAL, V. and KLOBOUKOVA, E. 1972: Genetic investigation in dyslexia. *Journal of Medical Genetics* 9, 48–52.

ZANGWILL, O. 1962: Dyslexia in relation to cerebral dominance. In Money, J. (ed.), *Reading Disability*, Baltimore: Johns Hopkins University Press.

—— 1978: The concept of developmental dysphasia, In Wyke, M. (ed.), *Developmental Dysphasia*. London: Academic Press.

ZANGWILL, O.L. and BLAKEMORE, C. 1972: Dyslexics reversal of eye movements during reading. *Neuropsychologia*, 10, 371–3.

ZERBIN-RUDIN, E. 1967: Congenital word blindness. *Bulletin of Orton Society* 17, 47–54.

ZETTERSON, A. 1969: *A statistical study of the graphic system of present day American English*. Lund, Sweden: Student Literature.

ZIGMOND, N. 1966: *Intrasensory and Intersensory Processes in Normal and Dyslexic Children* Doctoral Dissertation, Northwestern university.

ZURIF, E.F. and CARSON, G. 1970: Dyslexia in relation to cerebral dominance and temporal analysis. *Neuropsychologia* 8, 351–61.

Coopersmith, S., 149
Corah, N., 69
Corbollis, M.C., 85
Corkin, S., 100
Cotterell, G.C., 167, 218, 224, 234
Crane, A.R., 154
Critchley, E., 11
Critchley, M., 11, 26, 35, 68, 95, 96
Cromer, R.F., 135
Cronbach, C., 152, 195
Crosby, R.M., 90
Crowther, L., 43
Croxen, M.E., 68
Cruickshank, W.M., 188
Curry, L., 89

Darby, R., 76
Davie, R., 1, 2, 26
Decker, S.N., 36
De Fries, J.C., 36
De Hass, A., 76
de Hirsch, K., 61, 84, 90, 93, 175, 179
Dejerine, J., 4
Delacato, C.H., 198
Denckla, M.B., 29, 61, 71, 105, 110, 111, 146, 173
Desetto, L., 103
Deutsch, C.P., 2, 3, 79
Dimond, C., 73, 83
Doehring, D.G., 29, 35, 61, 68, 99
Donaldson, M., 107
Done, D.J., 92, 118
Dorman, M.F., 107
Douglas, J.W., 2, 69
Douglas, V.I., 225
Drasdo, N., 95
Dunlop, P., 84, 95
Dunn, A., 84
Dykman, R.A., 71, 225
Dykstra, R., 92

Eakin, S., 111
Edwards, R.P., 68
Eisenberg, L., 2, 13
Eisenson, J., 188
Elkind, D.A., 89
Elliott, C., 10, 34, 145, 152, 160, 163
Ellis, A.W., 76
Ellis, N., 10, 30, 61, 92, 103, 111, 115, 117, 118, 130, 131, 173
Elterman, R.D., 96, 98
Engleman, S., 3
Estes, W.K., 101

Fagg, R., 79
Farnham-Diggory, S., 15, 80, 94, 105, 113
Farr, J.E., 84
Faure, J.M.A., 71
Feingold, I., 194, 196, 199
Felton, R., 33
Fernald, G.M., 200
Festinger, L., 96, 97

Finlayson, M., 68
Finucci, J.M., 36, 37, 38
Fischer, M., 99
Firth, I., 107
Flax, N., 95
Fletcher, J.M., 135
Fowler, S., 95
Fox, B., 95, 113
Fransella, F., 154
Fraser, E., 2
Fredman, G., 9, 10
French, J.H., 28
Freundl, P.C., 104
Friel, J., 84, 174
Fries, C.E., 121
Frith, C.D., 112, 126, 132, 133
Frith, U., 6, 8, 10, 88, 105, 125, 133, 139, 169
Frostig, M., 89, 197
Fry, M.A., 115
Furness, M., 89

Gaddes, W., 14, 153
Galburda, A.M., 81
Gascon, G., 107
Gauntlet, D., 142
Gazzaniga, M.S., 80
Gelb, J., 121, 122
Gerhardt, 221
Gerver, D., 154
Geschwind, N., 68, 80, 81, 117, 123, 133
Getman, D., 96
Gibson, E.J., 113, 123, 125
Gillingham, A., 219
Gittelman, R., 194, 196, 199
Gleitman, L.R., 106, 110
Goetzinger, C.P., 89, 93
Goins, J.T., 90
Goldberg, H., 26, 35, 37, 84, 93, 95, 96, 99
Goldfuss, 166
Goldman, S.R., 117
Golinkoff, R.M., 117
Goodglass, H., 107
Goodman, K.S., 116, 129, 137
Gordon, H.W., 79
Goswami, U., 63
Goyen, J., 104, 158
Graham, E.E., 157, 159
Grant, S.E., 154, 155, 158, 159
Gray, J., 26
Green, J.B., 71
Gregg, L.W., 105, 113
Griffen, L., 97
Gruber, T.A., 78, 96
Guildford, J.P., 93
Gulliford, R., 2
Guthrie, J., 199

Haggard, M., 140
Hagin, R., 15, 37, 63, 84, 85, 88, 175
Hall, R., 89, 90
Hallahan, D.P., 198
Hallgren, B., 35

Hamilton-Fairley, D., 232, 233
Hammill, D.D., 93, 196, 198, 224
Hanley, J., 71
Harber, J.F., 92
Harding, C.F., 103, 107
Hardyck, C., 84
Harris, A.J., 84
Hart, S., 84
Hartley, G., 23
Haslum, M., 9
Hecaen, H., 84
Healy, A.F., 101
Heilman, K.M., 79
Helveston, E.M., 84
Henry, A., 93
Hermann, K., 37
Hermelin, B., 126
Hickey, C., 211, 215, 217
Hicks, C., 112, 113, 201, 227
Hinshelwood, J., 4, 35, 68
Hirst, L., 159
Hiscock, M., 81
Hitch, G., 112
Hockett, C.F., 140
Holmes, J.M., 62, 65
Hood, J., 130, 137
Hornsby, B., 199, 214
Hoshko, I.M., 29
Huelsman, C.R., 104, 158
Hughes, J.R., 38, 70, 71
Huling, M.D., 76
Hulme, C., 201
Hung, D., 122, 123

Imlach, R.H., 116
Ingram, T.T.S., 26 28, 35, 71, 84, 108

Jacklin, A.N., 27
Jakobsen, R., 121
Jansky, J., 61, 90, 174, 175
Joffe, L., 81, 162
Johnson, D.J., 27, 99, 207, 209, 226
Johnson, E.G., 76
Joos, L.W., 232
Jordon, D.R., 148, 173, 209
Jorm, A.F., 9, 10, 24, 33, 61, 65, 79, 106, 107, 137

Kalos, G., 159
Kaman, M., 109
Kanabe, G., 109
Katz, L., 104
Kavanagh, J.F., 106
Kawi, A.A., 69
Keefe, B., 75, 76, 84
Keeney, A.H., 15
Keeney, V.T., 15
Kellmer-Pringle, M.L., 1, 2, 14, 26, 27
Kemper, T.L., 81
Kendall, J.R., 130, 137
Kephart, N., 188
Kerr, J., 4

Kershner, J.R., 76
Kimura, D., 74, 75
Kinsbourne, M., 68, 81, 158
Kirk, S.A., 94, 126, 153, 209
Kirk, W.D., 126, 209
Klasen, E., 15, 159
Kline, C., 14
Knabe, G., 103
Knott, J.R., 65
Knox, C., 75
Kolers, P.A., 116
Koppitz, E.M., 90, 104
Kremenak, S., 94
Kussmaul, A., 4, 5
Kyostio, O.K., 126

Labov, W., 2
Large, B., 10
Larsen, S., 93
Leavell, V., 76
Lefton, P., 96
Legein, C., 96, 113
Leigh, J., 79
Leisman, G., 75, 96
Lenneberg, E.H., 77, 121
Leong, C.K., 76, 78
Leservre, N., 96
Lesgold, A.M., 117
Levin, H., 123, 125
Leviton, A., 64, 65
Levy, J., 80
Liberman, I., 93, 100, 105, 110, 113, 124, 136, 137
Lindgren, N., 121
Linn, J.R., 200
Loban, W., 115
Lovegrove, W., 87, 90
Lovell, K., 2, 89, 90, 199
Lyles, J.G., 69, 89, 104, 158
Lytton, H., 68

McBurney, A., 84
McCarthy, J.J., 99
Maccoby, E.E., 27
McGee, R., 24
McKeever, W.F., 76, 79
Mackworth, J.F., 87, 91, 94
McLaughlin, S.P., 80
McLeod, J., 99, 103, 157, 159, 161
McNeil, M.R., 81
McNinch, G., 93
McRare, R., 76
Makita, K., 122
Mann, V.A., 105
Marcel, A J., 64
Marcel, T., 64, 76, 133, 139
Mark, L.S., 113
Marshall, J.C., 63, 64, 65, 129
Marx, R.W., 153
Masland, R.L., 104
Matthews, B.A., 93
Mattingly, I.G., 106, 110

Mattis, S., 28
May, J.G., 75
Menyuk, P., 122
Messer, S., 122
Miccinati, J., 225
Miles, E., 215
Miles, T., 9, 19, 51, 61, 92, 104, 111, 117, 118, 130, 131, 159, 161, 162, 173, 199, 215
Miller, G., 103
Milner, B., 7, 80
Minden, H.A., 95
Mittler, P., 152, 158
Money, J., 26, 89, 124
Montgomery, D., 108, 112
Morency, A., 88
Morgan, W.P., 4, 68
Morrison, E.I., 92
Morton, J., 65, 67, 117, 130
Moscovitch, M., 77
Moseley, D.V., 26
Muehl, S., 70, 94
Murgatroyd, S., 201, 227
Myers, P.I., 196, 198, 224
Myklebust, H.R., 3, 27, 99, 207, 209

Naidoo, S., 26, 33, 35, 84, 93, 99, 159
Naylor, J., 2
Nelson, H.E., 104, 106, 138, 166
Netley, C., 104
Neville, D., 157
Newcombe, F., 64
Newell, D., 75, 76
Newton, M.J., 15, 19, 69, 71, 75, 84, 99, 101, 104, 163, 167, 173, 176, 209, 218
Noble, J., 72
Nodine, R., 96
Norman, R., 86

Obrzat, J.E., 76, 77, 79
O'Connor, N., 133
O'Donnell, P.A., 198
Olson, M.E., 76, 99, 113
Ornstein, R., 73, 79
Orton, S.T., 5, 35, 72, 83, 89, 200, 208
Osgood, C., 126
Otto, W., 107
Owen, F.W., 36, 38, 159

Panckhurst, J., 144, 159
Paraskevopoulos, J.N., 153
Park, G.E., 70
Pasamanik, B.P., 69
Paterra, M.C., 157
Patterson, K., 63, 65, 99
Pavlides, G. TH., 96, 98, 99, 146
Perfetti, C.A., 117
Perlo, P., 109
Petrinovitch, C.F., 84
Phillips, F., 109
Piercy, M., 101
Pierre, C., 100
Pirozzolo, F.J., 76, 96

Pollock, J., 216, 226
Porpodas, C.D., 140
Preston, M., 71, 79
Pumfrey, P.D., 2, 199

Quinlan, D., 101

Rabinovitch, M.S., 15, 76, 103, 108
Rajan, P., 76
Rapin, I., 28
Rapoport, J.L., 90
Rasmussen, J., 77
Ravenette, A.T., 2
Rawson, M.B., 37, 200, 208
Rayner, K., 76, 96
Rebert, C.S., 74
Reid, J.F., 26, 108
Reiton, R., 68
Richards, I., 101
Richardson, E., 93
Richmond, M., 88
Roach, M.A., 104
Robbins, M.P., 198
Robinson, 69
Rodgers, B., 9
Rogers, D.C., 104
Rosen, M.S., 69, 106
Rosenthal, R., 24
Rosinski, R.R., 117
Rourke, B.P., 62, 68, 76, 77
Routh, D., 113
Rozin, P., 106, 110, 123
Rubenstein, H., 109
Rubin, R., 69
Rubino, C.A., 95
Rudel, R.G., 77, 98, 100, 109, 110, 139
Rudnick, H., 95
Rugel, P., 75, 76, 103, 152, 160, 162
Rugg, M.D., 78, 80
Rutter, M., 1, 3, 6, 7, 8, 9, 10, 12, 13, 21, 26, 35, 68, 84, 154, 189
Ryan, T.J., 190

Sakamoto, T., 122
Sampson, O., 209
Satz, P., 14, 60, 61, 68, 77, 82, 83, 84, 89, 173, 174
Satz, R., 76
Savage, P., 158
Savin, H.B., 110, 125
Scheerev-Neuman, G., 114
Schiffman, G., 26, 35, 84, 93, 95, 159
Schroots, H.J., 100
Schulman, J., 64, 65
Segalowitz, S.J., 78
Senf, G.M., 104
Seymour, C.M., 93
Seymour, P.H., 35, 140
Shakespeare, R., 3
Shallice, T., 64
Shankweiler, D.P., 79, 81, 84, 93, 100, 105, 106, 110, 113, 129, 130, 137

Shave, D., 9
Shazam, M., 199
Shevill, H., 200
Shulman, M., 69
Silver, A.A., 15, 35, 37, 89, 93, 173, 175
Simon, A., 96
Sklar, B., 71
Sladen, B.K., 35
Slingerland, B.H., 173
Smith, F., 109, 116, 128, 137
Smith, P.A., 153
Snowling, M.J., 10, 63, 94, 112, 113, 114, 115, 132, 133, 139, 146, 163, 165, 169, 173
Sobotka, R., 75
Sommers, R.K., 76
Spache, G.D., 89, 134, 153, 159, 160
Sparrow, S., 76, 84
Sperling, G., 90
Sperry, R.W., 71, 80,
Spreen, O., 77, 108
Spring, C., 105, 111
Stanley, G., 89, 90, 99, 104, 131
Stark, L., 98
Steeve, A., 236
Steger, J.A., 107, 109
Stein, J.F., 95
Sterritt, R., 95
Stevenson, H.W., 9, 10, 37
Stillman, B.W., 219
Studdert-Kennedy, M., 81
Supramaniam, S., 111
Swinney, D., 75, 76
Symmes, J.S., 90

Tallal, P., 101
Tansley, P., 144, 159
Tarnopol, E., 15
Tarnopol, L., 15
Tayler, L.B., 76, 97
Taylor, M.L., 76
Temple, C., 137
Thomson, M.E., 15, 23, 33, 34, 58, 68, 76, 78, 80, 84, 85, 89, 92, 99, 100, 101, 104, 114, 118, 136, 137, 138, 139, 141, 150, 152, 156, 158, 159, 160, 161, 162, 163, 164, 173, 176, 202, 204, 206, 218, 225, 236
Tinker, C., 84, 97
Tizard, J., 1, 6, 41
Torres, F., 71
Tyler, S., 10, 34, 160
Tyson, 144

Tzeng, O., 122, 123

Underwood, D., 86

Valtin, R., 2, 93
van Deventer, A.D., 76, 79
van Nostrand, G.K., 61, 76
van der Wessel, A., 9
Vande Voort, L., 94
Vellutino, F.R., 13, 20, 89, 90, 92, 94, 100, 101, 104, 107, 109, 207
Venezky, R.L., 2
Vernon, M.D., 3, 29, 34, 59, 90, 97, 99, 199, 219
Vingilis, E., 133
Vogel, S.A., 116

Waller, E., 226
Waller, T.G., 116
Ward, L., 97
Warren, S.A., 76
Warrington, E.K., 64, 68, 106, 153
Watkins, E.J., 8, 14, 20, 80, 85
Watson, M., 131
Weber, R., 134, 137
Wechsler, D., 74, 84, 153
Wedell, K., 2, 41
Weigl, E., 133
Weinstein, R., 106
Wepman, J.M., 93
Werry, J.S., 226
Wexler, B.N., 69
Wheeler, T., 14, 20, 84, 85
Whitmore, K., 1, 6
Wiig, E.H., 104, 116
Wilsher, C., 38, 77, 79, 81, 82, 83, 92, 94, 101, 103, 118, 173
Wing, A.M., 138
Witelson, D.F., 76, 80, 158
Witelson, S.F., 76
Woolsey, M.E., 2

Yeni-Komshian, G.H., 76
Young, A.W., 76
Ysseldyke, J., 197
Yule, W., 6, 7, 8, 9, 10, 14, 35, 37, 154, 164, 189

Zangwill, O.L., 83, 84, 85, 96
Zeger, F., 9
Zerbin-Rudin, E., 37
Zigmond, N., 95
Zurif, E.F., 76, 100

Subject Index

acquired dyslexia, 63–67
adults, dyslexia in, 36, 52–55, 64–67, 240–246
Advisory Committee on Handicapped Children, 41
agressiveness, 17, 21–22
alexia, 4
Alpha to Omega programme, 214–215
ambidexterity, 84–85
anoxia, 69
anxiety, 17, 21–26
arithmetic, problems with, 18; subtests on WISC, 158–161
articulatory coding, 111, 132
assessments, 144–178, 164; attainments, 164–172; background factors, 146–147; behavioural/emotional difficulties, 148–149; developmental history, 147–148; diagnosis and, 199; educational history, 142–143; framework for, 145, intelligence, 150–164; and remediation, 191–194; sample reports, 178–190; screening procedures, 173–178; sensory mechanisms, 148; social history, 149
Aston Index, 176, 178–183
Aston Teaching Portfolio, 168–169, 228–231
at-risk birth, 69, 148
attainment, 165–167; error analysis, 167–172; measuring, 164–172
audio-phonic dyslexia, 28
auditory channel deficits. 170, 227
auditory coding, 129–133 (see phonological coding)
auditory discrimination, 93–94, 228–229
auditory dyslexia, 27–30
auditory evoked response (AER), 71
auditory perception, 92–94
auditory sequential memory tasks, 99–102, 161 (see also digit span)
auditory-visual integration (AVI), 94

Bangor Dyslexia Test, 16, 19, 175
Bangor Teaching Programme, 215–216
barriers to learning, 2–3

behavioural difficulties, 3, 17, 21–26; assessment, 148–149
Bender Gestalt test, 172
Benton Visual Retention Test, 172
binocular fusion, 95
birth history, 69, 148
bottom-up process, 88, 143
brain, cerebral dominance, 73–86; damage, 4, 63–68; EEG studies, 70–72; see also left hemisphere; right hemisphere
British Ability Scales (BAS), 34–35, 152–153, 155–156, 160–161
Bullock Report, 41

case histories, 44–55; assessment sample reports, 178–190
cerebral dominance, 72–86
Checklists of Basic Sounds, 168
Chinese language, 122–123, 130
Chronically Sick and Disabled Persons Act (1970), 40
Code of Regulations for Public Elementary Schools (1904), 1
coding, 104–108; subtests on WISC, 158–161
cognitive perspective, 86–119
comprehension, 136
computer-assisted learning, 246–251
contingent negative variation (CNV), 71
control groups, 63, 107, 135, 185–186
criterion orientated assessment, 145
criterion orientated screening, 177–178
cross-laterality, 83–85
cross-modal matching, 94

deep dyslexia, 64–66
definitions, 10–14
delayed versus deviant reading, 61, 137–138
developmental motor aphasia, 5
developmental alexia, 5
developmental history, 147–148
developmental word deafness, 5
diagnosis, assessment and, 144, 191
dichotic listening, 73–78, 81

digit span subtests, 158–162
digit span tasks, 99–101, 103–104
divided visual field studies, 73–78, 81
dyseidetic, 28, 31–33
dyslexia features, 16–21, 147
dysphonetic dyslexia, 28, 31–33, 106;
    expectancy tables, 154–156

Edith Norrie Letter Case, 233–234
Education Act (1870), 1
Education Act (1944), 40–42
Education Act (1981), 41–42
educational history, 149
electroencephalogram studies (EEG), 70–72,
    74–75
emotional difficulties, assessment, 21–26
English Picture Vocabulary Test, 157
error analysis, 127–128, 160–164
essay writing, 237–240
etiology, 61–119; cognitive perspective, 86–119
examinations, 242–247
eye movements, 95–99

families, inherited dyslexia, 35–40, see also
    parents; siblings
Fernald tracing techniques, 223–225
Finnish language, 126
flashcard techniques, 30, 217, 220
free-writing, 218–219, 237
Frostig Test of Visual perception, 89

genetic aspects, 35–40
Gerstmann syndrome, 68
Gillingham/Stillman Programme, 219–222
Goodenough Draw-a-Man test, 181

handeness, 82–85
handicap categories, 40–41
Hawthorne Effect, 195
hearing testing, 148
Helen Arkell Dyslexia Centre, 233–234
hemispheres function, 72–83
Hickey Programme, 221–223
Hiragana, 122–123

iconic memory, 87, 91
ideographs, 122–123
Illinois Test of Psycholinguistic Abilities
    (ITPA), 112, 126, 153, 160–161
incidence of dyslexia, 14–16
information processing, 86–88
inherited aspects, 11, 35–40
intelligence, dyslexia and, 12–13, low, 3;
    reading and 6–10; intelligence assessment,
    150–164; general intelligence, 150–153;
    intelligence and attainments, 153–157;
    subtest profiles, 157–164
inter-sensory integration, 80
IQ see intelligence
Isle of Wight study, 1, 6–8, 23, 154–157

Japanese language, 122–123

Kanjii, 122–123
Katakana, 122–123

laterality, 82–85
Left ear advantage (LEA), 75–77
left-handedness, 82–85
left-hemisphere, 27, 72–83
Left visual field advantage, 74–76
lexical access, 106, 111–112, 117–118, 123
local authorities, 37–39, 47
logogen model, 117, 130–132
logographic writing, 116
long-term memory, 102, 106, 114

Marshall's model, 129–130
maturational lag, 62–63, 74, 77–78, 82, 174
medical history, 149–150
memory, 91, 103–108, 110, 115, 119–120;
    assessment, 172–174; see short-term
    memory
minimal neurological dysfunction, 68–72, 148
mirror images, 72–73, 85
mixed-handedness, 83–86
morphemic knowledge, 164
morphology, 116
motor deficits, 25, 88–99
motor laterality, 85–86
multi-sensory teaching, 200, 208, 219–226
multiple regression, equations, 6–7, 255–257

naming, 110–112, 140
Neale Analysis of Reading Ability, 9, 136, 155,
    164–166
neurological aspects, 63–86, acquired dyslexia,
    63–65; cerebral dominance, 72–86; minimal
    neurological dysfunction, 68–72
neuronal migration deficit, 82
normative screening, 145, 174–177

ocular motor deficits, 95–99
official attitudes, 40–43
orthography, 121–124, 142
overlearning, 211

parents, anxiety, 251; emotional support, 251;
    encouragement, 2, 35; occupations, 149;
    role in remediation, 251–255
partial report tasks, 104
perceptual deficits, 89–100
perceptual skills, assessment, 172–173
phonemes, 121–123, 125
phonemic segmentation, 112–114
phonemic sequencing, 29
phonetic teaching, 4, 231–237
phonic analysis and synthesis, 28, 113
phonograms, 221–223
phonological coding, 128–133
phonological dyslexia, 64–67
phonological maturity, 124–125
phonological processing, 109–114
phonological route to reading, 129–130

Picture Arrangement subtests, 152, 158, 161–162
Piracetam, 79
Posner task, 111
pyscholinguistic models, 126–134
psychometric assessment, 145–146, 180–187

Raven's Matrices, 157
reading, 134–138; error analysis, 164–169; signs of dyslexia, 17; specific reading difficulty, 6–9
reading age, 6–18, 13; assessment, 164–172; reading development, 197, 203–204
redundancy, written language, 114
regression equations, 6–7, 147–148, 154–156, 255–257
regression to mean, 194
remediation, 191–251; assessment and, 191–194; computer assisted learning, 246; matching tasks to the learner, 226–231; multi-sensory teaching, 219–226; older dyslexics, 240–246; research, 194–207; role of parent in, 251–255; structured learning, 214–219; general principles, 207–214; phonetic teaching, 226–231; essay writing, 237–240; evaluating remediation, 194–207
right ear advantage (REA), 73–78
right hemisphere, 72–83
right visual field advantage (RVFA), 73–78

Schonell Graded Word Reading Test, 164–165
Schonell Spelling Test, 164–165
screening procedures, 173–178; criterion orientated, 177–178; normative, 174–177
SEARCH Test, 175
segmentation, phonemic, 112–114
self-esteem, 24–26
semantic errors, 138
semantic functions, 115–119
semantic memory, 103
sensory mechanisms, assessment, 147
sequencing, 94–97, 99–102, 135, 142, 154, 160
sequential programmes, 208
serial order, 100–102
sex differences, 26–27; dichotic listening, 75
short-term memory, 82, 94–95, 97–98, 109, 111, 100–109, 119, 135, 142–143, 160, 162, 172; capacity, 103–104; coding and, 104–107
sibling hostilities, 17, 23
simultaneous oral spelling (SOS), 220, 225
skills analysis, 141–142
Smith's reading model, 128–129
social background, 2
socio-physiological barriers, 2
sound blending, 176, 182, 229–230
sound discrimination, 179

sound matching, 229
sounds, checklist of basic, 168
specific reading difficulties, 6–9, 41
speech therapy, 231–233
spelling, 135, 138–140; error analysis, 169–172; signs of dyslexia, 17
spelling, tests, 166–167
Sperling tasks, 92
stage analysis, 86–88, 110
strephosymbolia, 5, 73
structured learning, 207, 214–219
subtest profiles, 152, 157–160
subtypes of dyslexia, 27–35
suburban areas, 2
surface dyslexia, 64–65
symptoms, 16–21
syntax, 115–119, 126
syllables, 204–206

task analysis, 143
teaching, 13; assessment and teaching levels, 191; computer assisted learning, 246; general principles, 207–214; group teaching, 188; matching tasks to the learner, 226–231; multi-sensory techniques, 219–226; parent's role, 251–255; phonetic principles, 4, 189; phonic approach, 231–237, research into, 196–207; see remediation
temporal-order perception (TOP), 100
Tizard Report, 41
top-down process, 88, 143
tracing techniques, 223–226
twins, 35–37, 55–60

verbal coding, 109, 111
Verbal/Performance discrepancy, 157–159
verbal processing, 109–111
visual channel deficits, 170
visual dyslexia, 28–33
visual evoked response (VER), 71
visual perception, 89–92
visual sensory store, 91–92
visual spatial dysfunction, 90–91
vocabulary subtests, 161–163
vowel difficulties, 136

Warnock Report, 41–42
Wechsler Intelligence Scale of Children (WISC), 7, 12, 36, 103, 108, 150–164, 255
Wepman task, 93
word blindness, 4, 39
word processing, 247–251
working memory, see short-term memory
written language, 121–140